Gigabit Networking

Addison-Wesley Professional Computing Series

Brian W. Kernighan, Consulting Editor

Gigabit Networking

Craig Partridge

ADDISON-WESLEY PUBLISHING COMPANY

Reading, Massachusetts   Menlo Park, California   New York   Don Mills, Ontario
Wokingham, England   Amsterdam   Bonn   Sydney   Singapore   Tokyo   Madrid   San Juan
Paris   Seoul   Milan   Mexico City   Taipei

The publisher offers discounts on this book when ordered in quantity for special sales. For more information please contact:

Corporate & Professional Publishing Group
Addison-Wesley Publishing Company
One Jacob Way
Reading, Massachusetts 01867

Library of Congress Cataloging-in-Publication Data

Partridge, Craig. 1961–
    Gigabit networking / Craig Partridge.
        p. cm.
    Includes bibliographical references and index.
    ISBN 0-201-56333-9
    1. Computer networks.   I. Title.
TK5105.5P3745   1993
004.6—dc20   93-28877
                                                                 CIP

ISBN 0-201-56333-9
Text printed on recycled paper containing 10% post-consumer waste.
1 2 3 4 5 6 7 8 9 10 CRW 96959493
First Printing, October 1993

To Lee, Tony, Katy, and Carolyn

Contents

Preface

Computing environments keep improving. Most improvements are incremental, changes such as a 50% increase in CPU speed or a doubling of memory capacity in a chip. Every so often the accumulated changes become large enough to transform some part of computer science. More powerful processors made it possible to share the CPU among several users, leading to multiprocessing operating systems like UNIX and MVS. The advent of timesharing transformed the study of operating systems. The advent of high-quality graphics has led to WYSIWYG interfaces.

Computer networking is undergoing such a transformation. The widespread use of optical fiber to transmit data has made tremendous increases in network bandwidth possible. Furthermore, greater CPU power, increasing disk capacity, and support for digital audio and video are creating demand for a new class of network services, which are not supported by today's networking protocols. The result of these trends is a world I occasionally describe as the *gigabit environment*, a computing milieu in which most or all of the components of a computer system are processing, storing, displaying, or moving data at speeds exceeding 1 gigabit per second. Although the gigabit environment does not yet quite exist (except, perhaps, at some supercomputer centers), it is fast approaching.

This book examines a critical part of the gigabit environment: the gigabit per second computer networks that make it possible to share vast quantities of data among many computer systems.

Since the mid-1980s considerable work has been done on designing, developing, and studying networks capable of transmitting data at gigabit per second rates, and by now much of this work has produced tangible results: prototype networks, proposed protocol architectures, influential studies identifying key research issues, and most important, increased industry and government funding for the construction and study of major research testbeds.

This book is based on that research and presents gigabit networking as we now know it. Key technologies, important protocols and applications, and where research is still incomplete, important unsolved issues are all presented. The goal is to give the reader a sturdy understanding of an important emerging field.

Who This Book Is For

The author expects the reader to have at least a nodding acquaintance with networking and computing, although the early chapters review essential topics. Beyond this prerequisite, the text is written to strike a balance between the needs of technical and academic readers and less-technical readers interested in getting a grasp of the field. When feasible, technical issues are introduced using non-technical terms and analogies, before delving into more detailed technical discussions. As a result, my hope is that this book will be useful to almost anyone interested in the topic of gigabit networks.

The author of any survey has to be selective about what material is presented. Inevitably, the result is a book that becomes one person's perspective on the field rather than a complete survey. But I have worked hard to try to make sure that this survey presents as broad a range of work as possible, given constraints on reasonable book length and time and resources to search out new work.

At the same time, I believe that anyone who takes the time to write a survey of a field should also give the reader some opinions about the strengths and limitations of the topics discussed in the survey. A survey without such a perspective is little better than a list of facts. So, scattered through the book are thoughts about important issues. I do not expect the reader to always agree with me.

Using This Book as a Textbook

This book was designed as a professional reference, but because much of its structure is based on a course I have taught for the INTEROP® conference for a number of years, it can be used as a textbook, for a graduate course on gigabit networking, or as a supplemental text for an undergraduate course in networking.

Because this text assumes a background in networking and focuses solely on gigabit networking, it is not sufficient as a stand-alone text for an undergraduate course. However, several chapters can serve as supplements to an existing text such as Tanenbaum's *Computer Networks*, Comer's *Internetworking with TCP/IP*, or Spragin's *Telecommunications*. Chapter 2 provides a useful tutorial on fiber optic networking. Chapters 5, 6, and 7 describe a number of high-speed networking technologies; and Chapters 9 and 10 may provide a useful perspective on protocol performance when studying the internetwork and transport layers. A study of flow control can be supplemented by Chapters 11, 12, and 13, which describe the difficult problems of performance guarantees.

For a graduate course on data networking, this book provides an introduction to a number of the key research issues in data networking and thus could serve as a useful textbook, perhaps supplemented by selected readings from the research literature.

Acknowledgements

As I wrote this book, I often became acutely aware that I knew less about gigabit networking than I had first thought. The field is exploding with new and interesting work. To help me fill gaps in my knowledge and improve the presentation of various topics, I've been able to lean on a number of people. Much of what is good in this book is due to their help. (All of what may be deemed bad about this book should be viewed as solely my fault.) I've tried to credit all those who helped, although I've no doubt missed a few.

Julio Escobar and Zygmunt Haas provided extensive comments on Chapter 2 that saved me from making a number of embarrassing mistakes. Chris Wilcox helped me better understand SONET. Bob Braudes, John Burruss, Norman Chang, Bruce Davie, Ole Jacobson, Joe Pagan, Steve Pink, Howard Salwen, and Jonathan Smith provided insightful comments on a number of chapters. Early in the writing of the book, both Dave Crocker and Brian Kernighan helped me work out a better presentation style in early drafts of Chapters 3 through 5, which helped immeasurably with later chapters. Simone Payment and Marty Rabinowitz of Addison-Wesley helped me with various issues of tasteful formatting.

A number of people provided advance copies of papers or reviewed pieces of the manuscript related to their work for accuracy. For their help, I'd like to thank David Anderson, Abhaya Asthana, Dave Banks, Dick Binder, Dave Borman, Charlie Catlett, Chris Cooper, Jon Crowcroft, Deborah Estrin, Greg Finn, Ed Foudriat, Sandy Fraser, Victor Frost, Mark Garrett, Rafael Gidron, Rich Gitlin, Bryan Gorman, David Greaves, Roch Guerin, Gerard Holzmann, Jim Hughes, Van Jacobson, Bob Kahn, Chuck Kalmanek, Jim Kurose, Larry Landweber, Will Leland, Paul Messina, Dave Mills, Biswanath Mukherjee, Joe Pasquale, John Renwick, Paul Rupert, Tim Salo, Chuck Seitz, Dave Sincoskie, Dan Stevenson, Dave Tennenhouse, and Lixia Zhang. Also thanks to Lawrence S. Brakmo for the data used to generate the slow-start graph in Chapter 10, and Mark Garrett for the data for the MPEG graph in Chapter 8.

I also want to thank the folks who got me into writing this book in the first place and helped me through the process. Dan Lynch all but dared me to put together a course on gigabit networking for INTEROP® 1990. Experience with that course and interaction with the hundreds of students who have taken it to date have helped shape this book. I met John Wait of Addison-Wesley when we were both stuck in the Houston airport by a snowstorm in 1987, and he and his team (Kim Dawley, Kathleen Duff, and Kathleen Habib) have since waited patiently for me to produce a book on networking. Brian Kernighan's help, both as series editor and in his comments on several drafts of this book, was immensely helpful. Thanks also to my employer, Bolt Beranek and Newman, for allowing me to undertake this work, and to the Swedish Institute of Computer Science, where I spent a very productive sabbatical year. Finally, thanks to my wife, Carolyn, who had to put up with losing her husband on many weekends and evenings as I pounded away at the keyboard.

Palo Alto, August 1993

Chapter 1

An Introduction to Gigabit Networking

1.1. Change in the Wind

Computers and the things we attach to computers, like networks and disk systems, always seem to be getting faster and less expensive. And every so often, this progressive improvement brings about big changes in the industry. When computers got powerful enough that people could use them at the same time, timesharing was developed. When the cost of computing components became low enough that individuals could afford them, personal computers appeared. When inexpensive local area networks like Ethernet were developed, distributed systems and distributed file systems came into being.

Another set of big changes is clearly on the horizon. Inexpensive computer central processor chips (CPUs) are rapidly getting as fast as supercomputers were a few years ago. Chips like the DEC Alpha [Sites 1992] have instruction cycle times of only a few nanoseconds. Chips will soon have instruction cycle times of a nanosecond or less, allowing them to perform billions of instructions per second (BIPS). These processors have enough computing power that many services now considered extremely compute intensive and feasible only on supercomputers and high-powered graphics workstations, like voice recognition, high-quality real-time computer graphics, handwriting recognition, and real-time animation and video, will be available on the average personal computer. Furthermore, it is becoming increasingly clear that these new services will use networks to carry their data.

Concurrently, there have been tremendous improvements in network bandwidth. Five years ago a 10 megabits per second (Mb/s) local area network and a 1.5 Mb/s long-distance line were both considered fast. Now local area networks are rapidly approaching 1 billion bits (1 gigabit or Gb) per second data rates, and

1

wide area networks are not far behind. Much of this advance is the fruition of nearly two decades of work on fiber optic signalling.[1]

At the same time, there have been tremendous changes in the telecommunications community. Telephone networks were built to carry largely analog telephone calls. But now an increasing fraction of the telephone network's capacity is being used to carry digital data such as faxes and computer network traffic. Numbers vary according to country and type of data included in the count, but in the United States, it is estimated that over 20% of the information flowing through the telephone network is digital data being sent between devices attached to telephone lines. Furthermore, although voice traffic is growing at only a few percent a year, data traffic is growing at over 20% per annum. This shift in traffic patterns is encouraging the telephone community to reexamine the role of data in telephone networks, and redesign its networks to better support digital data. This redesign is being encouraged by the realization that reengineering the phone networks also opens up possibilities for new telephone services, such as on-demand video.

These impending changes are having a potent effect on data communications. Networks (possibly telephone networks!) capable of handling billions or even trillions of bits per second will be interconnecting computers boasting new applications capable of generating or receiving gigabits of data. This image may be somewhat startling, but it is rapidly becoming very real. Researchers around the world, both in universities and industry, have been working on making these types of networks a reality for several years. Most of the key problems are understood and many of them have been solved.

The goal of this book is to present the problems and their solutions in a coherent study of gigabit networking. The purpose of this chapter is to sketch the forces that have motivated the development of gigabit networks and how researchers have come to think about gigabit networks, in preparation for the rest of the book.

---

[1] In abbreviations, a lower case b stands for bits, and an upper case B stands for bytes. (A byte has 8 bits.) So Gb is a gigabit and GB is a gigabyte. For consistency with industry practices, this book measures network data rates in bits but measures memory and packet sizes in bytes.

1.2. What Is Changing?

A number of changes are occurring in the data communications, computing and telecommunications fields that are encouraging the development of gigabit networks. Beyond encouraging the different disciplines to consider high-speed communications, the mutual interest in high-speed networks is leading to much greater cooperation between the historically disparate disciplines. We will look at the changes in each field separately and then talk about joint activities.

Computing

The field of computing appears to be entering a period of transition. A number of trends are encouraging changes in computers and their software.

From the technological perspective, there is a tremendous increase in the power and bandwidth of many parts of computing systems. At the very center of this improvement is the tremendous boom in the performance of processor chips. Processor performance is nearly doubling every year. By 1993, some inexpensive processors were capable of performing over 200 million instructions per second. These faster processors are making it ever easier to support powerful applications on inexpensive computing systems. Compounding this performance improvement is the slowly maturing field of parallel processing, which harnesses multiple processors in a single system.

Computer peripherals are also improving in performance. High-bandwidth disk systems have been developed. For example, a technology known as Redundant Arrays of Inexpensive Disks (RAID) combines a large number of the small inexpensive hard disks designed for personal computers into a large parallel disk array. These parallel arrays can be configured as gigabit-bandwidth file systems, from which large amounts of data can be read in parallel. Graphics systems can now display gigabits of data per second (a simple $1024 \times 1024 \times 32$ color graphics screen displaying data 30 times per second is displaying just over 1 gigabit per second). And later in this book, we will see a number of networking technologies such as HIPPI and ATM/SONET, capable of transmitting data at gigabit rates.

The emerging picture of computing systems of the future is therefore of powerful processors, capable of handling gigabits of data per second, coupled with peripherals like disk arrays, networks, and graphics systems also capable of handling gigabits of data. There are some serious technical challenges to making this system a reality. Between the fast peripherals and fast processor are pieces of the computing system that are proving stubbornly slow: notably memory (memory performance has not kept pace with processor performance) and computer buses (today's high-speed computer buses can typically handle only about 1 gigabit of data per second). Solving these problems will be one of the major challenges in computer science over the next several years, but it is widely expected these problems will be solved.

From the software perspective, the increasing power of computer systems is making a wide range of new applications possible. Computers now have so much computing power that applications previously thought to require exceptional computing power or bandwidth such as speech processing and multimedia (combined voice and graphics) applications, are appearing even on personal computers.

Data Communications

The primary goal of data communications is to facilitate the exchange of data between computing systems. As computing systems become increasingly powerful and versatile, data communications networks must evolve to support the new applications the computing systems can support. Of course, the ability to easily exchange data between computers has also had a tremendous influence on applications. Data networks led to the development of such applications and services as electronic mail (*e-mail*) and distributed file systems, neither of which was envisioned when data networks were first invented.

One of the most powerful ideas in data communications to date has been the notion of *internetworking*. In brief, the idea behind internetworking is that by developing a set of rules (*protocols*) for how computers (also termed *hosts*) communicate over a network, and rules for connecting one type of network to another, it is possible to build interconnected sets of networks (*internetworks*) in which any computer on any constituent network in the *internetwork* can communicate with any other computer. The development of the worldwide Internet, a global network connecting millions of hosts and several millions of users using the so-called TCP/IP protocol suite, is a testament to the power of the idea of internetworking.[2]

---

[2] It is important to distinguish between the term *internet* with a lower case *i*, which is any set of interconnected networks, and the global *Internet* (with a capital *I*), which is a particularly well-known internet.

(A less pleasant side of internetworking is that the idea is so appealing that everyone seems to want to develop his or her own set of internetworking protocols. So rather than one common internetworking protocol, the world currently has about half a dozen, including TCP/IP, the Open Systems Interconnection (OSI) protocol suite, Systems Network Architecture (SNA), and Novell's Netware. No good way has been found to pick from among the competing standards except to let users choose among them.)

The most popular of today's internetworking protocols offer a service designed to make it easy to send data between hosts and to facilitate the interconnection of different types of networks such as Ethernet and token ring. These protocols typically do not provide performance guarantees other than to try to ensure that data will be delivered if there is a viable path through the network between the sender of the data and the receiver.

The improvements in computing performance, however, are encouraging researchers to consider enhancing internetworking services. Computers are now powerful enough to support a number of interactive applications, such as simulation, multimedia conferencing, and virtual reality, and it would clearly be beneficial if these services could make use of internetworks. For example, the ability to have conferences between users on different machines, perhaps in different countries, is a far more powerful service than a conferencing system that permits conferences only on a single machine. To make these types of services available over a network requires at least a modest enhancement to internetworking protocols, so they can provide some types of performance guarantees to applications, (e.g., promising a voice application that it will always have enough network bandwidth that the voice will not sound broken at the receiver).

Telecommunications

For nearly a century, the primary purpose of telecommunications networks has been to support a communications network suitable for transmitting high quality voice sounds between telephones. These networks are carefully engineered to support the transmission of an analog or digital voice. Recently, however, the role of telecommunications networks and the telecommunications industry has been changing.

First, telecommunications networks are increasingly being used to transmit data, such as computer data and faxes, rather than voice. Currently in the United States, voice traffic in the telephone networks is growing at a meager 3% per year, while data traffic is growing at a rate of 20% per year. Although it will be several years before data surpasses voice as the major source of revenue, most telephone companies have long since concluded that data communications services are an important part of their current business and will be an even more important part of their future business.

Second, particularly outside the United States, the telephone companies have become heavily involved in delivering nontelephone services to customers. In most countries, telephone service is provided by a state monopoly that is often also the cable television (CATV) provider. These telephone companies are concluding that they would achieve considerable cost savings if they could consolidate their multiple delivery networks (i.e., the telephone and cable networks) into one integrated services network. In the United States, where the cable and telephone industries are separate, both cable and telephone companies have been quick to recognize the potential competitive advantages of being able to offer new services into their customers' homes.

Third, the world's telephone networks are now largely digital. Rather than transmitting analog voice, they transmit voice as a series of digital samples. The result is that the distinction between computer networks, which transmit bits between computers, and telephone networks, which transmit bits between telephones, is increasingly fuzzy.

Finally, the underlying nature of the telephone networks is changing. For a variety of reasons, telephone companies throughout the world have been slowly converting their networks from copper wiring to fiber. In the United States and Japan the long-distance networks have been almost converted from copper to fiber, and much of the local and regional telephone networks will be converted to fiber by the year 2000. Telephone companies have been installing fiber largely because it is more reliable, easier to maintain, has better error properties than copper, and requires less space to carry the same amount of data. But it is also true that the theoretical capacity of the fiber networks being installed is far more than voice traffic is ever likely to need.

The result of these trends is a telecommunications industry that finds itself with a surplus of bandwidth, a changing mix of traffic, and obvious commercial benefits from combining the various services it offers into a unified network.

Joint Activities

Observe that the interests of the three communities of computing, data communications, and telephones are converging. All three are interested in supporting new types of services or applications that combine some mix of computers, communications networks, and human users.

This emerging commonality of interests has led to a dramatic increase in the joint work between the various communities. Some of this joint work is the result of a mutual realization of the data communications community and the telephone community that they could not continue to ignore each other.

Probably the most notable joint activity is the set of gigabit testbeds in the United States. Each of these testbeds combines researchers from the telecommunications, the computing, and the data communications industries in joint research projects. Much of the credit for this joint effort is due to a small group of people who brought together the representatives of the different industries to collaborate in the testbeds.[3] However, a number of other cooperative gigabit activities have been established in countries throughout the world. (See Chapter 16 for a summary.)

Other joint activities are also in progress. For example, much of the standardization of Asynchronous Transfer Mode (ATM), a suite of communications protocols designed to support integrated voice and data networks, is being done through the joint collaboration of several standards bodies in the data communications and telephone communities.

As one might imagine, not all of these interactions are smooth. The goals of the different communities do not completely overlap. And in some cases, the communities approach problems from very different perspectives, making joint work difficult.

As a fairly benign (but useful) example of these differences, consider the question of what type of device will be attached to the integrated services network of the future. Many members of the telephone community use the telephone as their model system. Telephones are dumb custom devices engineered to

---

[3] Bob Kahn of the Corporation for National Research Initiatives is generally recognized as having played a key role in establishing these collaborations. Important recognition is also due to several project managers at the Advanced Research Projects Agency (ARPA) and the National Science Foundation (NSF), especially Ira Richer, Darlene Fisher and Paul Mockapetris, and David Farber of the University of Pennsylvania, who helped shape the collaboration.

send signals on a wire and play signals as they are received from a wire. The network is entirely responsible for keeping the signals clear. Because telephones are dumb it has proved relatively easy to mass produce them inexpensively. But if the devices attached to the network are dumb devices, then the network has to be engineered to provide precisely the types of signals the receiving devices expect. The computing community, which has watched as computers are incorporated into even the most mundane household appliances, finds it hard to understand why we should not assume any device connected to the network includes a general purpose computer, intelligent enough to manipulate the data it sends and receives. And many members of the data communications community, which has had such tremendous success with the idea of a single internetworking protocol that can provide a wide range of services, believe it is wrong to engineer a network for a particular application or small set of applications.[4]

1.3. Rules of the Road

When research on gigabit networking started in the mid-1980s, many researchers believed that gigabit networks were so much faster than existing networks that everything learned about networking would have to be discarded as no longer relevant. Now, after several years of study, it is clear that most of the lessons learned from earlier networks are applicable to gigabit networking as well. Some of these concepts are sufficiently important that they have shaped the presentation in this book.

Layering as an Architectural Abstraction

Over the past 20 years, the data networking community has found it very valuable to design protocols in terms of layered architectures. The term *architecture* must be emphasized here. Considerable experience suggests that layered implementations are a bad idea because they perform poorly. But as an architectural abstraction that helps clarify the roles of various protocols, the idea of layering has proved very valuable since it was developed in the mid-1970s by the ARPANET researchers and subsequently refined by the OSI standards teams.

---

[4] At this juncture it is probably appropriate to warn the reader that my background is almost exclusively in computer science and data communications. I have, however, tried throughout this book to be fair to the telephone community's perspectives as well.

The major advantage of layering is that it clearly delineates the responsibilities of the various protocols. This delineation helps define both how protocols interact with each other and the boundaries of a standards committee's job, which was one of the reasons that the OSI seven-layer model was developed.

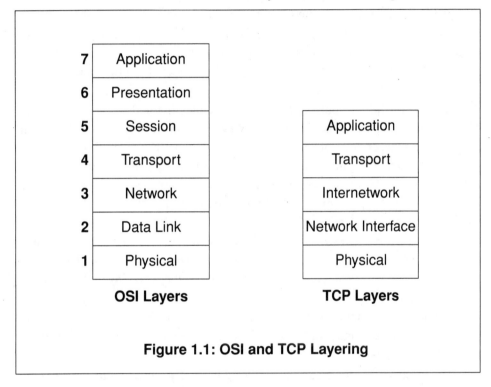

Figure 1.1: OSI and TCP Layering

To illustrate how layering can be used in an architecture, Figure 1.1 shows the seven-layer OSI architecture and the five-layer TCP architecture. Both architectures build up from the bottom. The lowest layer is the *physical layer*, which is the raw signalling media (the wire or fiber) over which data is sent.

In the TCP/IP model, the layer above the physical layer, typically referred to as the *network interface layer*, is viewed as containing all those mechanisms and protocols (signalling rules, frame formats, and media-access layer protocols) necessary to permit packets to be sent over the media. Above the network interface layer is the *internet layer*, which implements the protocols required to knit together divergent network technologies into a single virtual network, an internet. It may be useful to think of the internetworking layer as responsible for getting a packet or datagram through a series of networks between a sending host and a receiving host.

In the OSI architecture, the next layer after the physical layer, the *data link layer*, is responsible for signalling and framing. The layer above the data link layer is the *network layer*, which is generally thought to include both the media-access and internetworking protocols.[5]

The OSI and TCP/IP architectures come together again at the transport layer. The role of the *transport layer* is to provide a communications stream between two applications. Thus, the network or internet layer is responsible for getting data between hosts, and the transport layer adds the functionality needed to exchange data between applications.

On top of the transport layer, the OSI architecture adds three more layers. The *session layer*, which is now widely viewed as superfluous, was intended to assist in the management of the transport connection. The role of the *presentation layer* is to manage the formatting of data — to ensure that the data transmitted by the sender is interpreted correctly at the sender. The presentation layer is responsible for the problems of converting between the different data formats used on different systems. Above the presentation layer lies the *application layer*, which incorporates services designed to support a range of applications (such as a Remote Procedure Call service). The actual applications that use the OSI architecture are considered outside the scope of the seven layer model.

In the TCP/IP architecture, the application layer lies immediately above the transport layer. The notion in the TCP/IP architecture is that the question of what presentation protocol and what kinds of services to use is decided on an application-by-application basis.

The architecture for gigabit networking has not yet been defined. It may be the same as the TCP/IP or OSI architecture or it may be something completely different. However, the presentation of material in this book roughly follows a layered model.

Internetworking

Internetworking is probably the major networking discovery of the past 20 years. The strength of internetworking is its ability to link disparate network technologies into a single virtual network.

---

[5] The OSI model is somewhat fuzzy about where the media-access protocols fit in and originally did not include the notion of internetworking. It is clear, however, that these functions fit somewhere below the transport layer, and the network layer is the logical place.

No one network technology perfectly meets all the needs of all users and their situations. Some technologies like Ethernet are well suited for use as local area networks. Other technologies like satellite networks are well suited to provide wide area network services. Different technologies are more or less suitable for different office building layouts. As a result, different users will install different types of networks. But inevitably, one must make computers on two different types of networks communicate. To take a business example, the employees in one division may need to be able to exchange data with employees in another division, and the different divisions may use different networks. Internetworking protocols make it possible to connect the networks.

Another important advantage of internetworking is that it eases transitions from one networking technology to another. For example, if one is upgrading an office building from Ethernets to ATM, if all the systems run the same internetworking protocol, the building can be upgraded piecemeal (say, floor by floor). Because all the hosts support the same internetworking protocol, the hosts on the ATM network can still communicate with the hosts on Ethernets and vice-versa.

In brief, an internetworking protocol defines a data format for a common network-layer protocol and rules for transmitting this protocol over all known types of networks. Hosts send their data encapsulated in the internetworking protocol. Data that needs to cross network boundaries is transmitted through *routers*. For example, the IP (the Internet Protocol) is the internetworking protocol for TCP/IP. Methods for transmitting IP over various types of networks (Ethernets, token rings, etc.) have been defined. To send data, a host sends an IP datagram using the transmission rules of its local network (e.g., IP over Ethernet). If the IP datagram is destined for a host on another network (say, a token ring), the datagram will be sent via a router, which will remove the datagram from its Ethernet encapsulation and put it into the token ring encapsulation.

Beyond facilitating communication between disparate networks, internetworking has at least two other advantages. First, it permits users to choose the particular networking technology that makes the most sense for their situation. Second, it permits users to upgrade their particular portion of the network (e.g., to increase the bandwidth) without disrupting the rest of the network. (Observe that upgrading the internetworking protocol itself is extremely difficult — and done only rarely.)

Internetworking also has a disadvantage. There is a strong tendency to design internetworking protocols to support little more than the service offered by the least capable networking technology. Making the service minimal makes it easier to support. For example, it is widely believed that IP has proved far more popular than X.25 (another internetworking protocol) because IP is far easier to implement on LANs like Ethernets than X.25. As we move toward supporting new types of services for gigabit networks, one of the challenges is to retain the easy implementation of internetworking protocols like IP, while providing services beyond those of the least capable networking technologies.

Implicit in this book is the assumption that, like it or not, internetworking will be part of our future. As Chapters 2 through 7 will show, a huge variety of gigabit networking technologies are under development and it seems extremely improbable that any one technology will completely dominate. Each of the networking technologies has limitations that will make it inappropriate for some environments. The particular internetworking protocols may be different from those of today, but internetworking protocols they will be.

1.4. What Follows This Chapter

The rest of this book takes a generally bottom-up approach, starting with low-level media issues and building protocols and architectures on top of them. This approach follows my belief that, although the goal is to build an internetwork that liberates applications from the specifics of individual networks, we remain guided and limited by the capabilities of the networking technologies on which we build.

Chapter 2 is a general introduction to fiber optics, aimed at the nonengineer. It is intended to give the reader a good grasp of how fiber optics affect network design.

Chapters 3 through 6 are a detailed investigation of *cell networking,* including a full chapter (Chapter 4) on ATM which is the form of cell networking being deployed inside the telephone networks. Cell networking is technology that seems to have many advantages for gigabit networking, and it has been widely studied and implemented at gigabit speeds. At the same time, cell networking has some disadvantages; so to try to correct the balance, Chapter 7 looks at the modest but very interesting work done so far on noncell gigabit networks.

As an introduction and motivation to the second half of the book, Chapter 8 looks at gigabit applications and their requirements. As mentioned previously, part of the challenge of gigabit networking is to support new types of applications. Chapter 8 introduces the applications and their requirements in preparation for the remaining chapters.

Chapter 9 looks at problems of interfacing gigabit networks to computers The problems are not just in making the computers move data swiftly to and from the network, but also in enhancing the computers to support new applications, like multimedia conferencing, that gigabit networks will make possible.

Chapter 10 examines the problem of making today's protocols ready for gigabit networks. Then Chapters 11, 12, and 13 study how to enhance protocols to provide network support for real-time applications. Chapter 14 examines the surprising ways in which the performance of distributed systems will be affected by gigabit networks and some of the possible solutions to various performance problems. Chapters 15 and 16 conclude with a discussion of open problems in gigabit networking and suggestions for ways to keep track of ongoing work.

Further Reading

For an introduction to computer architectures, Hennessy and Patterson's [1990] book is highly recommended. For more information on disk arrays, and RAID in particular, see Patterson, Gibson and Katz [1988].

There are a couple of good textbooks on internetworking, both with TCP/IP and OSI. The most widely used are the first volume of Doug Comer's [1991] three-volume set of books on TCP/IP, and Andrew Tanenbaum's [1988] classic *Computer Networks*.

An early ARPANET paper [Davidson 1977] is generally believed to have been the first to mention layering. The OSI layering model was first presented by Zimmerman [1980].

David Irvin [1993] has written a useful article on some of the issues confronting the telephone industry, with a good set of references to further reading.

Chapter 2

Fiber Optics

2.1. Introduction

The development of gigabit networks has been closely linked to developments in fiber optics. Indeed, the advent of fiber optic signalling equipment capable of transmitting at several gigabits per second over long distances with very low error rates through optical fiber (typically known simply as *fiber*) showed that gigabit networks were feasible and has served as a goad to researchers.

Because fiber and its properties play an important role in gigabit networking, it is important to have at least a rudimentary understanding of the properties of fiber optic communication and how those properties affect the design of gigabit networks. Providing an overview of fiber optics is the primary purpose of this chapter.

Other transmission technologies are being improved so that they too are capable of transmitting and receiving at gigabit rates. Although less developed and less influential than fiber, these media are part of gigabit networking and are discussed briefly at the end of the chapter.

2.2. Essentials of Fiber Optics

The field of fiber optics has boomed over the past twenty-five years, since researchers began to examine the potential of almost lossless transmission using light in fiber. Much of the literature, unfortunately, is hard reading for the average computer scientist because it expects a background in the mathematics of physics. This section attempts to present the essentials of fiber optics in a few pages without resorting to mathematics much more complex than algebra and basic geometry. Suggestions for books that give a more complete treatment can be found in the recommended reading at the end of the chapter.

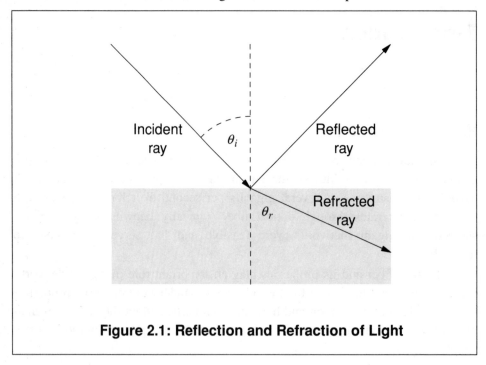

Figure 2.1: Reflection and Refraction of Light

Refraction and Fiber

It is an interesting property of light that when one sends light from one substance to another, two things happen: some of the light is reflected, and some of the light passes into the new substance. However, the rays of light entering the new substance are usually bent from their original angle (a phenomenon known as *refraction*). This behavior is illustrated in Figure 2.1. The arriving light (the *incident ray*) is shown hitting a boundary between two substances. Some light is reflected and some is refracted.

The amount by which a ray bends when refracted between two substances is determined by the *index of refraction* of each of the two substances and the wavelength of the light being sent. (Different wavelengths of light bend by different amounts — this phenomenon explains how prisms separate light into colors.) The index of refraction measures how much the light bends when it enters a substance. The ratio of the indices of the two substances determines how much light bends when moving from one substance to the next. In particular, the ratio of the sines of the angle of incidence, θ_i, and the angle of refraction, θ_r, equals the ratio of the two substances' indices of refraction. (Observe that both the angle of incidence and angle of refraction are measured from the perpendicular.)

The amount of light reflected and refracted varies, depending on the indices of refraction of the two substances through which the light is passing and the angle at which the light strikes the boundary between the two substances. If the light is shining perpendicularly, then the refracted light passes straight through. If the light is shining at an angle, some light is reflected at the same angle and some is refracted at a different angle. However, if the light is shining at an angle greater than a certain amount, called the *critical angle*, then the light is completely reflected (none passes through). The critical angle is the angle θ_i, whose sine is equal to the ratio of the index of refraction of the second substance divided by the index of refraction of the first substance.[1]

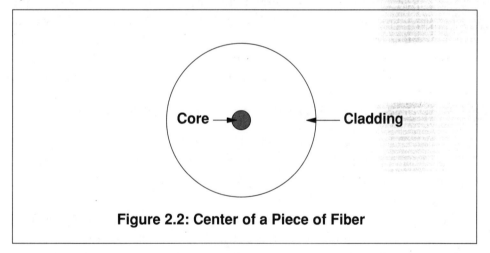

Figure 2.2: Center of a Piece of Fiber

Using the properties of refraction, it is possible to create thin strands of glass fiber that can transmit light over long distances. Figure 2.2 illustrates such a fiber. A strand of glass, called the *core*, is wrapped with another layer of slightly different glass, called the *cladding*. The core and cladding have different

---

[1] If the index of refraction of the second substance is greater than that of the first substance, there is no critical angle (the ratio is greater than 1). This is the case with window glass and air. Air has an index of refraction of about 1, and glass of about 1.45, for a ratio of 1.45. So although the amount of light reflected increases as the angle gets sharper (and this is why one can see reflections in glass), some light always gets through.

indices of refraction, with the core's higher than that of the cladding. As a result, light sent roughly straight down the core will stay in the core because any of the light trying to escape the core through the cladding will be reflected back into the core. By transmitting light through the core, it is possible to send bits in the form of pulses of light.

Bits Are Smaller, Not Faster

The index of refraction has another piece of significance. The index of refraction measures how fast photons travel in the fiber. For optical fiber, the index of refraction is around 1.45, which means the speed of light in fiber is about 0.69 the speed of light in vacuum or around 2.1×10^8 m/s.

Observe that the speed of light in fiber is not significantly different from the speed at which electrons propagate through copper. This observation is important — it means that if we were to transmit a single bit through the same length of fiber (as a burst of photons) and copper (as a burst of electrons), the bit would take the same time to get through the fiber as the copper. In other words, fiber is *not* faster than copper. Rather, what distinguishes fiber from copper is information density or bandwidth; one can pack more bits per unit of cable into a fiber.

An Example — Scaling Ethernet to Gigabit Speeds

To see how packing more bits into a unit of cable can affect protocol design, consider the problem of trying to scale up the Ethernet transmission rules to gigabit speeds. (For information on Ethernet see Metcalfe and Boggs [1976], and Boggs, Mogul, and Kent [1988]).

In Ethernet, every node is always listening to the network and may initiate a transmission only when the network is quiet. The network is a broadcast media (a cable) in which every node can hear transmissions from every other node. To guard against situations in which two nodes start sending simultaneously into a quiet network, nodes must listen to their transmissions, and if the data a node reads from the Ethernet does not match the data it is placing on the Ethernet, it knows that a *collision* has occurred. When a collision occurs, the node stops sending and waits a random time before trying to send again.

As Figure 2.3 illustrates, for Ethernet's collision detection and recovery scheme to work properly, the network must have a *minimum* packet size. Consider the example shown in the figure. Host A, at one end of the Ethernet cable, starts transmitting a packet. Host B is at the far opposite end of the cable. Just

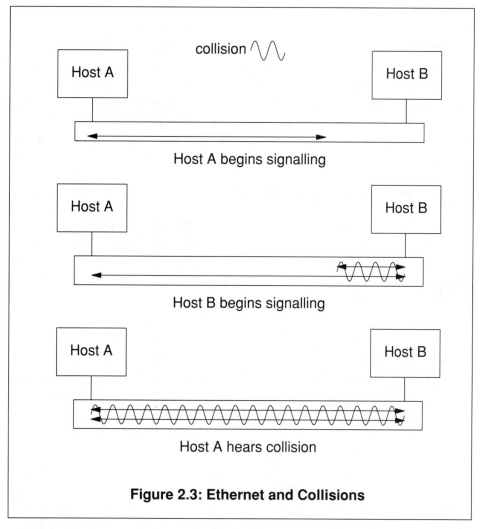

Figure 2.3: Ethernet and Collisions

before the first few of host A's bits reach host B, host B starts sending. (Keep in mind that until A's bits reach host B, the network will appear quiet to host B.) Now observe that host A will hear the collision only after the first few bits of host B's packet have traversed the wire all the way to host A. Thus, if we want to be sure that host A will hear a collision before it stops sending (and mistakenly assumes the transmission was successful), we need to make sure that host A transmits at least twice the cable length in bits. In a 10 megabit Ethernet, the minimum packet size is 64 bytes for a 5 km cable. But in a 1 gigabit Ethernet, the minimum packet size is about 6,400 bytes.

From an architectural perspective, 6,400 bytes is far too large for a minimum packet size. It would require small packets (e.g., 40 to 60 bytes long) to include thousands of overhead bytes as padding to protect against collisions, and this would cause inefficient use of the fiber's bandwidth.

The point of this example is that if we try to use fiber's high bandwidth, we will be unable to use some existing transmission schemes, like Ethernet. The particular lesson is that the cost of ensuring collision detection on high speed broadcast networks is sufficiently large that some other way to avoid collisions should be used.

Bandwidth Capacity of a Fiber

The bandwidth of a fiber is determined by the amount of light it can carry. Due to a number of physical factors, light currently passes easily through fiber in only three parts of the optical spectrum. These bands are each about 200 nanometers (nm) wide and are centered around the wavelengths of 0.85, 1.3, and 1.5 microns (a micron is 10^{-6} meters and abbreviated as μ).

Each of the three bands has about 25 terahertz (THz) of capacity. Standard signalling equipment can signal between 1 and 1.4 bits per Hz, so a single fiber could be used to transmit between 50 and 75 *terabits* per second!

(It may be useful to remember that a given color of light has a wavelength, λ, measured in meters (or fractions of a meter) and a frequency, f, measured in Hz, and that their product, $f\lambda$, must equal the speed of light, c. The frequency capacity of a band of the wavelength spectrum can be estimated by the equation

$$\Delta f = c\Delta\lambda/\lambda^2$$

where $\Delta\lambda$ is the size of the band (e.g., 200 nm), λ is the wavelength of light around which the band is centered (e.g., 1.5 μ) and c is the speed of light in the medium (2.1×10^8 m/s). The equation is the result of differentiating the equality $f = c/\lambda$ with respect to λ to get the change of frequency with respect to changes in wavelength. This equation is also used to determine the capacity of a piece of optical signalling equipment, if one knows the size of waveband at which the equipment operates.)

In reality, the achievable bit rate is somewhat less. Building fast signalling devices is expensive; it is more cost effective to build several parallel signalling devices that transmit at several different wavelengths on the same fiber, a practice called wavelength division multiplexing or WDM. WDM is analogous to the way the radio waves are multiplexed among multiple channels. And, like radio channels, some gap is left between signalling wavelengths to ensure the signals do not interfere with each other. But even if one leaves space between channels, a single fiber can be used to transmit tens of terabits per second.

Dispersion, Single-Mode, and Multimode Fiber

As a pulse of light travels through fiber, the pulse of light slowly spreads out. This phenomenon is known as *dispersion*.

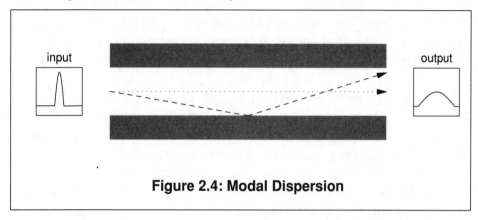

input

output

Figure 2.4: Modal Dispersion

Dispersion is an important problem because it limits the achievable bit rate over a fiber of a given length. (Conversely, given a bit rate, dispersion limits how long the link can be.) The farther a pulse travels in a fiber, the more it spreads out, until eventually it will interfere with the pulses ahead of and behind it, making it difficult to detect the signal. To avoid interference, one must either lengthen the interval between bits (reducing the signalling rate) or shorten the fiber by inserting some type of communications device that restores a clean pulse. Because the devices to restore the pulse can be expensive, and because the introduction of additional devices into a transmission path makes the path less reliable, finding ways to minimize dispersion is important. (More components in the path implies more places that the communications link can fail.)

There are three major types of dispersion: *modal*, *chromatic*, and *material dispersion*. Each is caused by different factors in fiber. Of the three, modal dispersion is probably the most important — the elimination of modal dispersion was a vital step toward high-speed communications.

One way to model modal dispersion is to think of it as a situation in which different photons in a pulse follow slightly different paths through a fiber.[2] The

_____

[2] Recall that light can be modelled as particles or wave forms and neither model is perfect. To keep the discussion simple, this section uses the particle model. The wave form model is

difference in paths means that different photons travel different distances and will reach the receiving end of the fiber at different times. For example, look at Figure 2.4, and compare the distance travelled by a photon that goes straight down the center of the fiber with the distance travelled by a photon that reflects several times off the core-cladding boundary. The difference in the distances travelled causes the signal to slowly spread out.

Modal dispersion gives its name to the two major types of fiber: *multimode* and *single-mode* fiber (also called *monomode* fiber). Multimode fiber suffers from modal dispersion; single-mode fiber does not. The difference between the two types of fiber is their geometry: typically multimode fiber has a big core of 50μ in diameter, and single-mode fiber has a small core of between 8μ and 12μ in diameter.

The number of different paths that a photon can take through the fiber is limited by two factors. The first factor is the critical angle between the core and cladding. Light striking at an angle less than the critical angle will pass through into the cladding. The critical angle in fiber is rather large, so only a small range of angles will reflect down the core. The second factor is that there is a limit to the total number of paths that photons of a given wavelength can take through a fiber and the number of paths is partly determined by the ratio of the wavelength of light being sent divided by the diameter of the fiber. The larger the ratio, the fewer available paths for the photons.

In multimode fiber, where the diameter is very large relative to the wavelength of light, several paths for photons will cause them to strike the core-cladding boundary at more than the critical angle and reflect down the fiber. In single-mode fiber, however, the diameter is almost the same as the wavelength of light and only one path works — straight down the center of the fiber. As a result, single-mode fiber suffers no modal dispersion.[3]

Although it does not suffer from modal dispersion, single-mode fiber still suffers from chromatic and material dispersion. Chromatic dispersion occurs

---

somewhat more accurate but requires the use of three-dimensional calculus to explain. For a good discussion, see Green [1993].

[3] The reader may wonder what happens if single-mode fiber is bent, say in a wiring closet. Does all the light going down the center run into the cladding and get lost? The answer is no; unless the fiber is very tightly bent, the light continues on through the fiber. This question points out one of the limitations of a presentation based on the particle model. When the diameter of a fiber is close to that of the wavelength of light being transmitted through the fiber, the particle model does not fully explain the light's behavior.

because, no matter how well tuned, a transmitting laser does not send all the photons at exactly the same wavelength of light. Different frequencies of light travel at slightly different speeds, so the photons sent at different wavelengths will spread out. Material dispersion occurs when impurities in the fiber cause photons to travel at different rates. Both chromatic dispersion and material dispersion have been substantially reduced by improvements in lasers and fiber fabrication, and it is currently possible to successfully transmit a high-bandwidth signal through a few thousand kilometers of fiber with almost no errors.

Repeaters and Amplifiers

Once dispersion has been minimized in a fiber, the next problem is a phenomenon known as *absorption*. As photons travel through fiber, some of them encounter impurities in the glass core or interact with the glass itself and are turned into other forms of energy, such as heat. As a result, a pulse can be thought of as being slowly absorbed by the fiber. The choice of the three signalling bands in fiber was dictated, in large part, by the fact that very little absorption occurs at those wavelengths. However, absorption does occur, and as a result, it is necessary to periodically amplify the signal.

Devices called *repeaters* and *amplifiers* are used to renew the strength of the signal. Both devices take a weakened signal from one piece of fiber and emit a signal of renewed strength out another piece of fiber.

Repeaters are optical-electrical devices, which take the signals from an input fiber, convert the signals into electronic bits inside the repeater, and then convert them back from electronic bits to optical pulses on the outbound fiber.

Although repeaters have the useful property that they can restore signals suffering from both disperson and absorption, they also have some annoying limitations. First, today's optical-electrical devices are capable of signalling only at a bit rate of a few gigabits per second, far slower than the theoretical maximum bandwidth of a fiber. So repeaters in a path limit the bit rate at which a pair of connected fibers can be used. Furthermore, to be able to convert pulses of light into bits, the repeater has to know something about the transmission patterns of the bits, so it can work out the bit clocking. Like all media, fiber grows or shrinks in response to changes in temperature. Changes in length change the time it takes for pulses of light to travel through a fiber. To deal with this phenomenon, the receiving end of the repeater looks for synchronization patterns to resynchronize its clock to the incoming bit patterns. However, the need for synchronization means that anyone using a fiber path that includes repeaters must use a transmission scheme that incorporates the synchronization patterns required by the repeaters. In other words, repeaters place limits on both bandwidth and signalling patterns.

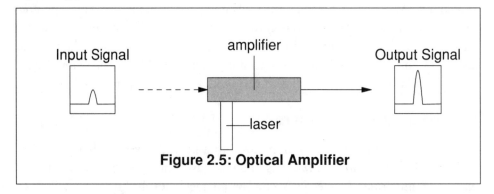

Figure 2.5: Optical Amplifier

A better alternative is *optical amplifiers*. Figure 2.5 illustrates an optical amplifier. A laser injects a regular amount of light into an amplifier, which excites the amplifier to just short of the point where the amplifier would transmit light into the outbound fiber. When a weak signal comes into the amplifier, it picks up energy as it passes through the amplifier and comes out strengthened. This amplification works particularly well for single-mode fibers because the incoming signal, though weak, has not suffered much dispersion. (Amplifying a dispersed signal simply amplifies the degenerate signal.) Note, however, that amplifiers add a little bit of noise to the renewed signal, so after several amplifications the signal may need to go through a repeater. However, it is currently possible to use amplifiers to create a path of single-mode fiber that crosses a continent (or an ocean) without requiring a repeater, yet can still be used to signal at gigabit rates.

There are two common types of optical amplifiers: semiconductor amplifiers and fiber amplifiers. Semiconductor amplifiers are essentially two mirrors that reflect light between them in a cavity. Entering signals pick up enough power to force a signal through the mirror on the outbound side. Fiber amplifiers are a length of fiber treated (or *doped*) with a rare element, into which the laser pumps light. Signals passing through the energized fiber are renewed. Different rare elements can be used. Erbium-doped fiber works well at the 1.5 μ wavelength, while praseodymium-doped fiber works well at the 1.3 μ wavelength. One important limitation of fiber amplifiers is that they can amplify light over only a restricted range of wavelengths, about 35 to 45 nm, or about 17% to 23% of the size of each of the fiber transmission bands.

Solitons

If a wave pulse is shaped in a particular way (the shape turns out to be the form of reciprocal hyperbolic cosine), the effects of dispersion and other physical phenomena in the fiber will counterbalance each other, with the result that the pulse suffers no dispersion (modal, chromatic, or material), regardless of how far it travels. These shaped pulses are called *solitons*, and they have only recently been discovered.

One modest technical problem with solitons is that they still suffer from absorption, and after a while, if too much of a pulse is absorbed, the pulse will break down. So solitons need regular amplification by fiber amplifiers.

Solitons offer the potential of sending extremely clear pulses of light through very long runs of fiber; in other words, the opportunity to use the full bandwidth of a fiber over almost arbitrary distances.

Single-Mode Fiber vs. Multimode Fiber

Single-mode fiber is so superior in its transmission properties to multimode fiber that one may wonder why anyone uses multimode fiber anymore. After all, multimode fiber suffers from dispersion and needs frequent repeaters to strengthen its signals.

However, multimode fiber is considerably more tolerant of errors in fitting the fiber to the transmitter or receiver attachments than single-mode fiber. (This is one of the reasons that multimode fiber is often used in cable TV networks.) As a result, where ease of termination is more important than maintaining a good signal quality over long distances (for example, if one is connecting computers to a nearby wiring closet), it seems likely that multimode fiber will continue to have an important role for some time to come.

2.3. Transmitters and Receivers

Transmitters and receivers are the generic terms for devices attached to a fiber to respectively transmit and receive signals. Transmitters are typically semiconductor lasers, fabricated in silicon or gallium arsenide. Similarly, receivers can be thought of as photodetectors, perhaps coupled with a filter to extract only the particular frequencies of light that are of interest.

Transmitters and receivers come in two varieties: fixed and tunable. Fixed transmitters and receivers are set to a particular wavelength of light at the time of manufacture. Tunable devices can dynamically select the lightwave frequency at which they send or receive. Fixed transmitters and receivers are a sufficiently simple idea that they require no further explanation, but the properties of tunable devices are important for some applications and will be briefly discussed here.

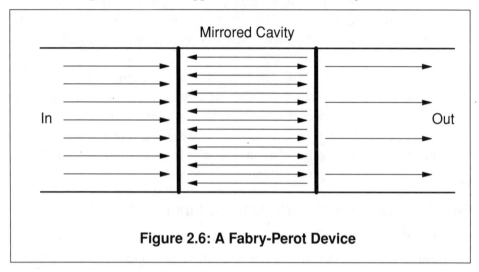

Figure 2.6: A Fabry-Perot Device

There are a number of ways to build tunable devices. For the purpose of illustration, we will look at one variety: *Fabry-Perot* lasers and filters, also known as *etalons*. The basic idea of a Fabry-Perot device is shown in Figure 2.6. A pair of mirrors is placed on each side of a cavity, into which light is injected from the left side. The entering light is reflected back by the mirror on the right, and the reflected light is in turn reflected back from the mirror on the left. On each reflection, some light is lost. At most wavelengths, after a few reflections, most of the light is gone. But for a particular wavelength, λ, the reflections cause a positive feedback loop to develop, such that light at that wavelength gets forced through the mirror on the right. The particular wavelength λ that the cavity selects is a function of the length of the cavity and the cavity's index of refraction. Thus, by mechanically adjusting the length of the cavity or by changing the index of refraction of the cavity's material, the value of λ can be changed.

If the cavity is placed in front of a power source, it provides a tunable Fabry-Perot laser. If the cavity is placed in front of a photodetector, it becomes a tunable Fabry-Perot receiver.

Most tunable lasers are variations on the basic Fabry-Perot model, with enhancements to improve the quality and power of the laser signal. There are, however, a wide variety of ways to build filters. Three types of filters other than

Fabry-Perot that are commonly mentioned in the literature are *Mach-Zehnder inferometers* (MZIs), *switched gratings,* and *acoustooptic tunable filters.*

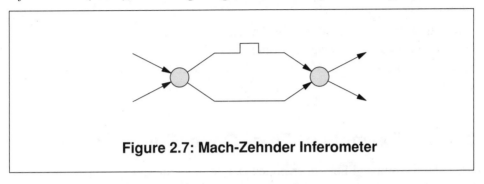

Figure 2.7: Mach-Zehnder Inferometer

The basic idea of an MZI is that beams of light are successively split in two and recombined, using a device like the one in Figure 2.7. Between the two splitting devices, there are two fiber optic paths, one slightly longer than the other. The difference in the lengths of the transmission paths causes the beams of light to arrive at the second device out of phase with each other. For certain wavelengths of light, this phase difference makes it possible to extract particular wavelengths of light by concatenating several MZI devices together. Furthermore, MZIs can be made to tune to selected wavelengths by changing the length of one of the paths using heat or opto-electrical devices.

A switched grating is a piece of finely etched glass combined with multiple photodetectors. The glass acts as a kind of prism, refracting light so that different wavelengths of light fall on different photodetectors. Choosing a particular wavelength of light is simply a matter of deciding which photodetector to listen to.

A more sophisticated way to build a grating is to build an acoustooptic filter. Acoustooptic filters use sound to select out the desired wavelength of light. Sound waves cause small variations in the density of a transparent material like glass. If one uses a material sufficiently sensitive to sound, these variations cause the material to behave like a grating and make it possible to select out a particular wavelength of light. By changing the wavelength of the sound, one can change the wavelength of light being selected.

Currently, a major problem with most tunable devices is that they all have limitations in important areas such as tuning ranges and tuning speeds. Fabry-Perot devices can typically tune over about a 35 nm range of wavelengths and take a few milliseconds to tune from one wavelength to another. Other filter designs have similar limitations. For example, switched gratings can tune very quickly from one frequency to another, but there is a limit to the number of photoreceptors that can be packed into a grating, and this limits the number of frequencies a grating can accept.

However, the field of tunable devices is still quite new. Optical textbooks written only five or six years ago often do not discuss the topic. As a result, it seems likely that we will continue to see improvement in tuning times and tunable wavelength ranges for some time to come.

2.4. An Example of Fiber Optic Signalling: SONET

Having outlined how fiber optics can be used for signalling bits, it is now time to demonstrate how fiber optic components can be used to build a network. As an initial example, we will examine the Synchronous Optical Network (SONET). SONET is a rather prosaic example because it is primarily a way to replace copper wiring with fiber. The goal is to achieve higher transmission rates in telephone trunks (by signalling at higher rates), while also using fewer wires (because one fiber can replace several copper lines) and employing a more flexible signalling protocol than is used for copper.

But SONET illustrates some of the basic transmission issues for fiber. It is also the transmission protocol used in telephone company fiber and, as a result, is likely to be one of the most commonly used transmission protocols over fiber. Furthermore, if one leases a fiber from one's phone company, it will probably use SONET framing. (It is possible to get so-called dark fiber that does not employ SONET signalling, but dark fiber requires the user to reimplement all the signalling services that SONET already provides.) Indeed, many researchers believe that because the telephone community will provide a large market for SONET signalling chips, SONET chips may become so readily available that everyone will use SONET signalling for point-to-point fiber links.

SONET and the SDH

SONET is part of a larger suite of telephony standards known as the *Synchronous Digital Hierarchy* (SDH), standardized by the *Comité Consultatif International Télégraphique et Téléphonique* (CCITT),[4] the worldwide telephony

---

[4] Recently the CCITT has been replaced by a new standards body, the Telecommunications Standards Board or TSB, but the relevant standards were issued by CCITT and, for the present, continue to be referred to as CCITT documents.

standards body.

The SDH was developed to support multiplexing on links capable of data rates of hundreds of megabits or more. The goal of the SDH is to develop a single set of multiplexing standards for high-speed links. Currently, there are three sets of standards for telephony multiplexing at lower speeds: the U.S. standard, the Japanese standard, which is very close to the U.S. standard, and the CCITT standard, which is used almost everywhere but the United States and Japan. For example, the United States uses a T1 standard for multiplexing together 24 64-Kb/s voice circuits onto a 1.5 Mb/s link, whereas the CCITT equivalent is an E1 circuit, which multiplexes 32 voice circuits at 2 Mb/s. Because of the different standards, international connection of telephone networks is sometimes awkward. Does one, for example, multiplex 24 or 32 circuits over a link between the United States and Europe? Also, telephone companies rent high-speed circuits from each other. For instance, to connect its phone network to the US, a telephone company in Sweden has to rent lines in a path through Denmark, the Netherlands, France, and the United Kingdom to get to a transatlantic fiber to the United States. If different phone companies have different transmission rates, then building such a concatenated circuit becomes difficult because each hop has a different signalling rate. By developing consistent multiplexing standards for higher speeds, much of this awkwardness can be eliminated.[5]

Table 2.1: SONET/SDH Transmission Rates		
Data Rate (Mb/s)	SONET STS/OC Designation	CCITT STM Designation
51.84	1	–
155.52	3	1
622.08	12	4
1,244.16	24	8
2,488.32	48	16

Table 2.1 shows part of the hierarchy of SONET/SDH transmission rates. Because SONET began as a U.S. standard and was then incorporated into the CCITT standards for SDH, there are three different ways to describe a given data rate.[6]

---

[5] Higher speeds made some of this integration easier. The protocols that integrate the different multiplexing rates into SONET all waste a few bits. But at high bandwidths, the waste of a few bits is far less important than it would be if bandwidth was precious.

[6] There are slightly different rules about what one can do with a circuit, depending upon

Under the SONET standard, the first data rate in the hierarchy is 51.84 Mb/s, it is designated *Synchronous Transport Signal level 1* (STS-1), or *Optical Carrier level 1* (OC-1). (The subtle distinction between an STS-*n* designation and an OC-*n* designation is that OC-*n* describes an STS-*n* bit stream after it has been converted to optical signals.) Numbering under the STS/OC scheme indicates how many STS/OC-1 circuits can be encapsulated at the given rate. For example, STS-12, at 622.08 Mb/s, equals 12 STS-1 circuits. In fact, an STS-12 line can be used as twelve multiplexed STS-1 circuits, four STS-3 circuits, or as a single-channel 622 Mb/s line. If the circuit is being used for a single channel, it is called a *concatenated* (or, in some circles, *clear channel*) line and designated by appending a *c* after the number, for example, OC-3c.

The CCITT data rates begin with 155.52 Mb/s, which is *Synchronous Transport Module level 1* (STM-1). Like the SONET numbering scheme, the CCITT scheme counts in multiples: so an STM-4 data rate is equal to four times the STM-1 data rate, and it is possible to translate between STM and STS values by simply multiplying by 3. For the rest of this book we will use the SONET OC terminology.

Although a whole range of multiplexing speeds has been defined, in fact only a limited set of them will likely be used. For example, complete standards for multiplexing telephone circuits over STM links currently exist only for OC-3, OC-12, and OC-48 (STM-1, STM-4, STM-16) data rates. The reason for this selective standardization is that the various telephone networks are not planning to change their multiplexing rates for lower speeds, and efficient multiplexing of both U.S. and CCITT low-speed circuits is possible only at some data rates.

The selective use of OC data rates is of some concern for people interested in using SONET for data communications, as some of the data rates not useful for telephony are very interesting for data communications. The most obvious example is OC-24, which has a data rate of 1.2 gigabits and is a logical data rate to use for links between gigabit-speed local area networks (LANs). Several proposed gigabit LANs have bandwidths between 800 megabits and 1 gigabit per second. If a SONET line is placed between two 800 megabit LANs, an OC-12 line is clearly too slow, but an OC-48 line is overkill. Without support for OC-24 inside the telephone networks, however, it is not clear there will be a market for

---

which *appellation contrôlée* is used to describe it. For example, the multiplexing rules for OC-48 and STM-16 are slightly different. However, these differences are not critically important for data communication uses and will therefore be ignored in this chapter.

OC-24 components. If the telephone networks do not support OC-24 then obviously they will not be buying OC-24 chips. Furthermore, if the telephone networks do not support OC-24, then users cannot lease OC-24 lines, so users will not buy OC-24 chips for their computers either.

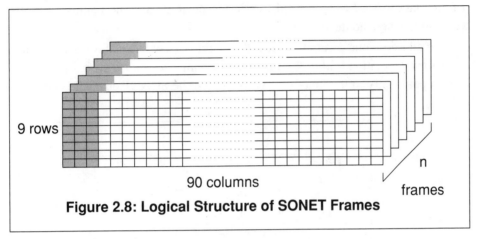

Figure 2.8: Logical Structure of SONET Frames

How SONET Works

SONET transmits data in frames. Each frame is logically thought of as a two dimensional chunk of bytes, with 90 columns and 9 rows (see Figure 2.8). For a given OC-*n* data rate, the unit of transmission is *n* frames. So OC-1 transmits data frame by frame, but OC-3 handles transmissions in groups of three frames. Somewhat confusingly, these larger groups of frames are also referred to as *frames*; the rule is that a single OC-*n* frame is made up of *n* OC-1 frames.

The first three columns (27 bytes per OC-1 frame) are reserved for transport overhead information. The first three rows are called the *regenerator section overhead* and the last five rows are called the *multiplexor section overhead*. Regenerator overhead is processed at each SONET repeater. Multiplexor overhead is processed at SONET multiplexors. (Repeaters simply renew the SONET signal on a fiber, but multiplexors combine and extract individual data channels from within the SONET frames.)

The fourth row of the transport overhead contains pointers. A key problem in multiplexing is that the lines attached to a multiplexor typically get out of sync with each other. Each line has its own clocking mechanism to manage its transmission and reception of bits, and for reasons such as the variation in fiber length mentioned earlier, the clocks of different lines will typically vary from each other. Now consider the problem of taking four OC-3 channels from different fibers and multiplexing them into one byte-interleaved OC-12 channel. It should be clear that the relative timing of when frames arrive from the different fibers will vary over time. The pointers are used to adapt to these variations. SONET permits data to start at arbitrary bytes in the payload, and the pointers indicate where in the payload the data starts.

In addition, one column in each 90×9 frame may be used for placing multiplexing information within the data (called *path overhead*). If this path overhead appears only in the first 90×9 frame, then the SONET channel is concatenated.

Frame	Frame	Interleave
A1	A2	C1
Parity	EOW	User
B1*	E1*	F1*
Regenerator Data Comm*		
	D1 thru D3	
Pointer	Pointer	Pointer
H1	H2	H3
Error Detect	Protection	Switching
B2*	K1*	K2*
Multiplex Data Comm		
D4 through D12*		
Zero Bytes		EOW-2
		E2*

Figure 2.9: SONET Transport Overhead Bytes

The structure of the three columns of SONET transport overhead information is shown in Figure 2.9 as defined for OC-1. At higher rates, the starred (*) bytes appear only in the first 90×9 frame; the other bytes may be repeated in later frames.

Most of the fields serve obvious functions. The A1 and A2 bytes form a frame alignment word, used for synchronization of the start of each 90×9 block. The C1 byte is used for interleaving STS frames (at rates greater than OC-3). The B1 and B2 bytes are error checks on the regenerator section overhead and the multiplexor section overhead, respectively. The E1 and E2 bytes are used to provide a 64-Kb/s voice channel for maintenance personnel in each of the regenerator and multiplexor sections. The F1 byte is a 64-Kb/s alarm channel. Bytes D1 through D3, and D4 through D12 provide data communications channels for network management between the regenerators and multiplexors.

The data communications channels are of some interest because they are used to signal between SONET equipment. Using these channels a user can instruct multiplexors to change the routing of SONET channels, making it possible to build a switched SONET network in which connectivity between different nodes of a SONET network is under user control.

It should be clear that SONET overhead is very carefully designed to meet the requirements of passing telephone data over long distances. For example, the presence of voice channels for maintenance personnel and alarm channels are probably unnecessary if SONET is to be used as the framing protocol between two nearby data communications devices in an office building. Some vendors have suggested that a stripped down SONET specification (largely a specification that says which overhead bytes to ignore) should be developed for local data communications framing. The major advantage of such a specification is that it should make it possible to build simpler (and presumably less expensive) SONET signalling hardware.

As of this writing, although the purpose of each of the bytes is specified, in many cases the format of their contents is not. So that they can deploy SONET now, users and vendors of SONET are developing private schemes for encoding some of the bytes. But the result is that two sets of SONET signalling equipment from different vendors may not interoperate.

The data portion of SONET is simply a collection of bytes, which is formatted as required by the higher level. Currently, standards exist for carrying multiplexed telephony circuits (at certain SONET rates) and for carrying data in the form of Asynchronous Transfer Mode cells. The ATM formatting is described in Chapter 4.

2.5. Another Example: WDM Networks

In contrast to SONET, wavelength division multiplexing networks use the special properties of optical fibers to build new types of data networks. The basic idea behind WDM networks is to divide up the bandwidth of a fiber into multiple channels, and then arrange for hosts that want to communicate to rendezvous on a particular channel. The rendezvous is made possible by pre-assignment or by tuning receivers or transmitters to the desired channel.

A major motivation behind WDM is the fact that it is currently possible to convert between electrical and optical signals at only a few gigabits per second. The goal of WDM is to make fuller use of the capacity of a fiber by employing multiple electrical-optical devices in parallel on different wavelengths. Some WDM proponents like to call these *terabit* networks, because the aggregate traffic can be measured in terabits per second. The author believes this is a modest abuse of terminology — the data communications community has typically described networks in terms of the data rate available to a single attached node. Using this terminology, WDM networks are gigabit networks (which seems sufficiently fast to brag about!).

Two key challenges arise in designing WDM networks. One challenge is to minimize the amount of time spent deciding which systems will communicate on which channels and maximize the time transmitting user data. The second challenge is to make effective use of the fiber bandwidth, both by packing the different frequency channels as close together as possible (a technique known as *dense WDM*) and by improving the effective tuning ranges of optical devices.

There are two major types of WDM networks. In *single-hop* WDM networks, all nodes can communicate directly with all other nodes. In *multihop* WDM networks, a node can communicate directly with only a few other nodes. To reach nodes with which it cannot communicate directly, a node must relay its messages through other nodes.

Examples of Single-Hop WDM Networks

Single-hop WDM networks are the simpler form of WDM networks. Their basic design is shown in Figure 2.10. Every node is attached to some sort of optical device that multiplexes all the inputs to all the outputs. One such multiplexing device is a *star coupler*, which can be thought of as a specially designed block of glass. Every output gets a copy of what every input is sending. Note that the effect of splitting the signal is to weaken it, so that if there are *n* nodes

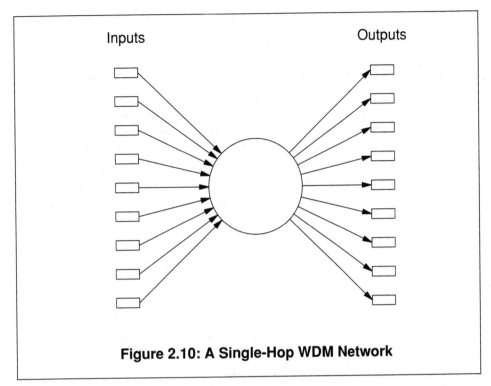

Inputs   Outputs

Figure 2.10: A Single-Hop WDM Network

attached, each gets 1/nth of the sender's signal. If *n* gets too large, this signal gets sufficiently weak to make signalling at high speeds hard, but current technology is sufficient to support at least a thousand nodes, each transmitting at about a gigabit.[7]

To help better understand the different types of single-hop networks, Mukherjee [1992a] has recently developed a useful taxonomy of WDM networks that distinguishes them by the types of transmitters and receivers they use. In this classification there are four types of networks:

1. *Fixed transmitter(s) and fixed receiver(s)* (FT-FR) networks have transmitters and receivers that can send and receive only on fixed channels. FT-FR networks are typically the least flexible networks, because each node is limited in the number of sending and receiving channels. FT-FR designs are better suited for multihop WDM networks, where the intermediate switches can shift signals from one channel to another. (For example, if host A sends on channel 12 and

---

[7] For several useful papers on these design issues, see Cheung and Winzer [1990].

host B receives on channel 23, one or more switches will be required to take the signal on channel 12 and retransmit it on channel 23, so B can hear it.)

2. *Tunable transmitter(s) and fixed receiver(s)* (TT-FR) networks have transmitters than can tune to different channels, but receivers that listen only on a particular channel. TT-FR networks are quite flexible because typically any node can talk to any other node. The major concern is collisions, as two transmitters attempt to contact the same receiver. These problems can be handled using either a standard collision resolution scheme (e.g., ALOHA) or special optical devices (called *protect-against-collision* switches) that suppress multiple transmissions on the same channel.

3. *Fixed transmitter(s) and tunable receiver(s)* (FT-TR) networks have transmitters that use a fixed wavelength but receivers that can scan a range of frequencies. Like TT-FR networks, FT-TR networks are quite flexible. The major design problem is figuring out to which channel to tune one's receiver. An important advantage of FT-TR networks is that they can easily implement multicasting (a group of receivers simply tunes to the same wavelength).

4. *Tunable transmitter(s) and tunable receiver(s)* (TT-TR) networks are probably the most flexible network architecture, but are arguably too flexible in that one must coordinate both transmitters and receivers to achieve connectivity, and this makes the access protocols rather complex to design.

Prototype single-hop WDM networks have been built using three different architectures (FT-FR, TT-FR, FT-TR). This section looks at two of these: LAMBDANET™, an FT-FR network, and one of the first WDM networks; and RAINBOW, one of the latest WDM networks using an FT-TR approach. (The best known TT-FR network is called FOX and is described in Arthurs et al. [1986].)

LAMBDANET

LAMBDANET was a project of Bell Communications Research in the mid-1980s [Goodman 1990]. The network interconnected *n* nodes using an FT-FR approach. Each node on the network had a single, fixed transmitter and *n* receivers, one for each sending channel. The receiver listened to all the channels all the time and pulled out the transmissions it wished. The prototype network connected sixteen hosts, with each channel having a bandwidth of 2 gigabits.

The obvious drawback of the LAMBDANET design is the requirement for n receivers at each node. This approach is clearly expensive (both in buying the receivers and locating them all on an interface board). However, the approach has some very interesting virtues. Multicasting is easy — everyone is always listening to every sender's channel. And there is no need to schedule transmissions — anyone can send at any time, because everyone has one's own channel. Furthermore, at the time LAMBDANET was built, tunable receivers were still very primitive. By using multiple receivers, LAMBDANET was able to test some of the ideas that would later be used in FT-TR networks.

RAINBOW

RAINBOW is a project of IBM [Janniello 1992]. The first version of the RAINBOW network, demonstrated in 1990 and 1991, was capable of sending at 300 Mb/s on each of 32 channels. The designers have often stated a goal of achieving 1,000 channels, each with 1 gigabit of bandwidth.

The RAINBOW network uses an FT-TR approach. Communication is achieved using a search protocol at the receiver. If host A wishes to communicate with a host B, A first tunes its receiver (a Fabry-Perot device) to B's channel. A then begins sending a polling signal, which contains both A and B's addresses, on its channel. On the receiving side, if B is not currently communicating with another node, then B's receiver is channel hopping, from one channel to the next, looking for poll messages that contain B's address. Thus B will eventually see A's poll message. When B sees A's poll, B transmits a start message on its channel. A, which had its receiver tuned to B's channel, will hear the start message and know it can start sending data.[8]

The RAINBOW design has a couple of advantages. It requires only one transmitter and one receiver. Also, it can support multicasting (multiple receivers all tuned to the same channel).

The current challenge in RAINBOW is to reduce the access time. Currently it takes around 10 milliseconds to establish a channel, because of limitations in the hardware to scan across and lock onto channels. This time is sufficiently long that RAINBOW is considered suitable for establishing only fairly

---

[8] There's an obvious deadlock in this protocol. What if A is trying to talk to B, while B is trying for C, and C is trying for A? RAINBOW fixes the deadlock problem by requiring hosts to give up if a connection isn't established after a while.

long-lived circuits. If hardware is developed that permits tuning within a few microseconds, the RAINBOW architecture could be used for packet switching.

Multihop WDM Networks

One way to avoid the need for fast, tunable transmitters or receivers is to build a multihop WDM network. In multihop WDM systems, transmitters and receivers typically are either tuned to a fixed frequency or capable of being tuned slowly and retuned only in response to a failure in the network or to adapt to a substantial change in traffic patterns.

Multihop WDM networks can be designed in a wide variety of ways. The essential idea is to build a connectivity graph among the nodes, so that the number of hops required to get between two nodes is kept small. This problem is tremendously interesting from a theoretical standpoint (for one thing, we can try optimizing the connectivity graph for metrics other than distance), but from a practical standpoint, few multihop WDM networks have been built.

TeraNet is one of the few. It is a multihop WDM network being built as part of the ACORN gigabit project[9] at Columbia University [Gidron 1992]. (Much of the early work on multihop WDM networks was done by Acampora of Columbia.) In TeraNet, computers are attached to the network through network interface units (NIUs). Each NIU has two fixed transmitters and two fixed receivers, all tuned to different frequencies. The frequencies throughout the network are arranged such that each frequency has exactly one transmitter and one receiver tuned to it. Thus each NIU can send to two NIUs and can receive from two (possibly different) NIUs. The task is then to arrange the NIUs so that there exists a path (via some number of NIUs) from each NIU to every other NIU in the network.

Obviously, there are a large number of possible TeraNet configurations. Figure 2.11 illustrates one possible configuration and a sample two-hop path from NIU-1 to NUI-4, via NIU-7. (Observe that multiple paths exist, and NIU-1 could also reach NIU-4 via a path through NIU-5, NIU-2, and NIU-6.) The configuration is interesting, in part because the NIUs are connected using multiple star couplers. Recall that the goal of WDM is to share the bandwidth of a fiber, so connecting each NIU to its neighbors using separate strands of fiber would defeat the point of WDM. Rather, several NIUs share an optical interconnection

---

[9] ACORN stands for Advanced Communications Organization for Research Networks.

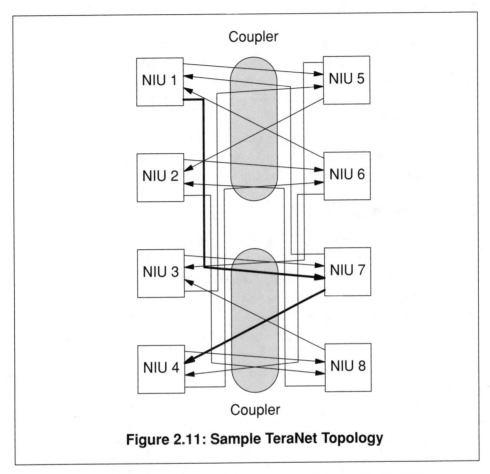

Figure 2.11: Sample TeraNet Topology

device. All the NIUs can share a single connection device, but TeraNet encourages using multiple connection devices, to reduce the number of times a signal must be split (thus, reducing the signal power required).

Because TeraNet uses fixed transmitters and receivers and each frequency is used by only one transmitter-receiver pair, it needs no protocol to mediate communication. Rather, it can transmit bits in whatever form it wants. In fact, TeraNet transmits data as fixed-sized packets, called *cells*, which will be discussed in detail in the next several chapters.

2.6. Other Media

The advances in high-bandwidth communications made possible by fiber optic signalling have encouraged engineers to try to improve the quality of signalling over other media. This section will look briefly at examples of two non-fiber optic media (radio, and microwave via satellite) that can signal at gigabit or near-gigabit rates.

The primary appeal of radio and satellite networks is that they can replace fiber in cases where installing fiber may be very expensive (e.g., over rough terrain or bodies of water) or provide backup to a fiber link.

Gigabit Radio Links

The LuckyNet gigabit testbed at AT&T Bell Labs has built a 2.4 gigabit per second (OC-48 bit rate) radio link between the Murray Hill and Crawford Hill laboratories, a distance of 23 miles [Gans 1991]. The design for the link calls for a bit error rate of just 10^{-11}, with the link being available over 95% of the time. (The major obstacle to high availability is a body of water between the two sites. During parts of the year, atmospheric conditions may cause interfering reflection off the water.)

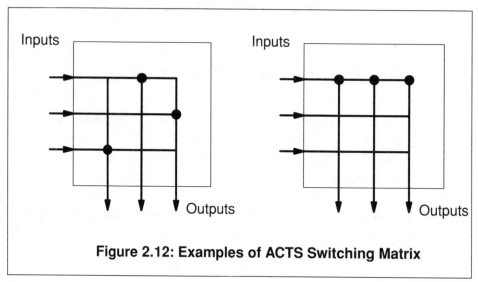

Figure 2.12: Examples of ACTS Switching Matrix

The Advanced Communications Technology Satellite

The Advanced Communications Technology Satellite (ACTS) is an experimental satellite that was launched by NASA in July 1993 [Balombin 1992; Bergamo 1992]. In one configuration, the satellite can support OC-12 bit rates via microwave to a number of sites within the continental United States. (The satellite can transmit formats other than SONET.) Data is transmitted over microwave channels as a sequence of OC-3 frames. The expected bit error rate of the microwave channels is less than 1 bit error in 10^{11} bits.

The channel is designed for a wide range of experimentation and supports both fixed and movable microwave beams. The movable beams may be tuned to different sites for different experiments.

At the heart of the satellite is a 3×3 microwave switching matrix (sketched in Figure 2.12). This matrix takes input from up to three up channels and determines how to distribute the inputs to the down channels. The matrix on the left of the figure shows each uplink connected to a different downlink, whereas the matrix on the right shows one uplink being broadcast to all the downlinks. The matrix can be programmed to change its configuration after each SONET frame, so that the frames of four OC-3 channels within an OC-12 uplink can be directed to different down channels.

The ability of the ACTS satellite to broadcast a single input channel to multiple output channels makes it more than a simple replacement for fiber otpics; it is an interesting vehicle for experimentation in the bulk distribution of information. Indeed, one of the experiments to be conducted on the ACTS involves the distribution of weather information from a central weather center to a number of sites across the United States.

2.7. Summary

This chapter has covered a lot of ground and a number of important points.

Fiber, especially single-mode fiber, is a transmission medium capable of transmitting a vast numbers of bits per second, with very few errors, over very long distances. Some other media, notably radio and satellite networks, are also capable of high speeds.

Fiber's transmission powers can be exploited in at least two ways. One approach is to treat it as a simple replacement for a large number of copper wires. This approach is being taken in telephone networks, in which copper wires are replaced with multiplexed fiber links using SONET. Another approach is to split the large bandwidth of fiber into multiple channels and do WDM. WDM gets around the bit-rate limitations of electrical-optical equipment. We examined some example networks that use WDM principles to build high-speed local area networks.

Further Reading

At least two good books surveying fiber optics have been written. The first book, by Personick [1985], is a good overview of the field written for nonspecialists but it is now slightly dated (in particular, it does not discuss tunable devices). The second book, by Paul Green [1993], is quite recent and designed to be a graduate engineering textbook. Green's book provides an outstanding coverage of the field as it currently stands but expects considerably more background in mathematics than Personick's.

A truly readable book on SONET has yet to be written. Sexton and Reid's [1992] book comes close but is occasionally difficult to understand and gives little attention to data communications issues. The brief description by Stallings [1992, pp. 546-557] may also be useful (though note that the encapsulation for ATM has changed since the book was written).

Mukherjee [1992a,1992b] has written a fine two-part survey of WDM network designs.

Chapter 3

An Introduction to Cell Networking

cell networking
switching
relay

3.1. Introduction

One of the important trends in gigabit networking is an increased interest in a technology now known variously as *cell networking*, *cell switching*, or *cell-relay*. A particular form of cell networking, Asynchronous Transfer Mode, is being developed by the CCITT and its successor, the TSB, as part of the Broadband Integrated Services Digital Network (B-ISDN) switching technology for future mixed telephone and data networks.

This chapter is an introduction to cell networking. The goal is to illustrate the range of capabilities of cell networks and present a few general concepts in preparation for the next three chapters, which study ATM, the particular link-layer cell network technologies being developed for wide area and local area networks.

① fix size

3.2. What Is a Cell?

The premise of cell networking is that all data should be transmitted in small, fixed-size packets, called *cells*.

In data communications networks, senders and receivers of data typically organize their data in *packets*, chunks of data with control information attached to them. (If this control information is at the front of the data, it is called a *header*, otherwise it is called a *trailer*.) To transmit packets over cell networks, a sender must break the packet into cell-sized chunks and transmit the cells across the network to the receiver, which must reassemble the data in the cells into a packet. This process is illustrated in Figure 3.1.

43

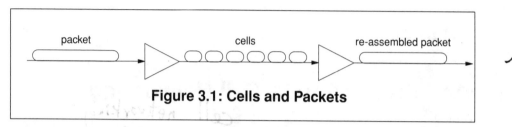

Figure 3.1: Cells and Packets

Different variations on cell networking use different cell sizes. Most network designs now call for cells that are 53 bytes long, a 5-byte header plus 48 bytes for data, because this is the size CCITT chose for ATM. However, cell networks have been built with cell sizes as small as 4 bytes and as large as 256 bytes; some of these networks are discussed in Chapters 5 and 6.

Size is important, it influence higher layer

The choice of size has some importance because the size of the data portion of the cell has an effect on the form of the higher layer protocols. To allow receivers to properly interpret the cell data they receive, each cell must contain a little bit of control information describing its relation to other cells in the data stream. For example, is this cell the beginning of a higher layer packet, the end of a packet, network management data, or user data? If cells are small, this control data must be absolutely minimized to avoid excess control overhead in each cell. If cells are larger, these requirements are somewhat relaxed, and for bigger cell sizes (128 bytes or larger) the amount of control information can be quite large. Thus the choice of higher layer protocols and how those higher layer protocols manage control information in cells can be affected by cell size.

size ↑ control ↓
size ↓ control ↑
higher layer decide size (manage control message

One reason to prefer small cell sizes is to reduce waste. When a sender breaks its data into cell-sized pieces, the last cell normally will not be completely filled. Indeed, if the sender chooses its data sizes without regard to cell size, on average half of the last cell will be unused. It is likely that most network systems will be tuned to try to keep cells largely filled, but one cannot be entirely sure.

Another reason to worry about cell size is serialization delay, the time it takes to put bits of data onto a transmission link. Serialization delay interacts with cell size in three ways.

Recall that one of the goals of many gigabit efforts is to allow voice, video, and computer data to run over the same network. In a mixed-traffic network, some types of traffic, most notably traffic from interactive voice and video conversations, will have tight limits on how long their data can take to get through the network.

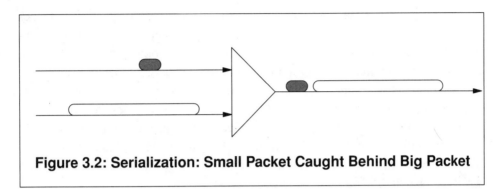

Figure 3.2: Serialization: Small Packet Caught Behind Big Packet

Choosing a small cell size can help meet those delay requirements. Consider the diagram in Figure 3.2. Two lines are feeding packets into a switching device that forwards the data out the line to the right. The top input line is carrying a time-critical packet containing a voice sample. The bottom line is carrying a big data packet. Because the voice sample arrives slightly after the big data packet, the voice sample is trapped behind the big data packet on the output line. If the big packet is very large, the voice sample could arrive too late.

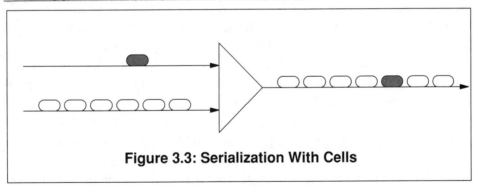

Figure 3.3: Serialization With Cells

Now consider the same example, but with the big packet broken up into cells, as in Figure 3.3. The time-critical cell has to wait only for the current cell of the big packet to be sent before it can be sent out itself.

Although it is possible to devise a system where the transmission of the the big packet is interrupted, this scheme wastes bandwidth by putting incomplete transmissions into the network and makes for substantially more complex interfaces that must be able to recognize and handle partial packets. Therefore, fixed-size cells are preferred.

Observe that if the cell size is too big, cells start acting like big packets, so the trick to keeping time-critical cells from being badly delayed is to keep cells

keep time-critical cell from being delay to long
→ small cell

relatively small. For these reasons, some experts argue that very small cell sizes are necessary (as small as sixteen bytes). One should keep in mind that this analysis assumes that the time spent to transmit a cell is nonnegligible (i.e., a cell takes long enough that the delay it might impose on cells stuck behind it matters). As network bandwidth increases, this concern will become increasingly irrelevant because the serialization delay caused by waiting for a single cell becomes negligible, even for larger cells. A 128-byte cell takes just a bit more than one *micro*second to transmit on a gigabit link, while the typical application is sensitive only to delays measured in milliseconds. So if all the links in the cell network are fast, the cell size can be large.

Another serialization issue is analog-to-digital conversion delays. Some parts of the telephony community would like to replace the current telephone network with cell networks. Voice is an analog input, which must be converted to a sequence of bits to be transmitted over a digital network. The need for conversion implies that at certain points in the telephone networks there will be devices that convert analog voice signals into digital samples placed in cells (and vice versa). To make the most efficient use of the cell network bandwidth, one would like to fill each cell completely with digital samples. Partially filled cells waste bandwidth and are therefore costly. Trying to completely fill a cell, however, introduces delay. The analog-to-digital conversion system must buffer up the converted signal until it has enough data to fill a cell. The larger the cell size, the more time the device must wait to get a full cell's worth of signal. Once again, small cell sizes reduce delay.

Yet another serialization issue is *forwarding delay*, the period between when a forwarding device starts receiving a packet and when that the device begins sending the packet on the next hop link. The forwarding device can be a router, but it can also be a host interface forwarding application data onto a network. There are two well-known ways to do forwarding.

One way is called *store and forward*: the device stores the incoming packet until it has the entire packet and then forwards it. In a store-and-forward system, every device in the path from the sender of the packet to the packet's receiver adds some delay due to the time spent storing the packet before forwarding the packet on. (This delay is very similar to that due to analog-to-digital conversion.)

The other way to forward is called *cut through*. In a cut through system, the device starts to forward the incoming packet out the next link while the packet is still being received on the inbound link. Cut through can almost completely eliminate storage delay, but is very difficult to implement. For example, cut through only works when the next network link is free. If the next link is already busy, then the forwarding device has to buffer the inbound packet until the outbound link is free. Also, if the inbound link is slower than the outbound link, the device can only forward the packet once it is sure that it will finish receiving the packet before it will finish sending! So a cut-through device has to have both cut-through logic and store-and-forward logic to handle times when cut through is not possible. Also, cut through requires very fast routing software that can look at the start of the packet and quickly figure out on which outbound link to forward the packet. Because of these technical challenges, implementations of cut-through routing are uncommon.

However, if one chooses the cell size properly, cell networks can perform almost as well as cut-through systems. Because a packet is fragmented into individual cells, a device can forward each cell as it is received and does not have to buffer up all the cells in a packet before forwarding them. To achieve good performance, the cell size must be chosen to balance the desire to have small cells, so data can be quickly forwarded, and the need to keep the cell size large enough that the cost of breaking up the packet into individual cells and the cost of routing the cells as individual data units do not exceed the benefits of cut-through-like performance.

cell is not rtx

3.3. Fragmenting Data into Cells

Cell network designs generally assume that cells are not retransmitted and that cells may be lost or their data corrupted in transit. Some cell networks permit reordering of cells, others require cells to be delivered in order, possibly with gaps when cells are lost.

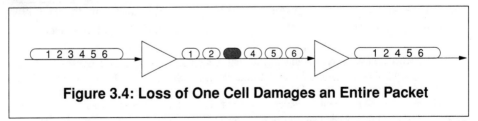

Figure 3.4: Loss of One Cell Damages an Entire Packet

It has been known for some time that technologies that fragment data into small pieces can have disastrously low performance if any of the pieces are lost in transit [Kent 1987]. Consider the following example of transferring a large packet, illustrated in Figure 3.4. The large packet on the left is broken up into cells over the middle link. Cell 3 is lost while traversing the middle link. The re-created packet on the right side is defective and will have to be discarded at the receiver. Because there usually is no mechanism in the cell network to detect and retransmit lost cells, the only way to recover the damaged packet is to retransmit the entire large packet again. Thus two copies of the packet will be sent because a single cell was lost. The throughput of the network is substantially reduced. Furthermore, if the loss rate is high enough, a cell in the retransmitted packet might be lost, causing another retransmission and even worse effective through-put.

One alternative to retransmitting the entire packet is to retransmit the individual cells that are lost. However, as noted previously, cell network designs assume that cells will not be retransmitted. This is because that retransmission schemes require that each cell be uniquely tagged, typically with a sequence number, so the receiver can request a particular cell be retransmitted and the receiver can properly identify the cell it is retransmitting. Unfortunately, at giga-bit rates, a sequence number would need to be about 8 bytes long,[1] and 8 bytes is generally felt to be too high an overhead (15%) in a 53-byte cell.

To avoid these fragmentation-related problems, it is necessary to ensure that cells will be transmitted over low-error, low-loss networks. Ensuring that the net-work has low-error and low-loss rates is a key design problem for builders of cell networks, as we shall see in Chapters 5 and 6.

3.4. Why Cells?

Variants of cell networks have been in existence since the 1970s. Examples of early cell networks include the slotted LANs developed at the University of Cambridge and a series of systems at Bell Labs culminating in the Datakit® switching system [Fraser 1993]. Why has cell networking suddenly become so

---

[1] A sequence number space should be sufficiently large that, even when it wraps around, there is no chance that two different cells currently being transmitted over the same connection have the same sequence number. To calculate the proper size for the sequence numbers, one must compute the maximum rate at which sequence numbers can be consumed and the desired delay (safety margin) between two uses of the same sequence number. This analysis has been done for the Transmission Control Protocol (TCP), and it was concluded that the sequence numbers should be 64 bits long [Jacobson 1992]. Although the TCP sequence space counts bytes and a cell sequence space would count cells, because cells are a small number of bytes long, a cell sequence number space would probably have to be similar in size to TCP's.

what's multicasting

important?

The primary cause for the rise of cell networking is that the telephony community (in the form of CCITT) decided to pursue a cell architecture for future telephone networks. However, the CCITT had at least three strong reasons to decide to choose a cell-based architecture. From its perspective, cells had the potential to

1. reduce the number of transmission networks;
2. provide easier support for multicasting; *why*
3. offer a better multiplexing scheme than ISDN for high speeds.

How cells can achieve these three goals was the subject of an influential paper by Turner [1986], and the discussion is important enough to repeat here.

The first issue is a desire to reduce the number of transmission networks. Currently each communications service, such as telephony, cable television, and computer data networks, has its own delivery networks. For example, the cable networks are designed to carry television signals and do not normally carry phone calls. This separation continues even though many of these networks are carrying information that is now, or will shortly be, digital (i.e., encoded in bits). Combining these separate networks into one has some clear advantages such as simplified wiring, economies of scale in network management, and easier integration of services.

(The motivations for the consolidation are not completely technical. Consolidating the different types of delivery networks has tremendous potential to increase the income of those information companies that manage to become the providers of the consolidated network.)

To reduce the number of transmission networks, one needs a networking paradigm that can support multiple types of services. It is essential that a network technology be able to discriminate among different types of traffic and ensure that less important traffic cannot dramatically interfere with traffic that has a higher priority. As shown earlier in the discussion of why cells have a fixed size, cell networks can limit the effect that one type of traffic may have upon another, by interleaving higher priority cells in the middle of lower priority cell traffic. This topic is an important one that we will return to in later chapters.

Another critical requirement for future gigabit networks is the ability to multicast data. Multicasting makes it possible for a single sender to deliver the same data to multiple recipients efficiently, which is necessary for services such as cable television. Although circuit networks can support multicasting, it is widely perceived to be easier to support multicasting using packetized services

How they know all is los ?

like cells.

The third issue in favor of cell networks is multiplexing. The telephony community is interested in scaling its Integrated Services Digital Network service to gigabit speeds and has realized that the standard ISDN model of providing a limited number of fixed-bandwidth circuits does not scale well.

One problem with ISDN is that fixed-bandwidth circuits are never quite the right size: an application almost always must ask for a circuit size that is larger than it needs. For example, Tanenbaum [1988] points out that the original circuit bandwidth of 64 Kb/s for ISDN was chosen because it was the channel size required for digital voice, but advances in digital voice transmission have dramatically reduced the amount of bandwidth required. Thus, a voice application will have to allocate a 64-Kb circuit even though a carefully coded voice circuit may require much less (possibly as little as 1 Kb/s).

A second problem with ISDN-style multiplexing is serialization time. Even if a gigabit application could allocate the over 16,000 64-Kb circuits required to create a gigabit channel, the application might find it difficult to use them effectively. Consider the problem of sending a single large chunk of data over the gigabit channel. There are two ways to send it. One way is to send all the data on a single 64-Kb circuit. This approach has the unfortunate effect of sending the data at 64 Kb/s, which is much slower (and takes longer) than the application wants. An alternative approach is to open multiple circuits and then slice the data into little pieces and send the pieces over different circuits (a practice known as *striping*). Striping typically requires complex receivers that can resynchronize the pieces sent over the various circuits. The complexity of the resynchronization usually makes striping an unsatisfactory solution.

One logical solution to the limitations of ISDN is to develop a service in which a single link is multiplexed using packets. Packet services have the advantages that they only use as much of the bandwidth as their applications require, and there is a tremendous amount of experience with packet concepts and technologies to build upon.

From the telephony perspective, fixed-size packets have at least one additional advantage. Wide area cell networks can be built in a way that closely resembles the topology of today's telephone networks. In brief, today's telephone networks make extensive use of aggregation to minimize costs. For example, instead of running thousands of 64-Kb/s wires between New York City and Washington, D.C., to handle the thousands of telephone calls that are typically being made between the two cities at any time, the telephone network runs a small number of high-speed wires and multiplexes (aggregates) the individual telephone conversations into those wires. At each end of the high-speed wire is a multiplexor is combined with a parallel routing device. The multiplexor takes the high-speed link and extracts the individual conversations. The routing device is responsible for routing each conversation's traffic to the right telephone. The routing device is a large, parallel processing device, because it is typically cheaper to replicate n 64-Kb/s switching devices than to build an $n \times 64$ Kb/s device.

One of the strengths of cells is that they work well with parallel processing devices. If there are multiple connections into a routing device, then the cells from the different connections can be forwarded in parallel because each will take exactly the same time to forward. All the cells are exactly the same length and require exactly the same type of processing. (Note that there is a big difference between this type of parallelism, which treats different connections in parallel, and striping, which scatters data from a single conversation across multiple connections.) For all these reasons, cells became an interesting technology.

3.5. Cell Routing

⌈ fast

⌊ less information

There are a number of ways to route cells through a cell network. The two most common are source routes and hop-by-hop addressing schemes.

The challenge is to find a routing scheme that is both fast (because the little cells must be routed quickly at high speeds) and requires a minimum of information in each cell (because the overhead space in a cell is limited).

Source Routes

When using source routes, the cell's entire route through the network is prepended to each cell in the form of a sequence of route elements. Each element in the source route is usually the number of the output port of a switch. When a cell enters a switch, the switch reads the first element in the source route to determine which output port to send the cell through, and then removes that element from the route. Figure 3.5 illustrates a source routed cell going through three switches with the route 2-2-1. One problem with source routing is that the maximum number of hops in the network must be limited, to ensure that the cell header does not get too large.

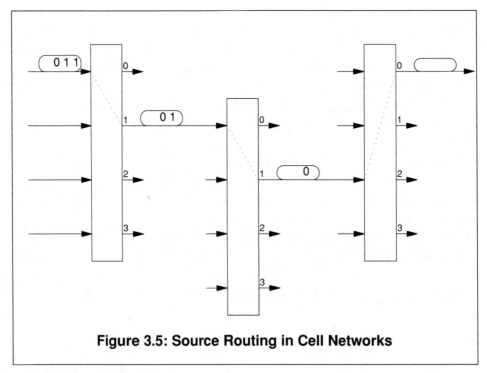

Figure 3.5: Source Routing in Cell Networks

Hop-by-Hop Routing

Hop-by-hop routing schemes use a fixed-sized header, which contains a *hop id*. When a cell enters a switch, the switch looks up the hop id in a table. The table contains three pieces of information: the hop id of the inbound cell, the output port from which the cell is to be sent, and a new hop id to replace the existing hop id.

An example of a hop id scheme is shown in Figure 3.6. A cell with hop id 27 enters a switch on port 2. A hop id table in the switch maps the inbound hop id to an output link and a new hop id, in this case output port 6 and hop id 94. Changing the hop id on a per-hop basis means that hop ids need be unique only on a per-switch basis, or if one maintains a table for each input port, unique on a per-link basis, and therefore can be rather small (a modest number of bits). One advantage of keeping the hop ids small is that they can be used as indexes directly into the table. (In other words, each lookup table is actually an array of memory, indexed by the hop id.)

There are a number of possible variations on the hop id scheme. One variation is for each connection to have a single hop id that is unique within the

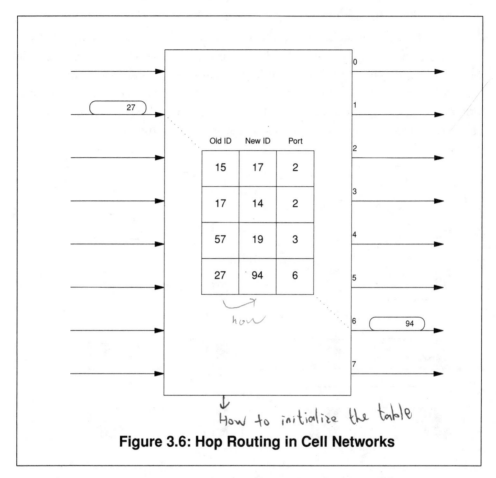

Figure 3.6: Hop Routing in Cell Networks

network, and does not change on a per-hop basis. Another variation is to use hierarchical hop ids, in which some parts of the network route according to one part of the hop id and other parts route according to another part of the id. For example, ATM networks use a two-level hierarchy that divides the hop id into a path id (for routing groups of cells together) and a circuit id (which routes individual cells).

3.6. Adaptation Layer Protocols

It is generally assumed that a cell protocol will be used in conjunction with an adaptation layer protocol. The purpose of the adaptation layer is to add features necessary to make the cell-based services useful to the higher layer systems

SAR

and applications that use them.

One reason that adaptation protocols are needed is to aggregate cells into larger data units. Applications tend to transmit data in discrete chunks (file blocks, video frames, etc.) that are far larger than a cell. These large chunks must be broken up into cell-sized pieces, which must then be reassembled into the original chunks by the receiver. This process is called *segmentation and reassembly* (SAR), and the protocols that perform this function are called *SAR protocols*.

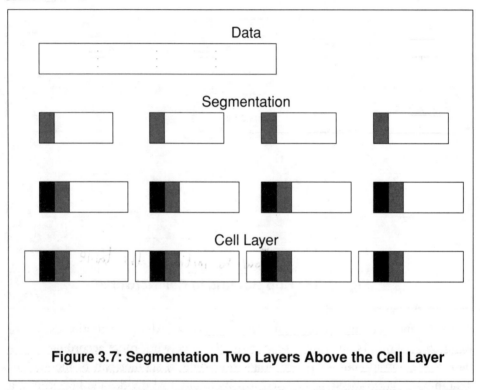

Figure 3.7: Segmentation Two Layers Above the Cell Layer

There is a strong motivation to place the SAR protocol(s) immediately above the cell layer to reduce the overhead in each cell. Figures 3.7 and 3.8 illustrate the problem. In Figure 3.7, the SAR protocol sits two protocol layers above the cell layer. The SAR protocol divides data into cells and then passes the cell-sized pieces to the layer above the cell layer, which must in turn add its own headers to each cell before placing the data into the cells. Therefore each cell contains overhead for both the SAR protocol and the protocol below the SAR protocol.

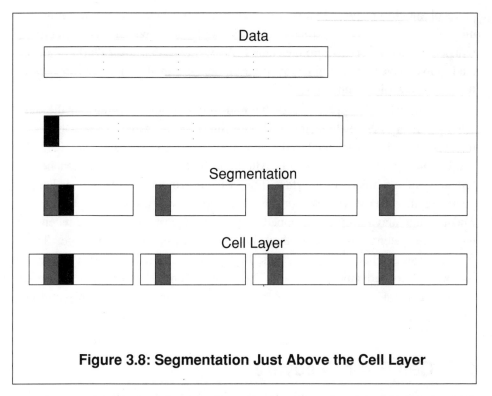

Figure 3.8: Segmentation Just Above the Cell Layer

In contrast, Figure 3.8 shows how overhead is reduced by placing the SAR protocol immediately above the cell layer. Each cell contains only the SAR header; the header of the higher layer protocol is amortized over the group of cells that contain the application's data unit.

Figures 3.7 and 3.8 highlight a fundamental design principle for adaptation layer protocols: *do not waste space in each cell!* Especially given that the typical cell size is only about 48 bytes, adaptation layer information uses up precious space that could otherwise be used to carry data. So keeping adaptation layer headers small is important.

The question of what functions an adaptation layer should perform, other than segmentation and reassembly and marking groups of frames, is a subject of debate. Chapter 4 will present examples of different adaptation layers that illustrate the range of functions that adaptation layers can provide. However, a general design principle that is useful to apply to adaptation layers is the *end-To-end argument* [Saltzer 1984].

The end-to-end argument was developed some years ago as a principle for dividing functionality among protocol layers. In brief, it states that a lower layer protocol should not provide a service that a higher layer protocol or application must also provide, on the grounds that the duplicate provision of the service is redundant: both layers will do the same task. Observe that this rule does not preclude lower layers performing functions in support of the higher layer service. Its goal is to avoid redundancy.

As an example application of the end-to-end argument, consider the question of delivery acknowledgement.[2] Some link-level networks acknowledge that messages have been delivered to the remote system. Is this a useful service? The end-to-end argument says it is not. Although the message may have reached the remote system's link-level interface, higher layer protocols at the sender have no guarantee that the message was delivered to higher layer protocols at the receiver. The message may have been dropped due to shortage of buffers at the receiver or the remote system may have crashed shortly after receiving the message. Therefore, to ensure reliable delivery, some higher layer service must still implement its own acknowledgement scheme. Thus, by the end-to-end argument, we can observe that link-layer acknowledgements are redundant and probably unnecessary.

3.7. Cell Error Recovery

No matter how well a network is designed and built, a cell occasionally gets dropped or has its data corrupted in transit. To deal with this occasional loss or corruption, various schemes for recovering from loss and errors have been developed.

One might wonder how serious it is to lose an occasional cell. The problem is that the loss may have larger consequences. As explained earlier in this chapter, a bad cell or the loss of a cell in a file block may necessitate the whole file block to be retransmitted. A lost framing cell in a video transmission may cause the video picture to be interrupted briefly. This problem is particularly severe for applications with bounded delivery times, because the missing data sometimes cannot be retransmitted within the time limit. For these reasons, there is an interest in finding ways to recover from losses and errors at the receiver.

---

[2] This example comes from the original paper on the end-to-end argument.

Error Models

Most of the work on cell error recovery has focussed on cell transmission over fiber. In such an environment, missing cells are typically the result of a queue overflowing in a switch. Corrupted cells are usually the result of a transmission problem in a fiber. However, as we saw in Chapter 2, errors in fiber transmission are extremely rare, and when they do occur, typically take the form of long bursts. Burst errors are usually easy to detect but hard to correct. So much data is damaged in the burst that one- or two-bit correcting Cyclical Redundancy Checks (CRCs) cannot correct the error. As a result, cells affected by burst errors can be treated the same as lost cells, and so the work in cell error recovery has typically focussed on how to recover from the loss of an entire cell, regardless of whether the loss was caused by queue overflow in a switch or by a burst transmission error.

Cell Recovery

How does a receiver try to recover the contents of a lost cell?

One (very wasteful) cell recovery scheme is to send every cell twice. The probability of cell loss is low, so sending two copies makes it extremely likely that one copy of the cell will get through. To avoid situations in which a small set of cells is dropped, one might keep the duplicate copies of the cells apart from each other in the transmission path. However, this scheme suffers from the obvious problem that it usually wastes a lot of bandwidth, because most cells are not lost. In fact, this trade-off is the general problem for cell recovery systems. Some redundant data must be sent to make recovery possible; however, if excessive redundant data is sent, too much bandwidth is wasted.

Shacham and McKenney [1990] have developed a recovery scheme that *exclusively ors* (XORs) a set of cells and appends the result (which is also one cell long) to the set. There are two variations. In the simpler variation, a single cell containing the result of XORing all the cells in the set is added to the set of cells. Then if one cell in the set is lost, XORing the other cells in the set will re-create the data in the missing cell. If more than one cell is lost, the cells cannot be re-created. The more sophisticated version arranges the cells in the set into a square block and both XORs the cells together and computes an XOR of the bit diagonals through the block. Both the XOR of the cells and the XOR of the bit diagonals (which may be more than one cell long) are added to the set of cells. This scheme can recover up to two lost cells per set.

Another recovery scheme has been developed by McAuley [1990], who proposed using a simplified Reed-Solomon code, called a Reed-Solomon burst erasure (RSE) code. Reed-Solomon codes are a popular encoding technique that sends h check bits along with every k bits of data. The h check bits along with the data in k are used to build h linearly independent equations. On transmission, the h check bits are computed such that the equations should all equal 0. On receipt, the equations are checked to see if they equal 0 and, if not, are solved to find the position whose value is in error and the correct value of that position. McAuley's simplification is to assume that the position with the bad value is known because the receiver knows which cell was lost, and therefore the receiver need solve only for the value of the missing cell. McAuley has described a method for implementing RSE in hardware at gigabit speeds.

Both McAuley's RSE code and Shachum and McKenney's XOR scheme have the useful property that they allow the recovery codes to be computed while data is being transmitted. There is no need to buffer cells prior to transmission while computing the recovery codes. However, if a cell is lost, the receiver may have to buffer some cells during the recovery process.

What about Bit-Error Correction (Correcting CRCs)?

Some researchers believe that focussing simply on losing entire cells is misguided. These researchers argue that if cell switching is to be a truly widespread technology its design should not be limited to fiber optic transmission systems. There is active research on transmitting data at gigabit speeds via satellite channels, microwave links, and copper wire. These media have different error properties from fiber, in particular a greater propensity for one- or two-bit errors, and it would be desirable to be able to transmit cells over these media. In addition, poorly installed fiber optic terminators can sometimes generate one- or two-bit errors in transmission. For these reasons, there is some interest in using simple error correcting CRCs in each cell.

Unfortunately, a major limitation of CRCs is that the number of bits required for an error correcting CRC is roughly portional to the log (base 2) of the length of the data to be protected. This relationship requires a far larger percentage of bits to protect small messages than to protect large messages. Given the trend to make cell sizes rather small, this relationship implies that deciding to use a CRC can substantially increase the overhead. For example, some ATM segmentation and reassembly protocols use a 10-bit CRC to protect their 48-byte payload, for a CRC-related overhead of about 2.5%.

An important question is whether the space devoted to the CRC is well used. For instance, assume that all errors are one-bit errors, that errors are independent, that the CRC can fix a single bit error in a cell, that cells are 48 bytes long, and the CRC is 10 bits. If the error rate averages 1 bit in 10^8 bits, we would send over 2 million CRC bits for every 384-bit cell saved by the CRC. It seems unlikely the CRC is worth the cost. However, there is another side to this argument. What if the damaged cell is so important that the data transmission has to be stopped until it is received — then the benefit of the CRC is not simply the recovered cell, but also that it solves the problem of losing a critical cell. The design trade-off here requires careful thought, which we will consider again when studying SAR protocols in Chapter 4.

3.8. Summary

This chapter introduced the notion of a *cell*, a fixed-size packet, and some of the basic issues and ideas in cell data transmission. Cells have the potential to serve as transmission scheme that can support a wide range of services, including voice, video, and data. This chapter illustrated why researchers believe cells could provide such a wide range of services.

However, using cells also requires a number of decisions, about cell size, routing mechanism, adaptation layers and error correction (if any). Making these decisions in an integrated way is difficult, as we shall see in Chapter 4.

Further Reading

The end-to-end argument, found in Saltzer, Reed, and Clark [1984], is required reading for anyone seriously interested in network or protocol design.

Much of the basic research on cell networking was done by Fraser, and his retrospective paper [Fraser 1993] is a wonderful window into the development of cell networks. Turner's [1986] paper came at the right time to encourage increased interest in cell switching. Some issues in cell networking are discussed on the USENET news group *comp.dcom.cell-relay*.

The standard presentation of problems with fragmentation and reassembly is Kent and Mogul [1987].

Tanenbaum [1988, pp. 206-210] has a good short description of how CRCs work. For a more comprehensive study of error detection and correction, see Blahut [1983].

Chapter 4

Asynchronous Transfer Mode

4.1. Introduction

Asynchronous Transfer Mode, commonly known by the slightly unfortunate acronym of ATM, is the most widely studied and implemented form of cell networking.[1] This chapter is an extended case study of ATM and is intended to give the reader concrete examples of the basic cell networking concepts discussed in the previous chapter.

The ATM standards are defined by CCITT. In the absence of CCITT standards, some interim standards for some aspects of ATM have been developed by a user and vendor group known as the ATM Forum. ATM is the underlying transmission system for CCITT's next-generation of ISDN, Broadband ISDN. B-ISDN is designed to provide subscriber communications services over a wide range of bit rates from a few megabits to several gigabits. The current ATM standards are designed to allow subscribers access to the telephone networks at speeds of up to 622 megabits/s and it is expected that eventually, gigabit speeds will also be supported, as the underlying ATM transmission system is clearly capable of gigabit speeds.

---

[1] In American English, ATM already has a well-established meaning as the acronym for automated banking or teller machines. More than one technologist has been surprised to discover that ATM was something other than a protocol for banking networks.

4.2. ATM Inside the Telephone Networks

Chapter 3 briefly explained why cell networking was attractive to the data and telephone communities as a service offering. However, ATM is also tremendously useful inside a telephone network. It is important to understand these internal benefits of ATM because the ATM standards occasionally reflect internal telephony requirements.

The telephone networks are changing in a number of ways. Two changes in particular appear to be important for ATM. First, the telephone networks are becoming increasingly computerized. Second, the introduction of high-capacity fiber has led to a tremendous consolidation of transmission lines.

The conversion of the telephone networks to digital technologies has brought increased computerization. Routing of calls, traffic management and other control functions are done by computer. Also, the increase in service offerings (call waiting, call forwarding, discount dialing plans, and the like) has meant the telephone networks must keep much more information about each subscriber on-line for billing and to make sure that phone calls to and from each phone are handled according to the services the user has purchased. As a consequence, a large amount of data communication takes place inside the telephone networks — to provide communication between the various telephone networks' computers. This traffic is carried over a separate data network that runs in parallel with the voice network. From the telephone companies' perspective, it would be nice if both the data network and telephone network could be built from the same technology.

The increased use of optical fiber in telephone networks has also led to increased consolidation of transmission lines. One fiber optic line typically replaces tens or hundreds of copper wires. As a result, telephone networks are now multiplexing far more circuits onto the same link and at higher bandwidths. This kind of multiplexing is difficult and expensive, and an opinion in the telephone community is emerging that it is easier at these speeds to multiplex separately addressed packets than to multiplex mixes of individual bits.

An important observation to make about these trends is that the telephone community is designing ATM to meet two sets of goals: (1) to meet its own internal needs for a more flexible transmission technology; and (2) to allow it to offer new services to users. In other words, ATM is, in part, a data communication technology developed by the telephone community for the telephone community. As a result, the ATM standards have occasionally clashed with the needs of the data communications community. At the same time, however, one should recognize that because ATM meets an internal telephony need, ATM will be implemented. What has not yet been determined is how much ATM technology inside the telephone network will affect the future of data communications (both cell based and otherwise) outside the telephone network. We consider this question more at the end of this chapter.

[handwritten annotations: ① hierarchy ② connected oriented ③ fiber optic network ④ low cost attachments]

4.3. ATM Conceptual Model

At least four major assumptions lie behind the design of ATM. The first is that ATM networks will be organized in a hierarchy, much like today's phone networks, with local user equipment connected to regional ATM providers, who in turn are interconnected by national or international ATM providers. The second is that ATM will be a connection-oriented service — a cell may not be sent until a connection (which in ATM terminology is called a *channel*) is established. The third is that the vast majority of the networks over which ATM will run will be fiber optic networks, with extremely low error rates. And the fourth assumption is that it is desirable to support very low cost attachments.

These assumptions closely mirror the current state of many of the telephone networks over which ATM is to be deployed. By and large, the major telephone networks provide a connection-oriented service. They have large fiber optic transmission fabrics. They are structured into a hierarchy. Finally, they have a low-cost equipment (telephones) attached to them. From these assumptions come a number of architectural principles critical to ATM.

First, ATM is designed to work in a hierarchical network. Although ATM networks are intended to be interconnected to each other, the method of interconnecting varies depending on where the connection point is in the hierarchy. ATM users' equipment connects to networks via a *user-network interface* or UNI. The twofold purpose of the UNI is to provide an interface to the user equipment that supports multiplexing (it is assumed that the user equipment may be multiplexing traffic from multiple users into the ATM network) and to protect an ATM provider's network from misbehaved user equipment. Connections between provider networks are made through a *network-network interface* or NNI. The goal of the NNI is to provide smooth interconnection between independently operated ATM networks that trust each other to be well behaved.

Because connection setup is required, ATM channel identifiers can be kept short (just 28 bits). Because ATM is hierarchical, the channel identifiers also have a hierarchical structure. Every channel identifier has two parts, a *channel* identifier, and a *path* identifier. At the edges of the network, where thousands of transmission links may be fanning out to users' homes and offices, cells are routed according to the full identifier (both *channel* and *path* portions). But the ATM backbone networks will typically have only a few high-speed (multi-gigabit or terabit) trunk links connecting each switch to its neighbors. In these backbone switches, the major routing task is to determine to which link to forward each cell. Because there are only a few links, only part of the identifier is needed to identify the next hop. For this reason, backbone switches are allowed to route just on the *path* identifier.

Another ATM architectural principle is to minimize errors and loss. The ATM loss and error model has been evolving. Originally the standards committees took the view that the ATM networks should strive to keep the loss rate comparable to the bit error rate of optical fiber (around 1 bit error in 10^{12} or better). More recently it has become clear that occasionally surges of traffic in an ATM network could possibly cause a switch to become briefly overloaded and drop a burst of cells. To minimize the effects of such overloads, ATM ranks cells, and the expectation is that high-priority cells will still get loss rates comparable to optical fiber loss rates.

To make low-cost attachments possible, the ATM standards bodies chose to prohibit cell reordering in ATM networks. Prohibiting cell reordering allows attachments (and possibly switches) to use simpler forms of buffering. In particular, reordering cells requires a random-access memory, but if cells are not misordered, the attachments can use FIFO memory. If cells are always in order, attachments may need no buffering at all. For example, an ATM telephone could conceivably just play the voice samples in the cells as they arrive. However, the ordering requirement does make some aspects of switch design more difficult.

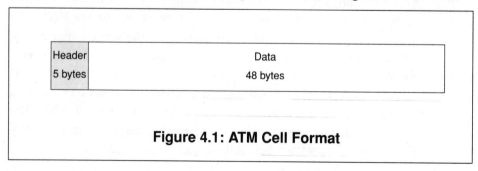

Figure 4.1: ATM Cell Format

4.4. ATM Cell Format

ATM cells are 53 octets (bytes) long, as shown in Figure 4.1. The first five octets are the cell header, which is used by the UNIs, NNIs, and switches to route the cell. The remaining 48 octets contain the cell data, which is formatted in one of the ATM adaptation layer formats described later in this chapter.

The data size of 48 bytes has no significance other than being the value on which the ATM standards committee compromised. The committee started with two camps, one of which wanted 128 bytes of data and the other of which wanted 16 bytes of data per cell. The larger cell size was designed to make ATM well-suited for data traffic. The smaller cell size was optimized for voice samples in a telephone network. After some negotiation, the two sides revised their proposals to 64 and 32 bytes and then split the difference. The result of this compromise is that the ATM cell size is considered a poor size for use with both voice and data. It is widely considered too large for voice, so voice will often be sent in partially filled cells. Two studies, using profiles of traffic from the Internet [Cidon 1992a; Caceres 1991a], suggest that the combination of 5 bytes of ATM overhead plus the frequent occurrence of packets that are only slightly larger than 48 bytes and thus leave the last cell in the packet largely empty can result in extraordinary overhead costs of 20% or more. (Overhead is measured as the number of bytes that contain no data divided by the total number of bytes sent.)

4.5. ATM Cell Header at the NNI

The ATM cell header has two formats: one is for cells being given to a UNI by an ATM user, the other is for cells crossing an NNI.

The format for the NNI is slightly simpler and thus will be discussed first. The NNI format has six fields, shown in Figure 4.2.

The Virtual Circuit and Virtual Path Identifiers

The first two fields in the ATM header at the NNI are the 12-bit *virtual path identifier* (VPI) and the 16-bit *virtual circuit identifier* (VCI).

An ATM connection is uniquely identified by the 28-bit address formed by the combination of the VPI and VCI. The VPI and VCI fields are distinguished to provide a two-level addressing and routing hierarchy.

To see how ATM uses the VPI and VCI, consider the following idea. Suppose that every ATM cell header contained a telephone number in the combined

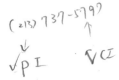

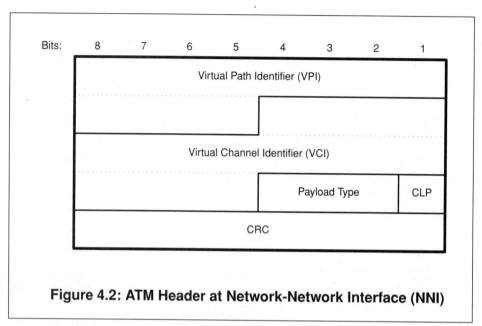

Figure 4.2: ATM Header at Network-Network Interface (NNI)

VPI and VCI fields. In most countries, a telephone number has at least two parts: a regional prefix plus a local number, such as (415) 555-1212, where 415 is the regional code and 555-1212 is the local number. Imagine that the regional code is placed in the VPI field and the local number in the VCI field.

At the edges of the ATM network, near the ends of connections, routing of these phone numbers will generally require that a switch examine the entire number. The switch needs to look at the VPI to determine if the phone number is local or long distance, and thus whether to route it to a local phone or to a long-distance switch. If the VPI is a regional code served by the switch, then the switch needs to look at the VCI to determine where next to route the cell.

In the interior of the ATM network, the switches may be forwarding only long-distance traffic. These switches need simply to examine the VPI field to determine where next to send a cell.

Except for two important differences, this example is essentially how the VPI and VCI work. The combination of the VPI and VCI is a unique address for a connection. And, depending on the location in the network topology, ATM switches route based on both VPI and VCI, or just on the VPI.

The two important differences between the example and ATM are these: first, the VCI and VPI are *not* telephone numbers; and second, the VCI and VPI have only local significance. Telephone numbers, if they are used for establishing connections, will be used only to help set up the connection. The actual VCI and VPI used for the connection will be entirely different numbers, which are chosen to make hop-by-hop routing through the ATM switching system easier.

One important way to make hop-by-hop routing easier is to make the hop identifiers small. The VPI and VCI fields are both intentionally small, small enough that individually they can be used as simple indices into routing tables. However, one problem with using small hop ids is that they cannot be used as global identifiers. Twenty-eight bits is small enough that the chance that two connections might accidentally use the same VPI and VCI is very high. But the cost of checking throughout the network every time a user wants to make a connection to find a unique combination of VPI and VCI is prohibitive.[2]

One solution to the problem of making the VPI and VCI unique is to make them unique on a hop-by-hop basis as described in Chapter 3. For each link, the two switches at each end agree on the VPI and VCI pair to serve as the hop id for each channel. When a cell passes through a switch, the switch changes the VPI-VCI pair from the pair used to identify the channel on the last hop to the pair used to identify the channel on the next hop. Switches that route only on the VPI change only the VPI and pass the VCI through unchanged. This allows the VPI switches to use even smaller hop ids.

Clearly collisions should never occur in this scheme. Each pair of switches knows which VPI and VCI pairs are in use on a given link and will not give a new channel the same VPI and VCI as an existing channel.

Payload-Type Field

Originally the payload-type field was two bits long and the ATM header had a bit reserved for future use. However, demands to use the reserved bit for various functions led to combining the payload field and the reserved bit to form a three-bit field that mixes several functions (not just tagging payload types).

The primary purpose of the field is to distinguish between user traffic and various forms of operations, administration, and management (OAM) traffic, as shown in Table 4.1.

---

[2] Today's networks solve this uniqueness problem by using very large addresses that are carefully structured to make sure that no collisions can occur. But these addresses can get very large. For example, ISO network addresses can be up to 160 bits long.

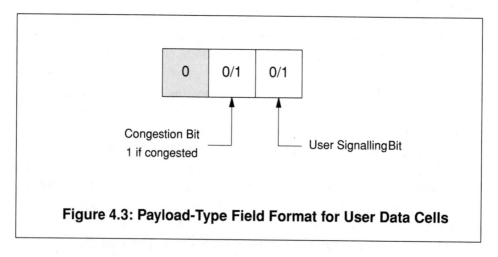

Figure 4.3: Payload-Type Field Format for User Data Cells

Table 4.1: OAM Payload Type Values	
Bit Pattern	**Definition**
1 0 0	OAM link associated cell
1 0 1	OAM end-to-end associated cell
1 1 0	Resource management cell
1 1 1	Reserved for future use

If the first bit of the field is 0, then the cell is a user data cell — a cell being sent from one user of the network to another. The organization of the payload type field is shown in Figure 4.3. In user data cells, the second bit is used to indicate if the cell encountered congestion in the network, and the third bit is a signalling bit available to the user. The signalling bit is used by one of the adaptation layers (AAL 5) to mark the end of each datagram.

If the first bit of the field is set, then the cell is some form of management cell (unless the bit pattern is 111, which is reserved for future use). The details of how the management cells will be used is still being determined.

Cell Loss Priority

The cell loss priority (CLP) field is a single bit. Setting the CLP indicates to switches in the network that, if by some mischance, the switch must drop some cells, this cell should be dropped before any cells that have the CLP cleared.

The CLP serves two roles. It is used to provide both modest flexibility in cell transmission with two levels of traffic priority and some protection against abusive users.

ATM networks are expected to support ATM connections with service guarantees. For example, a connection may be guaranteed up to 10 Mb/s of bandwidth when it needs it. However, most of the time, such connections will likely not use all the bandwidth they require. One way to encourage that bandwidth to be used is to allow ATM users to periodically send some extra data into the network, but to allow the network to drop this extra traffic if the network is overloaded. The CLP bit can be used to mark the extra traffic.

The other side of service guarantees is that there will likely be users who try to abuse the network, for example, by asking for a 5 Mb/s connection and then sending at 5.5 Mb/s, hoping the network won't notice. If the network does detect that a user is sending faster than the rate agreed to, the ATM standard permits the network to set the CLP bit in as many cells as necessary to reduce the number of priority cells (those with a zero CLP) to the agreed upon rate.

Header CRC

The CRC is computed only over the five-byte cell header. Because the header may change at each hop (the VCI and VPI will usually change and the congestion experienced bit in the payload type may change), the CRC must be checked and recomputed at each hop in the ATM network. The CRC polynomial is $x^8 + x^2 + x + 1$, which can correct a single bit error and detect a large class of multiple bit errors. The CRC may seem a bit strong (given the expected infrequency of errors, ATM probably only needs to do error checking, not error correction), but good error checking code would require about as many bits in the header, and this CRC has good error checking properties.

4.6. ATM at the User-Network Interface

The ATM header at the user-network interface is slightly different from the header at the network-network interface. The UNI header is shown in Figure 4.4.

The major differences are that part of the VPI field has been replaced with a generic flow control (GFC) field, and that the number of VPIs and VCIs that can be active at a UNI has been limited because of the bits taken up by the GFC.

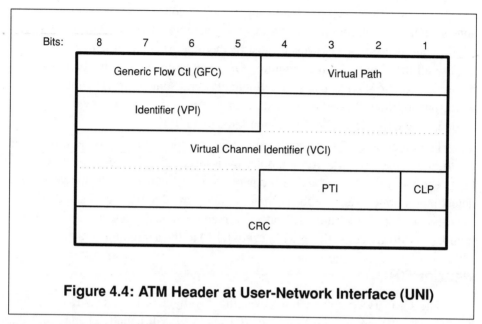

Figure 4.4: ATM Header at User-Network Interface (UNI)

Generic Flow Control Field

Users might connect ATM networks to shared access networks such as a Distributed Queue Dual Bus (DQDB) ring. The purpose of the GFC field is to give the UNI a four-bit field to negotiate with the shared access networks about how to multiplex the shared network among the cells of the various ATM connections. The values of the GFC fields are currently not defined, and the value of zero is always used.

Problems with the ATM UNI

There is some debate about whether the ATM UNI header format, in particular the GFC, makes much sense. Different shared network media will have different access protocols and so it is likely that each local network will require logic to convert the GFC values to its own internal access protocol formats. At best, the GFC is simply a set of standard values for expressing ATM priorities. It might have been better simply to decide that each technology would require a document defining how ATM priorities map into local access rules (such a document will have to be written anyway to map GFC values into local rules) and to have left the GFC out of the ATM header.

Another concern is that, by using bits for the GFC, the number of VCI and VPI values has been reduced. Furthermore, the UNI standard permits the provider to further limit the number of available VCIs and VPIs to users. Unfortunately, it seems that one place in a network where a large number of VCIs and VPIs will be needed is at an interface to a shared medium that has tens or hundreds of systems connected to it.

Finally, some researchers have argued that having two different ATM cell formats is generally a bad idea because it means that the ATM is not a *concatenative* protocol, one that looks the same everywhere in the network. IP, CLNP, and Ethernet are examples of concatenative protocols. The advantage of concatenative protocols is that communications devices can be plugged into the network wherever needed. With nonconcatenative protocols, like ATM, one has to worry whether the device matches the available interface. Furthermore, the UNI distinction is rather arbitrary. Networks tend to be connected in a number of ways so that one network's user is in fact an ATM service provider to another network. The existence of the UNI forces us to draw arbitrary boundary lines between users and providers when clear differences do not exist.

4.7. Adaptation Layers

So far, this chapter has described how ATM moves data from one endpoint to another. ATM sends data packaged into cells over a connection. However, to this point, nothing has been said about how the data is packaged into the cells. The protocols for packaging data into cells are collectively referred to as the *ATM adaptation layer*; the individual protocols are referred to as *AALs*.

The purpose of the adaptation layer is to efficiently package the various kinds of higher level data, such as datagrams, voice samples, and video frames, into series of cells that can be sent over ATM connections and reconstructed into the appropriate format at the receiving end. (The term *adaptation layer* is intended to describe the process of adapting data into a form suitable for ATM.)

Designing an Adaptation Layer

Before presenting each of the ATM adaptation layer protocols, it is useful to consider briefly some of the issues that arise in designing an adaptation layer. The first, and perhaps most obvious, question is, Given all the various forms that digital data can appear in, how many different adaptation protocols are required to support all the diverse types of data that one might send over an ATM network? This question is surprisingly hard to answer.

Some experts argue that no adaptation layer at all is required. Following this line of thinking, each application has its own ATM connection, and thus each application is free to package its data into cells in whatever format best suits the application. The major limitation of this approach is that it can compromise interoperability: if all applications can define their own formats, multiple different applications might perform the same service but be unable to interoperate. For example, one could imagine a world in which telephones from different manufacturers would use different ATM encapsulations; thus you could call someone only if both of you had the same type of telephone!

A slightly more interesting idea is to have only one adaptation layer. From an interoperability point of view, one adaptation layer is ideal; everyone can understand everyone else. Interestingly enough, designing a single adaptation layer that can be all things to all users, yet remains relatively simple, appears to be possible. Such a protocol was designed and tested by Escobar and Partridge [1991].

The CCITT took a somewhat different approach to designing the ATM adaptation layer. It chose to develop a small suite of adaptation layer protocols, with different adaptation protocols optimized for different types of applications. The different applications were envisioned to require different types of service. The four classes of applications that CCITT determined would need different services were:

1. *Constant bit-rate applications.* These applications send and receive data at constant bit rates. They also require that the delay from source to destination be bounded. Examples include telephones and some present data video systems.

2. *Variable bit-rate applications.* These applications send data at variable bit rates, but still require delay bounds.

3. *Connection-oriented data applications.* This class was intended to support applications that had historically used a network service like X.25.

4. *Connectionless data applications.* These applications currently use datagram networking protocols like TCP/IP or TP4/CLNP.

The CCITT gave numbers to the protocols that provide these types of services. Thus, ATM adaptation layer protocol 1 (AAL 1) provides constant bit-rate service, and AAL 2 provides variable bit-rate service.

Since this initial list was developed and approved, a number of changes have been made. The initial protocol formats for AALs 3 and 4 proved to be so similar that they have been merged into a single AAL; AAL 3/4. At about the same time, a large part of the data communications community came to the conclusion that CCITT's AAL 3/4 was not suitable for most data communications applications. As a result, AAL 5, also known for publicity purposes as the simple and efficient adaptation layer (SEAL) has been standardized. Finally, the need for AAL 2 is somewhat unclear, and so no standard for it has been developed.

ATM Convergence and SAR Protocols

[handwritten: SAR sublayer / convergence sublayer]

During the initial design of the ATM AALs, the CCITT decided that it made sense to divide each AAL into two parts: a *segmentation and reassembly* (SAR) sublayer, responsible for breaking data into cells at the sender and reassembling cells into larger data units at the receiver, and *a convergence sublayer*, responsible for helping to manage the flow of data to and from the SAR sublayer.

In retrospect, the two sublayers are so closely related that it is not clear that it is useful to consider them separately. (Indeed, AAL 3/4 appears to have suffered from being split into sublayers.)

AAL 1

The purpose of AAL 1 is to support a continuous bit-rate transmission. Some applications, most notably video, currently require continuous bit-rate data services. In addition, a continuous bit-rate service can be used to replace leased-lines.

AAL 1 SAR

As shown in Figure 4.5, the AAL 1 SAR formatting uses just a single byte at the start of each cell.

The byte contains four fields: a one-bit convergence sublayer indicator (CSI), a three-bit sequence count (SC), a three-bit CRC, and an even parity bit. To confuse the reader, the first nibble is also called the sequence number (SN) field because it used to just contain the sequence count. The second nibble is called the sequence number protection (SNP) field.

The CSI bit is provided to the AAL 1 convergence layer for signalling purposes. It is currently used to indicate boundaries of error correcting blocks in the

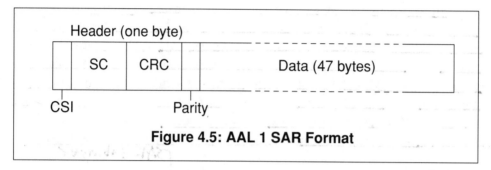

Figure 4.5: AAL 1 SAR Format

convergence layer.

The sequence count is a counter, modulo 8, incremented once for each cell. It is used to detect gaps in the cell sequence due to errors or loss.

The CRC is computed over the first nibble (the so-called sequence number field) using the polynomial $x^3 + x + 1$. After the CRC is computed, the parity bit is computed over the first seven bits and placed in the eighth bit. The receiver uses this information to detect errors (and optionally correct single bit errors) in the sequence number field.

In practice, AAL 1 would probably have been better served by a larger sequence space and less error checking. Recall that in ATM's loss model bit errors are rare, but burst of losses due to brief traffic overloads may occur. In this environment, a bit error seems far less likely than the chance that a group of exactly eight cells will be lost (causing the sequence number to fail to detect the loss).

AAL 1 Convergence Layers

Examined carefully, AAL 1 is very much like the fractional T1 service offered by phone carriers in parts of the United States. It allows users (and the phone network) to divide a large bandwidth transmission network into a number of smaller, fixed bit-rate ATM circuits.

Currently, all but one of the convergence layers proposed for AAL 1 are efforts to emulate what telephone circuits currently do internally in the telephone network. These convergence layers do not appear to be relevant to gigabit data communications.

The one convergence layer of interest is designed to support the delivery of video. (Recall that one of the benefits of ATM is its ability to support video and voice as well as data.) This convergence layer breaks the video data up into blocks of 128 cells. The blocks are organized as shown in Figure 4.6. Each row,

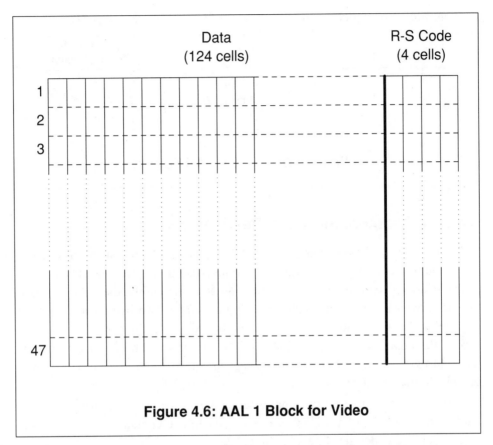

Figure 4.6: AAL 1 Block for Video

r, of the block is made up of the rth bytes from all the cells. The last four bytes in each row are a Reed-Solomon code, which can correct up to two bytes in error, or recover up to four bytes that have been lost among the 124 bytes in the row. There are 47 rows in a block (one for each byte of the data section of the AAL 1 cell), so, in the best case, this scheme can recover up to four lost cells.

AAL 3/4

AAL 3/4 is the result of standards efforts for two AALs. AAL 3 was intended to provide framing service for connection-oriented data protocols like X.25, and AAL 4 was intended to provide a framing service for connectionless protocols like IP. In practice, there is little or no distinction between framing for a connection-oriented protocol and framing for a connectionless protocol, so the two AALs were combined. Another important development has been the data communication industry's conclusion that AAL 3/4 is not appropriate for general computer-to-computer communication; hence the development of AAL 5.

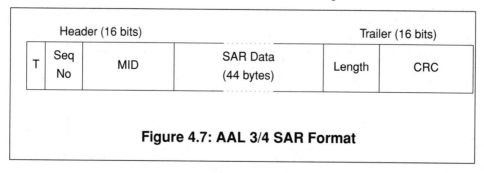

Figure 4.7: AAL 3/4 SAR Format

AAL 3/4 Segmentation and Reassembly

The AAL 3/4 SAR layer takes an AAL 3/4 convergence layer packet, segments the packet into a series of cells for transmission, and reassembles the cells at the receiver. To correctly do segmentation and reassembly, the AAL 3/4 SAR uses four bytes in each cell, as shown in Figure 4.7. A two-byte header contains a type field, sequence number field, and multiplexing identifier (MID). The two-byte trailer contains a length field and a CRC. In between header and trailer are up to 44 bytes of data. All the cells except for the last one in each packet must contain 44 bytes of data.

The type field is used to signal whether a SAR cell is at the beginning, the end, or in the middle of a packet, or is a single cell that contains an entire packet. The actual type codes are shown in Table 4.2.

Table 4.2: AAL 3/4 SAR Types	
Value	**Definition**
10	Beginning of Message (BOM)
00	Continuation of Message (COM)
01	End of Message (EOM)
11	Single Segment Message (SSM)

The ten-bit multiplexing identifier (popularly known as the MID) is intended to permit the interleaved multiplexing of multiple packets on the same ATM connection. If multiple packets are interleaved, each packet will have a different MID, so the receiving SAR can distinguish between the cells of the different packets. If no multiplexing is being done, then the MID is set to 0.

There is some debate about whether the MID is a bad idea [Tennenhouse 1990]. Multiplexing implies mixing traffic from different applications, possibly with different service requirements, onto the same ATM connection. Multiplexing multiple types of traffic is hard to do correctly, particularly if the number of applications being served is small. Multiplexing works better when the number of applications is large enough to permit statistical multiplexing and the law of large numbers helps out. But the number of applications required is far larger than a single ATM connection would normally serve. Some proponents of ATM believe that ATM's greatest strength is the potential it offers to reduce multiplexing. These proponents envision every data stream having its own ATM connection, so the ATM connection ID uniquely identifies the receiving application, and no further multiplexing or demultiplexing at the sender or receiver is required. The MID is obviously inconsistent with this goal.

The four-bit sequence number acts much like the sequence number in AAL 1 and counts sequential cells within a packet, modulo 16. Each packet has its own sequence space, so the sequence number can start at an arbitrary value at the beginning of each message. Furthermore, if the MID is being used, the sequence numbers are relative to the MID; different MIDs have different sequence spaces.

The six-bit length field counts the number of bytes of data in the data field. The length field must be 44 bytes except in SSM and EOM cells. The partial data in SSM and EOM cells must be in the front of the data field. In EOM cells, the length field may also be set to the magic number 63, which indicates that the packet is being aborted and should be discarded.

The CRC is a 10-bit code capable of correcting a single one-bit error in the cell. The CRC polynomial is $x^{10} + x^9 + x^5 + x^4 + x + 1$.

AAL 3/4 Convergence Layer

One AAL 3/4 convergence layer defines the format for all packets to be sent using the AAL 3/4 SAR layer. Its format is shown in Figure 4.8. The convergence layer uses a four-byte header and a four-byte trailer. The headers and trailers must be aligned to 32-bit boundaries, so the trailer may be preceded by up to 3 bytes of padding, to pad the data to a 32-bit boundary.

The common part indicator (CPI) is an eight-bit field intended to allow the convergence layer header to be redefined on a per-connection basis. Currently, the CPI field is 0, indicating the header and its fields are interpreted as follows.

The sixteen-bit buffer allocation size (BAsize) field indicates the maximum number of bytes required to store the convergence layer packet at the receiver. It

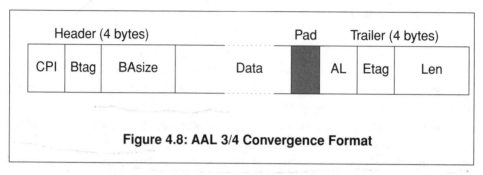

Figure 4.8: AAL 3/4 Convergence Format

is expected that some systems may start fragmenting and sending a packet over a connection before all the data has been passed down from the application. (The AAL specification refers to this practice *as streaming*.) In these cases, the BAsize field can be used to tell the receiver the maximum amount of buffer space to reserve for the incoming packet.

It is not clear how useful the BAsize field will be. Most interfaces today do no complex buffer allocation; they simply allocate a maximum size buffer for each incoming packet. So the BAsize field may be ignored by interfaces. A second concern is that the BAsize field is arguably too small. As ATM scales to gigabit speeds, hosts may want to send packets longer than 64 KB. The AAL designers propose to solve this problem by defining CPI field values that cause the BAsize field to count in larger units (e.g., 16-bit or 32-bit words).

The eight-bit beginning and end tag (Btag and Etag) fields are matching values used to allow the receiver to confirm (modulo 256) that the header and trailer of a convergence layer packet are in fact for the same packet. The fields repair a defect in the AAL 3/4 SAR. Recall that the SAR sequence number is only four bits long and may restart on each packet. Now consider a connection on which all the packets are two cells long and the sequence number restarts at 0 on each packet. Suppose a burst of errors causes two adjacent cells, the end of one packet and the start of the next packet, to be lost. Either the two cells were adjacent on a wire when a brief burst of bit errors occurred or the two cells were both part of a larger sequence of cells lost during a longer burst of errors or losses. What the receiver will get is the start cell for one packet followed by the end cell for the next packet. The sequence numbers will be in sequence, and if the connection is not doing multiplexing, the MIDs will match as well. As a result, the parts of two packets will be accepted by the SAR layer as an intact packet.[3] A number of similar scenarios can be imagined because the SAR

---

[3] This scenario is quite possible. Many data transfers send data in one direction and only send short acks in the other direction, so a connection may be carrying only short acks, which

sequence number space is too small to detect even modest bursts of losses or errors. The purpose of the Btag and Etag is to reduce the chance that the SAR layer will incorrectly reassemble pieces of multiple packets into one packet.

The alignment (AL) field is a byte of zeros to ensure that the trailer is 32 bits long.

The length field is the actual number of bytes that were sent in the packet. It must be less than or equal to the BAsize field. If the BAsize field is rescaled by the CPI field, then the length field is also resized. Because the AAL 3/4 SAR layer can compute the length of the packet by adding up the length fields in the SAR cells, the length field is probably redundant, but it may be a useful check that the SAR layer is working correctly.

Comments on AAL 3/4

The data communications community chose not to use AAL 3/4, but develop AAL 5 instead, largely because of concerns about performance and overhead.

Computers almost always prefer to send and receive data in big chunks rather than process the data in small pieces. Big chunks better amortize the fixed overhead costs of sending a packet. Unfortunately, AAL 3/4 requires that each cell be processed as it arrives (in particular, to examine the segment type field to see if the cell is the start or end of a message), which suggests the receiving computer will have to examine its data a cell at a time. One can avoid having the computer process each cell by building an interface that processes cells and interrupts the computer only when a complete message has arrived, but this approach makes interfaces more complex. Furthermore, AAL 3/4 would seem to have been willfully designed to make building a cell-processing interface difficult to build cheaply, with fields potentially being redefined by the CPI. As a result, to a computer manufacturer, developing a high-performance AAL 3/4 interface *why* seemed expensive. In retrospect, the performance concerns may have been somewhat overblown. There have been successful implementations of AAL 3/4 interfaces, and although they are more complex than AAL 5 interfaces, the difference in complexity is not extraordinary.

---

fit in one or two cells. Because the sequence number may be restarted with each packet and resetting a counter to 0 is easy, some interfaces may just reset the number to 0 for each packet.

The concern about overhead is more serious. The four bytes of AAL 3/4 SAR overhead in each cell, plus the five bytes of ATM header, means that 17% of each cell is lost to transmission overhead before a single byte of real data is placed in the cell! For small packets, the 8 bytes of AAL 3/4 convergence overhead is an additional penalty.

Furthermore, the AAL 3/4 specification has some design flaws. The MID in the SAR is arguably a mistake. The Btag and Etag clearly reflect a botched design of the segmentation and reassembly procedures, and utility of BASize field is very limited.

With the advent of AAL 5, it appears that AAL 3/4 will see limited use. A few services were defined on top of AAL 3/4 before AAL 5 was developed, the most notable of which are the IEEE 802.6 LAN (described in Chapter 6) and Switched Multi-megabit Data Service (generally known by its acronym SMDS or, in Europe, CBDS). SMDS emulates an IEEE 802 network over telephone circuits that use AAL 3/4 framing. However, both the SMDS and 802.6 standards committees are considering changing their specifications to use AAL 5, in which case AAL 3/4 will probably wither away.

AAL 5

AAL 5 was developed by the computing industry to try to provide a more efficient AAL for data communications than AAL 3/4.

The AAL 5 designers (led by Lyon and Lyles) had three major goals. They wanted a packet AAL with far less overhead than AAL 3/4. The AAL was to minimize the computer's cost in handling cells. If possible, the AAL was also to behave as much as possible like existing data communications interfaces like those for Ethernet and the Fiber Distributed Data Interface (FDDI), so that existing data communications software could easily be ported to support ATM.

The AAL they designed is shown in Figure 4.9. Its SAR layer is a single bit in the ATM header, which is set in the last cell of each packet. The convergence layer is just an eight-byte trailer in the last cell.

AAL 5 SAR Layer

The one-bit SAR layer is encoded in the payload-type field of the ATM header. If the cell is a user-data cell (the only type of cell that may contain AAL 5 data), the last bit of the payload-type field is used to signal whether the cell is the end of the packet. Putting the end-of-packet indication in the cell header is a

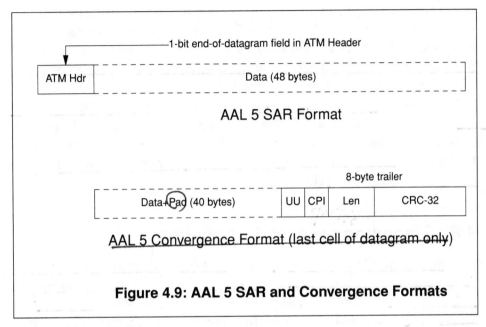

Figure 4.9: AAL 5 SAR and Convergence Formats

tremendous performance victory. The receiving computer can simply queue cells until it receives a cell with the end-of-packet bit set. When the last cell is received, the CRC and length get checked, and then the packet gets passed to the interface's computer.

AAL 5 Convergence Layer

Using the AAL 5 convergence layer, all the cells except the last cell of the packet are completely filled (all 48 bytes) with data. The last cell contains any data from the packet (if the packet's length was not exactly $40 + 48n$ bytes long for some n) at the start of the cell, and eight bytes of convergence layer trailer at the end of the cell. Any bytes between the end of the packet and the trailer are set to 0.

The trailer has four fields: a one-byte User-to-User Indication (UU) field, a one-byte Common Part Indicator (CPI), a two-byte length field, and a four-byte CRC.

The UU and CPI fields are currently unused and are set to 0. (In the original AAL 5 proposal, they were not even included).

The length field is simply the number of bytes of data in the packet (not including the padding between the end of the data or the trailer).

The CRC is a 32-bit CRC over the entire convergence layer packet, including the pad and the trailer. The CRC is extremely robust and can detect lost and misordered cells. Indeed, it has been shown that AAL 5, with just a bit in the ATM header and the 32-bit CRC, is at least as robust against errors as AAL 3/4. (See [Greene 1992] and [Wang 1992] for details.)

Indeed, the original AAL 5 proposal contained just the header bit and the CRC. The AAL committee asked for the length field and the UU and CPI fields to be added. (The designers of AAL 5 had felt there was no need for a length field because the approximate length of the packet could be determined from the number of cells in the packet.)

4.8. Signalling an ATM Connection

Before any ATM cells can be sent, an ATM connection must be established between the sender and receiver and a VCI/VPI must be assigned to the connection at each hop. A protocol that performs these tasks is called a *signalling* or *setup protocol*. Unfortunately, as of the summer of 1993, a signalling protocol still had not been defined for ATM. Some vendors have implemented proprietary signalling protocols but, until a standard is developed, interconnecting ATM switches from different vendors will be difficult.

ATM Forum and CCITT are both working on a signalling protocol called *Q.93B*, which is a modified version of the ISDN signalling protocol, Q.931. When Q.93B is finalized (probably in early 1994), it is expected to become the standard ATM signalling protocol.

One reason for this delay is that designing and implementing a signalling protocol is a complex task, one of the hardest in networking. Describing signalling protocols is also difficult and takes up all of Chapter 13 later in the book. To keep all the discussions of signalling together, and to make it easier to compare Q.93B with other protocols, a detailed presentation of Q.93B is deferred until that chapter.

4.9. Putting the ATM Bits on the Wire

ATM cannot be sent directly over a fiber optic link or a wire. Some rules for how ATM cells are to be encoded and ATM cell boundaries marked are required.

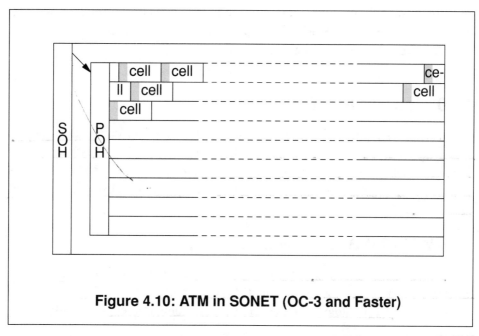

Figure 4.10: ATM in SONET (OC-3 and Faster)

Over long distances, such as within the telephone providers' backbones, the cells will be encapsulated inside SONET frames. (For details on SONET, see Chapter 2.) ATM cells are encapsulated in SONET using an ATM-specific protocol.[4] Standards only exist for SONET speeds of OC-3 and above.

In the encapsulation scheme each SONET frame contains a column of payload overhead (POH), followed by the ATM cells laid out in the rows of the payload as shown in Figure 4.10. The payload column is pointed to by pointers in the SONET overhead. Because neither the row lengths nor the total length of the SONET frame is an exact multiple of 53 bytes, cells may straddle row and frame boundaries. The bytes in a cell must line up with the SONET byte boundaries. Individual cells are located by looking through the bytes to find patterns that match valid ATM header patterns; that is, the bit pattern in the first four bytes is legal and the fifth byte is the valid checksum of the first four bytes.

However, SONET chipsets are currently too expensive to use to encode data for short distances. The expense is due to a large amount of chip logic to monitor the quality of the fiber optic link. This logic is essential for a long-distance link

---

[4] In other words, one can send ATM either in a particular SONET frame or something else, such as T1 or T3 channels, but not both.

and largely superfluous for a short-distance link. But as of the summer of 1993, no one had built a simple SONET chip for short links, and OC-3 SONET host interfaces were only just becoming available.

4.10. Issues in ATM

The process of writing the ATM standards is nearing completion and the process of developing and testing technologies to support ATM has been underway for a number of years, but a number of technical and quasi-technical issues surrounding ATM have yet to be fully resolved. This section examines a few of those issues.

How Will ATM Be Deployed and by Whom?

ATM is being jointly developed by two very different communities: the telephone community and the computer communications community. Beyond differences in terminology and perspectives, the communities differ radically in their attitudes toward time.

Changing a telephone system to support new services requires a lot of time. Often a large number of systems must be upgraded or replaced. In many countries, a lengthy regulatory approval process must take place before a new service can be offered to subscribers. As a result, and especially for large changes like replacing the interior of a telephone network with ATM, the telephone community plans in terms of taking more than a decade to deploy a service. On this schedule, ATM would not be widely available in most countries before the year 2005.

To accelerate the deployment of ATM, some telephone providers are beginning to install ATM switches in their offices and offer ATM as an add-on service over the existing phone network. This approach allows telephone providers to offer ATM more quickly, because it doesn't require replacing existing equipment. However, it makes ATM a special service requiring special wiring to the customer site rather than a universal service automatically provided to every home or office.

The computer communications community is much more dynamic. Its product cycle time is very short, measured in months or a few years. Indeed, many computer communications vendors, convinced that the telephone community's plans mean ATM is the technology of the future, are already building and selling ATM host interfaces and switches. This vast difference in time schedules has the potential to produce a number of problems.

First, there are already stresses on the standards process. Telephone standards bodies tend to work slowly, revising standards every several years. In the computing industry, several years is an eternity — standards are often developed in a matter of months. As a result, the official telephone standards process for ATM has fallen behind. The computer communications industry has had to develop its own quasi-standards group, the ATM Forum, which develops interim standards decisions while waiting for the official standards to appear.

Another problem is that the computing industry tends to make major changes in technology every ten years or so. If this trend holds true for ATM, the computing industry could be preparing to abandon ATM for a new generation of data communications technologies just as the telephone community is making ATM widely available. There is a possibility that the chance to provide telephone and data communications using one technology may be missed because ATM is deployed too slowly.[5]

ATM clearly has a role in the future of data communications. But the timing of the various deployments may have a strong impact on whether ATM's role is that of just another data communications technology or something more significant, such as the integration of the telephone and data communications networks.

What Exactly Is ATM?

ATM is a very general protocol, capable of providing a wide range of data services. One of the burning questions about ATM is, for which services will ATM actually be used? ATM looks very different depending on one's perspective. We will explore a couple of perspectives and their implications here.

One perspective is to treat ATM as just one type of networking service among many. The implication is that one should try to make ATM as compatible with other types of networks as possible. This approach requires fleshing out the ATM specification to address network-specific issues, such as defining the maximum transmission unit (MTU) for packets sent over an ATM network and

---

[5] Some people find this scenario hard to believe because they cannot envision the data communications industry failing to follow the telephone industry's lead. But the data communications industry is driven by the needs of the computing industry (which is arguably larger than the telephone industry) and has proved willing to ignore the telephone industry in the past.

developing schemes for multiplexing traffic between multiple hosts on the same VCI/VPI. The computing community appears to be taking this approach. AAL 5 was designed to make ATM interfaces look similar to existing network interfaces. Furthermore, standards groups have recently decided to encapsulate packets in the IEEE 802 packet format (the standard packet format for Ethernet, token ring, and FDDI) before sending them using AAL 5. This format makes it possible to distinguish between traffic to and from different hosts and to bridge packets between the existing IEEE 802 networks. (This standard can be found in RFC 1483 [Heinanen 1993].)

Another way to think of ATM is as a service that replaces bits on a wire with cells on a wire. ATM is available everywhere, and communities of people who want to communicate define rules for how to transmit their particular types of data over ATM. This appears to have been CCITT's perspective in the early years of ATM. Different AALs were defined for the various services that users might desire: AAL 1 for video, AAL 3/4 for data, and so forth. In this world, one does not use an ATM service, one uses a service over ATM, such as video over ATM or data over ATM, and a system using video over ATM generally cannot communicate with a system using data over ATM.

A third way to think of ATM is as an internetworking protocol in its own right: everyone uses ATM and any ATM device can communicate with any other ATM device. A number of researchers have found this particular approach very attractive, because it makes it possible to use ATM as both a network and a data bus. One could connect a diskless computer to an ATM network and could also attach a disk drive and video camera directly to a network, and the three devices could all communicate with each other using ATM. One could send video to be stored on the disk and read files from the disk into the computer for processing. This vision of ATM is becoming less and less feasible. ATM's nonconcatenative interface and the decision to use multiple AALs, both suggest that ATM will not be the same protocol for all the devices attached to an ATM network.

Different Visions

The important point of this section is that there is no single vision of ATM. What ATM is differs according to the perspective of the person talking. In large part, these variations simply reflect the fact that ATM is a new, still developing technology and some of the decisions that will determine exactly how ATM gets used have yet to be made.

4.11. Summary

Asynchronous Transfer Mode is the most developed form of cell networking. It delivers 48-byte cells with 5-byte headers over virtual channels. Its importance to the future of telephony would seem to ensure that it will play some role in the data communications networks of the future.

However, lingering concerns about ATM remain. Some of these concerns, such as the design of the UNI header and perhaps the cell size, can be addressed by the sweep of a standards committee's pen. Other concerns, such as the pace of deployment, are more problematic and may affect just how widely ATM is used.

Further Reading

The standard for ATM is CCITT Recommendation I.361. The AALs are defined in CCITT I.363. Outside recommendations to CCITT, AAL 5 is described by Green and Lyles [1992]. The ATM Forum has a hotline interested parties can call for information: +1 (415) 962-2585.

Händel and Huber [1990] have also written a fine book-length introduction to ATM, that, although somewhat dated, still has a very valuable perspective. A more current presentation is found in DePrycker's book [1993].

Most of the important work on how to design an AAL was (unfortunately) done after the initial drafts of the ATM AAL specifications were written. The first major study was by Escobar and Partridge [1991] and showed that a single bit to signal the end of each message was more efficient than the two-bit message type coding used in AAL 3/4. The study by Greene and Lyles [1992] showed that the AAL 5 format had superior error properties than AAL 3/4. Finally, Wang and Crowcroft [1992] showed that CRC-32 was a robust error check against cell misordering.

Chapter 5

Wide Area Cell Networking

5.1. Introduction

This is the first of two chapters on cell networking technologies. Here, we look at technologies for wide area cell networks.

As discussed in Chapters 3 and 4, a wide area cell network is built up of high-speed data links interconnected by high-speed cell switches. The data links simply convey cells, often bundled into SONET frames. The job of the switch is to route the cells between the links. So a large part of the problem of building wide area cell networks is designing the cell switches.

Switch design is a wonderfully rich topic. There are a number of different ways to design and build switches, and each design has its strengths and weaknesses. Indeed, an entire book could be written about switch design — one chapter can present only the most essential issues.

Because wide area cell switches are carrying traffic between user premises, they must route very large bandwidths (millions of cells per second) among a large number of links (a typical design goal is to support several hundred to a thousand links per switch). Furthermore, because these switches play a vital role in connecting sites together, they must be highly reliable.

To meet these design requirements, switch designers have tended to build switches around highly reliable parallel interconnection devices, often referred to as *switching fabrics*. A parallel interconnection approach is all but required because current non-parallel bus technologies are capable of moving only a few gigabits per second, which is far too little bandwidth to support several gigabit links.

5.2. Blocking

The fundamental problem in wide area switch design is *blocking* or *contention*. Blocking occurs when two or more cells contend for the same resource (a space in a buffer pool, a slot on an output line, a path through the switching fabric). If there are more cells than the resource can accept, the excess cells must be blocked from accessing the resource. The result of being blocked can be mild; for example, the cell may simply be delayed. However, the result of being blocked can also be quite severe: the cell may be discarded.

The obvious way to avoid blocking is to provide a surplus of each resource so a cell need never be blocked. But for large switches, handling millions of cells per second, the provision of extra resources can be extremely expensive or prohibitively hard to engineer or both. So any wide area switch design becomes a trade-off: how much transmission capacity can be achieved before the switch becomes too expensive? This critical trade-off is a topic that will come up several times in this chapter.

5.3. The Canonical Cell Switch

Figure 5.1 shows the canonical cell switch. It has n input ports and n output ports. Cells come in the lines attached to the input ports. A lookup is typically done on the cell header (e.g., the ATM VPI and VCI) to determine which output port to route the cell through, and based on this information, the cells are routed through the switch to the appropriate output ports, from which they are transmitted over the output lines. The switch is synchronous. In each clock cycle the switch routes one cell from each input port to its desired output ports. In short, a cell switch moves cells from input ports to output ports using a synchronized clock.

There are two widely accepted requirements on how a switch should move cells from input ports to output ports:

1.   A switch should drop cells only rarely, even given the worst possible mix of traffic at a high load. This requirement is needed because, in general, a cell is part of a larger data unit, and the loss of one cell can cause the entire unit to be corrupted. In other words, losing one cell usually makes many other cells as good as lost, so to minimize the effective loss rate, the actual loss rate must be quite low, on the order of 1 in 10^{12}.

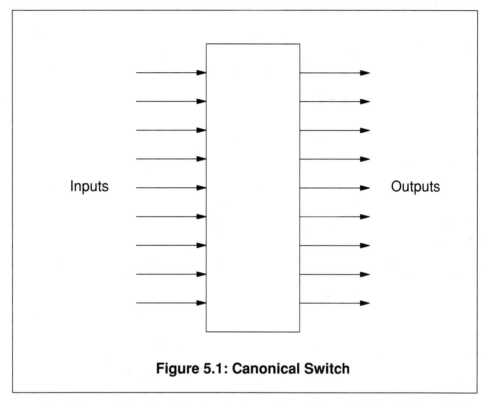

Figure 5.1: Canonical Switch

2. The switch should not reorder cells within a VCI. ATM prohibits reordering of cells within an VCI, and although this requirement causes switch designers some pain, it has been widely accepted.

Switch speeds and line speeds need not be perfectly coordinated, although they are typically multiples of one another. If the lines are faster than the switches, then demultiplexors are used to divide a line's traffic over multiple switch inputs, and multiplexors are used to combine several output ports into one output line. If the switch is faster than the lines, then input lines are multiplexed together, and output ports are demultiplexed into multiple output lines. Both types of multiplexing and demultiplexing are shown in Figure 5.2. On the upper left, a high-bandwidth line is being demultiplexed into three lines, and three middle lines are multiplexed together on output. At the lower left, two low-speed lines are multiplexed together into one switch input, and on the upper right, one output is demultiplexed into two low-speed lines. It is important to observe that demultiplexing on input is the harder operation, because the demultiplexer must ensure that all the cells on a particular channel are demultiplexed to the same

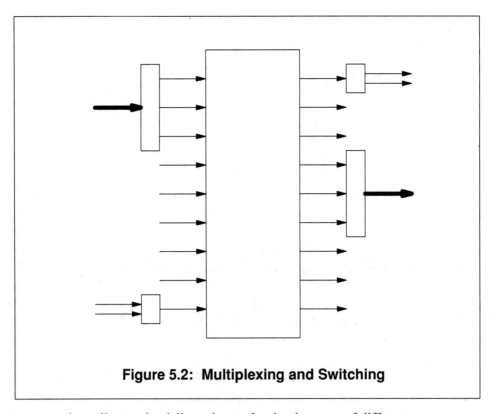

Figure 5.2: Multiplexing and Switching

input port, or else cells may be delivered out of order, because of different queue lengths (or blocking patterns) in the switch.

5.4. Buffering Strategies

Suppose that two cells enter the switch at the same time, both headed for the same output port. How do we handle blocking at the output port? There are five obvious strategies:

1. The simplest strategy is simply to throw away the extra cell. This is a poor approach. Consider that, on the next cycle, no cells may be destined for the output port for which the two cells contended last cycle. If the extra cell is saved, it can be transmitted on the output line during the next cycle. So throwing the extra cell away implies that the switch is throwing away cells that could have been transmitted.

2. Another strategy is to put extra buffers in the output port. If more than one cell arrives in a cycle, the extra cells can be stored. To avoid wasting buffer memory, there must be some limit to the number of cells that can be buffered. In realistic situations, the number of cells that need to be buffered is apparently modest (a few hundreds or thousands of cells), so this approach is quite reasonable. This strategy is called *output buffering* because cells are buffered at the output port.

3. If the switch passes back an indication of whether the cell successfully reached the output port, then cells that fail can simply stay in the input buffer and be tried again on the next round. This strategy is called *input buffering* because cells are buffered at the input port.

4. Unfortunately, most switch designs cannot signal if a cell successfully passed through the switch. In these switches, a variation of input buffering is often possible. In essence, the switch detects blocked cells inside the switching fabric and, via *recirculator lines*, passes them back to a special input port to be reinserted into the switch on a later cycle. One must take care to make sure that the recirculated cells do not become reordered with respect to other cells in their VCIs, but a number of strategies (some of which are discussed in detail later) can ensure that a cell does not become reordered.

5. Finally, it is possible to put buffering in the switch somewhere between the input port and the output port, an approach called *internally buffered* switches. However, managing buffers inside the switch is difficult and rather expensive (a parallel switch typically requires buffering in a lot of places in the switch), so this approach has received relatively little attention.[1]

Given that throwing cells away is a poor approach, the design choice is between output buffering and some form of input buffering. Which should one prefer? Both approaches are useful, but for different reasons. In this section, we consider why output buffering is useful.

---

[1] The one form of internally buffered switching fabric that has been experimented with is called a *Benes* network, which is described in Zegura [1993].

Why Output Buffering Helps — An Intuitive Argument

Consider a simple 2×2 (2 input by 2 output) switch. Cells at the input ports are labelled with the output port from which they are to leave the switch. Assume that every input port has a separate path to every output port, but the output port has a limit on the number of cells it can accept in a given switch cycle.

Now assume that this switch does input buffering in the following way: if two cells are destined for the same output port, one is randomly chosen to go through, and the other cell is put back at the head of its input port to try again on the next cycle. Any new cells arriving at the input port are queued behind the old cell so that there is no chance that cells within a VCI will get reordered.

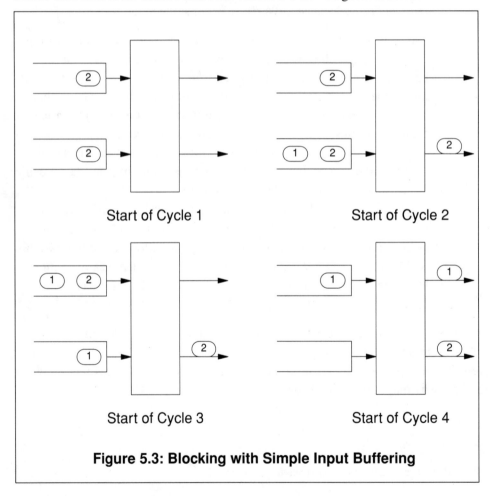

Start of Cycle 1   Start of Cycle 2

Start of Cycle 3   Start of Cycle 4

Figure 5.3: Blocking with Simple Input Buffering

Then consider the scenario shown in Figure 5.3. In cycle 1, two cells are both destined for output port 2. The cell at input port 2 is blocked and held over for cycle 2. At the same time, two new cells arrive, a cell on input port 2 destined for output port 1 and a cell on input port 1 destined for output port 2. The new cell at input port 2 must be queued.

In cycle 3, the cell at input port 2 gets out, but the cell at input port 1 is blocked. A new cell arrives at input port 1 destined for output port 1. Because input port 1 was blocked in this cycle, the new cell is queued.

In cycle 3, both the waiting cells get through to their output ports, and no new cells arrive. During cycle 4, the last cell will go through. So it takes four switch cycles to switch all the cells that were received in just three cycles.

Now suppose the switch were redesigned to accept two cells per cycle at the output port. If one cell arrives it is immediately transmitted; if two cells arrive, one is transmitted and the other is buffered. This switch uses a form of output buffering and, given same set of input cells as the last switch, behaves as shown in Figure 5.4. In cycle 1, both cells destined for output port 2 get to the output port. Because the output port can only transmit one cell, the second cell is buffered. As a result, both the cells that arrived in cycle 1 get through the switch on cycle 1. Overall, the output buffered switch takes one less cycle to handle the same traffic pattern as the input buffered switch.

The major difference in the two scenarios is that, with input buffering, a cell that could go through the switch is held up by a cell in front of it that has been blocked. This type of blocking is often called *head of line* (HOL) blocking, because the cell at the head of the queue is blocking those behind it. Output buffering avoids this type of blocking.

The key concern in output buffering is that the output buffers may fill and cells will have to be discarded. But input buffers can also overflow if cells are frequently blocked, and the chances of buffer overflow at the output ports is typically smaller than that the chances of overflow at the input ports.

Why Output Buffering Helps — A Formal Analysis

Some notable formal work has focussed on the importance of output buffering. This section sketches a little of this work, to complement the informal arguments of the previous section. The basic analysis in this section comes from a paper by Karol, Hluchyj, and Morgan [1987].

The next few pages will show two important results. First, the queuing delays for output queuing are largely a function of the arrival process and not

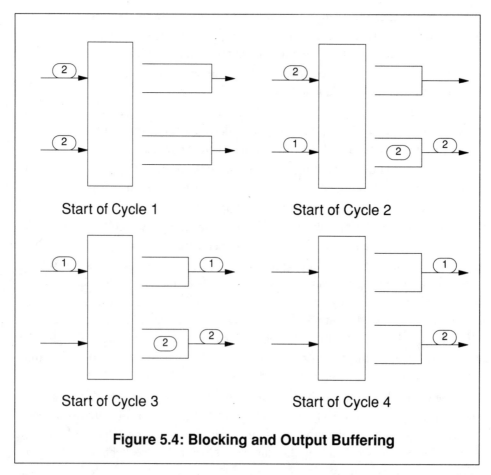

Figure 5.4: Blocking and Output Buffering

affected by blocking in the switch. Second, input queuing can cause severe blocking in the switch. This result suggests that queuing delays in the input queues will be longer. (Using a more complex analysis plus some simulation, Karol, Hluchyj, and Morgan showed that input queuing delays are indeed substantially longer and queues build up far sooner with input queuing.) Many of the methods and results presented here will be useful when discussing the merits of some of the switch architectures discussed later in this chapter.

One limitation of the following analysis is the assumption that cell arrivals are completely independent and unrelated to each other. In general, this assumption is known to be wildly optimistic. Real traffic comes in bursts, and as will be discussed later in the chapter, the bursts tend to increase the amount of blocking in the switch. The purpose of this particular analysis, however, is to show that even under the best possible traffic conditions, which minimize blocking, input queueing performs poorly, which suggests that for realistic traffic, the performance of input queueing will be abysmal.

Consider an $n \times n$ switch that has no internal blocking. Cells can block only when competing to exit at the output port. The goal is to model the performance of the switch using output buffering and using input buffering, to see which gives the better performance.

Mean Waiting Times in Output Queues

Modelling the performance of output queues is the easier problem of the two. Cells are sent directly through the switch from the input ports. Assuming that the traffic at the input ports is not correlated, arrivals at the output ports can be modelled as independent and identical Bernoulli processes with arrival probability ρ. A cell is destined for a particular destination with probability $1/n$.

In such a system, the probability that $k = i$ cells will arrive at the same time at an output port (in other words, that k input ports are sending to the same output port in a switch cycle) is

$$\Pr[k = i] = \binom{n}{i} \left(\frac{\rho}{n}\right)^i \left(1 - \frac{\rho}{n}\right)^{n-i} \tag{5.1}$$

where $0 \leq i \leq n$. Assume the switch size is infinite, so n approaches ∞. This equation becomes

$$\Pr[k = i] = \frac{\rho^i e^{-\rho}}{i!} \tag{5.2}$$

Using this equation, it is possible to derive the probability generating function for k

$$K(z) = e^{-\rho(1-z)}$$

The next step is to see that the size of an output queue is defined by a discrete-time Markov chain, in which, in each time period, the queue increases by k new cells and decreases by 1 cell, which is transmitted over the output line. So the length of the queue q at time t is

$$q_t = \max(0, q_{t-1} + k_t - 1) \tag{5.3}$$

This Markov chain has a probability generating function for the queue length of:

$$Q(z) = \frac{(1 - \rho)(1 - z)}{K(z) - z} \tag{5.4}$$

It is now possible to derive the waiting time for an arbitrary cell in a first-in-first-out (FIFO) output queue. When a cell arrives it must wait for all the cells already in the queue to be served before it can be sent. In addition, because each cell is part of a group of k cells appearing at the input ports, the cell has to wait for some number of its k fellow cells to be served. The probability generating function for time spent waiting for cells already in the queue is simply $Q(z)$. The waiting time for other cells in the same group is a function of the probability of a given group size and the chance (which is assumed to be uniform) that the cell falls in a particular place in the group. This probability distribution can be shown to have a generating function of

$$R(z) = \frac{1 - K(z)}{\rho(1 - z)}$$

Because the total waiting time for the cell is the sum of the waiting time for cells in the queue and the waiting time for cells in the same group, and these two functions are independent, the probability generating function for the total waiting time W is

$$W(z) = Q(z)R(z)$$

From the generating function one can derive the mean waiting time $\overline{w}$:

$$\overline{w} = \frac{n - 1}{n} \frac{\rho}{2(1 - \rho)} \tag{5.5}$$

This equation is nearly the equation for the mean waiting time for an M/D/1 queue. (An M/D/1 queue is a queue with Poisson arrivals and a fixed serving or forwarding time.) Given the assumptions about the behavior of arriving cells, it should be no surprise to see their behavior converge on a Poisson arrival distribution.

Looking over this analysis, one can observe that by pushing all contention problems to the output ports, the switch blocking problem has become a problem of managing buffer space in the output ports. Managing the buffer space, however, looks like a straightforward problem. Equation 5.5 suggests the queuing delays will be relatively short unless the load is high. (That is how M/D/1 systems behave.) Equation 5.4 shows it is possible to compute the expected queue length in the output ports and thus estimate how much queuing buffer space is required at the outputs to minimize loss. Indeed, this sort of analysis is precisely what designers of *crossbar switches* such as the Knockout and Gauss switches do.

Throughput with Input Queuing

There are a number of ways of analyzing the behavior of queuing at the input ports. We will consider just one, saturation analysis. Such analysis assumes that all the input ports always have a cell ready to be sent. When two or more cells block each other, one cell, chosen at random, gets through the switch and the other cells must try again on the next cycle. This analysis will show that the effective throughput of the switch is quite low. The low throughput suggests that the waiting time in the queues will be long whenever the arrival rate exceeds the maximum switch throughput and that eventually a large number of cells will have to be discarded due to queue overflows. One can contrast this result with output queuing, where the switch throughput is unlimited and the waiting time is simply a function of the arrival rate.

The saturation analysis closely parallels the output queuing analysis. The approach is to model the cells at the head of the input queues. At any time, t, there are b_s cells trying to reach output slot s. During the next cycle, one cell from the group b_s will be served, and some number of cells, a_s, destined for s, will reach the front of their queues because the cells in front of them were served. This model gives a Markov chain much like Equation 5.3:

$$b_s^t = \max (0, b_s^{t-1} + a_{s-1}^t)$$

At time t the value of b_s is simply the value of b_s at time $t - 1$ less the one cell that got through to the output port, plus the a_s new cells that have reached the head of their queues.

Now the problem has become one of deriving the distribution of new arrivals, a_s. This probability is

$$\Pr[a_2^t = i] = \binom{F_{t-1}}{i}\left(\frac{1}{n}\right)^i \left(1 - \frac{1}{n}\right)^{F_{t-1}-i}$$

where F_{t-1}, defined as the number of queues with new cells at the head at the end of time $t - 1$, is

$$F_{t-1} = n - \sum_{s=1}^{n} B_s^{t-1}$$

or

$$F_{t-1} = \sum_{s=1}^{n} a_s^t$$

The next step is to observe that, because F_t is the number of slots with new cells to send at the end of time t, the average throughput of the switch, α, can be expressed as $\bar{F}/n$, where $\bar{F}$ is the mean value of F. It can be shown that as n gets very large, a must become Poisson at rate α. Using this observation, one can build the probability generating function from the Markov chain model of b_s and find that the mean value for b_s is

$$\overline{b_s} = \frac{\alpha^2}{2(1-\alpha)}$$

when $n \rightarrow \infty$. And using the definition of F we can derive another form for $\overline{b_s}$:

$$\overline{b_s} = 1 - \alpha$$

Combining the two equations and solving for α shows that the mean utilization is only $2 - \sqrt{2}$ or 0.586! Thus if the switch stays loaded for very long, it can forward only a bit over half the traffic it receives.

5.5. Crossbar Switches

Crossbar switches are the ultimate in output buffered switches. As shown in Figure 5.5, each input port in a crossbar has a line to each output port. Because every input has a path to every output, there is no blocking at the input ports or in the switch. Any blocking occurs at the output ports.

All the complexity in a crossbar switch design is in the output ports. They must contain the logic to recognize cells directed at the output, and the logic to deal with possible traffic overloads, such as a cycle when all the input ports are sending to the same output port. The trick to designing a good crossbar switch is doing the sort of analysis done previously for output queuing and using the results of this analysis to minimize overloads and blocking at the output port.

Crossbars usually have very low blocking probabilities, but they have a key defect: they require a lot of circuitry (proportional to n^2 or worse) in each output port. Because costs grow quadratically with the number of ports, crossbar designs are generally suitable only for comparatively small switches. However, because the theoretical blocking performance of crossbars is quite good,

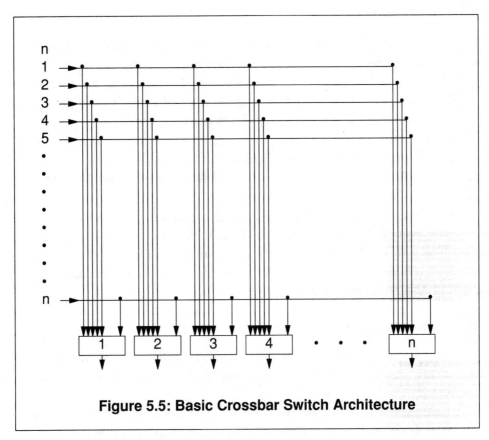

Figure 5.5: Basic Crossbar Switch Architecture

designers of large switches often compare the performance of their design with the expected performance of a large crossbar, using the crossbar switch as a realistic example of a "best-case performance."

Another advantage of crossbars is that designing them to support multicasting is relatively easy. Because every input is connected to every output, a special address can be used to tell a group of output ports to all accept copies of the same input cell in the same cycle.

This section looks at two example crossbar switches. The Knockout switch is one of the best analyzed crossbar designs and is often used as a standard against which to compare other designs. The Gauss switch is a newer design, simpler than the Knockout switch, yet with slightly better blocking performance.

Knockout Switch

The Knockout switch design was developed by Yeh, Hluchyj, and Acampora [1987]. The design calls for an $n \times n$ switch such as that shown in Figure 5.5. The switch simply connects all the inputs to all the outputs. The switch is *time slotted*; every clock cycle each input sends one cell to all the outputs. If an input has no cells to send, it sends a specially marked empty cell.

Each output port is a module consisting of a concentrator and a shared queue. The *concentrator* determines which cells to pass through to the shared queue. The *shared queue* stores the cells until they can be transmitted out the output port.

The Knockout switch discards cells if the concentrator receives more cells in a clock cycle than it can process or if the shared queue runs out of buffer space. The switch is designed so that the chance of such a loss is very small even if the load is high. The next two subsections examine how the concentrator and queue are designed to minimize loss.

The Knockout Concentrator

In the worst case, it is possible that all n inputs will send a cell to the same output in the same cycle. This observation implies that every output must be able to cope with receiving n inputs.

However, if we assume that the switch is forwarding data for lots of connections to lots of different destinations, the chance that all the inputs will be sending to the same output in the same cycle is quite small (see Eq. 5.3). Indeed, given a big enough switch and assuming cell arrivals are independent, the chance that the same output port will receive even a handful of cells in the same cycle is extremely small. So, if we are willing to assume that the connections are independent (and this is a bit of a leap of faith), it probably does not make sense to design all of the output port hardware to handle a large number of cells per cycle. Rather, it makes sense to design the hardware to support a limited number of cells per cycle and have a device to ensure that if, by some mischance, more than that number of cells arrives in a given cycle, there is some fair method for discarding the excess cells.

It is important that the method of discarding cells be fair. No input port's cells should get a substantial preference over another ports' cells. Otherwise, when the switch is heavily loaded (when it is most likely that multiple cells will be delivered to a single output), users of the switch will get different performance based on which input port their cells pass through.

The purpose of the Knockout concentrator is to take k cells in a cycle from the switch, where k can be any number from 0 through n, and output up to L cells, where L is the limit on the number of cells that the output hardware can handle in a switch cycle. If $k \leq L$, then the job of the concentrator is simply to recognize the k cells and pass them on to the rest of the output hardware. But if $k > L$, then the concentrator must fairly choose which L cells to pass through and which $k - L$ cells to discard.

The Knockout switch gets its name from the fact that the rules its concentrator uses to decide which L cells get passed through are similar to those of an L-elimination knockout tournament. (According to such rules, a player who loses L games is eliminated, or "knocked out," of the competition.) The basic component in the concentrator is a simple 2×2 switch that takes two cells in and outputs one cell on the "winning" output and the other cell on the "losing" output. If only one cell is input into the switch, that cell automatically is the winner. If two cells are input, one is randomly chosen the winner and the other is randomly chosen the loser.[2] The winning cell is passed on to another 2×2 switch where it competes with another winning cell. The losing cell is passed on to a 2×2 switch where it competes with another cell that has the same record of wins and losses that it does. The cell that wins all its matches goes out the first output from the concentrator. The cell that wins all but one match goes out the second output. The cell that wins all but two matches goes out the third output, and so forth, so that the cell that wins all but $L - 1$ matches goes out the Lth output. Any cell that loses L matches is discarded.

It should be clear from the knockout idea that all n inputs are initially candidates for the first output from the concentrator and that, over the lifetime of the tournament, $n - 1$ cells will at some point in time have lost exactly one match and thus be candidates for the second output, $n - 2$ cells will have lost two matches and thus be candidates for the third output, and so on. Thus one can subdivide the concentrator into L separate tournament modules, one for each output from the concentrator, and for the ith output, there will be $n - i + 1$ eligible cells. Because each 2×2 switch can only decide between two cells, this means each of the L modules needs to contain hardware for roughly n matches. Thus the

---

2 Actually, randomly choosing the winner and loser is just one possible way to design the 2×2 switch. The Knockout switch designers have suggested that even if the switch is deterministic and always chooses the cell on a particular input line as the winner, the system will still be close to fair because so few cells are dropped in the first place.

approximate complexity, in switching elements, of a Knockout concentrator at each output is only $n \times L$, and the switch as a whole scales as $O(n^2 \times L)$. If L can be kept small, that means the Knockout switch is close to a perfect crossbar design.

How large must L be? The goal is to keep L sufficiently large that the overall cell loss rate is acceptably low.

The probability that more than k packets will all arrive for the same output port in the same cycle is simply Eq. 5.1. To compute the effective loss rate, we must add up the chances of all the k values greater than L, weighted by the number of cells that must be discarded for a given value of k. Accordingly, the loss rate is proportional to

$$\sum_{k=L+1}^{n} (k - L) \binom{n}{k} \left(\frac{\rho}{n}\right)^k \left(1 - \frac{\rho}{n}\right)^{n-k}$$

If the input cells are assumed to be independent (a dangerous assumption) it turns out that for even small L (like 8) and large n (i.e., infinity), the loss rates at high loads are quite low. A switch in which L is 12 will have a loss rate of less than 1 in 10^{10}, even if n is infinite.

This result is the critical idea in the design of the Knockout switch. Although the Knockout switch is a crossbar, the concentrators at each output can be kept simple because L can be kept small.

The Knockout Shared Queue

The shared queue is designed to send one cell out the output port each cycle and to accept up to L cells from the concentrator to be queued. There are two important issues in designing the shared queue. First, one must determine how to move the L cells into the queue quickly (in one switch cycle). Second, it is possible that several successive cycles may each deliver a large number of cells into the output buffer, and one needs to figure out how big to make the output buffer so that, even if there are several heavy cycles, the buffers do not drop cells.

In the worst case, the shared queue has to be capable of accepting L cells in the same cycle. If L is more than two or three cells, making the memory paths fast enough to handle all the cells can be expensive. So the shared queue is actually L parallel queues, combined with a circular shifter. The shifter takes up to L cells and places them in the shared queues, but shifted up to $L - 1$ positions to the right. The shifter shifts the cell positions by the number of cells received in the last cycle. The purpose of the shifter is to evenly mix the arriving cells among

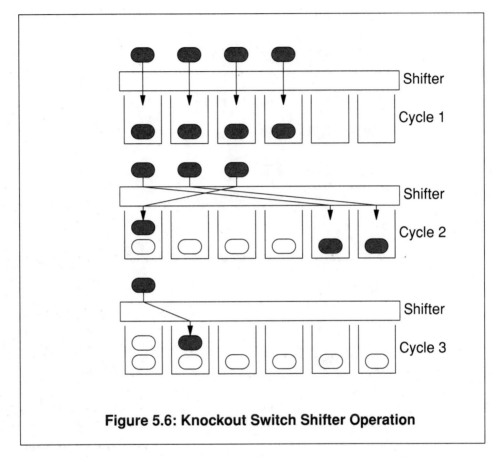

Figure 5.6: Knockout Switch Shifter Operation

the queues.

To see how the shifter works, consider Figure 5.6. The shifter takes six inputs. On the first cycle, four cells arrive and are placed in queues 1 through 4. In the second cycle, three cells arrive and are placed in queues 5, 6, and 1. In the third cycle, one cell arrives and is placed in queue 2. Observe that the shifting algorithm ensures that no queue contains more than one more cell than any other queue and that the newest cell always goes in the least-recently filled queue.

Cells are removed from the shared queue and transmitted out the output port according to the following algorithm. There is a rotating token among the queues. Whichever queue has the token holds the token until the queue has a cell to transmit. When a queue transmits its cell, it passes the token on to the next queue. Revisiting Figure 5.6, Figure 5.7 shows the shifter and shared queue working together. The token is shown as the box with a t below the output queue. Note that the shared queue algorithm always takes the next cell from the queue

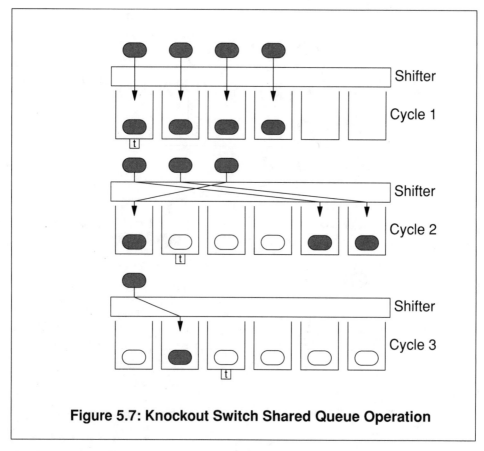

Figure 5.7: Knockout Switch Shared Queue Operation

that has been holding a cell the longest.[3]

Because the shared queue can accept up to L cells per cycle but send only one cell per cycle from the output port, it is clearly possible to overflow the shared queue's buffer space. (In the worst case, the switch could send L cells per cycle indefinitely.) Given that losing cells can severely hurt the performance of higher level protocols running over the cell network, it is important to make the shared queue large enough that the chance of loss is small.

If cell arrivals are unrelated, that is, if a cell arriving at an input port has an equal probability of going to any output port, then one can use the analysis of the

---

[3] Keep in mind that the token stops moving if a queue is empty. The first empty queue must be the next queue due to receive a cell. This feature ensures that the algorithm services the oldest cell next.

merits of output buffering earlier in this chapter to compute how big the shared buffer should be. (The following analysis is from Yeh [1987].) If the switch is infinitely large ($n \to \infty$), then Eq. 5.2 states that the probability of k arrivals at the output port is

$$P(k \text{ arrivals}) = \frac{\rho^k e^{-\rho}}{k!}$$

This equation is just the Poisson distribution. Now, to be conservative, assume that all k cells are always put into the shared queue (rather than just L). Because the time to remove one cell from the shared queue is constant, the queue can be modelled as an M/D/1 queue. The probability that the queue size will be of a certain length, q, in an M/D/1 queue is easy to compute, so all one has to do is choose q such that the probability that the queue length of the M/D/1 system is greater than or equal to q and is small enough that one is comfortable losing that many cells. For the Knockout switch, with $L = 8$, the designers found that a total of 40 buffers (5 per queue) was sufficient to guarantee a loss rate from both the concentrator and shared queue of less than 10^{-6} at loads up to 84% of capacity.

Gauss Switch

Like the Knockout switch, the Gauss switch is a crossbar. The Gauss switch, designed by de Vries, is currently being built by the Dutch telephone company. Its overall design is identical to the Knockout: all input ports transmit to all output ports, and the output port contains a concentrator that feeds into a queue.

The difference between the Knockout and the Gauss switches is that a Gauss concentrator has a simpler design, yet a slightly lower loss rate than a Knockout concentrator.

Figure 5.8 shows the Gauss concentrator. Each of the n input lines comes into a separate bus unit (BU) in the concentrator. Each BU is attached to a high-speed slotted bus.[4] At the top of the slotted bus is an empty slot generator (ESG), which generates L empty slots into the bus during each switch cycle. At the bottom of the bus is a set of buffers, which buffer cells until they can be sent out the output port, just as the shared queue buffers cells in the Knockout switch.

---

[4] The terminology in this book is slightly different from that of the Gauss designer.

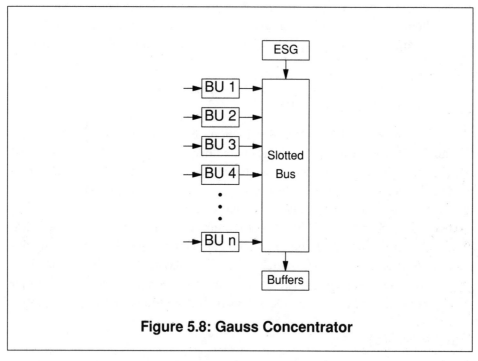

Figure 5.8: Gauss Concentrator

Each BU monitors the slotted bus, looking for an empty slot. If the BU sees an empty slot and the BU has a cell, the BU puts its cell in the slot and marks the slot as filled. The slotted bus then carries the cell down to the buffers pool where it is queued for output.

As described so far, the Gauss switch is much like the Knockout switch — the Gauss concentrator takes up to n inputs per cycle and places up to L cells into a queue for the output port. However, the Gauss concentrator is somewhat simpler, requiring just n buffers and a slotted bus per output port rather than the $O(n \times L)$ complexity of the Knockout concentrator. (One should, however, keep in mind that building a fast slotted bus may prove more expensive than building an $O(n \times L)$ concentrator.)

A more interesting property is that the Gauss concentrator also discards fewer cells than the Knockout concentrator. Recall that, in the Knockout concentrator, if more than L cells are received in a cycle, then the excess cells are discarded. In the Gauss concentrator, if more than L cells are received, then the excess cells are left in their respective BUs for the next cycle. If a new cell destined for the output port arrives at a BU that is holding a cell from the previous cycle, then the old cell is discarded. But if no new cell arrives, the old cell can try for a bus slot in the new cycle.

Exactly how many fewer cells the Gauss concentrator drops when compared with the Knockout concentrator depends on cell arrival patterns. If one assumes, however, as the Knockout analysis does, that the cell arrival patterns are independent, there is only a small probability that the next cell on an input is destined for the same output as the last cell at that input. In such an environment, Gauss design can significantly reduce the loss rate.

Problems with Crossbar Designs

The feasibility of building a useful Knockout or Gauss switch relies on the assumption that cell arrivals are not related to or correlated with each other. Because each cell's destination is essentially random, it is possible to design output concentrators that can accept a relatively small number of cells per cycle, and require rather small output buffers.

Unfortunately, in real life, cell arrivals for data traffic are related. Due to packet train effects [Jain 1986], it is highly likely that the next cell at an input port will be destined for the same output port as the current cell. Intuitively one can see that this is so by thinking about a packet that has been broken into cells and sent over a connection. All the cells in the packet will go to the same output port. Therefore if one cell in a packet is going to an output port, it is likely there are several more cells close behind it in the same packet and destined for the same output port.

The effect of related cell arrivals is to dramatically increase the likelihood that long output queues may develop. Attempts to simulate more realistic traffic through a switch [Giacopelli 1991] have found that maintaining a given cell loss rate may require ten times more buffering than an M/D/1 model predicts!

Another effect is to change the likelihood that more than L cells will arrive in a time cycle (affecting Knockout and Gauss designs) and increase the chance that a cell that is not served in one time cycle in the Gauss concentrator will be eliminated by a new arrival on the next cycle.

The implication is that one should be concerned about some of the design decisions in the Knockout and Gauss switches. Either one has to find some way to force data traffic to behave as if it is uncorrelated (an idea we will explore in the MONET switch design later) or we need more versatile switch architectures.

5.6. Batcher-Banyan Switches

Although the Gauss switch is simple, it still requires $O(n^2)$ components to build: n BUs at each of n output ports. For large switches (such as a switch designed to serve several hundred rooms in a large office building), it is useful to have a switch design that calls for fewer components.

Batcher-Banyan switches meet this requirement. They scale as $O(n \log^2 n)$. However, to achieve this modest improvement in scaling factor, yet keep the switch nonblocking, requires a switching fabric far more complicated than a crossbar.

The name *Batcher-Banyan* comes from the fact that such switches are built from two separate components: a banyan routing switch combined with a Batcher sorting network. Both components are discussed separately followed by examples of Batcher-Banyan networks.

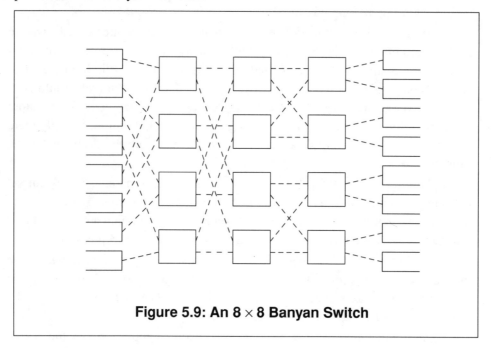

Figure 5.9: An 8 × 8 Banyan Switch

Banyan Switches

Figure 5.9 shows an 8 × 8 banyan switch. The input ports on the left are connected to the output ports on the right by a three-stage routing network. There is exactly one path through the network from each input port to each output port. Banyan switches get their name from the crossings of wires in the switch, which are fancied to be similar to the branchings of a banyan tree.

Cells are routed through the switch according to their output port. The *comparators* at each stage of the routing network are simple binary switches — based on a bit in the cell's destination output port, they route the cell out the upper or lower output wire.

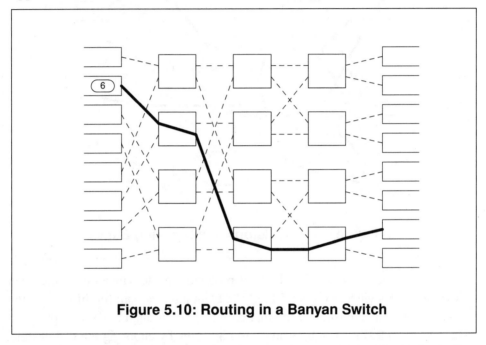

Figure 5.10: Routing in a Banyan Switch

Figure 5.10 illustrates a banyan switch that routes on the high-order bit in the first stage, the middle bit in the second stage, and the low-order bit in the third stage. The ports are numbered starting with 0. In the figure, a cell has arrived at port 1 destined for 6 (bit pattern 110). The heavy line shows how the cell will be routed through the switch. It is possible to build banyans that route on other bit patterns.

The typical banyan switch is synchronized. All the input cells enter the switch at the same time. A cycle is the time required to pass a round of cells through the routing network. It is possible to build unsynchronized banyan networks, but their performance is generally worse than that of synchronized banyans.

Because there is only one wire from the last stage of comparators to any output port, it should be clear that these banyan networks will block if two cells are sent to the same output port in the same clock cycle. What may be less clear is that blocking can occur even if all the cells are destined for different outputs, because the cells' paths may coincide for part of the way through the switch.

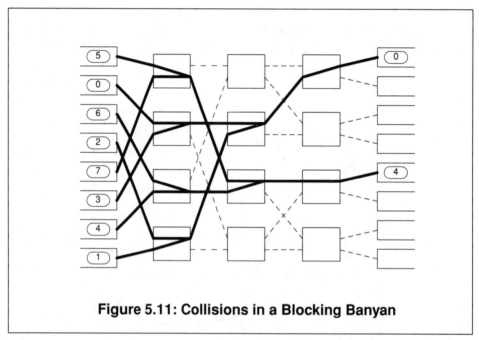

Figure 5.11: Collisions in a Blocking Banyan

To see the nature of the blocking problems inside banyan networks, consider the 8×8 switch in Figure 5.11. The eight inputs are all for different output ports, yet internal collisions mean that only two get through to their output ports. (In this example, the switch resolves all collisions by choosing the cell destined for the lower port number.) In general, half the cells reaching a stage of the switch can be blocked at that stage, so in the worst case, a switch has a throughput of only two cells.

However, collisions do not have to occur. Figure 5.12 shows the same eight inputs, but in an order such that all get through the switch.

Thus the banyan presents both an opportunity and a challenge. The opportunity is a routing switch that can provide a path from every input to every output without requiring $O(n^2)$ components. The challenge is to find a way to avoid or eliminate the banyan's awful worst-case blocking rate.

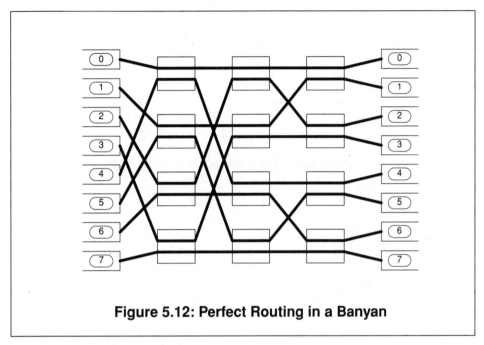

Figure 5.12: Perfect Routing in a Banyan

Batcher Sorting Networks

Batcher sorting networks are named for K. E. Batcher, whose paper [Batcher 1968] showed how to build sorting networks with complexity of $O(n \log^2 n)$ and pointed out that such sorting networks might be used to construct nonblocking switches.

Essentially, a Batcher sorting network does a merge sort in hardware. Recall that a merge sort takes two ordered lists and generates a single ordered list from the two lists. The challenge is to implement this sorting efficiently in hardware.

A Batcher sorting network is made up of simple two-input-two-output sorting elements such as that shown in Figure 5.13. Two values are entered on the left, and the sorting element sends the smaller value out its upper output, and the larger value out its lower output.

One method for making a sorting network from these sorting elements is to interleave the outputs of the sorters such that the inputs to the next stage of the sorting network are always *bitonic* sequences. Bitonic sequences are sequences that are juxtapositions of an increasing sequence and a decreasing sequence. Thus,

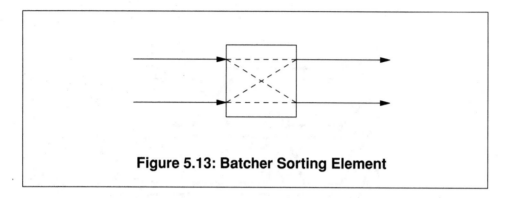

Figure 5.13: Batcher Sorting Element

$$1, 2, 3, 8, 7, 6, 5, 4$$

is a bitonic sequence, as is

$$8, 7, 1, 2, 3, 4, 5, 6$$

Furthermore, any bitonic sequence that has been arbitrarily split in two parts and had the two parts reversed is also bitonic.

One of Batcher's contributions was to show that if one took a bitonic sequence

$$x_1, \quad x_2, \quad x_3, \quad \ldots, \quad x_k, \quad x_{k+1}, \quad \ldots, \quad x_{2k}$$

and computed the sequence

$$\min(x_1, x_{k+1}), \quad \min(x_2, x_{k+2}), \quad \ldots, \quad \min(x_k, x_{2k})$$

and the sequence

$$\max(x_1, x_{k+1}), \quad \max(x_2, x_{k+2}) \quad , \ldots, \quad \max(x_k, x_{2k}) \cdot$$

that both of these two sequences are also bitonic, and no number in the first sequence is greater than any number in the second sequence. From this observation, it is possible to build a sorter with $O(n \log^2 n)$ complexity.

The basic idea behind a bitonic sorter is shown in Figure 5.14, which sorts the list 8, 5, 4, 3, 1, 2, 6, 7. Sorting a list of n elements yields two bitonic sequences of length $n/2$. Sorting these two sequences gives four sequences, each of length $n/4$. After $\log n$ stages, each sequence is of length 1, and the entire list has been sorted.

But how does one get a bitonic list to start with? The trick is to build a bitonic version of a merge sorter. Figure 5.15 illustrates the idea, by sorting the list 3, 5, 4, 8, 7, 2, 6, 1 into 8, 5, 4, 3, 1, 2, 6, 7. In the first stage, adjacent

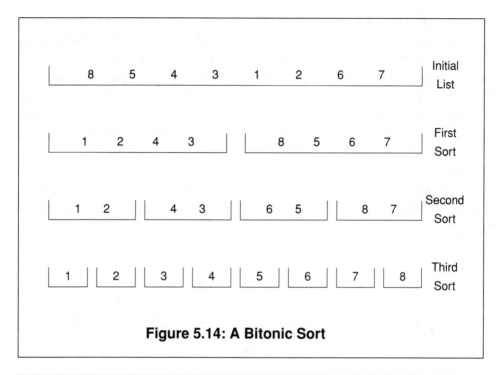

Figure 5.14: A Bitonic Sort

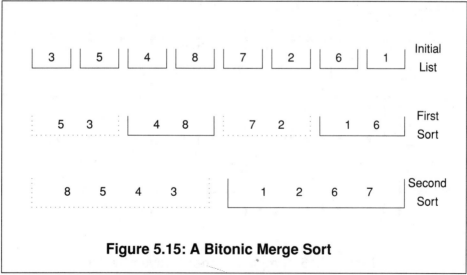

Figure 5.15: A Bitonic Merge Sort

numbers are combined and then sorted by a single bitonic sorter to create sorted lists of length two. Note that the lists in the dotted boxes are in descending order and come from a sorter that sorts in reversed order. For the second stage of the merge sort, adjacent boxes are combined to make lists of length four. Because one list is ascending and the other is descending, these new combined lists are bitonic. The combined lists are each put into two-stage bitonic sorters that yield sorted lists of length four (again the sorters alternate between being ascending and descending). Finally, the two lists of length four are combined to create the sequence $8, 5, 4, 3, 1, 2, 6, 7$.

In general, merge sorting a list of length n requires $\log n$ stages, each of which is a bitonic sorter; thus the complexity of the total sorter is approximately $n \log^2 n$.

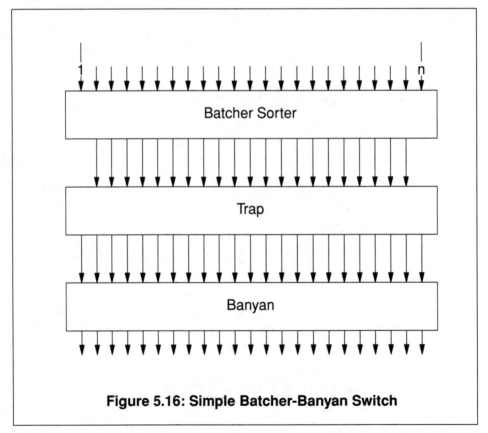

Figure 5.16: Simple Batcher-Banyan Switch

A Simple Batcher-Banyan Switch

If one can sort cells efficiently using a bitonic sorter, it is then easy to make a banyan switch nonblocking. One simply sorts the cells in the bitonic sorter, scans the sorted list for multiple cells to the same output (which may collide), then passes the sorted list of cells as inputs into the banyan, after compressing the sorted list into a list of cells with no gaps. If the inputs to a banyan switch are sorted and there are no gaps (inactive cells) between cells, then there will be no collisions in the banyan. (A pretty proof of this property of banyans can be found in the appendix to Lee [1988].)

This idea is the essence of a Batcher-Banyan switch and is shown in Figure 5.16. On each switch cycle, each input line at the top puts one cell into the Batcher sorter. The Batcher sorts the cells and passes them onto the trap module. The trap module detects duplicate cells to the same destination and selects one cell for each destination to pass on to the banyan. The trap then compresses the list of sorted cells so there are no gaps and places the cells on the input lines into the banyan switch. The banyan routes the cells to their appropriate outputs.

The feature that tends to differentiate Batcher-Banyan designs is the design of their trap modules. The challenge of the trap module is to avoid discarding cells when there is more than one cell for the same destination while making sure cells do not get reordered.

Starlite

Starlite was one of the earliest Batcher-Banyan switches, built in the early 1980s [Huang 1984]. The outline of the Starlite is shown in Figure 5.17.

Cells come in the input lines at the top and on each cycle enter the cell switch through a concentrator. The Starlite designers assumed that, on average, only some of the n input lines would have cells to put into the switch. So the first stage of the switch is a concentrator which eliminates empty cells (e.g., cells entered by input lines that have no traffic) and passes on the remaining m ($m \leq n$) cells as inputs to the Batcher sorting network. After the cells are sorted the *trap* module detects multiple cells to the same output port. If more than one cell is destined for the same output port, the extra cells are injected into the sorting network again on the next switch cycle via *recirculator lines*, which pass cells back into the sorter. Finally, the trap network passes its sorted list of cells (with only one cell per output port possible) to an *expander* that expands the sorted list into a pattern that will not block in the banyan network.

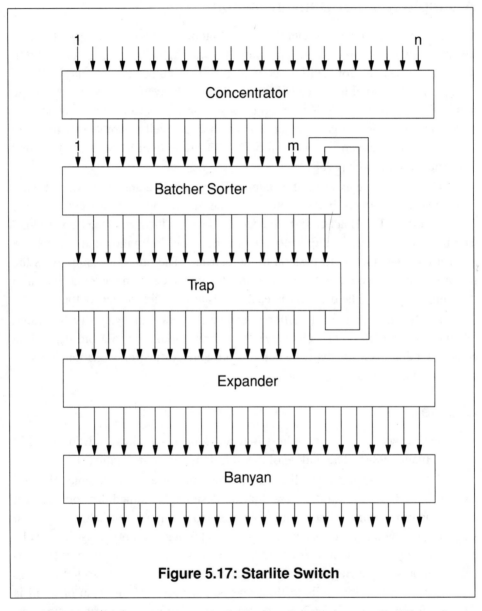

Figure 5.17: Starlite Switch

The concentrator, sorting network, trap, and expander are all different types of bitonic sorters. The concentrator sorts such that full cells are sent to the m outputs, and empty cells are sorted out. The sorting network is a standard bitonic network as described earlier. The trap network has a little logic to detect multiple cells to the same address and tags the extra cells such that a bitonic sorter will sort them to one end of the trap's output lines. The expander network takes m inputs and, using a sorter, expands them to their proper positions among the n output lines.

The motivation for the concentrator was the observation that, on average, many of the n inputs will be idle, and by removing the empty cells generated by the idle inputs, a less complex sorter with m inputs and outputs can be used. One question that the Starlite paper does not address is whether the advantage of the smaller sorter is outweighed by the chance that the number of active inputs will be greater than m and the concentrator will have to discard active cells.

Analyzing the cost of each of the sorters, we observe that the Starlite switch is made up of four sorters, each with complexity between $m \log^2 m$ and $n \log^2 n$. Thus the overall complexity of the switch is $n \log^2 n$.

Other important features of Starlite, beyond the number of chips required to build it, are the recirculator lines and Starlite's ability to support multicast cells.

The recirculator lines are one way to solve the problem of blocking, while avoiding the need to discard cells. By reintroducing duplicate cells found in the trapper into the next switch cycle, one can minimize loss. One problem with recirculators is how to ensure that cells do not get reordered. Consider the example shown in Figure 5.18. Two cells on the same input line are destined for output 8. Due to blocking, the first cell gets recirculated to enter again on the same cycle as the second cell. It is important to make sure that the first cell gets through first, or else the two cells may get reordered. The Starlite design does not describe how to ensure that reordering does not occur, but the usual approach is to use a priority system, so that the first cell, once recirculated, gets a higher priority in the trap section than the second cell.

The Starlite does multicasting by a two-stage copy network placed above the concentrator, as shown in Figure 5.19. The first stage is a sorting network. New cells entering the switch are put into input ports on the left. *Copy cells* are put into the input ports on the right. Copy cells are special cells that contain the channel id of the cells they want to copy and the destination port to which the copy is to be sent.[5] The sorting network sorts the cells based on their source addresses, so that each new cell appears next to cells that want to copy it. The copy network then duplicates each new cell into all of its copies and injects the cells into the concentrator.

---

[5] Starlite actually used cells with a source and destination address, but the principle is the same.

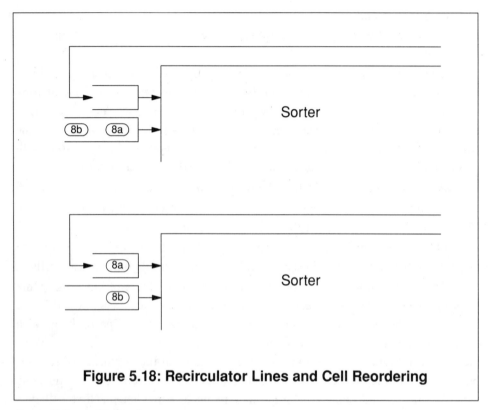

Figure 5.18: Recirculator Lines and Cell Reordering

Sunshine Switch

The Starlite switch is essentially an input buffered switch. Blocking in the switch causes cells to be put back at the head of their queues, via the recirculator lines. Given the advantages of output buffering, one would prefer to design a Batcher-Banyan switch that is output buffered.

The Sunshine switch is close to the state of the art in Batcher-Banyan switches. Its name is a pun on the name of the Starlite switch, after which the Sunshine switch is patterned. Although not completely output buffered (the Sunshine also has recirculator lines), the Sunshine is closer to an output-buffered switch than the Starlite. The Sunshine switch is an experimental prototype switch built by Bell Communications Research.

The Sunshine switch design is shown in Figure 5.20. The similarities to the Starlite should be clear — a Batcher sorting network with a trap network and recirculator lines. But the Sunshine switch uses a set of k banyans in parallel to route the cells and has changed the location of the concentrator. It has also

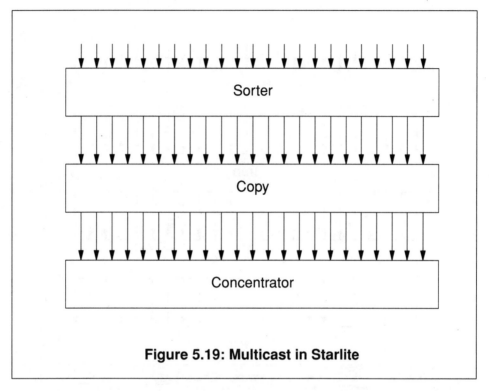

Figure 5.19: Multicast in Starlite

replaced the expander network with a selector network. Other important features of the Sunshine switch are that it supports multiple cell priority levels, and that each output port can accept up to k cells in a switch cycle.

Cells enter the Sunshine switch from n inputs at the top and enter a Batcher sorting network. Each cell is tagged with its output port number and a priority. The Batcher network sorts the cells in increasing order according to their tags. (As a little hack, the first bit in the tag is a 0 or 1 depending on whether the cell is empty or full, so that empty cells all sort to one end.)

The Batcher network is followed by a trap network that sees if more than k cells are destined for the same output, by comparing the destination of the cell in position i with the destination of the cell in position $i - k$. If the destinations are the same, then the cell in position i will have to be recirculated for another round and is specially marked for recirculation.

The concentrator network takes the output of the trap network and resorts the cells, so that cells destined for recirculation are sorted by their priority (rather than destination). In the remote chance that there are more cells to be recirculated than recirculator lines to carry them, the excess cells will be discarded. By

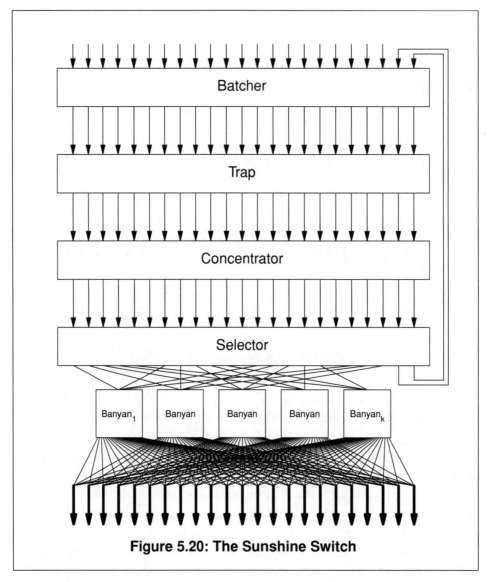

Figure 5.20: The Sunshine Switch

sorting the cells to be recirculated by priority, the concentrator ensures that, if any cells are discarded, it will be those cells with the lowest priority. Cells that are recirculated also have their priorities increased, so that, on the next cycle, they will get through the switch in preference to other cells from the same channel that are behind them.

The selector takes the outputs of the concentrator and routes them either to the recirculator lines or into the parallel banyans. The k adjacent outputs are routed to different banyans, so that up to k cells may be routed in parallel. Each banyan can send to every output port, so a single output port may receive up to k cells in a cycle.

The Sunshine switch supports multicasting but does it in each input port rather than by building a special copy network. Each input port contains a processor that recognizes cells for multicast ports and makes the appropriate number of copies.

The Sunshine is primarily an output-buffered switch, using k banyans to deliver cells in parallel to the output ports. However, it also uses recirculator queues, so there is an element of input buffering in the switch.

5.7. Input Buffering Revisited

Earlier in this chapter we compared output buffering and input buffering and concluded that output buffering, in large part because it avoided HOL blocking, offered higher performance. We have also noted that some of output buffering's good performance depends on traffic behaving in a fairly random fashion (which it typically does not).

In recent years there has been some work on devising more sophisticated input buffering schemes that reduce HOL blocking. For example, the primary reason for HOL blocking is that the input queues are FIFO. Cells behind the cell at the front of the queue cannot be serviced, even if they are for different output ports than the front cell. An obvious way to improve performance would be to allow cells deeper in the queue to try to get through the switch if the first cell is blocked. Using this approach, input-buffered switch throughput can be improved to be nearly competitive with an output-buffered switch: a saturated switch can achieve about 90% throughput compared to the 58% throughput of simple FIFO input queues.

A more interesting approach is to use special input buffering to avoid HOL blocking and also improve the intermixing of traffic, so the traffic looks more random (thus reducing the chance of loss at the output queues). This approach was taken in the MONET switch.

MONET — A Blocking Banyan with Input Buffering

MONET was a prototype switch design by Robinson and Carvey [Robinson 1990]. (The switch has never been built.) The basic idea behind MONET was to extend the blocking banyan switch used in the Butterfly® and Monarch™ multiprocessors to the problem of switching ATM cells.

A blocking banyan network is essentially a banyan switch with no sorting network in front of it. Cells are passed through the switch in a two-stage cycle. In the first stage, each input port examines the first cell in its queue and tries to establish a path to the appropriate output port. If more than one cell is destined for the same output port, one input port will establish a path and the rest will fail and have to wait for the next cycle. In the second stage, the input ports that successfully established a path transmit their cells through the switch.

Because there is no sorting network, blocking banyans have collision rates far higher than normal input-buffered switches. Because the potential rate of collisions is high, blocking banyans cannot discard cells that block. Rather, the switch must signal to the input ports whether the cell has successfully passed through the switch, and cells that fail to get through must be saved to try again on another clock cycle.

The high collision rates also imply that, unless strong efforts are made to minimize collisions, a blocking banyan switch may suffer from very poor throughput, especially at high loads. The MONET designers dealt with the collision problem in three ways.

First, they designed the switching fabric to run somewhat faster than the input and output links the switch served. As a result, a modest amount of blocking in each cycle was acceptable, because the switch had a higher capacity than the input and output lines.

Second, they put some extra paths into the switching fabric. By providing some redundant paths through parts of the fabric, the chance of collisions was reduced.

Finally, the MONET designers used input buffering to shape the traffic patterns entering the switch. They observed that the MONET switch would be connected to SONET networks; so instead of receiving cells one at a time at an input port, the input ports could be designed to work in groups of cells (where a group was all the cells in a SONET frame) once per SONET frame cycle. This observation suggested a way to shape the input traffic patterns.

The MONET design calls for the input ports to place the cells in a SONET frame into multiple queues, one queue per VCI. (All cells using the same VCI are in the same queue.) On each switch cycle, the input port randomly chooses the cell at the head of one of the VCI queues to send. If the cell gets through, it is taken off the VCI queue; otherwise the cell stays in the VCI queue and will be tried again in some later cycle. Essentially, this approach can be viewed as mixing the input traffic so it tends to look less correlated.

Using these techniques, the MONET designers were able to simulate a variety of bursty and highly correlated traffic patterns (such as a pattern of n arrivals all destined for the same output port each cycle) entering a saturated switch and still achieve throughputs of 0.95.

5.8. An Optical Cell Switch

The basic problem in cell switch design is how to connect all the input ports to all the output ports without collisions in the switching fabric. If you think about switching that way, it begins to sounds like the problem of designing a WDM network.

Figure 5.21 shows a prototype cell switch designed (but not yet built) at Bell Communications Research [Cisneros 1991], which uses a set of optical star couplers to interconnect the input and output queues of a cell switch. The switch has k input and output queues and m optical stars.

As with any WDM system, the major problem in the optical switch is to coordinate transmissions through the star couplers. Each input queue has m tunable lasers. Each output queue has m fixed receivers, and all receivers at a given output queue are tuned to the same wavelength. (Note that since all the receivers are tuned to the same wavelength and each input has only one laser to each star, it is not possible to use the optical fabric to multicast from one input to multiple outputs through a coupler.) Transmissions are coordinated through the collision resolution device (CRD). On each cycle, each input queue informs the CRD to which output the cell at the head of the input queue is destined. Because a star coupler can forward only one cell to a given output (each output listens to only one wavelength), the CRD must detect cases of multiple queues sending to the same output. The CRD then notifies each queue whether or not it may send its cell on this cycle.

Since the CRD's function is relatively simple, it is possible to improve switch performance by running multiple CRD cycles per cell cycle and keep all

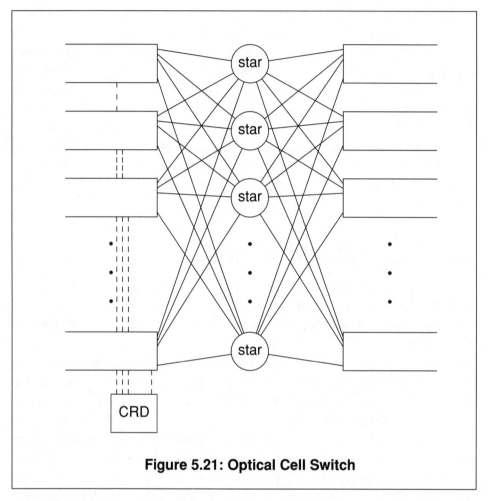

Figure 5.21: Optical Cell Switch

m optical stars busy in parallel. To maintain cell ordering, (because two cells from the same connection may be passing through two different star couplers in parallel), cells are placed in the output queues in the order of the star couplers they came from.

An important design problem is getting optical technology, especially lasers, capable of switching wavelengths in less than the time it takes to transmit one cell. This is a difficult problem, but the designers of this switch believe it will soon be feasible.

5.9. The Cost of Port Controllers

So far this chapter has not said much about the part of the port controllers that actually receive and transmit data over the lines connected to the switch, because these devices are usually pretty dull pieces of hardware. At their simplest, they are often just a transmitter or receiver chip, a lot of memory, and a processor to manage the queues and run some line management software.

However, it is important to keep in mind that the port controllers represent the vast majority of the *cost* of any switch. Consider that typically only a handful of chips implement the switching logic but there are *n* input port controllers and *n* output port controllers.

Because switching logic design is intellectually more challenging (and certainly more mathematically interesting) than designing port controllers, lots of papers have been published about switch design but very few about port controller design. It is important to keep in mind that the port controllers are there, too.

5.10. Summary

A key difference between cell switches is whether they are input or output buffered. Output-buffered switches such as the Knockout and Gauss switches typically have better performance. Because Batcher-Banyan switches tend to be input buffered, considerable care has to be taken to make them perform well. The Sunshine switch uses parallel banyans to approximate the performance of an output-buffered switch. The MONET switch achieves high performance using a sophisticated input queue management scheme. Finally, we observed that a lot of the cost of a switch is in its port controllers rather than the switching fabric, and a good designer will keep these costs in mind.

Further Reading

The literature on cell switching is voluminous. Many of the key papers, including several of the papers mentioned in this chapter, have been collected in Dhas, Konangi, and Sreetharan [1991] Lee's paper [1988], although it concentrates on copying for multicasting, is also a good introduction to the idea of Batcher-Banyan switches. The paper by Karol, Hluchyj and Morgan [1987] comparing input queuing and output queuing is also useful reading for understanding the theory behind various switch designs.

Chapter 6

Local Area Cell Networks

6.1. Introduction

The last chapter surveyed wide area cell networking technologies: large switching systems designed to provide wide area interconnection. This chapter examines gigabit-speed local area cell networking technologies: a variety of technologies intended to connect end systems such as computers, printers, video servers, and even voice systems like telephones, within a building or campus. Often, technologists distinguish building networks and campus networks by referring to building-sized networks as local area networks (LANs) and campus networks as metropolitan area networks (MANs). In practice, the technology for the two types of networks (at least as far as gigabit cell networking is concerned) is identical. Indeed, some of the networks surveyed are alternately described as MANs or LANs depending on whose paper is being read. So this chapter treats cell technologies for LANs and MANs together.

The survey is divided into two parts. The first part examines shared media networks for local area networks. These networks use ring- or bus-based technologies in which all nodes on the network are attached to the same cabling.

The second part looks at local area cell switching technology. The major distinction between these switches and the switches presented in the last chapter is that local area switches are designed to connect host systems together over short distances, whereas wide area switches tend to connect networks over long distances. This difference makes feasible some different design decisions, which we will briefly consider.

6.2. Shared Media Cell Networks

Shared media cell networks are networks in which the network's physical media (fiber or copper) is accessible to multiple systems. The usual logic for shared media networks (also called *multiaccess networks*) is that no single system is likely to use the entire media bandwidth for very long, so sharing the bandwidth among multiple systems is a useful cost savings. Also, the use of a shared media tends to make support for multicasting easier, because all the systems are listening on the same wire.

The major concern in a shared medium is making sure that, when multiple systems are competing for the medium's bandwidth, all the systems get an equitable fraction of the available bandwidth.

Shared media networks can also have trouble supporting performance guarantees. If several different systems on the same media all want to reserve part of the bandwidth to support applications with performance guarantees, how are their reservations to be coordinated?

Cell networks often solve the allocation and reservation problems by establishing methods for arbitrating the right to send a cell. However, the methods for arbitrating access can vary widely and have different consequences.

Shared Media Networks at Gigabit Speeds

Moving to gigabit speeds has an important impact on the design of shared media networks.

Recall the discussion of Ethernet performance in Chapter 2. It illustrated an important characteristic of the evolution of local area networks to gigabit speeds: the propagation delay in a fiber stays constant, but more and more bits can be packed into the fiber. This trend has an important implication: access techniques, such as Ethernet's, whose performance can be influenced by the length of the network (or the number of bits that can be in the network at any one time) will have difficulty achieving high performance, because the relative length of the network is increasing. One interesting feature of the networks in this chapter is how their access techniques try to achieve high performance.

Another point of difference in the various networks is their range of chosen cell sizes. At high speeds, particularly over short distances, cell size is not an important issue. Local bandwidth is cheap enough that completely filling cells is typically not considered important, and the difference in serialization times between a 53-byte cell and a 256-byte cell is less than 2 μs, small enough that no system is likely to care about the difference.

Cambridge Backbone Ring

The Cambridge Backbone Ring (CBR) was developed as a collaborative project between the University of Cambridge[1] and Olivetti Research [Greaves 1990]. It is of interest because, Cambridge arguably has more experience with cell LANs than any other organization, dating back to the first Cambridge Ring in the 1970s [Hopper 1977]. Furthermore, the CBR has been in operation for some time, and there is considerable experience using it to support gigabit applications.

The CBR is a ring network in which the ring's round-trip delay is divided into a number of *frames*, which rotate around the network. Special five-bit synchronization patterns are inserted between frames to equalize timing and filling odd space left if the ring delay is not an integral number of frame times.

Header	Full Monitor Type	Data 4 × 228-bit slots	Response Quality	CRC
4 bits	12 bits	1152 bits	8 bits	12 bits

Figure 6.1: CBR Frame Format

The CBR frame format is shown in Figure 6.1. Each frame contains four *slots*, where each slot contains one cell (both data and header). In the CBR a cell is 36 bytes long, of which four bytes are a header containing 16-bit source and destination addresses, and 32 bytes (256 bits) are data.

The *header* of a CBR frame is a special four-bit code, which is sufficiently distinct from the synchronization pattern to be recognizable even in the case of bit errors. Following the header are twelve bits of control information, three bits for each cell: a full-empty bit that indicates if the frame is filled; a type bit that indicates the data's priority and whose use is not fully defined; and a monitor bit, whose use is explained later in this section.

---

[1] Popularly known as Cambridge University.

The control bits are followed by four cells and then by eight more bits of control information. These eight bits contain two bits of information for each cell: the response bit, which can be used for retransmission of damaged cells; and the quality bit, which is used to indicate when corrupted cells have been detected in a frame. The control bits are followed by a twelve-bit CRC that is computed on the entire frame except for the header and CRC itself.

To send data over the CBR, a system looks for an empty slot by scanning the full-empty bits in each frame. When it finds an empty slot, the system inserts its data and sets the full-empty, the monitor, and the quality bits. The system can also set the response and type bits if it chooses. The addresses in the cell header are set to the addresses of the sending and destination systems.

When a system recognizes its address as the destination address in the cell header, it copies the data from the slot and sets the response bit.

When a system recognizes its address as the sending address in the cell header, it must clear the full-empty bit and make the slot available for reuse. Note that it is possible for a system to fail while it has slots in use on the network. To ensure that these slots get freed, each ring has a monitoring station. When a frame passes the monitoring station, the monitoring station copies the monitor bit into the full-empty bit for each cell and clears the monitor bit. After two passes by the monitoring station, this scheme will have cleared the full-empty bit even if the sender fails to do so.

The CBR supports multicasting by allowing multiple receivers to listen for cells addressed to a special destination address.

Every system on the ring computes the CRC for each frame. If the system discovers the CRC is bad, the system clears the quality bits for all the slots. In this manner, bad slots can be detected. Every time a station changes a slot, the CRC must be recomputed. Observe that by sharing the CRC over four slots, an error in one slot can corrupt all four slots. The CBR designers felt that errors would be sufficiently rare in fiber optic networks that it made sense to save bandwidth by using a single CRC, rather than using a CRC per slot.

The CBR designers wanted to make it possible for low-cost workstations to attach to the CBR, albeit at lower bandwidths. So the CBR allows systems to selectively receive only from one slot position in the frame. Each system maintains a table mapping destination addresses to slot positions. To send, a system looks up the slot position being read by the destination and inserts the cell into a free slot in that position. (Observe that for this system to work, each system must be able to send in any slot.)[2]

---

[2] There is a chance in this scheme that all the low speed stations will end up using the same slot position to receive in and waste three-quarters of the ring's bandwidth. The initial CBR

Ring networks have historically prevented systems from hogging all the network bandwidth by permitting systems to only have one packet (or cell) in transit at any given time. However, relatively long propagation delay in gigabit networks and the desire to allow systems to use large portions of the bandwidth required the CBR designers to permit a system to have multiple slots in use at one time.

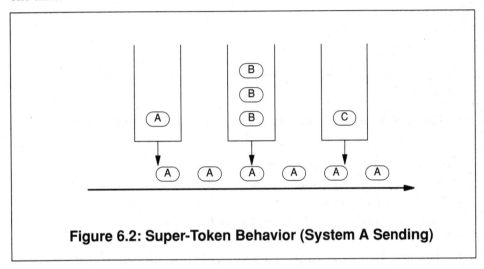

Figure 6.2: Super-Token Behavior (System A Sending)

Unfortunately permitting a station to use multiple slots can cause *super-token* behavior. Figures 6.2 and 6.3 illustrate the concept of a super token. System A is sending a burst of cells onto an otherwise inactive network. Figure 6.2 shows that, while system A is sending, the shared network is in use and systems B and C are unable to send. As a result, data begins to build up in the queues at systems B and C. (Note that in this diagram, unlike those of the previous chapters, the cells are labelled with the system they are coming *from* rather than the system they are destined for, to better illustrate the super-token concept.) Finally, system A empties its queue, and now system B is able to send (Figure 6.3). But system C is now blocked by system B's traffic, and its queue will continue to build up until system B finishes. The result of this kind of behavior is that each system gets access to the network in big clumps, rather than on a per-cell basis. The network acts very much like a network that uses a single token to control which hosts get to send. Thus the term *super token*.

---

design does not fix this problem, but an enhanced CBR has been designed that tries to mix traffic evenly among slots.

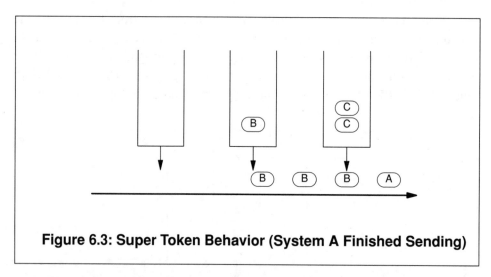

Figure 6.3: Super Token Behavior (System A Finished Sending)

It may not be immediately obvious why the super-token behavior persists. Looking at Figure 6.3 one might reasonably wonder what happens if system A sends a cell. Would that cell not get mixed into system B's cells, and thus, over time, could one not expect the token to get broken up? There are two reasons that tokens tend to persist.

The first reason has to do with how cells get cleared from the network. Recall that the CBR is a ring, so all cells sent out the right side of the figure loop around the ring and come back in from the left. These cells' slots are considered full until the sender clears the full bit. If system A sends for long enough, all the cell slots on the network will contain system A's data and will appear full to any system except system A, which is clearing the slots. System B gets to send only once system A stops refilling its cleared slots with more cells. Once system A stops sending, unless it gets a new cell to send very quickly, it will pass on all its free cells to system B, which then monopolizes the network in its turn.

The second reason tokens persist has to do with how higher layer protocols tend to work. To keep senders from sending data faster than receivers can accept it, higher layer protocols typically use some form of flow control to limit how much data a sender can transmit before receiving an acknowledgement. This observation implies that the reason system A stopped sending data in Figure 6.3 is that all of its higher layer protocols have sent as much data as they can without an acknowledgement. (The receiving systems could not acknowledge the data received because system A was hogging all the cell slots.) Until the systems to which system A was sending gain access to the network, system A's higher protocols will wait for acknowledgements and have no more data to send. Thus higher layer flow control tends to cause super-token behavior because the only way a system can get more data to transmit is to give up the super-token so that its receivers can send acknowledgements.[3]

To avoid super-token behavior, the CBR does not permit stations to fill successive slots. Also, when sending systems free a slot they have just used, they may not refill the slot but must pass it on.

Observe, too, that by permitting a station to use multiple slots and optionally supporting retransmission of cells, the CBR may cause retransmitted cells to arrive out of order at the receiver. This behavior violates ATM's expectations but the CBR predates ATM. Furthermore, there is no requirement (except perhaps market pressure) that a cell network conform to ATM's requirements.

The CBR has limited support for performance guarantees. Each station may transmit on all the slots in the ring, once every n ring rotation times, so the maximum delay is roughly bounded. There is no way to allocate a particular share of the ring bandwidth. However, just the simple delay constraints are apparently sufficient to allow experimentation with multimedia applications. (See Hopper [1990]).

The CBR is a good example of a cell ring network. It illustrates the basic problems (such as super-token behavior and the need for hosts to use multiple slots per ring revolution) that any ring designer must confront.

One feature that the CBR does not have is slot removal, in which the receiver frees the slot or an erasure station detects and frees slots that have been read. Freeing slots permits other nodes to reuse the slot as the slot goes around the ring between the receiver and the sender. Because, on average, a cell travels only halfway around the ring to get from its sender to its receiver, having the receiver free the slot will typically double the effective bandwidth of the ring. See Sharon and Segall [1992] for one slot reuse scheme and references to others.

---

[3] Some protocols do not require acknowledgements. They are relatively rare. It is also worthy of mention that flow control can cause super-token behavior in point-to-point networks. Super-token behavior was first observed by Van Jacobson as a phenomenon on the Arpanet.

IEEE 802.6 (DQDB)

The Distributed Queue Dual Bus (DQDB) standard is a joint standard of the Institute of Electrical and Electronic Engineers (IEEE) and the American National Standards Institute (ANSI) [IEEE 1991], usually referred to either by its acronym or its IEEE standard number (802.6). It is derived from an earlier technology called QPSX. DQDB is of interest largely because its standards committee worked carefully with the ATM standards bodies to ensure that DQDB local networks would interconnect with ATM long-distance networks. DQDB's cell and header sizes are the same as that of ATM, the header formats are almost identical, and AAL 3/4 and the DQDB MAC protocol are identical.

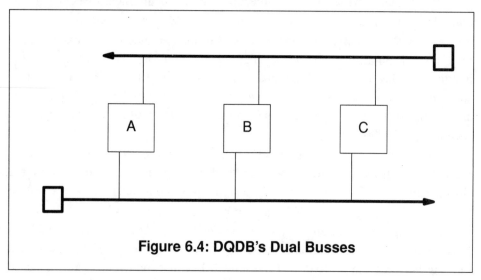

Figure 6.4: DQDB's Dual Busses

In a DQDB network, every system is connected to two unidirectional busses, as shown in Figure 6.4. The two busses transmit in opposite directions, so there exists a transmission path from every system to every other system. The busses are slotted, and each slot can hold one 48-octet cell plus a 5-octet cell header. The slots are generated by devices at the head of each bus and transmitted "downstream."

The dual bus architecture is typically implemented over a physical ring network, as shown on the left of Figure 6.5. The advantage of this approach is that if a link between two nodes fails, then the ring can reconfigure itself to be a true bus, where the two end nodes are the nodes on either side of the failure (as shown on the right of Figure 6.5).

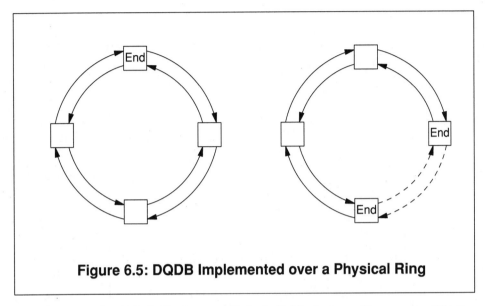

Figure 6.5: DQDB Implemented over a Physical Ring

Like the CBR, DQDB places cells in individual slots. However, unlike the CBR, slots are not grouped into frames. In addition, to support traffic with real-time delivery requirements, DQDB allows slots to be permanently reserved (or according to the language of the DQDB standard, "prearbitrated").

The DQDB slot format is shown in Figure 6.6. The fields are identical to ATM format at the UNI with three important exceptions:

1. The four-bit generic flow control (GFC) field has been replaced by an eight-bit access control field (ACF), which is used to control access to the DQDB busses.

2. Instead of a VPI and VCI, DQDB just has a VCI.

3. The control bit fields are slightly different. DQDB has a two-bit priority field and a two-bit payload field, but the ATM UNI has a three-bit payload field and a one-bit cell loss priority field. Originally, these control bit fields were the same, but the change to ATM to accommodate the user signalling bit in the payload field caused the two standards to diverge. (The DQDB standard had been issued before ATM was changed.)

Access to slots is managed using the ACF and the VCI. There are two different modes of operation, one for regular traffic, the other for reserved (real-time) traffic.

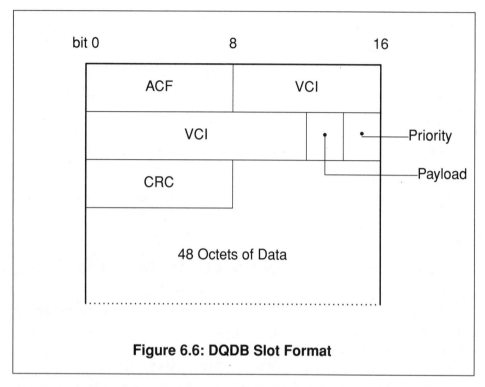

bit 0   8   16

ACF | VCI

VCI | Priority

CRC | Payload

48 Octets of Data

Figure 6.6: DQDB Slot Format

For regular traffic, DQDB uses a distributed arbitration scheme. To send a cell, a system must reserve a slot on the appropriate bus (i.e., the bus on which the sending system is "upstream" from the destination).

To reserve a slot on one bus (call it the sending bus for this cell), a system examines cells on the *other* bus (the reservation bus), looking for a slot in which a request bit in the ACF is 0, and sets that bit to 1. DQDB supports three levels of priority, so three possible bits can be set, depending on the priority the system assigns to the cell it wants to send. The request bit indicates to systems upstream of the sender on the sending bus that a slot has been requested at a given level of priority. The sending system then waits for its free slot on the sending bus and, when the free slot comes, fills the slot with its cell and sets the VCI.

Free and empty slots are distinguished by two bits of the ACF.[4] The sender

---

[4] Two bits are required to distinguish full slots from empty slots because there are two types of slots: regular slots and prearbitrated slots. Therefore the network has to distinguish between full and empty regular slots and prearbitrated slots, which requires three distinct values.

employs counters to determine which free slot it should use. The sender keeps a count, for each priority level, of the requests for slots that it has seen on the reservation bus. Whenever the node sees a request bit of the same or higher priority level turned on, it increments the counter. Whenever the node sees a free slot of the same or higher priority level on the sending bus, it decrements the counter. When a node requests a free slot, it copies the request counter into a countdown counter. This counter counts down as it sees free slots on the sending bus until its counter is 0. The system then places its cell in the next slot. If higher priority requests are made on the reservation while the countdown counter is being used, then the countdown counter must be incremented, to let the higher priority traffic through first. Keep in mind that because both buses may be used for sending and reservations, two sets of counters must be maintained. Note that this queueing scheme is distributed — the management of the slots is done separately at each system, by observing traffic and requests on each bus.

Unfortunately, the DQDB allocation scheme does not fairly allocate slots. If two systems are sending at the same time, it is extremely unlikely that the systems will share the bandwidth equally. To see why this might be so, look back at Figure 6.4 and consider a situation in which systems A and B are both transmitting long (multiple-cell) messages to C. Assume the network was initially idle and that system A started sending its message first. In this situation, system A's requests for free slots are immediately served because its counter of previous requests is always 0. Then system B starts sending. To send, system B makes a request on the top bus. Until system A hears system B's request, system A will keep filling slots, and when system A hears system B's request, system A will let just one free cell through and then resume filling slots. Only when system B finally sees the free slot can it send its cell and request another free slot. Thus the amount of bandwidth that system B receives depends upon its physical distance from system A. Finding a perfect solution to this problem is rather hard, so DQDB uses a heuristic one. Every so often, a system is required to let a free slot that the system had reserved go past. Forcing systems to occasionally skip using a free slot means that a system accidentally hogging the bus (like system A in the example) will slowly yield its bandwidth to other systems.

Another problem with the DQDB scheme is that, at high loads, the time to get the right to send a cell depends on the length of the bus. Because the time to serialize a cell is much shorter than the time it takes for a bit to travel the length of the bus, the result is that the time required to send a cell is heavily influenced by the bus length.

DQDB handles real-time or prearbitrated traffic differently. Each stream of prearbitrated traffic is given a unique VCI. Reserved slots are generated by the head of the appropriate bus with their VCI fields set to the VCI of the channel using each slot. A bit in the ACF is set to indicate this slot has been preassigned. The sending node watches for preassigned slots with the right VCI and puts its cells into those slots. Note that even though the mechanism for using prearbitrated cells has been defined, the DQDB standard currently does not define how to set up VCIs. So, currently, this service is useless.

Addressing in DQDB is a little strange. Prearbitrated slots use the VCI field, but this leaves no space in the header for addressing regular slots. So DQDB defines one VCI to be special (the VCI of all ones) and requires each system to reassemble all the cells sent on the special VCI back into packets and then examine the destination address in each packet to see for which system the packet is destined. Packets are fragmented into cells using the segmentation and convergence layers of AAL 3/4 (using a distributed MID assignment algorithm, to ensure no two systems use the same MID). The data contents of the AAL 3/4 convergence layer data unit is a packet in IEEE 802 format. The DQDB standard permits systems to use one of six different address formats in the 802 header; most of these schemes support multicast addressing.

The result of this addressing and adaptation layer cake is that DQDB can simultaneously support two types of traffic: reserved traffic using cells and regular IEEE 802 style packets. This dual type of service has considerable appeal. However, the down side is that DQDB is hardwired to use AAL 3/4 (with its high overhead), whereas the data communications community largely favors AAL 5 (SEAL).[5] Furthermore, although the DQDB cell service was originally intended to be completely compatible with ATM, the standards have now diverged slightly. Originally it had been thought that because DQDB would seamlessly interconnect with ATM wide area networks and provide transparent support for the ATM data oriented AAL, DQDB had an inside track to become the local area network of the late 1990s. Now, it appears that DQDB picked the wrong AAL and may not interconnect quite so perfectly with ATM. Its future is unclear.

---

[5] The 802.6 standards committee is considering revising DQDB to support AAL 5 but this change will presumably take some time to effect.

HANGMAN

HANGMAN is a prototype gigabit cell LAN built by the Hewlett-Packard Laboratory in Bristol, England [Watson 1992a]. Its design is different from both the CBR and DQDB in a couple of respects.

First, rather than connecting systems directly to the fiber optic cable, HANGMAN connects them via devices called *nodes*. Each node connects several systems to the fiber. By providing an extra device between each system and the network, the HANGMAN designers had greater flexibility to experiment with access techniques and special protocol implementations.

Second, HANGMAN uses a large cell size: 256 bytes. The designers of HANGMAN were most interested in optimizing performance for local area traffic (which tends to use large packets) and felt that interfacing with outside cell networks with smaller cell sizes, such as B-ISDN, was less important than achieving good local area performance. As a result, they chose a cell size they thought would be efficient for local data transfers.

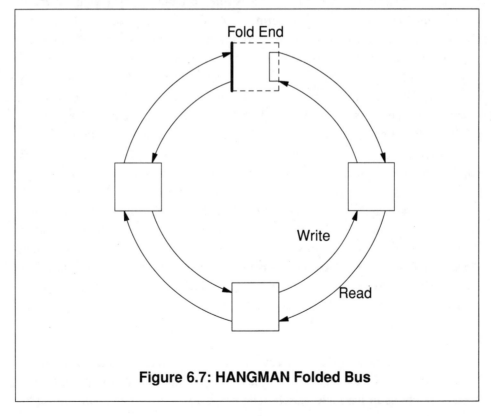

Figure 6.7: HANGMAN Folded Bus

Third, the physical architecture of HANGMAN is a logical folded bus implemented over a dual ring, rather than the ring of the CBR or the dual bus architecture of DQDB. Each node is attached to the bus twice, with one attachment on the write bus and one on the read bus, as shown in Figure 6.7. At the head of the bus is an intelligent slot generator that sends empty slots onto the write side of the bus, where nodes place their data into the slots. Slots loop back via a fold node onto the read side of the bus, where the nodes read the data from slots. If a link between two nodes in the ring is severed, it is detected and the nodes on either side of the break become the new head and fold nodes.

Like DQDB, HANGMAN can have fairness problems. Nodes near the head of the bus have unequal access to the bus. To fix this problem, HANGMAN uses an access protocol called S (for *simple*) [Limb 1990]. In short, S calls for each node to have a counter, which counts down every time a slot is sent. When the counter reaches 0, the node must stop sending. The counter is refilled if the node observes an empty slot on the read bus (indicating that no node could use the slot). The value to which the counter is filled is called P. The value of P can be different for each node, which permits HANGMAN the flexibility to allocate bandwidth unevenly across the nodes, if appropriate. Observe that the S protocol largely avoids dependencies on the length of the network.

Normally, S allocates bandwidth and delays waiting for the bus slightly unevenly, depending on the position of the node and the traffic on the network. However, in the worst case, when all nodes are trying to send all the time, S becomes almost perfectly fair, giving each node an equal share of the bandwidth.

HANGMAN can also provide nodes with guaranteed shares of the ring bandwidth. The slots are grouped into cycles of 2048 slots, and a node can ask the slot generator to mark certain slots in each cycle as reserved for that node's use. To mark a slot, the slot generator puts the node's address in the source address field of each slot and marks the slot as reserved for synchronous traffic. To find its slots, a node simply reads the source addresses of the synchronous slots. A nice feature of HANGMAN is that nodes can request which slots within a cycle they would like to reserve. So if a node knows that it wants to transmit a datagram that is two slots long, once each cycle, it can ask for the two slots to be adjacent in the cycle. Each reserved slot in a cycle represents about 500 Kb/s of bandwidth.

Recall that each HANGMAN node connects several hosts to the network. This architecture led the HANGMAN designers to experiment with putting some special functions in the node. Each node has its own processor. This processor was initially added to make it easier to manage and configure each node, but it also makes it easier to experiment with adding new functions into the node.

In its current incarnation, HANGMAN does all the protocol processing up to the transport layer in the node, rather than the attached systems. The major advantage of this approach is that special devices like cameras and video screens can be directly connected to a node (without the need for a computer in between). Also, making the node do all protocol processing minimizes the problems of multiplexing the various systems' traffic in the node.

Addressing in HANGMAN is done using 16-bit node addresses. The address of all ones is used for broadcasting.

The most interesting aspect of HANGMAN is that it was designed without regard to compatibility with ATM. As a result, it gives a bit of a non-ATM perspective to cell network design.

Manhattan Street Network

The Manhattan Street Network (MSN) is a very different type of cell LAN. Developed at Bell Labs [Maxemchuk 1985], the MSN is a fully connected mesh network. The major advantage of a mesh network is its great flexibility in routing.

A 4×4 MSN is shown in Figure 6.8. Links transmit in one direction, and alternate links go in opposite ways. The vertical links are sometimes called *avenues* and the horizontal links are sometimes called *streets*, to evoke the similarity of the MSN architecture to the way streets are laid out in the borough of Manhattan in New York City. Each node gets its address from its location in the mesh. The first number identifies its street (or row) and the second number identifies its avenue (or column). Thus, node 0/1 is one avenue over and two streets up from node 2/2.

A node can send a cell into the network from one of its outputs if the node receives an empty cell on one of its inputs. The network will route the cell from node to node until it gets to its destination.

Exactly how the cell gets routed is probably the most interesting problem in designing the MSN. For example, rather than going one left and two up to get from node 2/2 to node 0/1, one could go two down and one left. There are a number of possible ways to route (see Maxemchuk [1987] for several examples). The simplest is to simply compute the offsets, r and c between the current node (r_{now}/c_{now}) and the destination node (r_{dst}/c_{dst}), according the following formulas (for a 4×4 MSN):

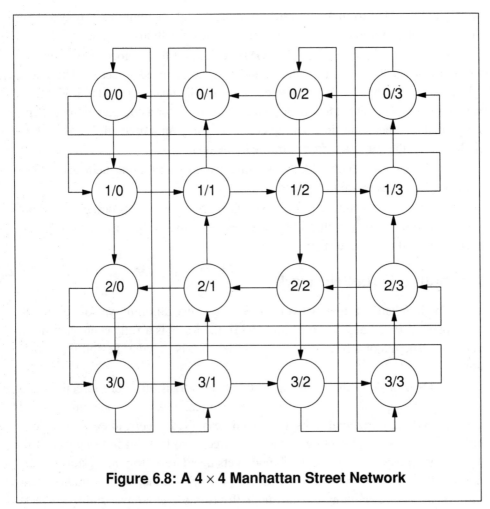

Figure 6.8: A 4 × 4 Manhattan Street Network

$$r = 2 - \left[(2 - \delta_c(r_{\text{now}} - r_{\text{dst}})) \bmod 4\right]$$

$$c = 2 - \left[(2 - \delta_r(c_{\text{now}} - c_{\text{dst}})) \bmod 4\right]$$

The values δ_c and δ_r are either +1 or −1 depending on the direction of the street or avenue of the destination node. So δ_c is +1 if c_{dst} is even (the avenue goes down) and −1 if c_{dst} is odd. Given r and c, the current node routes the cell according to the rules in Table 6.1. According to these rules, a cell sent from 3/2 to 0/0 could follow the route shown in Figure 6.9. These particular routing rules do not always give the optimal path, but are probably the simplest set of rules to implement and usually give a nearly optimal path.

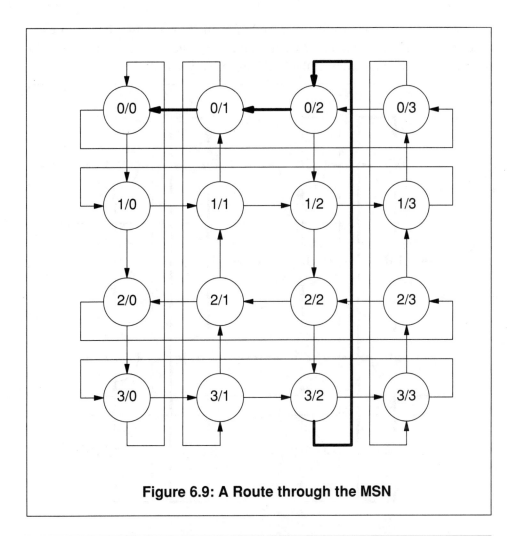

Figure 6.9: A Route through the MSN

Table 6.1: Simple Routing Rules for the MSN	
Condition	**Routing Rules**
$r > 0, c > 0$	Route either down or left.
$r > 0, c < 0$	Route right. If you cannot route right, route down.
$r < 0, c < 0$	Route either up or right.
$r < 0, c > 0$	Route up. If you cannot route up, route left.
$r > 0, c = 0$	Route down.
$r = 0, c > 0$	Route left.

What if two cells arriving at a node (recall there are two inputs to each node) both prefer the same path? Or if a link in a route has failed? In these two situations, the mesh topology of the MSN proves very valuable.

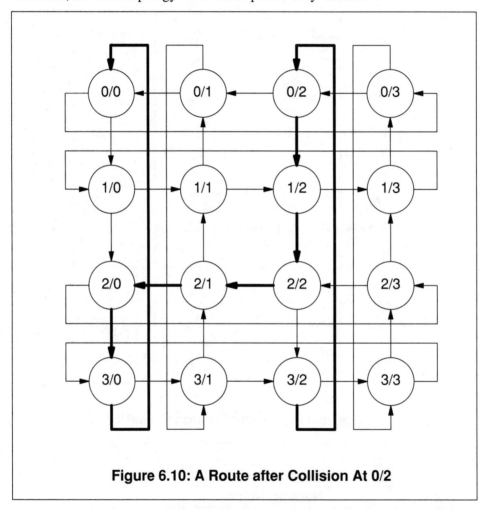

Figure 6.10: A Route after Collision At 0/2

If two cells want to use the same path (i.e., the cells collide), the node randomly sends one cell along the desired path and routes the other cell out the other path.[6] The misdirected cell is then routed normally at the next hop. The result is that the cell will follow a longer path but it will still get to its destination. Figure

---

[6] This random routing is reminiscent of hot-potato routing developed by Paul Baran [1964].

6.10 shows what might have happened in the previous example if the cell had collided with another cell at node 0/2.

A link failure requires a slightly more complicated procedure. Because every node has two inputs and two outputs, if a link fails, then one node will have two inputs and only one output and another node will have one input and two outputs. The node with two inputs and one output poses a problem: if two cells arrive, there is only a path to forward one and the other will have to be discarded. This is the only situation in which the MSN can lose cells. To keep this situation from happening, the MSN has a mechanism to restructure itself after a link failure so that no node has more inputs than outputs. The mechanism works as follows:

- If a node stops receiving cells on a row link, it stops transmitting on its column link.
- If a node stops receiving cells on a column link, it stops transmitting on its row link.

When a node stops transmitting, it effectively shuts down the link it was transmitting on, which causes the receiving node on that link to perform the link failure procedure itself. Except in exceptional outages (multiple link failures), the result is to remove a single cycle of four links from the network. Figure 6.11 shows the result if the link from 2/2 to 2/3 fails.

The major advantage of the MSN is its rich connectivity, which allows it to survive multiple link failures. This rich topology also means that, for large networks, the network tends to perform well even under high loads if the traffic is well mixed. Some cells collide, but enough redundant paths exist that these collisions do not seriously impact performance.

The MSN also has some major disadvantages. It does not support multicasting or broadcasting, nor does it support a guaranteed service. There are traffic patterns that will cause the MSN to send some cells over very long paths, with bad results for applications that require guaranteed performance. A final potential concern is that the MSN permits cells to be reordered.

6.3. Local Area Switching Technologies

In addition to shared media LANs, several researchers and companies have developed local area cell switches.

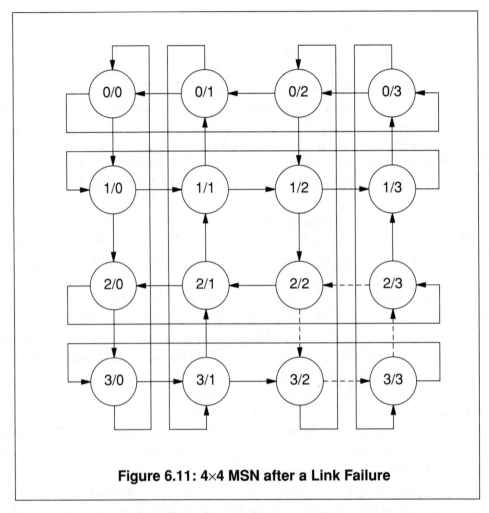

Figure 6.11: 4×4 MSN after a Link Failure

Many of these switches have a Batcher-Banyan architecture just like the wide area switches described in the last chapter. The only major difference is that a local switch tends to be much smaller than a wide area switch. A local switch may support between 8 and 32 inputs and outputs, whereas a wide area switch may support thousands.

The smaller switch size also makes simpler technologies that scale relatively poorly, like busses and crossbars, more appealing.

Beyond their smaller size, local area switches are also distinguished from wide area switches by the relatively short length of fiber between the switch and the hosts it serves. Because the distance and thus the transit delay is short, it is possible for the switch and its hosts to more closely coordinate their buffer management, with some interesting results.

The AN2 Switch

The AN2 switch is a research ATM switch being built by Digital Equipment Corporation's Systems Research Center. It is a small (16×16) switch specially designed to take advantage of the properties of a local area switch.

The AN2 is a crossbar, an architecture made possible by the switch's modest number of ports. The crossbar is fast enough to permit individual ports to transmit data at speeds as high as a gigabit per second.

The switch uses a combination of traffic segregation, input buffering, and hop-by-hop flow control to eliminate loss between switches. ATM traffic through an AN2 switch is divided into two types: continuous bit-rate and variable bit-rate virtual circuits.

Continuous bit-rate circuits must preallocate bandwidth at each switch. The allocation method groups cells into virtual frames of 1,000 cells, and each continuous bit-rate circuit is allocated certain cells in each frame. All unallocated cells in a frame plus those cells allocated but not used are available to variable rate circuits. By scheduling the continuous bit-rate cells, AN2 avoids contention on continuous bit-rate circuits, but contention can still arise among variable rate circuits. If too many variable rate circuits offer data at the same time, some cells might have to be discarded.

To prevent loss in variable rate circuits, the AN2 combines input buffering with hop-by-hop flow control, using the mechanism shown in Figure 6.12. At each switch, each virtual circuit keeps a window counter. Every time the virtual circuit sends a cell to the next switch, the counter is decremented. If the counter is 0, the circuit may not send and must buffer any cells it receives. When the next switch forwards a cell on, it sends back an acknowledgement. When a switch receives an acknowledgement for a virtual circuit, it increments that circuit's counter. Acknowledgements are sent in the GFC bits of the ATM header.

One way to think of this scheme is to observe that the AN2 implements window flow control on a hop-by-hop basis. Window flow control requires a virtual circuit to maintain buffer space equal to the round-trip time of the hop. (The buffer space should equal the round-trip time for two reasons. If the buffer space is less than the round-trip time and if the circuit is sending at the maximum rate, then it will have to stop sending and wait for an acknowledgement, even if it is the only circuit currently using the link. If the buffer space is greater than the

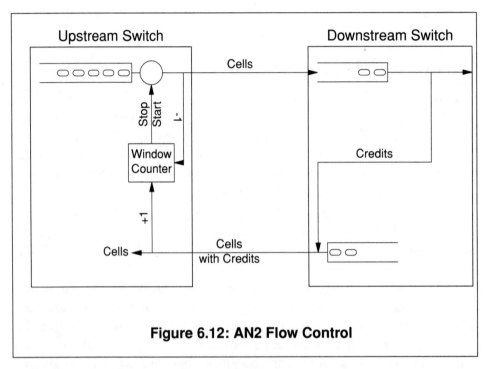

Figure 6.12: AN2 Flow Control

round-trip time, then the sender can overfill the link and cause congestion before it runs out of credits.) Over a long distance so much buffer space can be expensive. But over local area distances the buffer costs are quite small. At OC-3 speeds, 1 kilometer is only 4 cell times long, and a kilometer at a gigabit is only 24 cell times. Even if the switch supports a few thousand virtual circuits per link, the amount of memory required for buffering is only a few megabytes of RAM.

Finally, groups of AN2 switches can automatically learn of each other's presence and generate routes between themselves and the hosts they serve. This capability was first developed for the *Autonet* packet network, which influenced the AN2 design [Schroeder 1991]. The automatic configuration is achieved using a flooding algorithm, in which all the switches in the network exchange topology information using a special protocol. Note that this service works only if all the switches in the portion of the network being configured are AN2 switches or implement the AN2 flooding protocol.

6.4. Summary

There are a wide variety of ways to build local area cell networks. Shared media cell networks can be built as rings (the CBR), folded buses (HANGMAN), dual buses (DQDB), or fully connected mesh networks (MSN). The different networks and designs have different advantages: some offer guaranteed performance; others are more robust in the face of errors. Local area cell networks based on switches are also possible and we examined one switch (AN2) that takes advantage of the short length of local area links to prevent cell loss with hop-by-hop flow control.

Further Reading

The CBR is part of a larger networking program at Cambridge focussed on networking and multimedia technologies. Some information on these programs can be found in Zielinski et al. [1991] and Hopper [1990]. The two best DQDB references are the standard itself [IEEE 1991], and the paper on how the standard solves the fairness problem, by the designers of the fairness algorithm [Hahne 1990]. The S access scheme used in HANGMAN is being replaced by an improved scheme called $S++$, which is described in Watson et al. [1992b].

Getting more information about local area switch designs is rather hard. Ian Leslie [1991] has written about a switch being used at University of Cambridge. But most of the commercial vendors of local ATM switches have been rather reticent about describing important details of their switch design. The discussion of of AN2 is derived largely from a couple of lectures given by Chuck Thacker, its primary designer.

Chapter 7

Gigabit Packet Networks

7.1. Issues in Packet Network Design

Far more work has been done in the past few years on gigabit cell networking technologies than on gigabit packet network technologies. This disparity of effort is somewhat surprising, because building fast packet networks is generally considered simpler than building fast cell networks. The best explanation for the situation appears to be another case of that classic engineering disease of solving yesterday's problems.

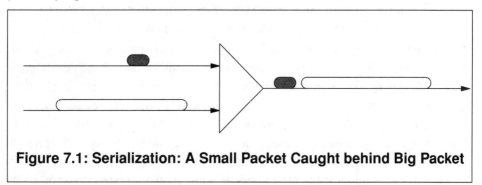

Figure 7.1: Serialization: A Small Packet Caught behind Big Packet

Recall that Chapter 3 pointed out that one motivation for cell networks was to solve the serialization problem shown in Figure 7.1. The packet coming in the top line contained time-critical data that could be trapped behind the big packet coming in the bottom line. The time-critical data could be delayed so much that it was no longer useful.

Serialization problems are a serious issue for today's slower packet networks. For example, on an Ethernet, a maximum-sized packet of 1518 bytes takes a little over 1 ms to transmit. Given that access to the Ethernet is statistical and there is no way to ensure that a particular packet will not get caught behind several others, a real-time packet can easily get delayed by several milliseconds. For these reasons, experiments with packetized voice over Ethernet such as the Etherphone have typically been done on Ethernets with very low loads.

However, at higher bandwidths, this problem largely goes away. At 1 gigabit, a maximum-sized Ethernet frame takes about 12 μs to transmit, which is such a short time that all but the most time-sensitive applications will not notice. Human beings are sensitive to delays of tens of milliseconds, so this delay is one-thousandth of the size a person might notice. Expressed another way, the real-time packet would have to get caught behind about 1,000 big packets before a human user might care. And it is not hard to devise network access protocols that ensure that a real-time packet gets served within 1,000 packet times. (The topic of interference and packet sizes is considered in greater detail in Chapter 13.)

Another concern for packet networks has been support for *isochrony,* the ability to send data, especially voice samples, at fixed intervals. Variable packet sizes make it difficult to send data at fixed intervals. However, as we shall see in later chapters, the desire for isochrony is historical rather than technical. The major requirement for real-time traffic is simply that its delay be bounded.

So when looking at technologies for gigabit packet networks, three features are of particular interest. First, a technology obviously needs to achieve gigabit or near gigabit speeds. Thankfully, this problem is reasonably easy, and a number of approaches are possible. Second, it would be nice if a technology had mechanisms to provide at least rough bounds on how long it takes for a packet to pass through the network, because if the technology does not explicitly provide delay bounds, implementors will have to write software to use the network in such a way that some bounds are provided. Third, it would be very useful if the technology supported multicasting, to allow easy support for multicast conferencing.

7.2. Local Area Packet Technologies

There are a wide variety of ways to build local area packet networks. WDM is one approach. As Chapter 2 pointed out, if the time to search through the channels were improved, the RAINBOW architecture could be used to support packet transmission.

This section looks at three other approaches: switched point-to-point networking (HIPPI), interconnected hubs (ATOMIC), and rings (CSMA/RN).

HIPPI

Strictly speaking, the High-Performance Parallel Interface (HIPPI) is not a networking protocol at all; it is a point-to-point connection technology, designed to connect two devices (typically a supercomputer and a peripheral) at either 800 or 1600 Mb/s over a cable no more than 25 meters long.[1] But HIPPI has turned out to be very important for experimentation in gigabit data communications, because it was the first standard way to connect devices at high data rates and because it can be used in conjunction with a switch to provide a gigabit LAN service [Tolmie 1993].

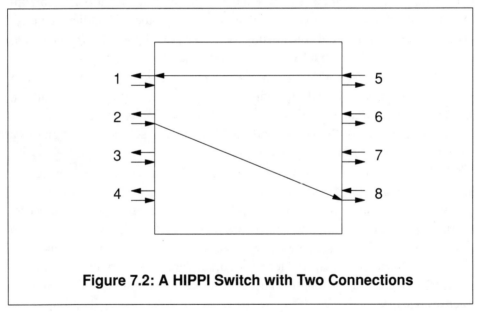

Figure 7.2: A HIPPI Switch with Two Connections

HIPPI is a standard produced by the ANSI X3T9.3 committee, chaired by Don Tolmie. It defines a simplex packet framing protocol, based on a connectionlike scheme. To send data, a device requests that it be connected to the destination device. An example of two connections through a switch is shown in Figure 7.2. This connection causes all packets sent by the sending device to go to

---

[1] An implementors' agreement called *Serial HIPPI* exists for operating HIPPI over fiber to distances of 10 kilometers.

the receiving device. HIPPI does not allow multiple connections to be multiplexed over a line at the same time. When a device is done sending, it asks to end the connection. If a connection cannot be established, because the destination is already connected to another system, HIPPI allows the requesting device to either wait for the destination to become free or be notified that a conflict exists and it should try again. Note that, for simple, point-to-point links between two devices, HIPPI can just establish a single, permanent connection.

Packets are sent as as a sequence of *bursts*, where each burst is a group of 1 to 256 words. At 800 Mb/s the words are 32 bits wide. At 1600 Mb/s the words are 64 bits wide. Only the first or last burst in a packet (but not both) can be less than 256 words. The HIPPI cables are very wide, so the clock rate on the cable is just 25 Mhz (40 ns per word). Packets can be up to two bytes short of four gigabytes long. An indeterminate packet mode (i.e., arbitrary length) is also supported. Every HIPPI packet contains a higher layer protocol identifier (identifying the upper layer protocol contained in the packet) and up to 1016 bytes of control information. (Each burst has 8 bytes of overhead.)

The control information section of the packet is used to support a variety of HIPPI modes. Currently, HIPPI defines how to use the control information to support the transmission of IEEE 802.2 protocol data units and IPI-3 disk and tape commands via HIPPI. (In support for IPI-3 one can see HIPPI's origins as a channel protocol for supercomputers.)

When sending variable length packets through a switch, the usual procedure is to establish and tear down a connection after every packet (or every few packets), to allow maximum multiplexing of the switch. As a result, part of the packet overhead is the time required to get a connection request to the switch and get an answer back and for the sending device to handle the connection setup and teardown. The connection setup and teardown times depend, in part, on the length of the HIPPI cable, and for long distances the times can be quite long — tens of microseconds.

HIPPI also lacks support for multicasting. For protocols that use multicasting to find services, HIPPI can support a special multicast port that actually just directs multicast transmissions to the port of a server which has agreed to provide the services. But this workaround does not comfortably serve multicast services like video and audio conferencing.

Overall, two things make HIPPI interesting. First, that it exists and is widely used — it will be a gigabit attachment technology for some years to come. Second, the HIPPI designers were relentless about keeping the technology simple, to make implementation straightforward. As a result, HIPPI is a good example of just how easy it can be to implement gigabit speeds. Certainly, a 32-bit data path clocked at 25MHz is very comfortably within the state of the art.

Fibre Channel

Another switched interconnection technology being proposed for use as a network is Fibre Channel. Fibre Channel is expected to become an international standard from the International Standards Organization (ISO) sometime in 1994. The Fibre Channel designers have been more aggressive than the HIPPI designers about supporting different types of connections. For example, beyond IPI-3 and 802 framing, Fibre Channel supports the Small Computer System Interface (SCSI) and IBM's block multiplexor channel protocol (FIPS60). As a result, the Fibre Channel protocol is generally viewed as more complex than HIPPI's.

The ATOMIC LAN

ATOMIC is a gigabit LAN built by USC Information Sciences Institute, based on a multiprocessor interconnection chip technology called *Mosaic*, developed at CalTech [Dally 1987].

The Mosaic technology is built around a chip that links eight 0.5 gigabit communications channels to a simple packet switch and a 16-bit processor. The chips are typically connected into a 4×4 or 8×8 mesh reminiscent of the Manhattan Street Network. An example is shown in Figure 7.3. (Observe that, unlike the MSN, the edge chips in the Mosaic mesh are not connected to each other.) Depending on the version of the chip, each channel operates at between 500 and 800 Mb/s.[2]

Mosaic routes packets in a mesh by putting two counters, an x counter and a y counter, at the start of each packet. To route a packet from one chip to another, the offset in x and y between the two chips in the grid is computed and placed in the counters. The chips route the packet from hop to hop using the counters. First the packet is routed in the x direction, subtracting or adding 1 for each node passed until the x counter goes to 0. (One subtracts 1 going right, and adds 1 going left.) When the x counter goes to 0, it is removed and the chip

---

[2] Like the proponents of "terabit" networks, the ATOMIC proponents sometimes sum all the channel capacities and quote the aggregate bandwidth (which is around eight gigabits) rather than the bandwidth available to each node.

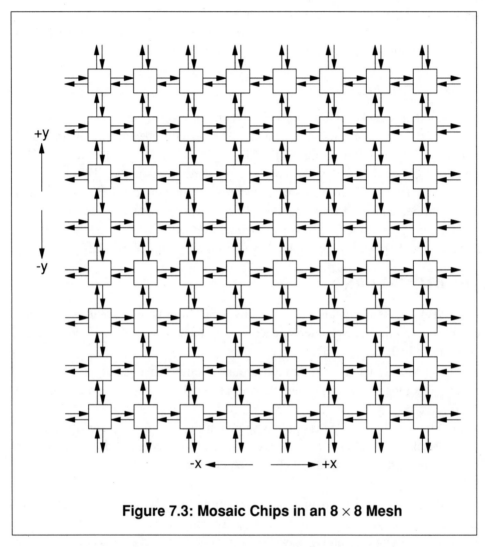

Figure 7.3: Mosaic Chips in an 8 × 8 Mesh

places the packet on the y axis. The packet is then routed in the y direction until the y counter goes to 0. The packet is then at its destination. The y counter is removed, and the packet (now free of its x, y counters) is delivered to its host.

If hosts are attached to the edges of a mesh, then the Mosaic routing does not always work. For example, in the ATOMIC network shown in Figure 7.4, host A can reach host D using the Mosaic route of (2,-2), but D cannot get to A, since any route from D must go up at least 1 in the y direction before it can go in the x direction, and Mosaic requires the x direction be traversed first.

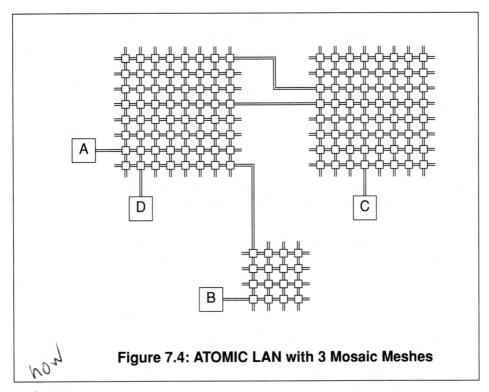

Figure 7.4: ATOMIC LAN with 3 Mosaic Meshes

The ATOMIC architecture enhances the Mosaic routing scheme by supporting multiple source routes. For connectivity, ATOMIC extends the Mosaic routing scheme, to allow for multiple pairs of counters to be prepended to a packet. Therefore when the first source route is completed, the chip at the receiving Mosaic processor simply checks if another pair of counters is on the packet, and if so puts the packet back on the network. Thus D can now reach A with a route of [(4,0), (0,-4)]. This enhanced routing scheme both allows for multiple routes through a Mosaic mesh (thus making better use of its multiple paths) and also allows ATOMIC to use individual Mosaic meshes as concentrators, by providing a mechanism for routing between concentrators. For example, host B can communicate with host C using a source route of [(1,0), (0,-4), (0,-5), (4,0), (0,-5)].

Mosaic supports variable sized packets of even lengths. The mechanism works in the following way. When the header of a packet arrives at a Mosaic chip, the next hop is determined from the header, and assuming the path to the next hop is not already in use, the chip records that data from the packet's input port is going to the output port to the next hop. The chip then proceeds to forward the packet along this path, until it reaches the end of the packet, which is indicated by a special *tail* marker. At this time, the chip discards its path information for the packet and makes the output port available to other packets.

If two packets are trying to go out the same port, one packet is blocked until the other packet finishes using the port. Mosaic does byte-by-byte flow control between chips, so blocking a packet means refusing to accept the next byte from the prior chip. This chip in turn refuses new bytes from its predecessor, so blocking a packet rapidly causes the packet's flow to stop all the way back to the sender. Exactly how much of the bandwidth in a concentrator will be lost due to these collisions is unclear. Studies using completely random traffic suggest that about 50% of each channel's capacity may be lost. Because traffic is not completely random, but rather tends to have hot spots, the expected loss will probably be somewhat higher.

Note that because the Mosaic chips do byte-by-byte flow control, if the data channel is to be fully used (i.e., have no dead time), the distance between two chips can be no more than 0.6m. This distance is obviously too short for building a network. In particular, requiring that a computer be no more than 0.6m from a Mosaic concentrator and that concentrators be no more than 0.6m apart is not reasonable. To deal with this problem, the Mosaic chip has been augmented with a *Slack* chip, which implements window flow control over a link and permits multiple bytes to be outstanding.

ATOMIC requires that every concentrator have at least one host that serves as an *address consultant*. The address consultant learns the topology of the entire ATOMIC network by flooding the network to learn where all the connected nodes are. The address consultant uses this information to build a routing table that shows how to route between any two hosts. When a host wishes to send data to another host, it asks the address consultant for a route. Depending on the connectivity between the concentrators, there may be multiple routes between any two hosts. To allow for traffic balancing on links between concentrators and recovery from connectivity failures, the address consultant may respond to the same request with different paths at different times.

Multicasting in ATOMIC is done using the processors in each Mosaic chip. In each concentrator, one or more processors are assigned the job of replicating packets. The address consultant tells the processors where to send packets addressed to a particular multicast address. The consultant then tells hosts to transmit multicast addresses to the designated processors.

The major virtues of ATOMIC are its topological richness, which makes it extremely robust and offers the opportunity for sophisticated balancing of traffic loads, and its support for multicasting. ATOMIC does not, however, provide support for bounding delay, and because packets may block internally in the meshes, it can lose a lot of its bandwidth to collisions.

The CSMA/RN Ring

It is rather surprising but true that no prototype gigabit packet ring network has been tested yet. A number of designs are currently under development, and one, the FDDI follow-on, may become a standard. As yet, however, none has been built.

The oddity of the situation is that gigabit packet rings make a lot of sense. For example, token rings like FDDI that control token rotation times, can easily bound packet delay times. And as the bandwidth increases, some of the limitations of short token rotation times, such as the low throughput and efficiency *why* shown by Jain [1990b], go away. Furthermore, any ring network can trivially support the multicasting facilities by simply sending a multicast packet round the ring, so that each node on the ring can pick up a copy of the packet.

Of the various proposed gigabit packet ring designs, one that has been fairly carefully studied and simulated by its authors is the Carrier Sense Multiple Access/Ring Network (CSMA/RN), developed by a team at Old Dominion University [Foudriat 1991]. The CSMA/RN also has a somewhat novel access protocol, which highlights some of the issues in gigabit ring design.

The essential design of a CSMA/RN interface is shown in Figure 7.5. Data from the ring comes in on the right and is put into a short delay buffer (about a hundred bits long). The signal from the ring is also passed directly to the controller, bypassing the delay buffer. The controller manages the flow of data, using the advance information about what is coming in from the ring.

If a packet on the ring is addressed to the controller's host, the controller routes the packet's data from the delay buffer to the host's input line, until the entire packet is removed from the network.

If the ring is active (i.e., data is being transferred), data already on the ring always takes precedence over putting new traffic on the wire. So although the ring is active, the controller simply forwards any data not destined for the controller's host onto the output line to the ring.

If the ring is quiet, the controller is allowed to start sending data from the host onto the ring. However, if the controller hears data coming in from the ring, while the controller is sending (the essence of carrier sense), the controller must do something to deal with the collision. In CSMA/RN, the controller stops

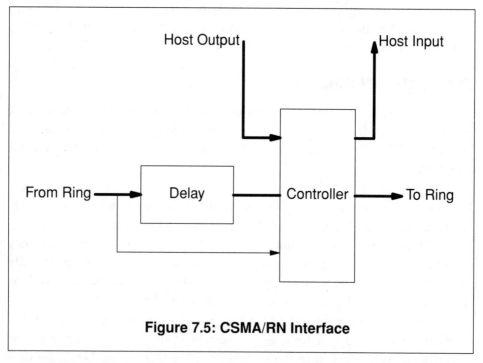

Figure 7.5: CSMA/RN Interface

transmitting the host's packet after putting a truncation marker on the end of it, indicating the packet is incomplete and the rest of it will be sent later. Keep in mind that the controller has time to stop transmitting its packet because the data from the ring is going through the delay buffer. After the controller sends the truncation marker, it can forward the data from the ring as it emerges from the delay buffer.

If the CSMA/RN used cells, one could make the delay buffer equal to one cell time, and then the controller would know that, if the ring was quiet, it had time to send at least one cell. But because the CSMA/RN uses variable size packets, the designers had to solve the problem of collisions. They had a choice of approaches.

One approach is to abort the packet being sent. The controller puts an abort token on the end of its packet, and the packet is discarded when it reaches its receiver. The problem is that this scheme wastes bandwidth by sending partial packets that get discarded.

An alternative approach is to combine the delay buffer with the host's transmission buffer. When a collision occurs, the new data from the ring is placed behind the to-be-transmitted packet in the transmit buffer. The difficulty with this scheme is that it effectively increases the ring size when there are collisions and makes the transmission time around the ring more variable. The variability in transmission time can be bounded by choosing an appropriate maximum packet size and limit on the maximum number of stations on the ring. For example, at a gigabit, a maximum packet size of 1500 bytes (about the maximum Ethernet packet size) with a maximum of 100 stations on the ring (the Ethernet limit for one cable) implies a maximum variation in transmission time of just 1.2 ms.

The CSMA/RN approach tries to strike a balance. If an entire packet gets onto the ring, its transmission time is constant, because it has priority over other packets trying to get onto the ring. And by allowing variable sized packets, without aborting them, the CSMA/RN tries to maximize use of the ring's bandwidth. But, in the worst case a packet may get chopped into lots of little fragments and take a long time to get onto the network. These fragments will waste some bandwidth with their headers and truncation markers. However, considerable though simplified simulation[3] strongly suggests that, even with an offered load of a gigabit per second, the collision rate is quite low. So CSMA/RN looks like it may be a good design: offering statistically bounded delays for variable sized packets.

One other feature about CSMA/RN worth noting is that it removes packets at the receiver. As a result, the bandwidth in the ring can be reused, which on average can be expected to double the effective data rate. Removal also reduces the chance of collisions by keeping packets on the ring for less time.

7.3. Wide Area Packet Technologies

Wide area packet networks are typically built by interconnecting some number of forwarding devices. Two models have been used. In one model, the forwarding devices are routers, and the routers are directly connected to each other. In the other model, the forwarding devices implement some sort of media access protocol to create a virtual network, and the routers are attached to the network through the forwarding devices. Examples of both types of networks are

---

[3] The simplification is that although the designers tested the design with a range of packet sizes, loads, and access patterns, they assumed random independent arrivals and addresses and only varied packet sizes between runs, not within a single run. Varying the packet size seems unlikely to make a big difference — the most important issue for collisions would seem to be whether another packet is coming, not how big it is. However, independent arrivals and addressing will tend to make the traffic load better mixed than it would be in real life and slightly reduce the chances of collisions.

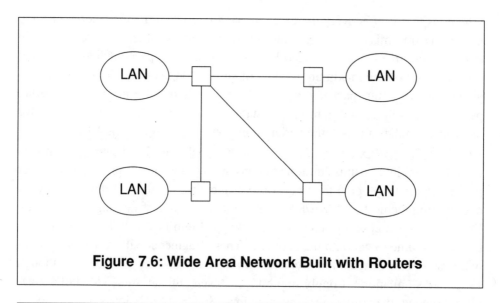

Figure 7.6: Wide Area Network Built with Routers

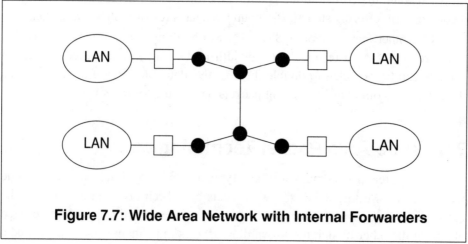

Figure 7.7: Wide Area Network with Internal Forwarders

shown in Figures 7.6 and 7.7.

Neither architecture has a consistent advantage and both are used widely today. The router-only approach is widely used in the Internet. Frame Relay and X.25 networks use forwarding devices.

The major stumbling block to building either type of wide area network is the difficulty of implementing routers or forwarding devices that can route packets at gigabit data rates.

Routing Packets at Gigabit Rates

Any device that routes packets can be viewed as composed of three parts:

1. a set of network interfaces that connect the various networks to the device,

2. one or forwarding processors that decide where to send each packet,

3. a connection fabric that interconnects the network interfaces and forwarding processor and moves packets between interfaces as directed by the forwarding processor.

To forward packets at gigabit rates, all three parts must operate at gigabit speeds.

Building gigabit network interfaces is certainly feasible. This chapter has already talked a little bit about how to connect to networks at gigabit data rates, and Chapter 9 will discuss how to build gigabit interfaces in detail.

Developing forwarding processors that can decide where to send packets fast enough to keep pace with gigabit data rates is also not particularly hard. Researchers have known for several years that, with careful design, it is possible to use relatively inexpensive processors to forward packets at rates consistent with gigabit speeds. The statement may be a bit surprising and requires a bit of explanation.

Forwarding a packet is typically a matter of doing some simple consistency checks on the packet header (more complex checks like CRCs are typically done by the receiving interface), determining the next step in the packet's route to its destination, and possibly updating the packet header. Observe that the packet's destination address is usually found in the packet header, so the header is the only part that needs to be examined in the process of forwarding a packet. In other words, the process of deciding how to forward a packet is a matter of reading and updating a few words of memory and then arranging for the entire packet to be transmitted out an interface.

As an example of how simple forwarding a packet can be, consider Figure 7.8. The figure contains an excerpt of some code to forward an IP datagram written in the C programming language. This particular implementation was done by Van Jacobson and is taken from Jacobson [1990c]. The code starts by converting the buffer pointer (m) into a pointer to an IP header (ip) and storing the buffer length in a register (len). The packet is quickly checked to see if it is of the correct type and without options, and then the route is looked up in a small cache. In most cases, the route will be in the cache so a complete route lookup in a large routing table can be avoided. (In a study, Feldmeier [1988] showed that even a

```
register struct ip *ip = mtod(m,struct ip *);
register u_int len = m->m_len;
register u_int dst;
/*
 * check IP version number & header length.  Min length header
 * with correct version is special-cased (we know we won't have
 * to deal with src route or other IP options).
 */
if (*(char *)ip != ((IPVERSION << 4) | sizeof(struct ip)/4)) {
    ...
} else
    dst = ip->ip_dst.s_addr;

/* find (or create) cache entry for this destination */
cache = &ipfwd_cache[HASH(dst)];
if (cache->dst != dst) {
    ...
}

if (rt = cache->rt) {
    /* packet not for us -- forward it */
    register int i;
    register struct ifnet *dest_ifp;
    /* update time-to-live and checksum */
    i = ip->ip_ttl;
    if (--i <= 0) {
        ...
    }
    ip->ip_ttl = i;

    i = (int) ip->ip_sum + 256;
    ip->ip_sum = i + (i>>16);
    dest_ifp = rt->rt_ifp;
    if (dest_ifp->if_mut < len)
        ip_output(m,rt);
    else
        (dest_ifp->if_output)(m,rt);
}
```

Figure 7.8: Code to Forward an IP Datagram

small routing cache of about 200 entries would typically achieve a cache hit rate in excess of 90%.) Assuming a cache hit, the IP header is updated and the datagram is forwarded out an interface. The lines highlighted in gray are the approximately twenty lines of the code that would be executed when forwarding a typical IP datagram (i.e., a datagram without options and a cache hit). Even though there must also be code that manages the inbound and outbound interfaces, it is clear that IP processing is quite cheap. As Chapter 9 will show, this code can be quite small. Therefore, even if one is being conservative, it is safe to assume that a total of 200 instructions is sufficient to forward a packet, including both device drivers and the code that decides how to route the packet.

Table 7.1: Packet Sizes and Gigabit Data Rates		
Packet Size in Bytes	Number of Packets per Second Equal to 1 Gb/s	Instructions per Second Required
64	1,960,000	392,000,000
128	980,000	196,000,000
1,024	122,100	24,420,000
8,192	15,500	3,100,000
65,536	1,910	382,000

The number of packets that must be processed at gigabit rates depends on the packet size. Table 7.1 shows a selection of common packet sizes, along with the approximate number of packets of that size per second that must be processed at gigabit rates. The far right column shows the approximate number of instructions per second (at 200 instructions per packet) required to forward that many packets. Note that as the packet sizes get large, the number of instructions the processor must execute becomes very small. On most networks the average packet size is about 128 bytes. This requires nearly 200 million instructions per second to keep up with 128-byte packets at gigabit speeds, but relatively inexpensive processors such as the DEC Alpha 21064 can perform that many instructions per second. With larger packet sizes, the processing requirements become very easy to achieve. For instance, an Intel 486 processor, commonly used in personal computers, would probably be sufficient to forward 1024-byte packets at gigabit rates. In general, processing power does not appear to be a problem for forwarding devices.

Copying data between interfaces is the critical problem. In general, for a router or switch to support n interfaces, each capable of sending and receiving at 1 gigabit per second, the router must be able, in the worst case, to copy data at n

gigabits per second. Designing a data bus capable of moving many gigabits of data per second between interfaces is difficult. Cell switches solved this problem by moving data in parallel. A crossbar or Batcher-Banyan switch uses parallel gigabit paths to get data from input ports to output ports. But cell switches bene-fitted from fixed size cells. Making a parallel switch for packets with variable lengths is much harder. The packets will take varying amounts of time to pass through each stage in the switch, which tends to increase the contention in the switch and reduce its utilization.

To date, implementors have chosen not to even try to implement switches but rather to develop specialized busses to move data between interfaces. This section looks at two different approaches: the plaNET switch, which uses a ring-shaped bus, and the Bell Labs router, which uses parallel busses.

plaNET — A High-Speed Packet Router

Originally called the Paris switch, the plaNET switch is a gigabit switch developed by Cidon and Gopal of IBM [Cidon 1988; Cidon 1992b]. It is an eight-port switch, with a ring-shaped bus. Although plaNET supports a number of routing schemes, packets are typically transmitted using source routing.

An outline of the plaNET switch is shown in Figure 7.9. Links are attached to the switch using adapter cards. When an adapter receives a packet from the link, it places the packet on the bus. The packet is relayed around the bus from adapter to adapter. Each adapter examines the packet, and if the packet's source route indicates it is destined to be transmitted by that adapter, the packet is copied into the interface's output queue. To support multicasting, multiple adapters can copy the same packet. The receiving adapter does not remove the packet from the bus, but passes a copy of the packet on to the next adapter. The adapter that put the packet on the bus is also responsible for removing it from the bus. To ensure regular access to the bus and avoid collisions, adapters gain access to the bus according to a round-robin scheme.

The plaNET bus supports a data transfer rate of six gigabits. The switch was designed to support links with data rates up to 800 Mb/s, so the data rate of the bus is higher than aggregate data rates of the eight links connected to the switch. An interesting feature of the bus is its serpentine structure. If the bus had been implemented as a simple ring connecting each adapter in turn, there would have been an extra long hop in the ring between the top and bottom adapters. This extra length would be enough to complicate the timing of the bus, so an interwoven bus topology was used to keep all the hops roughly the same length.

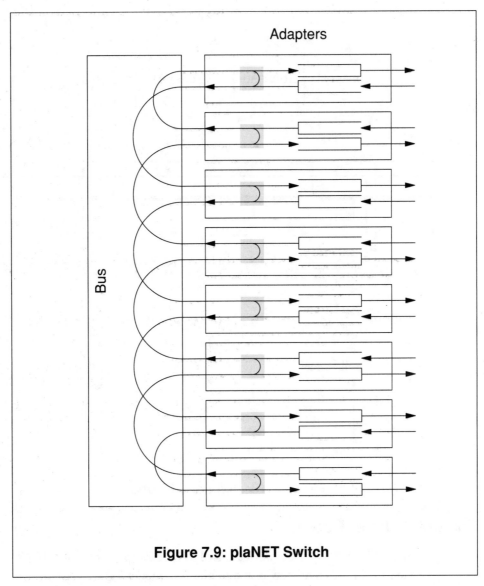

Figure 7.9: plaNET Switch

In conjunction with plaNet, IBM has developed a local distribution network called ORBIT. ORBIT networks make it possible for multiple hosts to share access to a plaNET adapter.

Developed in the late 1980s, plaNET was one of the first (if not the first) gigabit switches, and it is widely viewed as having shown that, if one designed the switch carefully, achieving gigabit speeds was feasible.

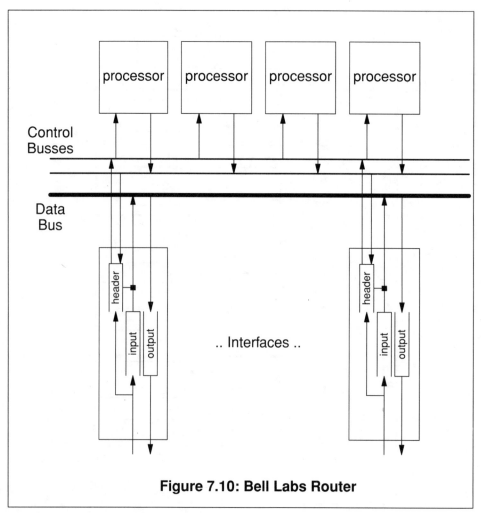

Figure 7.10: Bell Labs Router

The Bell Labs IP Router

A team at AT&T Bell Laboratories has developed a prototype gigabit IP router [Asthana 1992]. An overview of the router is shown in Figure 7.10.

The router uses multiple special purpose processors to forward packets. When an interface receives a packet, it strips off the IP header and forwards the header to one of the processors. The processor updates the header, finds a route and outbound interface for the packet, and sends the updated header and forwarding information back to the interface. The interface then transfers the updated packet to the outbound interface.

The router supports multiple processors, and tests with a four-processor prototype suggest that four processors achieve a performance of about 3.5 times the speed of one. (The small loss is due to the fact that the router uses the processors in round-robin order, and sometimes a processor finishes routing ahead of a preceding processor and must wait for its predecessor to finish.) Each processor is a specially designed 3 MHz processor capable of forwarding 60,000 packets per second,[4] so the four-processor system can forward about 210,000 packets per second, which is enough for gigabit rates if the packet sizes are large. The router designers expect to improve the processors to run at 20 MHz, which would yield a more impressive forwarding rate of 1.4 million packets per second.

Messages between the interfaces and the processors travel over different busses (the control busses in the figure) from packets being moved between interfaces (which travel over the data bus). The two types of interactions have very different characteristics. The headers exchanged between interfaces and processors are very small messages that have to be carefully arbitrated to ensure that assignment of headers is properly distributed among the processors. (If the assignment is imbalanced, some processors will be underutilized, reducing the forwarding rate.) The transfer of packets between interfaces typically takes the form of long messages, whose delivery can be less rigorously scheduled. By separating the busses for the two types of transfers, the router designers were able to optimize each bus for the type of message it carries. The initial prototype actually uses a surprisingly slow data bus that runs at just over 1 gigabit per second. But because the bus is used purely for transferring data, that is apparently enough for gigabit rates.

The Bell Labs router's packet rate and data bus rate just barely qualify it as a gigabit router, but its architecture is probably a precursor of the router designs we are likely to see in the future. Multiple inexpensive processors will process packet headers in parallel to achieve very high forwarding rates, and specialized data busses will be used to move packets between interfaces at high data rates.

---

[4] Note that if 1 Hz = 1 instruction cycle, this processor is forwarding an IP datagram about once every 50 instruction cycles, so the 200-instruction cycle estimate made earlier is certainly conservative!

How to Connect the Forwarders

How are packet forwarding devices like the plaNET switch and the Bell Labs router to be attached to each other? Traditionally, the devices have been connected using lines rented from the telephone companies. For high speeds, that implies the forwarders will be interconnected by lines running SONET. Indeed, because providers of alternative media like satellites and microwave tend to follow the telephony lead on protocols, those media will likely support SONET framing. So SONET appears to be the leased-line protocol of the future. How should forwarding devices send packets in SONET?

The obvious (and probably the most likely) approach is to encapsulate the packets in AAL 5 and ATM and use ATM over SONET to send the packets.

An alternative is to define other protocols for use over SONET. Defining alternatives is not particularly hard; SONET is simply a protocol for delivering frames of bytes between two points. All one has to do is define a protocol for using the bytes. Proposals exist for encapsulating HIPPI packets in SONET; others may follow.

7.4. Summary

The development of gigabit packet networks has lagged behind the development of gigabit cell networks. However, with the exception of wide area networks, where the problems of building fast forwarding devices are an obstacle, there is no clear technical reason for the lag.

For local area networks, several promising approaches have been noted. Prototypes of WDM networks (covered in Chapter 2), switched point-to-point networks (HIPPI), and the ATOMIC network exist. As the sketch of the CSMA/RN illustrates, building a gigabit ring network does not appear to be hard.

For wide area packet networks, the major task is designing and building gigabit packet routers and switches. The hardest problem in these devices is finding a fast bus architecture and then building the hardware around it to achieve gigabit per second data rates. Two prototype systems were examined: the plaNET switch, which uses a simple but very fast bus, and the Bell Labs router, which achieves good performance by separating the data bus from the control bus.

Further Reading

For more information on the costs of forwarding packets, see Clark et al. [1989b] and Partridge [1990a].

The HIPPI article by Tolmie and Renwick [1993] has pointers to the relevant HIPPI standards. The HIPPI mailing list is *hippi-ext@think.com*. The Fibre Channel standards are being developed by ANSI X3T9.3. There is also a Fibre Channel e-mail list (*fiber-channel-ext@think.com*).

Chapter 8

Gigabit Applications

8.1. Introduction

The preceding chapters have shown that there are a variety of ways to build networks that can transmit data at gigabit rates. It is now time to start considering what protocols and applications will run over those networks.

The goal of this chapter is to examine the applications that will use gigabit networks, especially applications of the future. This study of applications and their needs begins the process (which will extend through much of the rest of the book) of designing protocols to meet the needs of gigabit applications.

8.2. Classic Applications

With a few important exceptions, the applications used on today's data networks are relatively insensitive to variations in bandwidth and delay. (In contrast, applications on telephone networks are fairly sensitive to these variations.) Transport protocols like the Transmission Control Protocol (TCP) recognize and dynamically adapt to changes in network delay and available bandwidth. And network services like e-mail and file transfer that use TCP can make do with whatever bandwidth is provided to them. Usually, no one cares if a file transfer goes a little faster or a little slower. However, some applications would benefit from higher bandwidths.

Interactive services, such as remote login, and remote graphics services like *X Windows* benefit only slightly from higher bandwidths. Interactive services typically send little packets containing user keystrokes. The major benefit they receive from high bandwidth is reduced interference from big packets, which take less time to transmit at high speeds. Also, for graphics interfaces, occasional bandwidth intensive activities like refreshing a screen (which tends to dump a screenful of bits onto the network) go more quickly.

Another service that benefits from higher bandwidth is distributed file systems like the Network File System (NFS). Distributed file systems make it possible for a networked system to treat files on another system's disks as its own. The system that actually maintains the files is typically called a *file server*, and the system requesting access to the files is called a *client*. Mechanically speaking, the way distributed file systems work is that the client requests blocks from the file (or in some schemes, a complete copy of the file) from the file server, and the file server sends the requested information. File blocks are relatively long (typically several thousand bits), so higher bandwidths improve performance. For example, consider that an 8 Kb (1 kilobyte) disk block takes 8 ms to transmit on a 10 Mb/s Ethernet, or roughly half the time (on average) it would take to read the block off a disk. But if the network bandwidth is 1 gigabit, then 8 Kb take only 80 μs. These times matter because, in most cases, an application on the client is waiting to read the file block. So application performance on the client depends heavily on how fast the file server can provide pieces of files. Higher network bandwidth reduces the time it takes for replies to get back from the server and thus improves client performance.

The file server and client performance issues are representative of a broader issue. As computing systems get faster, their peripherals have to get faster with them. Amdahl's rule states that processors need a bit of I/O for each instruction cycle. Processors will soon have instruction cycle times of a nanosecond or less, which implies that they will need a gigabit per second of I/O. Perhaps a stronger argument is that these fast processors will typically process between 64 and 128 bits of information (combined instruction plus data) per instruction, so they will be processing up to 128 gigabits of data per second. For such a system, a gigabit is simply the rational bandwidth for its network connection.

8.3. New Applications

In general, the new applications that gigabit networks make possible need either high bandwidth or low response times (or both) to work effectively. Gigabit networks clearly meet the need for high bandwidth. And gigabit networks can help provide good response times by keeping serialization times low.

The new applications can be roughly divided up into two groups. The first group is distributed computations that need good performance between computers. The second group is interactive distributed applications that wish to deliver lots of information to human users in times consistent with human response times. The next two sections look at both types of applications.

8.4. New Computing Applications

Although computers are continuing to get faster, they are also getting more specialized. This specialization is particularly true for high-end computing systems like supercomputers and multiprocessors. Some systems are very good at vector processing, others are good at parallel processing, and still others are good at graphics.

Many interesting computation problems can be broken up into subproblems that would perform best on different systems. In other words, a single problem might have two steps, where the first step is best performed on a vector processing system but the second step is best performed on a highly parallel system. Often, however, a lot of data must be maintained across stages in the process. Gigabit networks can help improve performance by quickly moving data between the different systems.

An example of such an application is allocating work within a chemical plant. The idea is to optimize use of highly expensive equipment within the plant. For this application, time is money. The faster the application can plan the proper division of work over the equipment, the more quickly the plant can put the plan in place. The problem has two parts: first, a cost matrix that measures the costs of doing operations on various pieces of equipment must be calculated; then, based on the cost matrix, an optimal assignment of work must be found. Computing the cost matrix turns out to be well suited to vector processing systems. But finding the optimal assignment is better done by parallel systems. In an experiment by Carnegie-Mellon researchers, a Cray Y-MP was used to do the calculation of the cost matrix, and a Thinking Machines Connection Machine 2 (CM-2) was used to find the optimal assignment. The large cost matrix was transferred using an 800 Mb/s HIPPI link between the two computers [Catlett 1992].

The chemical plant application is largely a one-way data transfer: data goes from the Cray to the CM-2. That is useful, because the time to send a bit across a network is far longer than an instruction cycle on these high-speed machines. If the cooperating systems have to spend a lot of time waiting to receive data from each other, the improved computation times may not matter much.

However, even with network delays, it is sometimes productive to use gigabit networks to link multiple high-performance systems into a larger parallel processing system. For example, researchers at UCLA are experimenting with running a parallel model of interactions between the atmosphere and an ocean. The purpose of this model is to simulate tens of years of interactions. In the simulation, one supercomputer (a CM-2) simulates the ocean, another supercomputer simulates the behavior of the atmosphere, and the two simulations exchange information about the state of their side of the atmosphere-ocean boundary. Each unit of simulated time takes about 100 ms for each of the two simulators (ocean and atmosphere) to compute, and the amount of data about state boundaries that has to be exchanged before the next time cycle can be simulated is about 5 to 10 megabytes. To keep the simulation running briskly, the time to transfer these megabytes between simulators should be kept short. On a 10 Mb/s Ethernet, the transfers would take several seconds — a long time relative to the 100 ms computation cycle. A gigabit network can transfer the data in under 100 ms, a time more consistent with the computation times.

The primary feature of these new computing applications is their need for large bandwidths. The effective performance improvement of the chemical plant analysis depends on moving the cost matrix quickly from the Cray Y-MP to the CM-2. The distributed climate modelling application needs high bandwidths to move state information between processors in a reasonable time.

8.5. Applications with Humans in the Loop

A number of gigabit applications involve real-time interactions with human beings. From an applications perspective, human beings have the interesting properties that they can absorb a lot of information (in particular, visual information) and that they are sensitive to delays.

A particularly exciting area of human-in-the-loop applications is *multimedia* applications. Multimedia applications combine sounds, video, and computer graphics in an interactive environment. Examples of multimedia applications include conferencing, in which participants can use their computers to see and talk with each other, and *telepresence* or *virtual reality*, in which the application gives the user the illusion of being in another place. One of the challenging aspects of these applications is that studies suggest human users tend to remember the failings of a system more than its successes. A multimedia application that has occasional lapses in audio or video quality will be remembered as giving poor quality even if most of the time the audio and video are quite good.

Unfortunately, with the exception of audio (which is emphatically not a gigabit application), only a limited number of human factors studies examine how people respond to various types of media. (Apparently this lack of research is due, in part, to the rapid change in media display technologies — a study with one technology is quickly made obsolete with the development of another display technology.) To sketch some of the requirements of applications that interact with people, this section will start with a study of the human factors of sound and then use some of the results from sound to help build a model of interactions for other types of data like video.

Sound

Transmitting sound over gigabit networks is probably the least interesting application, because the data requirements for sound are quite small (as little as 16 Kb/s for telephone-quality speech, and recent developments in wavelet compression are driving this value even lower). However, in large part due to the widespread availability of voice service through the telephone networks, the human factors of interactive voice systems are well studied. So the primary purpose of this section is to understand the human factors of voice, with an eye toward applying this information to less well-studied applications.

Table 8.1: Bandwidths for Various Types of Audio	
Type of Audio	**Bandwidth**
Telephone speech	16 Kb/s
Audioconferencing speech	32 Kb/s
Near-CD quality audio	64 Kb/s
CD-quality audio	128 Kb/s

Table 8.1 illustrates the current bandwidth required for the high-quality transmission of various types of audio.[1] In each case, the bandwidth listed represents the bandwidth needed to achieve a quality of sound that users rate as excellent.[2] The various data rates represent increasing quality of sound.

---

[1] High quality is typically measured by asking listeners to rate sound quality on a 5-point scale, and treating sound rated at an average of 4.5 or better as high quality. If one is willing to accept lower quality, the bandwidths can be even lower.

Telephone speech represents what users consider high-quality sound over a telephone. Audioconferencing speech requires slightly higher bandwidth to accommodate the audio overtones that indicate that the speaker is in a room. (The sense of being in the same room with the speaker has proved important for the ambiance of conferencing.) Near-CD audio is audio quality that users find hard to distinguish from the quality of the audio of compact disks, and CD quality is the bandwidth required to achieve full CD quality.

None of the bandwidths (except, perhaps, the CD-quality audio) in Table 8.1 is particularly large, even in the context of today's networks. Local area networks typically sport bandwidths in excess of 10 Mb/s, and wide area networks often offer connectivity at rates in excess of 64 Kb/s. What makes audio interesting are its timing constraints and its ability to cope with loss.

Audio has three sets of timing constraints. First, audio must be sampled and played at regular intervals or it will sound choppy or distorted to a listener. Second, when using interactive audio (e.g., a telephone call), users are sensitive to how long voice samples take to get through the network. Third, users are sensitive to when they hear themselves (e.g., when the earpiece on their telephone plays back what they have said).

Audio devices are typically designed to generate or play samples at fixed rates. For example, telephone voice takes the form of eight-bit samples taken every 125 μs (8 KHz). CD audio uses sixteen-bit samples approximately every 22.7 μs (44.1 KHz). As a result, transmitted audio data takes the form of a continuous stream of samples. Data in this form is sometimes referred to as *continuous* or *isochronous media*. One of the properties of continuous media is that its data must be played out under fairly tight time constraints. Once sample n is played, sample $n+1$ must be played a fixed interval (e.g., 125 μs) later, plus or minus a small variation. Indeed, if sample $n+1$ is not available to be played at the right time, it is as good as lost. Playing the sample at the wrong time would make the audio sound worse than not playing the sample at all. Indeed, the general practice is to suppress late samples. This observation brings up an important point — any network that is to support continuous media needs some set of rules to assure that, given sample n, a system can know when to expect sample $n+1$, so that the playing times of the samples can be properly synchronized.

Users are also sensitive to round-trip delays in audio links. As anyone who has made phone calls that passed through multiple satellite links can attest, a

---

2 Data from Nick Jayant of AT&T Bell Laboratories.

conversation between two or more people relies on timing cues. If the time delays are too long, these cues are lost. For example, if someone tries to interrupt a speaker, the speaker on hearing the attempted interruption will typically pause briefly. However, if the interrupter does not start speaking during that pause, the original speaker will start to speak again. If the network delay is too long, the interrupter will not have heard the speaker pause in time, and so the interrupter will start to speak at about the same time the speaker starts speaking again. Such abortive interactions can make conversations difficult.

Table 8.2: CCITT G.114 Delay Recommendations	
One-Way Delay	**Characterization of Quality**
0 to 150 ms	"acceptable for most user applications"
150 to 400 ms	"may impact some applications"
above 400 ms	"unacceptable for general network planning purposes"

The question of what is an acceptable round-trip delay was studied at Bell Labs in the 1960s by Riesz and Klemmer [1963; 1967]. These studies tested delay in such a way that aspects of delay could be isolated from the audio equipment attached to the network.[3] In the tests, a number of users' were told that some of their phone calls would be routed over paths with extra delays, and that if they were unhappy with the delay, they could press a button to get a reduced delay. Over the course of several weeks, calls were routed over paths with round-trip delays of 600, 1200, 1800 and 2400 ms. What these studies showed was that users are quite comfortable with round-trip delays of 600 ms; in most weeks, they never requested a better delay. Higher delays showed considerably higher levels of user dissatisfaction. A later study by Brady [1971] generally confirmed these results, though Brady notes that users' tolerance to delay decreased with time.

These studies suggest that for interactive voice, round-trip delays of at least 600 ms are acceptable. Much more recently, the CCITT has issued a set of recommendations (G.114) for planning networks to achieve good-quality voice. These recommendations summarized in Table 8.2 suggest that round-trip delays of up to 800 ms are acceptable to a large number of applications. (Note that

---

[3] Isolating the audio equipment is important. Echo cancellers and other devices on the audio line may interact with delay in ways that degrade voice quality. Measurements that include features of the audio equipment therefore often measure equipment limitations rather than user sensitivities. Some delay studies use the term *pure delay* to make clear they are trying to isolate delay effects from equipment issues.

Table 8.2 reports values in one-way delays, although the earlier literature uses round-trip delays, which can be considered twice the one-way delay.)

It is important to keep in mind that these values are for two-way conversations. If all the voice is going in one direction (e.g., a lecture), then there are effectively no timing constraints.

A third timing issue occurs when users hear themselves. There is considerable evidence that users get disoriented if they hear something more than 100 ms after they have said it. (In other words, the earpiece must play sounds spoken into the mouthpiece of the telephone in less than 100 ms.)

Audio Timing and Its Implications

A couple of lessons can be drawn from the audio timing information. First, any system for sending continuous media over a network needs to be cognizant of the sensitive timing of samples. Samples must be transmitted in a timely fashion to avoid loss of samples due to late delivery and to ensure that the output device has access to samples at regular intervals. Note that, typically, some loss of samples is acceptable though the amount of permissible loss varies from application to application. Human ears and eyes apparently can smooth over occasional glitches from missing samples.

Second, people seem to have a range of sensitivities to delays. For conversations, relatively long delays (up to 400 ms one-way) are acceptable. However humans expect to hear themselves speaking far faster (in about 100 ms). Why there should be this factor of four disparity in two activities that involve listening to speech is unclear, but the result is consistent with other studies that indicate that comfort with delay varies widely with activity. For example, studies of user productivity and response time show a wide variation in user sensitivities. (See Chapter 7 of Shneiderman [1992].) Based on these sorts of studies, Shneiderman [1992] suggests that some of the sensitivity to delay is actually learned on an application-by-application basis, which is consistent with Brady's findings that users have a learned sensitivity to audio delays.

From a networking perspective, where engineering the network delay is a hard problem, this variation in sensitivity in delay is somewhat frustrating. If gigabit networks are to be designed to support real-time applications like voice, some target delays are required.

In the absence of better evidence, this book will take the view that for conversations human users are generally tolerant of the delays specified in Table 8.2, namely one-way delays of up to 400 ms and round-trip delays of up to 800 ms for conversations. For applications requiring closer interaction with the system (such as hearing oneself on the telephone and interacting with simulations), we will assume that users are less tolerant and desire delays closer to 100 ms. Note that this approximation is fuzzy. Typing at a keyboard certainly would seem to qualify as close interaction with a system, yet studies indicate the comfortable delay ranges are more akin to those of conversations. The networking community could clearly benefit from better human factors studies, even if they show that users' sensitivity to delay varies on an application-by-application basis.

It is also important to keep in mind that these time limits are generally goals, not fixed constraints. An occasional audio sample can fail to arrive within the time bound, because a modest level of loss in an audio stream will not be noticed.

Video

The transmission of images, moving or still, is one of the largest bandwidth consuming applications currently known.

Video is almost invariably transmitted in a compressed form, for the simple reason that compression is so effective. Commercial compression algorithms can achieve 26-to-1 or better reductions in the average number of bits transmitted. However, the amount of data that must be sent for each video frame can vary wildly. This variation presents an problem. To avoid flickering video, frames must be displayed at fixed intervals apart at a rate of 30 frames a second or faster. All the data for a given frame must fit into a fixed interval's worth of bandwidth, or like audio samples, the data for the frame will arrive too late to be displayed.

Figure 8.1 illustrates this problem for a sequence of five frames. The dark line shows the amount of bandwidth each frame would require to transmit all of its bits within a single frame interval. The dashed line shows the actual bandwidth available to the video stream. Frames 2 and 4 need more bandwidth than is available, but Frames 1, 3, and 5 do not use all the bandwidth.

Currently, video encoders solve this problem in the way shown in Figure 8.2. They select a given bandwidth at which to transmit (based on the bandwidths of virtual circuits available and the quality of the video signal desired). Then the video is coded so that when a particular frame's data exceeds the available bandwidth, enough information is sent to make a respectable image, and extra data to touch up the image is sent along with data from successive frames (the gray areas in the figure). Intuitively one can think of the encoder as keeping track of two images, the frame information the receiver currently has and the

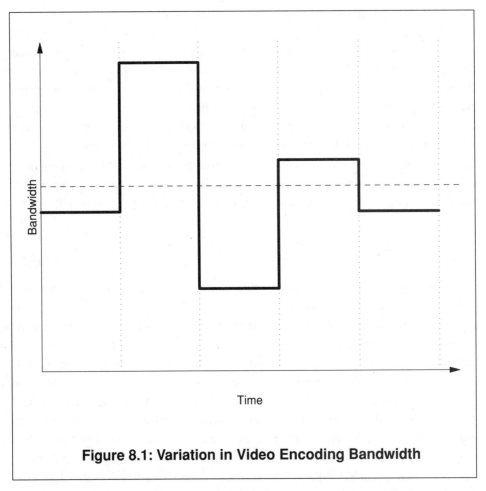

Figure 8.1: Variation in Video Encoding Bandwidth

frame as it should actually appear, and whenever a new frame's data does not use all the bandwidth, the remaining bandwidth is used to send data to touch up the receiver's frame and bring it closer to the correct image.[4]

Encoders work this way because, to date, the standard way to transmit video is over a fixed-bandwidth channel (such as a leased telephone line). However, more recently, considerable attention has been given to designing the network to handle variable data rates and designing video transmission schemes that

---

[4] This intuitive description is emphatically a simplification. Actual video encoders have far more complex algorithms that make sophisticated decisions about how to mix updates from previous frames with data from the current frame and how to modulate the encoding scheme's parameters to stay within the maximum available bandwidth.

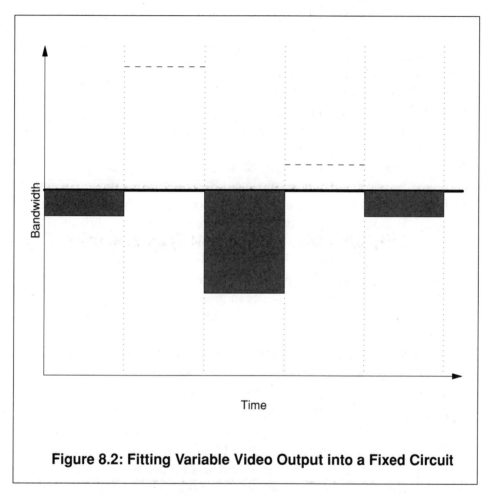

Figure 8.2: Fitting Variable Video Output into a Fixed Circuit

generate variable amounts of data. These transmission schemes are termed *variable bit-rate* (VBR) video.

An Example: MPEG

The Moving Pictures Experts Group (MPEG) is a standards group that meets under the auspices of the International Standards Organization (ISO). The group has developed a set of standards for the transmission of compressed variable bit-rate video. The goal of the MPEG group is to develop a scheme for storing digital video (with its audio), but studies suggest it will also serve well as an encoding scheme for transmitting video over networks. Currently MPEG coding schemes are defined only for low bandwidths (1.5 Mb/s) but higher bandwidth standards offering higher fidelity images, are expected. In any case, MPEG is a good example of how variable bit-rate video encoding behaves.

In brief, MPEG codes video using three frame formats: **I**, **P**, and **B** frames. **I** (*image*) frames are complete bit images of a single frame and are sent periodically to bound the effect of compression (and transmission) errors. The exact number of **P** and **B** frames that can be sent between **I** frames is configurable. **P** (*predicted*) frames update the image (using a predictive algorithm) from the last **I** or **P** frame. In other words, given a starting **I** frame, a series of following **P** frames will try to track changes in the frame. To further reduce the amount of data required to transmit the image, there are **B** (*bidirectional*) frames. **B** frames describe a frame in terms of the differences between either the last and next **I** or **P** frames. It is simplest to think of the **B** frame as describing the difference from either the last high-quality image (generated from an **I** or **P** frame), or the next high-quality image, depending on which image the current image differs the least from. Note that because a **B** frame can reference forward or backward, both the last and next **P** or **I** frames must have been transmitted before the **B** frames can be sent (which can be a bit confusing). The ratio of **B** and **P** frames is configurable.

Figure 8.3 shows a graph of a sample MPEG data stream for 60 frames.[5] The sequence starts with an **I** frame and then follows a pattern of two **B** frames followed by a **P** frame (or every twelfth frame, an **I** frame).

One feature of the MPEG encoding scheme is that it can tolerate the occasional loss of a frame. If a **B** frame gets lost, one can guess what the image will look like and proceed on until the next **P** or **I** frame arrives to provide a corrected image. And in the case of lost **P** frames, the next **I** frame will correct any problems in the predicted image. In most cases, an image changes only slightly from frame to frame so a decoder can simply guess that the missing **P** or **B** frame would not change the current image.

Clearly the effects of losses in the MPEG data stream are most severe if an **I** frame is lost. Also, some types of video data are more important to perceived picture fidelity than others. For example, getting image outlines correctly placed is typically considered more important than getting colors exactly right. As a result, there has been interest in encoding video such that less important data in

---

[5] Data for this graph was kindly provided by Mark W. Garrett and Antonio Fernandez of Bellcore. The graph is derived from the MPEG encoding of several frames of the movie *Star Wars*.

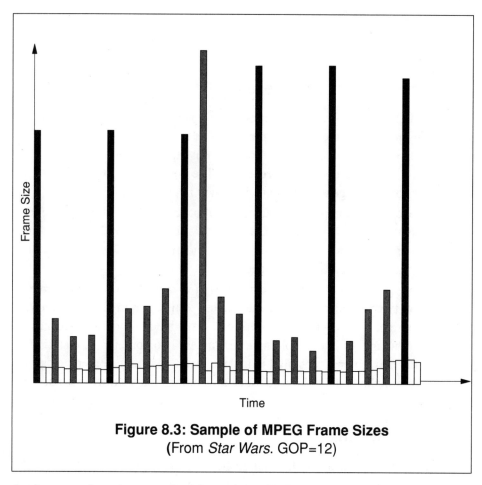

Figure 8.3: Sample of MPEG Frame Sizes
(From *Star Wars*. GOP=12)

the frame updates is segregated from the more important data. The less important data can then be put in lower priority packets or cells, such as ATM cells with the CLP bit set. This type of encoding is called *layered encoding*. The MPEG standards do not include rules for layered encoding, but extensions for a layered MPEG have been proposed [Pancha 1992].

H.261

Another video encoding standard that has been proposed for networked video is H.261, a CCITT standard. H.261 is similar in spirit to MPEG: full image information is interleaved with predictive updates. The major difference is that, rather than sending a full I frame periodically, H.261 sends image updates for regions of the screen. These region updates are interleaved with predictive updates such that all the regions of a screen are regularly updated. The major advantage of H.261's encoding is that it makes the data stream substantially less variable.

A Comment about Compression

The high degree of compression of video images in standards like MPEG is achieved by permitting the received picture to be an imperfect copy of the original (a practice known as *lossy compression*). For regular entertainment use, this type of compression is perfectly acceptable. The compression is tuned to throw away pieces of the image that the human eye will not notice.

However, lossy compression can cause problems. For one thing, if one tries to compress the image too much (i.e., to too low a bandwidth), the received picture quality may be very poor. Also, for some scientific work, lossy compression may throw out critical parts of the image.

A more general problem with compression is that increasing the degree of compression typically also increases the amount of time required to do compression. In extreme cases, video encoders can take hundreds of milliseconds to compress an image. If one is holding a real-time video conference, that kind of coding delay may be unacceptably high. As a result, real-time conferencing systems may use higher bandwidths to reduce the coding delays between sender and receiver.

Video Bandwidths

The amount of bandwidth required by a video application varies widely, depending on such factors as the size of the picture, the desired quality of the image, and whether the image is in black and white or color.

Currently computer scientists tend to focus on the expected qualities of high-definition television (HDTV), which are similar to what computer monitors are expected to be able to achieve. Uncompressed, HDTV requires something over a gigabit per second of bandwidth. Lossless compression (i.e., compression that does not result in a reduced fidelity picture when the images are uncompressed) can reduce the bandwidth by about 50%, to a bandwidth in the several 100 Mb/s. Informal research reports suggest that lossy compression may achieve compression of 50:1 or better, resulting in bandwidths of 20 Mb/s.

The suggestion is that for scientific applications that require the very highest fidelity images, HDTV may require several hundred megabits per video stream. For applications like conferencing, the requirements may be only a few tens of megabits per user, though note that if there are several users (a conference of six to eight people), the bandwidths become an appreciable fraction of a gigabit.

Examples of Multimedia Applications

To provide some sense of how audio and video can be used to develop interesting applications, this section briefly describes some multimedia applications. One of the most interesting applications is conferencing — allowing people at different locations to talk with each other via a combined audio and video link. In fact this technology is already selectively available from a number of telephone providers.

Because computer graphics interfaces continue to mature and the cost of video cameras continues to decline, it is clear that within a few years, the average PC could serve as a conferencing station, allowing individuals to participate in multimedia conferences. A large number of experimental multimedia conferencing systems have been built, including the Touring Machine project at Bellcore and an executive conferencing facility serving the NTT Laboratories in metropolitan Tokyo. Both systems are being used for experimentation with the human factors of conferencing.

Because each user may generate her own multi-megabit video stream, a conference of modest size can rapidly consume well over 100 megabits of bandwidth. There have also been experiments with especially large screens, the size of the wall of a room. These large screens can give the illusion of combining two conference rooms into one large conference room. Obviously, providing high-fidelity images on a screen measuring several square meters requires a lot of bandwidth.

The next two examples come from geology. By and large, geologists are trained to do their work in the field — to analyze interesting rock formations by actually seeing them, often from multiple perspectives. However, some interesting geological locations are not easily amenable to field work.

One such location is the surface of Mars. To allow geologists to study the surface of Mars, NASA has developed software that uses satellite photos of the Martian surface to generate three-dimensional (3D) images of the planet. Using a special apparatus, including a headset which incorporates a 3D stereoscopic display, a geologist can be given the sensation of being on the Martian surface. This application is a good example of a virtual reality application.

Another geologically interesting but hard to reach location is below the Earth's crust. Scientists at UCLA are developing an application that allows users to examine 3D images of the Earth's crust, based on seismic data, satellite images and other information about the Earth's surface.

The challenge of these geology applications is that computing the images to provide to the scientists can take a long time. Unfortunately the applications are most useful if the scientist can interact with them and get new views on demand (by typing at the keyboard in the crust application or by turning one's head in the Mars application). The Mars simulator is currently almost fast enough (users report that it works well provided one does not turn one's head too fast), but for the crust application it currently takes weeks of computing to develop one image. The plan for the crust application is to reduce the time to develop an image down to less than a second, by using several supercomputers in parallel and then combining their outputs at a display. The combined data streams from the different computers will be about one gigabit per second of data.

8.6. The Impact of New Applications

The primary goal of this chapter is to try to characterize the needs of gigabit applications, with particular attention to new requirements that may lead us to use new protocols.

The general message of the preceding sections is that many new applications have one or more of the following needs:

1. Some applications need a certain amount of bandwidth to maintain high-quality service (be it good-quality audio or video or simply timely file server response).

2. Some applications have limits on how long data can take through the network. For example, interactive voice conversations work best if one-way delays are less than 400 ms.

3. Continuous media applications have timing requirements about the spacing between samples played at the output device.

The first two needs translate fairly easily into requirements upon gigabit networks. It should be possible for applications to request a certain guaranteed amount of bandwidth, though exactly how to describe the required amount of bandwidth is a difficult problem that will be considered in detail in Chapter 11. Second, it should be possible to allow applications to request guarantees about network delays.

The last need, for controlling spacing at the output devices, is less easy to translate into a requirement. The telephone networks meet this requirement by designing the entire telephone network to preserve the intersample spacing as it is transmitted by the sender. Originally, many researchers thought that this strictly timed approach would be required if data networks were to support continuous media. But recently some innovative experiments with *adaptive applications* have shown that strict timing is not required within the network.

Adaptive Applications

The essential idea of an adaptive application is that instead of requiring the network to make strict performance guarantees, the application asks for loose performance guarantees, and the application continuously changes its behavior to accommodate how the network is currently delivering its data.

An example of an adaptive application is the **vat** voice-conferencing system developed by Van Jacobson and in experimental use on the Internet. In its simplest form, **vat** can be used like a telephone: two people talking to each other, but through their computers instead of telephones and using the Internet in place of a telephone network.

The challenge of supporting a phone conversation is maintaining the correct spacing between samples. To avoid garbled output due to variations in transit times through the network, adaptive applications buffer the voice samples at the receiver. The intersample timing is recreated by the receiver before the samples are played. There are a number of ways to restore the spacing. **Vat** recreates the timing by having the sender timestamp each sample. The receiver uses the timestamps to restore the intersample spacing.

The trick in adaptive applications is to make the receiving buffer large enough that even samples that take a relatively long time to get through the network will arrive in time to be played. Thus if network delay for a sample varies between 50 and 100 ms, the receiver should have a buffer that can store up to 50 ms worth of data. Voice samples that arrive at the sender in less than 100 ms are buffered until 100 ms have elapsed since they were sent and then are played. In this way the buffer both restores intersample spacing and buffers out variations in network delay. The time (in this example, 100 ms) at which the voice samples are played is called the *playback point*.

Choosing the right playback point is a difficult problem. If the receiver chooses a playback point that is too early (i.e., makes the buffer too small), then many voice samples will arrive too late to be played and the voice quality will be poor. If the receiver is conservative and makes the playback point too late, then the speakers in the network phone call will sound far away from each other, making conversation more difficult. Compounding this problem is that the delay over data networks changes with time, so the playback point that was just perfect at the start of the conversation may be too short (or too long) later in the conversation.

Vat deals with this problem by changing the playback point, during the conversation, in response to the network delays it observes. If vat discovers that a lot of voice samples are arriving late, it increases the playback point. If vat observes that all the voice samples are arriving well before they are played, it moves the playback point back. Vat shifts the playback point during intervals of silence in the audio stream, so the changes are almost invisible to the listener.[6]

In another form of adaptation, Garrett and Vetterli [1993] have shown that, if given feedback about expected loss rates inside the network, a video coder can change its layered encoding scheme to maximize the quality of the received image in the face of the expected loss.

Effect of Adaptive Applications

Adaptive applications could have a major impact on how networks are designed to support real-time applications. Instead of building a network that carefully bounds delay and strictly preserves intersample spacing, one can build a network that gives approximate guarantees to applications and expects applications to adapt to variations. Indeed, strict guarantees about bandwidth may not be needed either. The major effect of briefly lowering bandwidth to an application is to increase the network delay suffered by the application's data. Adaptive applications can adapt to those increased delays.

Exactly how widespread adaptive applications will be is unclear. The essential requirement for an adaptive application is some memory for buffering and a processor to handle spacing issues at the receiving device. Some researchers have argued that adding memory and a processor to receiving devices is not desirable; they point to the success of the telephone network model where the telephone is an extremely simple attachment device. However, in an age where almost every consumer device includes one or more pieces of silicon, it

---

[6] Listeners typically do not notice if a pause is slightly longer or shorter than usual. The one notable exception is music. Experiments with musicians playing along with music sent over the network show that minute changes in rests can really confuse the musicians.

seems likely that most receiving devices on networks could support adaptive applications.

Experiments with adaptive applications on the Internet have shown two important results. First, even on regular data networks like the Internet, which have no special support for real-time transmission and have traditionally been viewed as hostile to real-time applications, adaptive voice and video applications have worked well. Successful conferences with participants on several continents have been held. However, there have also been some glitches when network load grew high. For instance, there was a voice conference held within greater Boston, where the playback point (and thus the perceived delay) grew to several seconds. The implication is that adaptive applications make it much easier to support real-time applications and place far fewer restrictions on how networks handle data, but that some network assistance will be required to support high-quality real-time applications. So the timing and bandwidth needs discussed in earlier sections still apply, but we can be a bit more casual about how we achieve them.

8.7. Summary

There are three important messages from this chapter. First, a wide range of applications, from the mundane file server to fancy multimedia applications will benefit from gigabit networks. Second, although the human factors of multimedia are imperfectly understood, all evidence suggests that human users can comfortably work with a wide range of network delays, and that in any case, comfortable delays are well in excess of 100 ms (a relatively long time). Third, even though multimedia data such as audio and video streams have typically been thought of as fairly inflexible in their bandwidth and timing requirements, adaptive applications have shown ways to manipulate this media to adapt to variability in networks, largely without sacrificing output quality.

Further Reading

Charlie Catlett [1992] has written a useful survey article on gigabit applications, with a focus on supercomputing. For a general discussion on user interface requirements, Shneiderman's [1992] book is highly recommended.

Chapter 9

Making Hosts Ready for Gigabit Networks

9.1. Introduction

It is widely accepted that gigabit networks will have an effect on the operating systems and architectures of the computers, or *hosts*, to which they are attached. The combination of higher bandwidth networks and increased application requirements for both bandwidth and performance guarantees suggests that we will expect more from our computers.

This chapter studies the particular problems of making hosts and their operating systems ready for gigabit networking. The focus of this chapter is on two essential problems. First, we will look at the generic issues related to getting data off the network and through the system to applications at gigabit rates, a problem sometimes referred to as *throughput preservation*. Second, we will consider how an operating system might provide the needed support for performance guarantees. The problem of making particular network protocols and their implementations run fast is deferred to the next chapter, which studies the question of whether the current protocols are suitable for gigabit rates.

It is important to keep in mind in this chapter that, although networking is important, it is not the only thing a host does. The sharply increased use of networks, through applications like distributed file systems (e.g., the Network File System), distributed graphics (e.g., X windows), and the use of networked multimedia systems, has made networking far more important, arguably an essential piece of a host. But there are other important parts to a host. So, in the quest to improve performance, the goal is to find techniques that improve networking performance without seriously jeopardizing the performance of other parts of the host system.

9.2. The Model Machine

One common mistake when studying the problem of interfacing hosts to networks is to assume networks are getting faster while hosts stay the same as today's systems. This kind of thinking typically leads to disastrous visions of plugging a gigabit network into a 20 MHz personal computer and desperate calls for special hardware to mediate between the massive network bandwidth and the poor, overworked CPU.

In reality, gigabit networks will be (and are) attached to much more powerful machines. By the late 1990s, workstation class processors are expected to have instruction cycle times of about 1 nanosecond and be capable (at peak rates) of performing 1 to 2 billion instructions per second (BIPS).[1] (See, for example, the DEC Alpha processor [Sites 1992], whose designers are quite clear about their goal of achieving such high clock rates.)

Amdahl's rule of thumb states that each instruction per second requires a byte of memory and a bit of I/O. Given general trends in memory costs, it is not unreasonable to expect these 1 BIPS processors to have close to 1 gigabyte of main memory. And developments in fast file systems, parallel disk systems such as Redundant Arrays of Inexpensive Disks (RAID), and file caching, make clear the feasibility of building file systems that can move data at gigabit rates. So the puzzle for this chapter is not how to make all the parts of the host fast — many will be fast already. Rather the problem is how to make sure that networking is fast, too. The next several sections look at key pieces of the system and how they might be optimized.

9.3. The Costs of Moving Data

In its simplest form, all networking does is take data from an application and send it over a network or take data from a network and give it to an application. As a result, a large part of the cost of networking is the cost of moving data between the network interfaces, the host operating system, and the networked applications.

---

[1] To make their terminology parallel with *giga*bits, some researchers have taken to referring to GIPS, for *giga* instructions per second. This term is a linguistic barbarism (a misuse of the prefix *giga-*) and is inconsistent with current terminology (which counts instructions in thousands, millions, billions, and trillions).

Unfortunately, as a number of studies have shown, the relative cost of moving data and, in particular, copying data is increasing. For example, Ousterhout [1990] examined operating system performance on Reduced Instruction Set Computer (RISC) processors and found that data copies were far slower than the processor's rated performance would lead one to suspect. The reason data copies are becoming expensive is that memory speeds have not kept pace with improvements in processor performance (see, for example, the discussion by Hennessy and Patterson [1990, pp. 426-427]). Because memory speeds have not kept pace, currently a processor can execute as many as four instructions in the time it takes to read one word from main memory.

Newer processors like the Alpha and the Pentium contain a number of features that try to hide this disparity in speeds. One feature is *super-scalar* architectures, which permit multiple independent instructions to execute in the same clock cycle. Thus if an instruction is loading data from memory and the next instruction is doing something unrelated to the instruction loading memory, both instructions can execute in parallel. Another feature is *scoreboarding*. In a scoreboarded architecture, instructions that load data into a register do not wait for the data to come back from memory, but rather mark the register as awaiting data. The processor then continues to execute new instructions. The register gets filled with data when the memory access completes. Only if an instruction accesses the register before the memory access has completed does the processor stop execution (or *stall*). Both super-scalar architectures and scoreboarding are of primary benefit when reading data. For writing data, processors typically cache writes to memory, so that unless there are a lot of writes at once, the processor does not have to wait for the write to complete.

Each of these features, however, is of limited help if the task is copying a lot of data (e.g., a buffer of application data) from one place in memory (such as the application's memory) to another (e.g., networking buffers). When copying large amounts of data, the processor's ability to copy is limited not by how fast it can issue read and write instructions, but by the peak speed at which the system memory can serve those instructions. An important feature of any host's operating system is that it be designed to minimize the number of times that large amounts of memory have to be copied, because these copies are limited by the system's memory speed, rather than its processor speed.

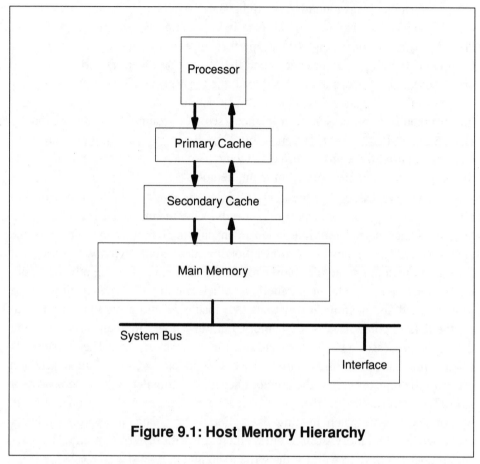

Figure 9.1: Host Memory Hierarchy

Memory Hierarchies

The last section talked about host memory as if it was a single collection of memory chips. In fact, as Figure 9.1 shows, memory architecture is typically organized in a hierarchy.

In general, memory chips run a spectrum from small, fast, and expensive to big, slow, and cheap. All the factors go together. Improvements in speed tend to force one to make memory chips that hold less memory and cost more.

Now consider the problem of a hardware designer trying to get memory for a very fast processor. Getting memory that is fast enough to keep up with the processor means buying small, expensive memory chips. Unfortunately one has to buy a lot of these chips to provide enough memory for the processor. (Remember part of Amdahl's rule: one instruction requires a byte of memory. A

1 BIPS processor will need a gigabyte of main memory.) Buying lots of small, expensive chips rapidly gets very expensive.

One way to reduce the cost is to build a hierarchy. Buy some fast, expensive memory and put it close to the processor as a cache. Then buy lots of somewhat slower, but bigger and cheaper, memory and use that as main memory. If one can keep the most frequently used instructions and data in the cache, the memory will look fast to the processor even though most of the memory is slow. A designer who wishes can use multiple levels of caching, with each cache representing a trade-off in memory speed, price, and size.

Caching does not come free. A major problem is keeping all the caches consistent with main memory. In general, updated data in caches must be written back to main memory, and data from peripherals must pass through main memory on their way to the cache to be accessed by the processor. But typically, caches are a performance win. What makes caches a performance win is *locality*, the fact that instruction and data access patterns are generally predictable.

Unfortunately, from a networking perspective, caching is not always a help. Networking code often violates the locality assumptions. The best example is what happens when a packet arrives. When a packet arrives at an interface, it typically interrupts some other activity on the processor. This often forces the processor to load new instructions to process the interrupt. Furthermore, to handle the packet, which is not in the processor's data cache, the processor has to pull the packet's data over the bus into its cache to read the packet header. Getting the new instructions and the packet data makes little or no use of the memory cache and thus causes the processor performance to suffer.

A Bad Example: Network Buffering in 4BSD

The networking code in 4BSD UNIX system (4, 4.1, 4.2, and 4.3BSD) has had a large influence on how networking protocols are implemented. Yet it manages memory in a way that tends to force excessive data copying. (In fairness to the researchers that developed the first BSD networking implementation, their goal was to get a working reference version of the protocols to work. Furthermore, many of these problems have been repaired in 4.4BSD. The old scheme is well known, however, and provides a good example of well-meant code that cannot cope well with today's requirements.)

The BSD system buffers networked data in fixed-size memory buffers called *mbufs*. Each mbuf can store 112 bytes of data, the result of dividing pages into 128-byte chunks and then using 16 bytes for overhead information. In special cases, a larger page-sized buffer can be allocated.

Mbufs were designed to make the common protocol operation of adding or deleting headers easy. Mbufs can be chained into linked lists, and data within an mbuf is located via offset and length counters in the mbuf header. To delete data from the front or end of an individual mbuf, one just updates the offset and length pointers. To delete entire mbufs, one simply deletes the mbuf from the chain. If there is space, data can be added to an mbuf by copying into the mbuf and then updating the length and counter pointers. If no space is available, a new mbuf to contain the data can be allocated and added to the chain. For both adding and deleting, a minimum of work is required.

When an application sends data, it calls one of four variations of the *send* system call with a pointer to a buffer of data and the amount of data in the buffer to be sent. The BSD system copies the application's data into a chain of mbufs and then passes this chain to the appropriate protocol stack for transmission. The code implementing the protocol stacks prepends the appropriate headers before passing the augmented chain to the network interface driver for transmission. The network interface driver typically then instructs the interface hardware to copy the mbuf chain into the interface's memory and transmit the packet.

Receiving data is roughly the reverse of the sending process. When an interface receives a packet, it signals its device driver to have the new packet copied into an mbuf chain. This chain is then passed to the appropriate protocol stack where its protocol headers are removed. The remaining chain of user data is then passed up to a queue, where it waits for the application to read it. When the application calls the *recv* system call (or its variants) the data is copied from the mbuf chain into the buffer the application specifies.

From this description, it should be clear that for both inbound and outbound data, a piece of application data is read and written at least twice in its entirety while traversing the path between the system call and the network interface hardware (or in the other direction from interface up to application). The reads and writes are done during the two copies: between application buffer and mbuf chain and between mbuf chain and network interface memory.

Another problem with the BSD approach is that the use of small buffers encourages cache misses, as the copying code moves from one buffer to the next and changes the section of memory being accessed.

The BSD approach is by no means uncommon. A number of operating systems copy data multiple times between different buffer pools, and not just for network interfaces but for other peripherals like disks as well.

Two Problems with Layered Code

Another limitation of the BSD mbuf architecture is that a high-level routine (e.g., the *send* system call) is copying data into buffers before it knows how the lower layers want to access the data. As a result, the way the data is buffered is often wrong, and the data must be recopied into the proper format in lower layer routines.

For example, the author once had the experience of writing a device driver for a network interface that required packet data to be transferred to and from the interface in a single buffer. Unfortunately, the BSD code delivered the packet data as a chain of mbufs. As a result, the device driver needed an additional data copy between mbuf chains and large packet buffers to accommodate the requirements of the interface.

This example is one of many instances where layered coding can hinder performance. Networking particularly is afflicted with these kinds of problems because many people naively believe that the famous OSI seven-layer architecture, which includes strict rules about abstract interfaces between protocols, requires layered implementation. In fact, the OSI seven-layer architecture was developed to allow different parts of the networking standardization to be assigned to different committees, and the abstract interfaces made it difficult for one committee to accidentally place requirements on another committee [Zimmerman 1980]. Designing code around the principles used to assign work to standards committees is clearly not wise software engineering. Even though it was recognized many years ago that improved performance is possible by combining code for multiple protocol layers [Clark 1982], many people continue to blindly layer their protocol implementations.

One common result of layering an implementation is that the implementation does unnecessary data copies. Looking at the BSD code again, it includes a memory copy that is clearly unnecessary and an artifact of a layered implementation. If a reliable protocol is sending data, then the protocol must keep a copy of the data, in case the data must be retransmitted. The easiest way to keep a copy is simply to tell the lower layers not to discard the mbuf chain after copying the chain to the interface. The BSD implementation, however, has no way to convey special instructions about buffer management between layers. The result is that the upper layers must make an extra copy of the mbuf chain.

9.4. Reducing Memory Copy Costs

Given that memory copies cost a lot, how can copies be minimized? The fundamental problem is to find a way to copy data directly from the applications' buffers into the interfaces that transmit the data onto the network. We will look at two ways to achieve this goal: memory mapped buffers on the interface and copy-on-write memory management combined with direct memory access.

The Afterburner Interface

Suppose that one implemented a network interface so that it looked like part of a processor's main memory, and the interface's memory was used as kernel buffer space. Then the two-copy process of copying data from application memory to kernel buffers and then from kernel buffers to interface memory could be implemented as a single copy from application memory to interface memory. Similarly, for inbound packets, data could be copied straight from interface memory to application memory. The number of memory copies would be halved, and because memory copying is relatively slow, performance would presumably improve. (In fact, in test cases, performance has been shown to nearly double.)

The performance advantages of such an interface were pointed out by Jacobson [1990c] in his proposal for a WITLESS interface. (WITLESS stands for a *W*orkstation *I*nterface *t*hat's *L*ow-cost, *E*fficient, *S*calable, and *S*tupid.) Jacobson had studied protocol implementations and concluded that a large amount of the time spent sending and receiving packets was lost in the device drivers that took a long time to control the interface (e.g., start transmissions and receive new packets) and move data from the operating system to the interface hardware. His WITLESS design was intended to minimize both the memory copying and control costs. Based in large part on Jacobson's ideas, Banks and Prudence [1993] of Hewlett-Packard implemented an experimental FDDI interface they called *Medusa*, and then a general interface design called *Afterburner*. Both interfaces are for HP 700 workstations.

The Afterburner design is illustrated in Figure 9.2. On the left side, the board is plugged into a memory bus with a 32-bit data path. (The Afterburner is actually plugged into the graphics bus and maps its memory into the processor's I/O memory space, to avoid both having to support error correction, which was required of memory interfaces in the HP 9000 series 700 workstation, and difficult interactions with the processor's memory cache.) At the center of the interface is a triple-ported video memory, with two serial ports and one parallel port. The parallel port is used to support fast access to the graphics bus, and the two

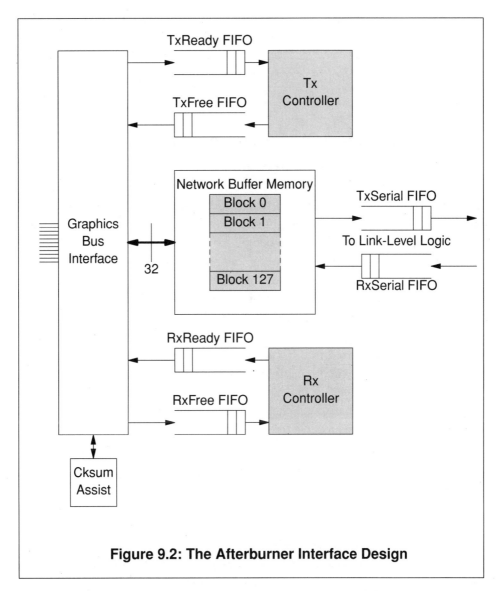

Figure 9.2: The Afterburner Interface Design

serial ports provide transmitting and receiving paths to the link-level chipset (not shown) off the right side of the interface. (The link-level chipset contains the network-specific hardware to put data onto the network, such as ATOMIC or ATM over SONET encoding hardware.) Memory is organized in fixed-size eight-KB buffers. Fixed-size buffers have the dual advantage of making memory management simple (no fragmentation concerns) and making it possible to specify a buffer's length and address in a single word.

Figure 9.3: Afterburner FIFO Control Word Format

To transmit a packet using the Afterburner, a host can read a word from the free transmission buffer (TxFree) FIFO, which contains the address of a free buffer. The host fills the buffer with the packet header and the application data, and then writes a one-word message containing the high bits of the address combined with the length of the buffer in the low-order bits (as shown in Figure 9.3) into the transmission ready (TxReady) FIFO. The transmission controller takes packets from the ready FIFO and streams their data onto the network out the transmission serial port of the buffer memory. When the buffer has been sent, it is freed by placing it back in the TxFree FIFO. Receiving works similarly. Inbound packets are placed in the receive ready (RxReady) FIFO. The processor is interrupted only when the FIFO goes from empty to nonempty (multiple packets should be serviced in the same interrupt due to context switching costs discussed later in the chapter). When the host is done with the buffer, it writes the buffer address into the receive free (RxFree) FIFO.

Observe that because all control communications take the form of atomic single-word writes and reads, there is no need for ready semaphores or other complex driver support.

Experiments with the Medusa interface (which is essentially an Afterburner for FDDI) have shown two impressive results. First, by comparing the throughput using the Medusa interface with the old-style BSD mbuf code against revised code that uses the Medusa's memory as the source of kernel buffers, it was shown that eliminating one memory copy effectively doubled throughput. Second, a relatively slow workstation (1990 vintage) with the Medusa interface was capable of transmitting at full FDDI bandwidth with processing time left over. Achieving full 100 Mb/s FDDI bandwidth had previously been thought to require a far faster workstation. Experiments using two Afterburner boards cabled together (with no link-level chipset) have achieved nearly 200 Mb/s throughput.

Copy-on-Write with DMA

The Afterburner/WITLESS approach to data copying is often referred to as *programmed I/O* since the I/O data copies are done by the processor. Another way to design computer systems is to make it possible for data copies to be done between interfaces without disturbing the processor, using a technique known as *direct memory access* (DMA). For these systems, several implementors have had success at minimizing data copies using a combination of a virtual memory technique called *copy-on-write* (COW) to manage the data buffers and a DMA network interface.

Copy-on-write is a technique to permit pages in a virtual memory system to be shared inexpensively. If two or more applications or an application and the operating system both want access to the same page of data, both are given pointers to the same page and the page is marked copy-on-write. If a user of the page tries to change (or write to) the page, then the page is copied and the user is given a private copy, so that the user's changes do not affect the data of the other users of the page. Because most sharing is done to allow multiple access for reading (for example, multiple instances of the same program sharing the same instructions and static data structures), COW can generally reduce the amount of copying required in a virtual memory system [Smith 1989].

DMA is a data transfer technique in which interfaces on a bus can transfer data to and from the processor's memory without disturbing the processor. DMA schemes are typically optimized for moving bursts of data (e.g., 32 words of data) at a time. This is a mixed blessing: although it makes copying memory without disturbing the processor possible, it sometimes limits processor access to main memory during the data burst and often requires complex setup code be executed to do a transfer.

However, despite some of the limitations of DMA, high-performance implementations have been achieved by combining a copy-on-write with DMA. The essential idea is that, when an application asks for data to be transmitted, the operating system marks the pages containing the application's data as copy-on-write and uses those pages as the operating system's data buffer. So instead of copying data from application space to operating system space, the data is shared. The operating system generates the packet headers in a bit of operating system memory, and then instructs the interface to DMA the headers and data from the shared pages into a packet buffer and send them. Assuming the application does not write to the pages containing the data it just sent, forcing the pages to be copied, this scheme, like programmed I/O, requires just one memory copy — the

DMA of the data into the interface. (If the application does not cooperate and writes on the page before the data has been sent, then performance is typically rather poor.)

On the inbound side, the operating system keeps the interface informed about what pages are free. When a packet comes in, the interface DMAs the packet data into a free page and then notifies the operating system that a packet has arrived. The operating system removes the packet headers and, if the application's receiving buffer is page aligned, simply changes the application's page table, replacing the receiving buffer's page with the page containing the packet. Note that this scheme requires that the application take care to use only buffers that are page aligned and an integral number of pages long, so some application cooperation is required. In some cases, however, language compilers and loaders can be modified to recognize data buffers and align them properly without changing the application.

Like the Afterburner approach, this approach to interface design has yielded high performance.

Eliminating All Data Copies?

Both the Afterburner/WITLESS approach and the COW/DMA approach reduce the number of required data copies for inbound or outbound packets to one copy between application space and interface memory, using either programmed I/O or DMA.

It is worth noting that researchers have considered trying to eliminate the data copy altogether. The basic idea is to combine the page management technique of the COW/DMA approach with the on-board memory of the Afterburner/WITLESS approach so that the interface memory can be used as regular pages in the application memory space. The application would preallocate some interface pages to use as its sending data buffers. Thus by placing data in its buffers the application is automatically placing data in the interface memory, ready to be transmitted. Similarly, inbound packets would not have to be DMAed; they would already be in pages that could be remapped into the receiving application's space.

This approach is feasible, but has one major drawback. If interface memory is of limited size, then it may have to be managed by the applications that use it. In particular, applications would have to carefully manage the network buffers they use, with calls to the operating system to allocate and free buffers as needed. Many system designers feel that part of the goal of an operating system is to conceal these sorts of hardware-specific issues from applications.

9.5. Other Processor-Memory Interactions

Data copying is usually the most costly interaction between processors and memory, especially if the packets being sent are large. But other interactions can affect performance, too. Indeed, for small packets, for which very little data copying is done, the costs of these interactions often represent most of the cost of sending a packet. The three most important of these interactions are these:

1. *Branch misses*. Most processors try to predict the next instruction they will perform. Conditional branches (e.g., `branch-if-equal`) may cause one of two instructions to be performed, depending on the result of testing the condition. Processors have to guess which instruction will be performed and often take a substantial performance penalty if they guess wrong.

2. *Context switches*. When a processor stops executing code for one task and starts executing code for another task, it has to save the state of the old task, and then load the state and code for the new task from memory. This changing of state and code is a context switch.

3. *Interrupts*. Interrupts occur when a device like a network interface signals a processor to indicate the device needs to be serviced.

It may not be immediately obvious, but the cost of all three types of interactions has some basis in the relationship between processors and memory. This section considers each factor in turn.

Minimizing Branch Misses

Most modern processors are pipelined. A pipelined processor performs instructions in stages, where each stage is part of an assembly line of operations necessary to complete an instruction. For example, in a three-stage pipeline, an instruction must pass through all three stages to complete. The performance advantage of pipelining is that, if done carefully, stage 2 can be working on instruction $i + 1$, while stage 3 is working on instruction i. Critical to making a pipeline work is knowing which instruction will be done next. In the three-stage pipeline, the processor needs to be working three instructions ahead (loading instruction $i + 3$ into stage 1 as instruction i completes stage 3).

Conditional branches are instructions that cause the processor to retrieve the next instruction from one memory location or another based on some condition. Until the branch is completed, the processor cannot know which instruction will be performed next. To try to limit the effects of branches, most processors guess which way the branch will go. If the processor guesses wrong, the pipeline has to be cleared and the proper instructions must be loaded from memory or cache.

Branch misses are probably the least serious performance problem. The interaction with memory is typically mild; the processor must simply load a few new instructions. They are mentioned here first to point out that processors are pipelined (which becomes important when discussing interrupts) and because of some interesting, if largely preliminary, work on branch prediction.

Processors tend to have rules about which way they will guess that a conditional branch will go. For example, the DEC Alpha processor assumes that branches backward in memory will be taken and forward branches will not be taken. Smart compilers then generate code to try to maximize the chance that the processor's assumptions will match the code's behavior.

In many cases, the compiler cannot know which branch is more likely. Yet correctly predicting which way to go matters: studies have shown that even if a branch goes one way slightly more often, arranging the code so that the processor correctly chooses the more likely path yields a large performance improvement.

Operating systems typically contain a number of conditional branches that test for rare conditions, like invalid parameters to a system call or a device error. The implication is that improving the quality of branch prediction (and reducing branch misses) may improve operating system performance.

Clearly the best way to optimize branch predictions is to run an operating system, measure the frequency with which it takes various branches and then recompile the operating system code using the measurements to correctly organize the branch instructions. Recently a technique known as *profile based optimization* (PBO) has been developed that allows this cycle of measurement and recompilation to be done automatically. A measurement of the system is taken and then fed into the compiler, which generates code that reflects the last profile. In fact, PBO does more than just improve branch predictions. If two pieces of code are frequently executed one after another, PBO moves the two pieces of code together to increase the chance they will be in the cache at the same time. Preliminary studies using PBO on the UNIX operating system have suggested that selected pieces of networking code can go as much as 30% faster if the branches are predicted correctly [Speer 1993].

Minimizing Context Switches

Context switches are typically very expensive because they require both new code and new data to be loaded in the processor cache. (The new code typically wants to reference data not currently in the cache.) The effects of context switches can be severe. Mogul and Borg [1991a] showed that a context switch could take hundreds of instruction cycles to complete and that the cache hit rate will be lower (and performance degraded) for as many as 400,000 instruction cycles after the context switch.

In a perfect system, no more than one context switch should be needed to send a packet and one context switch plus an interrupt to receive a packet. On the transmission side, the context switch is between the sending application and the operating system that creates and transmits the packet. On the receiving side, the context switch is between the code that receives and processes the packet for the operating system and the application code that uses the data in the packet. In very simple systems, the context switch on transmission may not be required. The application can be given direct access to the network interface control registers and memory. In multiprogrammed systems, however, some operating system software is typically required to manage access to the shared interface.

Unfortunately, most systems are not careful about avoiding context switches. Many older operating systems were built using multiple-priority schemes in which inbound packets pass through code that operates at various priority levels. For example, a packet may be taken off the board at a high interrupt level, its packet headers processed at a middle interrupt level, and then given to the application at the lowest interrupt level. Dropping down between priority levels typically requires a context switch, so this scheme (which is similar to that of 4.2BSD) requires two context switches after the packet arrives.

Newer systems often do no better. For example, several new systems (MACH, OSF, and the Next operating system) use a *microkernel* operating system design. Microkernels try to minimize the size of the operating system by limiting their services to a set of critical functions like process management, memory management, and interrupt handling, and they move all other services like networking, and disk and file system management, into special servers. As a result, an inbound packet will have to go through the microkernel interrupt handler and then the network server before reaching the application it is destined for. Each transition, to the interrupt handler, to the network server, and to the application, requires a context switch, so the system will absorb three context switches.

Minimizing Interrupts

Interrupts have the effect of a compounded context switch. (They also break the instruction pipeline, but that effect typically is not as serious as the context switches.) When the interrupt occurs, the processor must put aside its current work to run the code to handle the interrupt. Jumping to the interrupt handling code represents a context switch. And if the interrupt presages the arrival of new data, then a new application may have to be awakened to receive the data (another context switch). Furthermore, because the data is new, it typically will not be in the cache, so the application will suffer cache hits reading its data.

There are a couple of ways to minimize interrupt costs. First, and perhaps most obvious, is to require the operating system to do as much as possible in response to an interrupt. For example, the Afterburner interface encourages this approach by interrupting only when the receive FIFO goes from empty to non-empty. If multiple packets are in the receive FIFO, the Afterburner expects the operating system to retrieve all of them in response to one interrupt. A second approach is not to interrupt after packet transmissions. Network interfaces have historically interrupted the operating system to signal that a packet has been sent and its buffer can be freed. But the operating system typically has enough buffer space that it need not be notified immediately if a buffer can be released. Several new interfaces, including the Afterburner and the OSIRIS ATM interface (discussed later in this chapter), suppress transmission interrupts.

9.6. Multiprocessor Architectures

Many people believe that the key to high-performance systems is to use multiprocessor architectures, but work on making networking fast on multiprocessor systems is still in its infancy. This section will just briefly outline what appear to be the hard problems.

Figure 9.4 shows a fairly standard multiprocessor architecture. Processors are connected to some sort of connection fabric — a bus, a switch, or a ring. Each processor has some local memory. Processors communicate with each other and their peripherals, like the network and disk controllers shown in the upper right, using the connection fabric. It is important to note that the communication between processors over the connection fabric is very much like networking between processors, with all the same problems. Communicating between processors often requires interrupting the processors, causing cache misses. As a result, a central problem in parallel processing is finding ways to

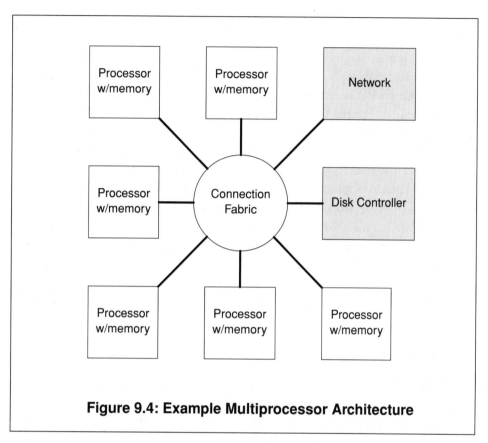

Figure 9.4: Example Multiprocessor Architecture

divide work among processors so that their communications costs are minimized.

From a networking perspective, an important problem is that an application's data is likely to be scattered across the several processors participating in a parallel implementation of the application (a situation known as *striping*). Thus when the application decides to send a packet, data for that packet often will have to be collected from multiple processors. Collecting the data requires contacting each processor and getting it to transfer the requisite piece of memory. So sending a single packet may require multiple (expensive) communications between processors.

Similar problems occur on the receiving side. A single application may be running on multiple processors, and each processor may need some fraction of the data in the packet. So the receiving code needs to be able to figure out how to properly stripe the data across the processors. If the data is striped incorrectly, then the various processors may lose considerable time rearranging the data among themselves.

Although it is often hoped that multiprocessors could improve performance on protocol processing by doing pieces of the processing of each packet in parallel, as the next chapter will show, the actual protocol processing that must be done on each packet is rather small. As a result, processing the same packet in parallel does not appear to make sense — the cost of dividing the processing among the processors almost certainly exceeds any performance benefit. A more promising approach that is only beginning to be studied is to use parallelism to process different packets on different processors [Bjorkman 1993], much as the Bell Labs router uses multiprocessing to forward packets in parallel.

The need for considerable internal communication, the problems of getting striping right, and the shortage of opportunities for using parallelism in networking code make it difficult to get high performance from multiprocessor systems. Indeed, many multiprocessor systems currently report data transfer rates that are slower than those achieved by some PCs. These results are disturbing, but it is probably too early to worry. Implementers are still learning how best to use multiprocessors.

Outboard Processors

Outboard processors are a sort of special form of multiprocessing. The general idea is to build a network interface that includes a processor. The higher layer protocols are then implemented on the interface processor, thereby freeing the host processor from doing protocol processing.

Experience with outboard processors has been mixed. Some outboard processors, such as the Stanford NAB [Kanakia 1988] and the CMU CAB [Arnould 1989], have improved the performance of the systems they were attached to, either by improving protocol performance or by reducing overall system load or both. However, at least as many outboard processors have made their host systems perform less well.

Looking at experience so far, it appears that the capacity of an outboard processor to improve performance depends on at least two factors: the complexity of the interface between the outboard processor and the host, and the relative speeds of the outboard processor and the host processor.

Outboard processors must typically be very tightly integrated with the host operating system. To see why, consider an application trying to open a TCP connection. Using an outboard processor, the operating system must request that the outboard processor open the connection. Furthermore, the operating system has to exchange a certain amount of state information with the outboard processor, such as which application has asked for the connection and how errors in opening the connection should be reported to the operating system. This sort of interface is typically more complex than the interface to regular network interfaces, which simply send and receive packets. The result for some outboard processors has been that the processing time required to manage the outboard interface rivaled the time it would take to simply perform the network protocols in the host.

Another problem area is the speed of the outboard processor. In general, outboard processors are caught in a curious economic dilemma. The purpose of the outboard processor is to offload the host processor. But if the outboard processor is too expensive, then the customer would typically be better off buying a more powerful host processor instead. The challenge is to find an outboard processor that is substantially less expensive than the host processor, but has enough processing power to do protocol processing as fast as the host processor can hand it data. Often no processor meets both requirements.

9.7. What about Cells?

So far, this chapter has not talked about attaching hosts to high-speed cell networks. There are two reason for delaying the discussion until this point.

First, designing a high-speed cell interface requires a hardware designer to be aware of both the cost of copying data and the high cost of interrupts and cache misses. Given the high cost of an interrupt, it is apparent that interrupting a host on a per-cell basis is probably not reasonable. The interface will have to assemble cells into packets (i.e., do AAL processing) before notifying the host that a packet has arrived. Clearly the packet should be assembled in such a way as to minimize host copy costs.

Second, there are some innovative ideas about how to take special advantage of trends in processor and multiprocessor design to improve performance of systems connected to cell networks. These ideas could only be discussed after the issues of connecting to processors and multiprocessors.

An OC-12 ATM Interface

A couple of ATM over SONET interfaces have been described in the literature. An OC-3 interface was developed by Traw and Smith [1993] at the University of Pennsylvania (UPenn), and an OC-12 interface at Bellcore by Davie

[1993a]. The Bellcore interface is named the *OSIRIS* interface, for an Egyptian god who was broken up and then put back together again. Both interfaces were developed under the auspices of the Aurora testbed project. The UPenn interface was designed to interface to an RS/6000 workstation and does ATM segmentation and reassembly on the interface. The OSIRIS interface was designed to interface to a TURBOchannel™ bus on a DECstation 5000™ and does segmentation and reassembly using host memory. Although both interfaces have strengths, the OSIRIS interface is somewhat easier to explain and less like the interfaces described earlier in the chapter, hence it will be the example used here.

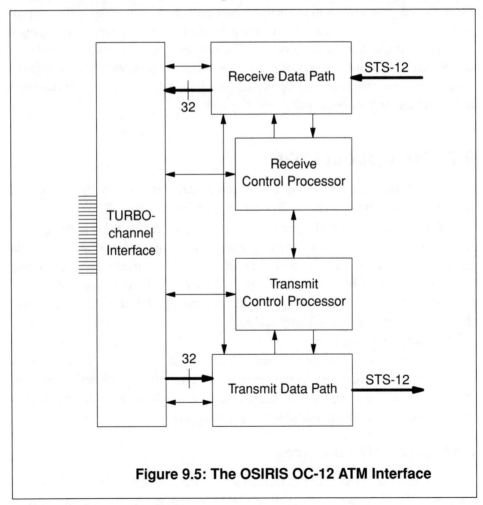

Figure 9.5: The OSIRIS OC-12 ATM Interface

The general outline of the OSIRIS interface is shown in Figure 9.5. The receiving and transmitting data paths are largely independent, and each data path is managed by a microprocessor (an Intel 80960CA). The OSIRIS interface is designed to support experimentation with ATM; the inclusion of the microprocessors provides greater flexibility for deciding how to order cell transmission and reception among different virtual channels and generally permits more flexible host-interface interaction. At the same time, the processors are not quite fast enough to do all of the processing of each cell (which arrive and depart at the rate of about one every 23 instruction cycles), so most data movement is handled by hardware and the processors' role is to coordinate the data transfer rather than handle the data themselves. The TURBOchannel is optimized for DMA transfers, so all data is moved using DMA.

On transmission, the operating system notifies the interface when a buffer of data is to be sent. The operating system provides the interface with the location and size of the buffer, the ATM VCI over which the data is to be sent, and the priority of the data. The interface then DMAs and transmits cell-sized chunks of the buffer. Data for cells is DMAed as needed to avoid having data transfers from large, low-priority buffers interfere with data from high-priority buffers. (That is, starting to transfer data from a large buffer does not mean the entire buffer has to be copied before other data can be considered.) The rules for choosing which buffer will provide data for the next cell are handled by software in the transmission control processor.

Similarly, on reception, after the cell headers have been removed from the inbound cells, their data is DMAed into buffers in main memory. As on transmission, the order in which cells are DMAed is determined by the control processor. Note that, because the receiving and transmitting parts of the interface are both doing DMA, their DMA requests may compete. To deal with this problem, the interface allows the receiving logic to tell the transmitting logic to stop doing DMA, so that bus bandwidth is freed to get received cells off the interface and into host memory.

The OSIRIS interface was designed to use AAL 3/4, and thus moves data in 44-byte chunks across the bus, but its design is equally well suited to AAL 5. Inbound AAL 5 data can be copied directly into buffers and the host notified when a cell with the user signalling bit set is received. Note that there's some similarity between copy cells using DMA and copying words of data using programmed I/O. Copying the contents of AAL 5 cells into a buffer is much like copying bytes into a buffer, the interface is just copying data in bigger units.

Desktop ATM Networks

The idea of thinking about cells as very large bytes is a natural introduction to another idea: desktop ATM networks.

The ATM payload of 48 bytes is similar to the cache line size of many architectures. The cache line size is the amount of data that can be moved in one transfer from memory to or from the processor cache, and it is typically the most efficient unit of data transfer between CPU and memory. This observation, plus the similarities between multiprocessor connection fabrics and networks mentioned earlier, has led researchers to suggest replacing the multiprocessor connection fabrics with ATM networks.

One such experiment is the desk-area network (DAN), developed at the University of Cambridge [Hayter 1991]. Essentially, the DAN uses a small ATM switch as the bus for a computer system. All peripherals like disks, consoles, and memory communicate with the processor or processors via the switch. The switch and everything attached to it are under the control of the system's operating system.

A Cell Coprocessor

Another way to make use of the similarity between cache line sizes and cell payloads has been proposed by Tennenhouse. He is building a cell networking interface that acts as a coprocessor. The advantage of a coprocessor is that it is directly connected to the main processor and thus bypasses the entire memory hierarchy. Data arriving at the coprocessor is copied directly into the processor's registers or cache, and data leaving the processor goes directly to the coprocessor.

9.8. A Summary of System Performance Issues

Earlier in the chapter we noted that improving networking performance should not be done at the expense of the performance of other parts of the host system. The preceding several pages have shown two important ways to improve network performance:

1. *Minimize copies.* Given the disparity in memory and processor speeds, copying data from one piece of memory to another is one of the slowest operations a processor can be asked to do. Experiments with interfaces like the Afterburner, which make it possible to minimize data copies, have yielded substantial performance improvements.

2.   *Minimize cache misses and costly operations like interrupts and context switches that force cache misses.* Processors are dependent on good cache performance. The very nature of networking, which involves getting data from outside the host (and thus, by definition, getting data from outside the cache), makes a certain number of cache misses unavoidable, but minimizing cache misses remains an important goal.

Observe that both improvements are related to the performance gap between processors and memory and that neither improvement is specific to networking. Indeed, a team of operating system researchers at the University of Washington has identified precisely these two problems as part of a general suite of performance problems that must be addressed in operating system design [Anderson 1991]. The implication, therefore, is that improvements to networking code should generally improve overall system performance and vice versa.

9.9. Support for Real-Time Applications

It is now time to look at the second challenge that gigabit networks pose for hosts and their operating systems: how to support applications like multimedia conferencing that have real-time requirements. The general topic of making operating systems better able to support real-time applications has received considerable attention in recent years, as interest in multimedia systems has increased. To bound the discussion here and keep the book focussed on networking issues, we will look solely at the question of how hosts can support real-time applications that use a network.

One type of real-time applications is *embedded systems*, in which a system is completely programmed to provide a single service, such as air traffic control or rocket guidance. These systems have very tight time constraints and disaster can strike if a system fails to meet those constraints. However, multimedia conferencing and other real-time applications that are most likely to be used over gigabit networks have far less stringent requirements. As Chapter 8 showed, failing to meet an application's constraints is annoying but not disastrous. Furthermore, the system on which these applications run is likely to be time shared; it will not be devoted to a single service. Thus, real time in this context means finding some way for general purpose systems to meet the timing requirements of some special (but not critical) applications.

Networked real-time applications are particularly hard because, in many situations, the participating hosts have imperfect control over when data is delivered. Some local area network technologies like DQDB can deliver data on exact schedules, but if data travels over several networks in an internetwork then precise timing schedules are hard to achieve. Instead, as Chapters 11, 12, and 13 will explain in more detail, the internetwork will probably provide some weaker guarantee, such as that all data will get to its destination within a delay interval, t, of being sent. The data may arrive more quickly than t, but that is acceptable provided there is some memory to buffer the data in. Because memory is cheap, that is a fair assumption. So we are looking for techniques to support real-time requirements that will work even if the data delivery system has some variation in delivery times.

How Hard Is the Problem? DECspin and vat

In 1990, two brothers named Palmer at Digital Equipment Corporation decided that a good way to learn about the requirements of real-time applications would be to implement a real-time application on a regular host and see what application requirements the host could not meet. So they took some workstations running UNIX and connected them to an FDDI network and implemented a voice and video conferencing system on them. The conferencing program ran like any other application, with no special support from the UNIX or the workstations' hardware.

Much to the brothers' surprise, the conferencing system worked! Up to eight people could hold a successful conference on a network using DECspin [Palmer 1992]. The DECspin experience is not unique — in recent years, a number of researchers have discovered that their unmodified workstations and PCs are capable of supporting real-time applications like voice and video conferencing and real-time animation. Quality is typically imperfect, but often satisfactory.

Furthermore, some experimenters have shown that these real-time applications can be run over networks with extremely variable delays. The best example of such an application is the vat voice conferencing system discussed in Chapter 8. Vat is being used over the Internet, a network well known for its highly variable delays.

The performance of both vat and DECspin can suffer if the computers they run on are running a number of compute-intensive tasks at the same time a conference is taking place, but they still illustrate several important points. First, the computing power and data moving capabilities of even inexpensive computers are now sufficient to support real-time requirements. Second, in many cases, the real-time requirements can be met without special assistance from the operating system. Third, the success with adaptive applications like vat is a reminder that there is some flexibility in many real-time requirements — playback points can be varied or extra buffering can be used to recover from variations in data delivery times. Given these insights, it is now time to look at some approaches to supporting real-time requirements.

Workahead Scheduling

Anderson [1993] has developed a way to think about networking streams of audio and video information that he calls the *continuous media resource model*.

In the model, output devices on a host are viewed as devices that read data from a buffer at regular intervals. So, for example, an audio output device might read an eight-bit voice sample every 125 μs. The goal of the system is to ensure that the output device never finds its buffer empty (a situation called *starvation*).

It is assumed that the network can guarantee a maximum delay, D, from the time a piece of data is sent by the sender (time t_0) until the data is received at the receiver. The receiving application sets the playback time and buffering for the output device such that the output device will always be reading data D time units after the data was sent. It is straightforward to prove that in this environment the data to be played should always have been received before the output device needs it. So the only way the output device can starve is if the receiving application fails to place data received into the output device's buffer in time.

One way to ensure that the output device's buffer is always filled in time is for the operating system to schedule the execution of the receiving application so that the application always runs just before the output buffer is read and places new data in the output buffer. However, this approach can lead to inefficient use of the processor. Figure 9.6 shows how scheduling can affect two applications. The shaded boxes represent processor time given to a low-priority application that is ready to run starting at cycle 4. The white boxes are processor time given to a real-time application that is scheduled to move one piece of data from the input buffer to the output buffer just before each read by the output device (the output device reads at times 2, 4, 6, 8, and 10). Observe that the low-priority application does not finish until the end of cycle 8, because it must be continually interrupted by the real-time application to make sure there is data in the output buffer for the output device.

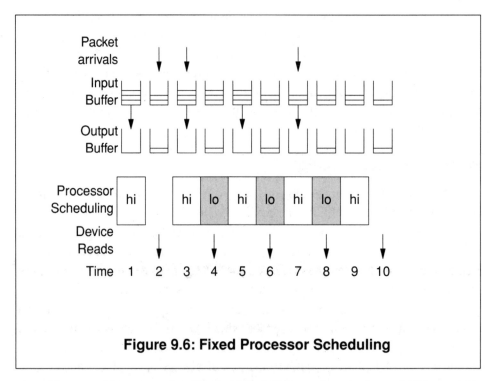

Figure 9.6: Fixed Processor Scheduling

Contrast this approach with the scheduling approach shown in Figure 9.7. If there is no other work to be done and data is waiting to be processed, the operating system allows the real-time process to continue to run and move data from the input buffer to the output buffer. Anderson calls this practice *workahead* scheduling. The advantage of this approach is that, because the real-time application has been able to move several pieces of data to the output buffer by time 4, it can permit the low-priority application to run to completion and still have enough time to get new data into the output buffer in time to be read at cycle 8. Overall system responsiveness is improved because the low-priority application finishes far earlier.

What makes workahead an improvement is the practice of letting the real-time process run for additional time in the processor whenever data needs to be processed and there is no competition from other processes.

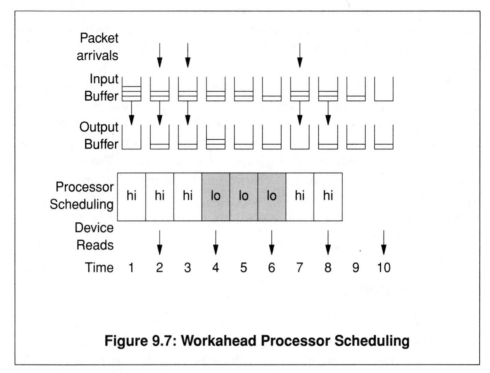

Figure 9.7: Workahead Processor Scheduling

Extending Workahead Scheduling

Workahead scheduling requires careful coordination between the operating system and real-time processes to work correctly. For the scenario in Figure 9.7 to work, the operating system has to know that the real-time application has worked ahead and need not access the processor while the low-priority application is running. One can further extend the idea of workahead scheduling to reduce the coordination required.

Suppose the operating system divides access to the processor such that it schedules applications in cycles of time τ. In other words, a real-time application is promised it will get a scheduled share, s units of time in the processor, in every cycle of τ units. As before, the goal is to make sure that the output device does not starve.

In the worst case, a piece of data sent at time t_0 will arrive at time $t_0 + D$ at the receiving host. If at time $t_0 + D$, the receiving application has just relinquished the processor, it may not run again until nearly 2τ time units later. (The value is 2τ to cover the case where the application ran at the very start of one cycle and will run again at the very end of the next cycle.) The receiving application can ensure that the output device does not starve by setting the play-back point to $t_0 + D + 2\tau$ and requesting a time slice s sufficient to move enough data between input buffer and output buffer to keep the output device running for time 2τ.

A scheme similar to this one has been used successfully in the real-time control systems for linear accelerators.[2] The advantage of this scheme is that scheduling is simpler. The operating system need make sure only that sometime in the cycle, τ, the real-time application gets its share s. No other communication between the application and operating system need occur. The drawback of this scheme is that it increases the delivery time to the user. But processors are now sufficiently fast that the cycle time, τ, could be set to a period equal to a few million instruction cycles and still add a delay of only a modest number of milliseconds to the delivery time.

9.10. Summary

This chapter has touched on a lot of ideas. The basic lessons are fairly simple, however.

To keep up with high speeds (of both networks and other peripherals like RAID file systems), operating systems need to minimize data copies and avoid costly cache misses. A variety of schemes, such as programmed I/O to interface memory and DMA combined with copy-on-write, were presented for minimizing data copies. Suggestions were also made of ways to avoid cache misses. More generally, careful programming that avoids poor buffering techniques and poor locality is essential, and it was pointed out that highly modular or layered programming may not be the best approach.

The other major observation is that supporting many real-time applications appears to be increasingly easy as processors get fast enough that relaxed scheduling techniques can be used.

Further Reading

For another example of where layering harms performance, see Crowcroft et al. [1992].

---

[2] Personal communication from Van Jacobson.

The standard book on computer architecture is Hennessy and Patterson [1990]. It examines the disparity between memory and processor performance, discusses pipelining and conditional branches, and briefly discusses high-speed I/O subsystems.

The Ousterhout [1990] survey on operating system performance, and the paper by Anderson et al. [1991] are good studies of how operating system performance is affected by changes in computer architecture. There are a number of good introductory books on operating systems. My favorite is Silberschatz [1994].

For a wonderful survey of high-speed interface designs see the February 1993 issue of *IEEE Journal of Selected Areas in Communications*. This issue includes an insightful discussion of the "do's and don'ts" of interface design by Bob Metcalfe.

The July 1993 issue of *IEEE Network Magazine* includes studies on high-speed host systems. One is a thought-provoking article by Smith and Traw on using *clocked interrupts* (a variant of polling) — the idea is to have a timer that wakes up at regular intervals and processes the interface and application queues. The idea has elements of the extended workahead approach described earlier and can be shown to reduce interrupt costs. This issue also includes a description of the Afterburner interface.

Other than Anderson's work, the operating system work on real-time issues that has received the most attention is the work on real-time Mach [Tokuda 1990]. This work is closer in spirit to classic embedded systems than Anderson's.

Chapter 10

Today's Internetworking Protocols

10.1. Internetworking

Probably the most successful idea in data networking over the past twenty years has been the concept of *internetworking*. Internetworking is a method for interconnecting networks, regardless of the particular link or MAC layer protocols that the individual networks use. (Internetworking can thus be distinguished from *bridging*, because bridging works only between networks with similar or identical MAC layers.)

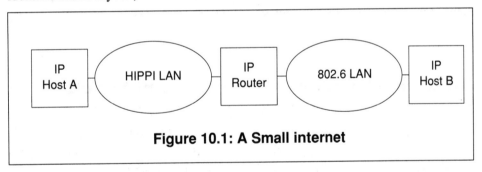

Figure 10.1: A Small internet

What makes internetworking possible is the development of internetworking protocols like IP and ISO's Connection-Less Network Protocol (CLNP). To create an internetwork, one implements the internetwork protocol on every constituent network in the internetwork. Hosts on the constituent networks then use the internetwork protocol's services (rather than the particular local network's protocols) as the primary means of communication. For example, Figure 10.1 shows an IP internet made from two networks, a HIPPI LAN and an IEEE 802.6 LAN. If Host A on the HIPPI LAN wishes to communicate with Host B on the 802.6 LAN, then Host A creates an IP datagram destined for B and sends that datagram in a HIPPI frame to the router. The router takes the IP datagram out of the HIPPI frame, reencapsulates it in 802.6 cells, and transmits those cells to Host B. Host B receives the datagram by removing the IP datagram from its 802.6 encapsulation.

The great advantage of internetworking is that it makes it possible to plug together arbitrary networks. If one person buys a HIPPI network, a second person buys an ATM network, and a third person buys an ATOMIC network, and all three want to communicate, they do not have to build a device that converts between the HIPPI, ATM, and ATOMIC protocols. Rather they need simply to support an internetwork protocol on each of the three networks.

Occasionally, people have argued that things would be a lot easier if the computing community just adopted one networking technology, like ATM, and could thus dispense with the need for an internetworking protocol. The idea may sound seductive, but it is rather improbable. The one-size-fits-all approach is rarely successful. Different networks like ATM, HIPPI, and ATOMIC meet different needs, yet their users will likely want to be able to communicate with each other. As a result, it seems reasonable to assume that internetworking is here to stay, and we should think about how to scale internetworking protocols to gigabit speeds.

10.2. Gigabit Speeds and Today's Protocols

A few years ago researchers thought that protocols like TCP/IP and OSI used on today's internetworks would have to be completely replaced to achieve gigabit speeds. Indeed, some went so far as to claim that everything learned about networking to date had to be thrown out.[1] It is now clear, however, that these expectations were premature. Today's internetworking protocols have proved quite capable of transmitting at gigabit speeds, with some modest tuning. And many of the design principles and rules of thumb that we have learned over the past two decades of data networking continue to apply to gigabit networks.

There is a challenge, however. Today's protocols are not perfectly suited to supporting multimedia applications. These applications require performance guarantees that today's protocols generally cannot provide: guarantees about maximum delay or minimum bandwidths.

---

[1] See, for example, Leiner [1988].

To better understand where the challenges lie in developing gigabit protocols, this chapter looks at how today's protocols function on gigabit networks. This study tries to serve two goals: first, to learn the various techniques for making protocols go fast and how these techniques may affect gigabit networking protocols; and second, to point out the limitations of today's protocols and, by studying those limitations, highlight the important new protocol features that need to be developed as networks move to gigabit speeds.

Surveying all the protocol suites currently in use (TCP/IP, OSI, AppleTalk, Novell NetWare, etc.) is clearly beyond the scope of the chapter, so we will focus on one protocol suite that has been particularly well studied: the TCP/IP protocol suite (also known as the Internet protocol suite), named for its two most popular protocols, the Transmission Control Protocol and the Internet Protocol.

10.3. Architecture of TCP/IP

The TCP/IP protocol suite, developed by a team of researchers in the late 1970s, is the internetworking protocol used on the Internet, a global network covering all seven continents, connecting millions of computers and users, and incorporating a tremendous variety of different network technologies.

The basic architecture of TCP/IP is shown in Figure 10.2. At the center of the protocol suite is the Internet Protocol. IP is a datagram protocol, offering best-effort delivery of datagrams between hosts attached to an IP internetwork. A *datagram* is a packet formatted according to the rules of the internetworking protocol. *Best-effort delivery* means simply that IP makes a reasonable effort to deliver datagrams to their correct destination with their data uncorrupted, but IP is permitted to occasionally lose, corrupt, misdeliver and reorder datagrams.[2]

Each host on an IP internetwork has one or more IP addresses. (A host may have more than one address when it is attached to more than one network, such as a host connected to both a HIPPI LAN and an 802.6 LAN.) To direct a datagram to another host, a sending host sends the IP datagram to one of the destination host's IP addresses. IP addresses are 32 bits long and are typically written as four decimal numbers, one per byte, separated by dots (e.g., 128.89.1.192). The 32 bits are divided into three parts: a *network identifier*, a *subnet identifier*, and a

---

[2] Because IP is the best known datagram protocol, the definition of datagram has been slowly changing to mean an internet packet delivered via a best-effort service. But other internet protocols like X.25 also use the term *datagram* for their packets.

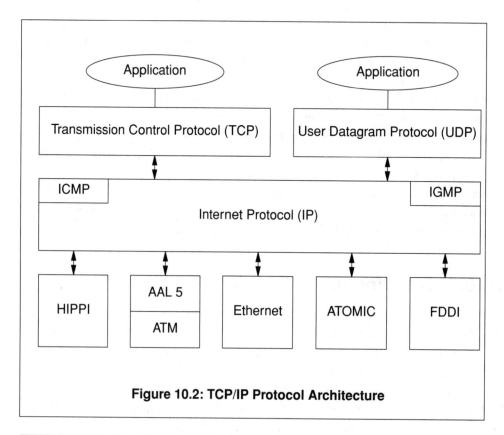

Figure 10.2: TCP/IP Protocol Architecture

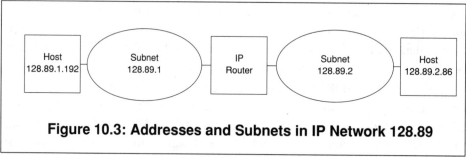

Figure 10.3: Addresses and Subnets in IP Network 128.89

host identifier. Individual instances of a networking technology (e.g., a cable or a fiber) are called *subnets*, and the subnet identifier uniquely identifies the piece of cable (e.g., a particular Ethernet segment) on which a host lies. The host identifier uniquely identifies the particular host within the subnet. The network identifier identifies a set of interconnected subnets managed by the same organization. Figure 10.3 illustrates this idea, by showing two subnets of network 128.89, connected by a router. IP also supports special addresses for broadcasting (sending a datagram to every host on a network or subnetwork) and multicasting (sending a copy of a datagram to selected hosts anywhere in an internetwork).

IP requires that for each subnet technology, such as Ethernet, HIPPI or FDDI, there be a standard way to encapsulate an IP datagram into the technology's framing protocol and map an IP address into the technology's addressing scheme. So, for example, *Request for Comments* (RFC) 894 defines how to place IP datagrams into Ethernet frames, and a companion document, RFC 826, defines an address resolution protocol (ARP) that is used to translate IP addresses into Ethernet addresses on an Ethernet. Standards also exist for some gigabit technologies. The rules for encapsulating IP in HIPPI networks are defined in RFC 1374, and the rules for encapsulating IP over ATM (using AAL 5) are defined in RFC 1483.

Subnets are connected using IP *routers*. If two communicating IP hosts are on different subnets, the routers' job is to forward IP datagrams between the hosts. In brief, a router is a device that accepts an IP datagram from one subnet, determines the next subnet the datagram needs to traverse to get to its destination, and places the IP datagram on that subnet (using the new subnet's encapsulation). Routing is done hierarchically based on the IP address. If a datagram's destination is within the same network, then routing is done on the subnet and host id. If the destination has a different network identifier than the network or networks the router is in, then routing is done based solely on the network identifier. Because the network topology may change due to line failures or reconfigurations, routers exchange topology information with each other using special routing protocols.

IP also includes two supporting protocols, which actually use IP to carry their messages. These protocols are the Internet Control Message Protocol (ICMP), which is used primarily to carry error messages related to IP transmissions between routers and hosts, and the Internet Group Multicast Protocol (IGMP), which is used to support multicasting.

IP simply provides delivery of datagrams between hosts. To actually deliver data between applications, an additional level of service is required. To provide this service, the TCP/IP protocol suite defines a number of transport protocols, of which the two best known (and most widely used) are TCP and the User Datagram Protocol (UDP).

UDP is a very simple protocol that just adds application addressing to IP, in the form of source and destination *ports* (sixteen-bit identifiers) [Postel 1980]. A port and IP address uniquely identify a particular application using UDP. UDP is unreliable — it just places a UDP segment inside an IP datagram and relies on IP to deliver the UDP segment to the receiving host's UDP implementation. UDP does have a checksum to check that IP has not corrupted the data in transit, but use of the checksum is optional.

TCP is far more sophisticated. Like UDP, TCP adds application addressing, again in the form of sixteen-bit ports. However, TCP provides a reliable service, namely, the in-order delivery of a stream of bytes [Postel 1981]. Like UDP, TCP relies on IP to deliver TCP segments to the receiving TCP, but TCP also requires the receiving TCP to acknowledge segments received. If a segment is not acknowledged within a timeout period, TCP will retransmit the segment. Segments are numbered to uniquely identify them. There is a limit (known as the *window size*) on the number of unacknowledged segments that may be outstanding at any time, to bound the amount of buffering of unacknowledged segments that must be done at sender and receiver. To determine when to retransmit a segment, TCP dynamically estimates the round-trip time by measuring the time it has taken for earlier segments to be acknowledged.[3] In addition, to guard against corruption of data by IP, TCP checksums every segment.

An application uses either TCP or UDP (or both) depending on the application's needs. Applications like file transfers or remote login, which require correct transmission of data, use TCP. Applications that do not require reliable delivery or require multicast delivery use UDP. (TCP does not support reliable multicasting, because the problem of reliable multicasting over internets has not been solved.)

10.4. Techniques for Going Fast

In 1987, Greg Chesson gave a talk in which he suggested that TCP/IP and OSI might never go faster than 10 Mb/s [Chesson 1987]. Until that time, few researchers had seriously investigated the performance limitations of TCP/IP. Chesson's talk inspired several researchers, most notably Jacobson, to take a serious look at the problems of making protocols run fast. The product of this

---

[3] The art of dynamic round-trip time estimation is widely misunderstood. It is, in fact, possible to very accurately estimate the round-trip time, even over networks with moderately high loss rates. The TCP algorithm combines a filter to weed out misleading samples using an algorithm known as Karn's algorithm [Karn 1991] and an estimation function that computes both the mean round-trip time and its variance [Jacobson 1988].

research has been a number of techniques to improve protocol implementations.

Some of those techniques, such as memory management and interrupt handling, are related to operating system performance and were discussed in the last chapter. However, other techniques are more specific to network protocols. Those techniques are discussed here.

Better Lookup Techniques

Looking over the sketch of the TCP/IP protocol architecture in the last section, one should note that there are several cases where a piece of information has to be looked up in a table. TCP must find the connection block for each segment received. IP must find a route to be able to send an IP datagram. In the general case, each of these lookups has a worst-case cost of $O(\log_k n)$, where n is the number of routes or protocol control blocks in the table, and k is some base indicating the fraction of the blocks that can be eliminated on average by each comparison.[4] This cost may not seem very high, but keep in mind that, except for the checksum computation on the packet, all the other protocol activities such as adding and removing headers are at worst $O(1)$ operations. Lookups therefore represent a very large fraction of the cost of protocol processing, and finding ways to minimize lookup costs are important.

There are two obvious ways to try to reduce lookup costs: (1) where possible, use caches of frequently used information to avoid general lookups; and (2) find lookup algorithms with very good average running times. Not surprisingly, work has been done on both problems.

The trick to building an effective cache is to maximize the hit rate in the cache, while minimizing the costs of searching and maintaining the cache. These goals are often in conflict, because the best way to maximize hit rates is often to make the cache larger, while the easiest way to minimize cache maintenance costs is to keep the cache size small. Caches are most effective when one can find some pattern to the lookups that make it possible to keep the cache small.

Interestingly enough, networks exhibit precisely the kind of traffic patterns that are likely to make caches effective. As Jain and Routhier [1986] observed, packets in networks often travel in *packet trains*, clumps of packets all headed for the same destination. In their study they found that about 30% of all packets on a

---

[4] In certain situations, one could use perfect hashing to achieve an $O(1)$ lookup cost, but perfect hashing requires prior knowledge of all the values that may be placed in a hash table. (See [Lewis 1991, pp. 288–291].)

network had the same destination as the previous packet. Mogul [1991b], in a study of traffic patterns in hosts, showed that about 70% of the segments received by UDP and TCP are destined for the same port as the last segment. Furthermore, both Mogul and Jain and Routhier also found that if a packet is not going to the same destination as the last packet, it is often a response to the last packet.

The studies strongly suggest that caches of just one control block or route may actually achieve very high hit rates. These caches are often called *one-back caches* because they cache the entry found for the packet one back in the packet sequence. A one-back receiver cache keeps the control block that the last packet was destined for. A one-back sender cache keeps the control block from which the last packet was sent. Jacobson [1990c] has implemented a one-back receiving cache for the TCP in 4.3BSD, and Partridge and Pink [1993] have implemented both one-back receiving and one-back sending caches for UDP, also in 4.3BSD. Both projects have reported significant cache hit rates and performance improvements.

Although the one-back caches give very good performance, some fraction of traffic still misses the cache and requires a lookup. One possible way to reduce the lookup cost further is to make the cache somewhat larger. For example, Feldmeier [1988] extended the work on packet trains and, based on traffic measurements at a number of routers, showed that a cache of only 20 routes was likely to yield a cache hit rate of over 90%. If the cost of a lookup is not too horrible, a 90% hit rate may be sufficient to make the average cost of a lookup so low that it is not worth optimizing further.

There are cases where the traffic is sufficiently skewed in its behavior that the hit rates are much lower. One example is in transaction processing, an application in which thousands of users are regularly accessing a single system. (A good example of a transaction system is a group of airline reservations agents making and changing reservations in a central database.) Trying to find efficient protocol control block lookup schemes to support transaction processing led McKenney and Dove [1992] to thoroughly study various lookup approaches. They concluded (using some industry standard transaction benchmarks) that the best lookup scheme is hashing using open chaining, where the head of each hashed link list keeps a cache of the last accessed control block. Jain [1992] has similarly looked at the problem of developing good hash algorithms for efficient route lookup in routers.

Looking at the work on reducing lookups to date, the major success has been in using caches effectively. Although the work of McKenney and Dove and

Jain holds promise for improving lookup times in large tables, it is probably not yet safe to declare that problem solved. Note, too, that we have not discussed ways to keep routing tables small. In fact, ever-expanding routing tables are becoming a moderate problem — they are big and expensive to maintain. The problem of trying to reduce routing table sizes is one of the motivations for a new version of IP.

Reducing or Eliminating Checksum Costs

Having reduced the cost of lookups, it is now time to look at the other major performance cost: checksums. The last chapter talked about reducing the cost of copying data by eliminating extra copies and observed that there was a penalty each time memory was accessed, due to the likelihood that data was not in the cache and the mismatch between CPU and memory rates. The checksum presents a very similar drain, because computing a checksum requires that each byte in the packet be read and added (in some fashion) into the sum.

The first step to optimizing a checksum algorithm is to try to do the sum using the host machine's native word size (to optimize memory accesses) and native byte order (to minimize byte swapping costs). Both the TCP/IP checksum and TP4 (the ISO transport protocol number 4) can be parallelized in this manner.

The TCP/IP checksum is a sixteen-bit one's complement sum over the segment (with odd lengths being padded by a zero byte). This sum can be done independent of byte order. Consider the sequence of hex bytes:

$$0x80, 0x81, 0x82, 0x83, 0x84, 0x85$$

which are added as sixteen-bit words into a sixteen-bit sum:

$$0x8081 \,\hat{+}\, 0x8283 \,\hat{+}\, 0x8485 \;=\; 0x878A$$

where $\hat{+}$ is one's complement addition. Now compare this result with the sum when the bytes are reversed:

$$0x8180 \,\hat{+}\, 0x8382 \,\hat{+}\, 0x8584 \;=\; 0x8A87$$

The sums are the same except that their bytes are reversed. To see why this is always true, note that the carries are the same in both cases: from bit 15 to bit 0, and from bit 7 to bit 8. (Recall that one's complement addition requires that carries be added back into the low-order bit.)

The TCP/IP checksum can also be done using any word size of sixteen bits or greater. For example, consider summing 32-bit quantities. One can simply add the 32-bit numbers using one's complement addition and, when the 32-bit sum has been computed, fold and add the high 16-bits of the 32-bit sum to the low bits and get the 16-bit sum. Like the byte-ordering example, this summation works because the carries work: carries from bit 15 go to bit 16, and carries from bit 31 go to bit 0. Like the 16-bit sum, the 32-bit sum can be done independent of word order. (This feature has been used to implement a vectorized checksum on Cray computers [Braden 1988].)

Many RISC processors do not support an add with carry.[5] On these systems, however, it is possible to accumulate word-sized sums using quantities that are half the word size and letting the carries accumulate in high bits of the word. Periodically, the carries get folded into the sum. For example, one could do 64-bit additions of 32-bit values on a 64-bit machine and let the carries accumulate in the high-32 bits of the running sum. Every 32 additions, the high bits would be folded with low bits to avoid losing carry bits.[6]

Once the checksum additions have been optimized to the host's native word size (or close to it), another optimization is possible. Jacobson observed a few years ago that RISC processors are capable of performing two instructions per clock cycle, of which only one operation can be loading data from memory or storing data to memory. As a result, in a copy loop of instructions of the following form,

---

[5] One can detect that a carry has occurred by simply comparing the sum with both operands, and if the sum is less than either operand, a carry must have occurred. So, to simplify the CPU, the carry bit is left out. But testing for the presence of the carry is usually more expensive than the algorithm of accumulating carry bits described here.

[6] The OSI TP4 checksum can be optimized using similar algorithms. In brief, the TP4 checksum (developed by Fletcher [1982]) requires the computation of two eight-bit values, s_0, and s_1, in parallel. If the bytes in a message are $b_0, b_1, \cdots$, for each byte, b_i, the values are incremented according to the following rule:

$$s_0 \leftarrow s_0 \hat{+} b_i \qquad s_1 \leftarrow s_1 \hat{+} s_0$$

In other words, s_0 is the sum of the bytes, and s_1 is the sum of the intermediate values of s_0. It should be clear that s_0 could equally be computed as a sixteen-bit quantity and then folded into an eight-bit quantity at the end. It much harder to see, but also true, that s_1 can be computed using sixteen-bit values [Sklower 1989]. Unfortunately, computing s_1 in the larger bit size typically requires two additions, with the result that the TP4 checksum requires three additions per word (one for s_0 and two for s_1) rather than TCP/IP's one, with the result that the TP4 checksum implementations to date have all been substantially slower than implementations of IP checksums. But the techniques for performance improvement are the same.

```
load [%r0],%r2    !load data r0 points to into r2
store %r2,[%r1]   !store r2 into location
                  !pointed to by r1
```

there is space for two instructions (since each instruction is a load or store requiring a separate cycle). The trick is to put the instructions for the checksum into those slots;

```
load [%r0],%r2     !load data r0 points to into r2
add %r5,%r2,%r5    !add to running checksum in r5
addc %r5,#0,%r5    !add carry into r5
store %r2,[%r1]    !store r2
```

Because the two instructions would otherwise be unused, this trick effectively means that performing the checksum comes for free. This interleaving of instructions may seem to be specific to RISC processors, but it sometimes works well on CISC processors too, due to interactions between the CISC processors and their memories.

Because the combined checksum and copy runs as fast as a simple copy loop, it makes sense to replace the data copy from user space to interface buffers described in Chapter 9 with a combined checksum and copy. Systems that use DMA instead of programmed I/O can achieve the same effect by putting checksumming logic into the DMA path, so data is checksummed as it is DMAed into the interface.

Moving the checksum code to a checksum and copy routine requires some careful recoding of the protocol code, particularly on the receiving side. Historically, protocols have computed the checksum to confirm that the protocol data and headers had not been corrupted, before copying data to the application's buffers. If the checksum and copy code are combined, the checksum must be checked after the data has been copied to the application's buffers. Furthermore, all updates to the protocol's state variables must be delayed until the copy is done.

Two more controversial suggestions also have been made for improving checksum performance.

One suggestion is simply to leave the checksum out, especially if packets are to travel only over the local LAN, which is assumed to be error free. There are at least three known problems with this suggestion. First, techniques such as subnetting (which makes a collection of networks look like one virtual network) hide topology information and make it very hard to determine if a packet will actually stay on the local network. Second, LANs are often not error free. For example, a few years ago there were a number of Ethernet interfaces that would periodically corrupt a few bytes. Unfortunately, some distributed file system protocols, to try to improve performance, turned off the UDP checksum. The result was that system administrators would periodically discover random bits of their distributed file system had been corrupted. Third, if the checksum comes for free as part of the data copy loop, given it serves a useful function, why take it out?

A second suggestion is to move checksums to the end of the packet, a practice known as trailing checksums or *trailers*. The idea behind trailers is that if the checksum is at the end, the sending machine can start sending the packet before the checksum computation is finished, whereas if the checksum is in the start of the packet, the sender cannot send the packet until the checksum has been computed and put into the header. Trailers have no effect at the receiving host because the host cannot release data to the receiving application until it has confirmed the checksum is correct, which requires all the data to have been received and summed. Also trailers require that the delivery of data to the sending interface be predictable — if the operating system is interrupted as it is passing data to the interface, and the interface is already putting the data onto the network, fragmented packets may result.

Prediction

Having greatly reduced the costs of lookups by using caching and all but eliminated the cost of doing the checksum by including the checksum in the copy loop, it is now time to look at optimizing other TCP functions.

There is a line of argument that, because TCP has so many features like retransmissions, window sizes, and urgent data, it must be expensive to implement. The problem with this line of argument is that it assumes that the number of features equates to lines of code executed per TCP segment. In truth, TCP behavior is highly predictable, and one can take advantage of this predictability by optimizing the frequent path through the TCP code in both the receiving and sending TCP implementations.

Figure 10.4 illustrates the number of fields in the TCP header that change on a per-segment basis.[7] The shaded fields do not change. The source and destination ports are set at connection setup, and because TCP connections currently

---

[7] This figure is adapted from Figure 3 of Jacobson [1990a].

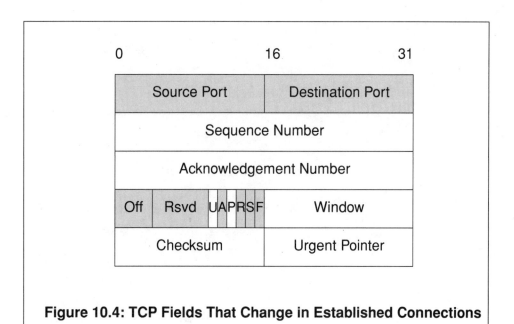

0 16 31

Source Port	Destination Port
Sequence Number	
Acknowledgement Number	

| Off | Rsvd | UAPRSF | Window |
| Checksum | | | Urgent Pointer |

Figure 10.4: TCP Fields That Change in Established Connections

either always use options or never use options, the data offset (Off) remains constant, as do most of the control bits. But Figure 10.4 does not tell the whole story. In situations in which no segments get lost or reordered (which is most of the time), the sequence number changes by the amount of data in the last segment received, and the window size typically does not change. The urgent pointer is only used if the urgent bit (U) is on, and it usually is not, and the PUSH bit (P) can be ignored if the receiver passes data up to the application promptly. The result is shown in Figure 10.5. Almost none of the fields change in unpredictable ways.

These observations led Jacobson [1990b] to develop an algorithm for TCP receivers called *header prediction*. Header prediction looks for segments that fit the profile of the segment the receiver expects to receive next; namely, segments that

1. are for connections that have been established,
2. have only the acknowledgement bit (A) and optionally the push bit (P) set (other bits on would indicate urgent data or that the connection was being closed),
3. are the expected next segment in the sequence (i.e., data in this segment starts where the last segment left off),

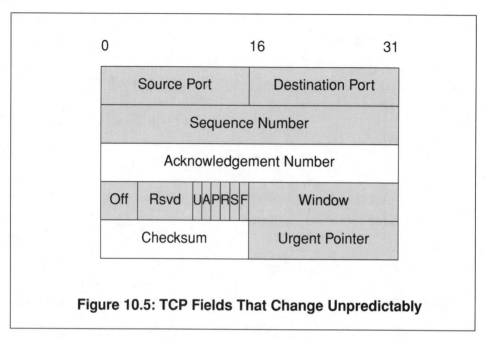

Figure 10.5: TCP Fields That Change Unpredictably

4. have not changed the window size,

5. are for connections that are not retransmitting data (if the connection is retransmitting, acknowledgement processing requires more effort),

6. are either acks for data or new data arriving, but not both (again processing both acks and data in one packet is more complex, and most connections are sending one way at a time).

Once the control block for the connection has been located, these tests require five comparisons. A data packet that meets all the conditions (and most will) then requires just a handful of instructions (largely the instructions to strip the header off) and can then be passed up to the application. Thus the incremental cost of receiving a TCP segment, after connection lookup and performing the checksum, is tiny — a handful of instructions.

Header prediction is an algorithm for the receiving TCP, but similar predictive schemes work for optimizing sending. On the sending side, an application typically writes its data to some sort of *connection handle*, a file descriptor or socket. This connection handle can be designed to map directly to a control block (thus eliminating the control block lookup). And because the TCP destination is set, the control block can also cache the IP route (thus eliminating the routing lookup). Furthermore, just as the incoming segment can be predicted, so the outgoing segment can be predicted. The sending TCP can keep a template TCP header, whose sequence number is incremented as segments are sent and whose acknowledgement number is updated as segments are received. As a result, sending becomes a matter largely of copying the template header onto the front of the TCP data, filling in the checksum (computed as the segment's data was copied), and sending the segment.

Prediction schemes are not limited to TCP. Similar schemes could presumably be used for TP4 (though apparently no one has tried). Predictive algorithms have also been used to optimize a UDP implementation [Partridge 1993].

More Data in Flight — Sequence Numbers

Recall that Chapter 2 explained that bits do not travel faster in fiber. Fiber just makes the bits shorter, allowing more bits to be packed onto the link in a given unit of time. The amount of time required to send a single bit across a continent on a gigabit network is not substantially smaller than the time required today. What has changed is that the number of bits that can be in flight at any time has grown by a factor of 1,000. The amount of data that can be in flight is often referred to as the *delay-bandwidth product*, because it equals the network delay multiplied by the network bandwidth.

One implication of a big delay-bandwidth product is that protocols' window sizes and sequence spaces need to be made larger. Recall that the receiver's window size bounds how much data the sender can transmit over the connection before receiving an acknowledgement. Clearly it should be possible to negotiate a window size that is as large as the delay-bandwidth product of the path; if the path is otherwise idle, a single connection should be allowed to fill it. For a gigabit path, that delay-bandwidth product is often measured in megabytes. Unfortunately, today's protocols, including TCP, typically allow window sizes of no more than 64 kilobytes. However, this problem is easy to fix, and an option has been defined to allow TCP's window size to be extended [Jacobson 1992].

Sequence numbers are used to uniquely identify segments, so that, if segments become reordered or lost, the receiver can restore proper ordering and correctly identify missing segments to the sender for retransmission. Sequence numbering is done using wrap-around counters (counters that count up to a certain value and then wrap around to restart at 0). It is critical to the correct operation of protocols like TCP that it be effectively impossible for two different segments in the same TCP connection to use the same sequence number at the same time. TCP handles this problem by expecting IP to bound the maximum packet lifetime and then making the sequence numbers big enough that the sequence space will not wrap for a long time. Unfortunately, TCP was designed in the 1970s, when 10 Mb/s was considered fast, and given an IP maximum packet lifetime of 120 seconds, the TCP sequence space was made 32 bits long and counts in bytes. It takes about 1,700 seconds at 10 Mb/s to send 2^{31} bytes. Unfortunately, at gigabit speeds, it takes 17 seconds to send 2^{31}. The TCP sequence space has become too small.[8] But like window sizes, this problem is fairly easy to fix, and options have been defined to extend the TCP sequence space.

The Current Situation

It is now time to pull together the work on checksumming, header prediction, and caching and lookup techniques and assess the suitability of today's protocols for transmitting at gigabit speeds.

The cost of sending a datagram can be divided up into a fixed part and a variable part. The fixed part is the header processing (handled by header prediction), the various table lookups (handled by caches and good lookup algorithms), plus time in the device driver and any interrupt costs and context switches incurred getting data between the network interface and the application. If one adds up all these fixed costs, they amount to around 150 instructions for both sending and receiving a TCP/IP datagram. The variable per-packet cost is the cost of handling the data, which can vary from segment to segment. This cost is the cost of doing one data copy and checksum, or roughly the maximum speed that the processor can copy data or the host can DMA data.

Putting the fixed and variable costs together, it is apparent that the time required to process a large TCP/IP datagram should be close to the time required to copy its data, provided the cost of interrupts is not very high. (Recall Chapter 9 discussed how to minimize interrupts.) A BIPS CPU should have no trouble sending TCP/IP at gigabit rates, and indeed, some implementations on some processors do very well now. For example, Cray's standard TCP/IP implementation has been measured sending data 790 Mb/s.

---

[8] Note that because TCP counts bytes rather than segments, it consumes the sequence space very fast. However, even protocols like TP4, which assign sequence numbers to segments, can quickly run out of sequence numbers. TP4 like TCP has a 32-bit sequence space, and one can easily wrap the space by sending TP4 segments with small amounts of data in each segment.

Dave Clark of MIT best summed up these results when he said. "If going fast is the goal, I have difficulty understanding what the problem is." Simply sending at gigabit rates is quickly becoming a solved problem.

A Comment about "Lightweight" Protocols

While some researchers were off tuning up TCP/IP implementations, other researchers had begun work to develop what they called *lightweight* protocols [Doeringer 1990]. Essentially the original idea behind lightweight protocols was to develop simpler protocols that could run much faster than existing protocols like TCP/IP. A notable example of a lightweight protocol is XTP [Strayer 1992].

The result of the efforts to improve TCP/IP is that the notion of a lightweight protocol has become much less interesting. First, the protocol overhead is now so low (150 instructions) that reducing it further is unlikely to make a noticeable performance difference. Second, it has proved quite hard to find parts of TCP that could be eliminated without compromising the protocol's ability to handle certain classes of errors. What the preceding analysis suggests is that eliminating those functions is not worth it — they cost almost nothing (except a few bits in the header) to support because, when they are not used, they do not affect performance.

10.5. Limitations of Today's Protocols

Having shown that today's protocols can indeed transmit data at gigabit rates, it is now time to identify the limitations of today's protocols. Going fast is not enough. Protocols need to be able to control the larger amounts of data in flight and provide new services like performance guarantees.

More Data in Flight — Flow and Congestion Control

The last section noted that large delay-bandwidth products required changes in the sequence spaces and window sizes. A more important problem posed by gigabit delay-bandwidth products still needs to be addressed; namely, it takes a long time (measured in bits) to tell a sender to slow down. For example, if a TCP is sending data at a gigabit per second between New York and Los Angeles and the receiver in Los Angeles tells the sender in New York to slow down, the sender in New York will continue to transmit for about 30 ms (about 3 million more bits of data) before it hears the request from Los Angeles. If the data is sent via satellite, the delay and amount of data sent before the sender hears the request to slow down are even larger (more than 10 million bits).

There is a natural temptation in this scenario to focus on the amount of data sent, but that is misleading. A few million bits is less than a megabyte of data, which is not very big. The problem is the interaction between large bandwidths and long feedback delays. To see why this is so, consider the behavior of the slow-start algorithm.

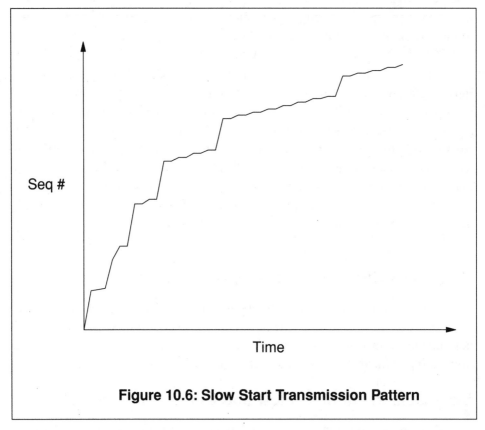

Figure 10.6: Slow Start Transmission Pattern

The slow-start algorithm is the flow and congestion control mechanism used by TCP. In brief, slow-start requires each TCP connection to continuously probe the network to try to learn the amount of bandwidth currently available to the connection. The probing algorithm requires the sender to keep a *congestion window*, which is the estimate of how much traffic the network can actually take. This congestion window is managed using a two-part algorithm. In the first part, the sender starts by sending one segment and waiting for the segment's acknowledgement. When the acknowledgement comes back, the sender sends two segments, and waits for their acks, after which the sender transmits four segments. This exponential growth of the congestion window continues until the sender finds that a segment has been lost (which is assumed to indicate the segment has been discarded from an overloaded queue). When a segment is lost, the sender keeps a record of the size of congestion window and starts the exponential sending pattern again from a window size of 1. But in this second stage, the sender grows the window exponentially only up to one-half the previous congestion window. After that, the sender grows the window linearly, cautiously probing toward the bandwidth at which data was previously lost. This cautious pattern of probing gives the slow-start algorithm its name. If one examines TCP sequence numbers versus the time they are transmitted, slow-start gives the jaggy transmission pattern shown in Figure 10.6. Although it may look a bit ugly, the pattern actually hovers fairly close to the mean bandwidth available to the connection.

Now consider doing slow-start on a gigabit link and assume that, through some fluke such as a brief burst of datagrams from another source, one of the TCP segments gets lost early in the first exponential growth stage. On the next cycle, the TCP will grow its congestion window exponentially up to one-half the previous window and then grow linearly toward the gigabit bandwidth of the link. Unfortunately, linear growth takes a long time, and on a long-distance link the window size will not reach the size appropriate for gigabit speeds for anywhere between a several seconds to several minutes.[9] That is a long time to adapt.

The problem is not with slow-start. Slow-start is an algorithm designed to adapt to network paths with bandwidths ranging as low as a few hundred bits per second up to gigabits. In this environment, the algorithm has to be conservative. Consider that if slow-start were optimistic and started out by sending a full gigabit window of about 6 megabits of data and there turned out to be a 9.6 Kb/s link in the path, it would take over ten minutes to transmit the first window's worth of data. That is at least as bad as taking a few minutes to scale up to a gigabit. It also is fairly clear that the slow-start algorithm would work quite well if it knew a

---

[9] A brief explanation of the numbers is in order. Assume the round-trip delay is 60 ms (about what it might be across a continent), and the link has an available bandwidth of 1 gigabit. If the packet size used is 576 bytes (4,608 bits), the correct window size for the channel is $(1,000,000,000 \times 0.06)/4608$ or about 13,000 packets. If the window size is growing linearly from 1, it will take 13,000 round trips or 780 seconds or 13 minutes to get the correct window size. If the packet size is large (16 KB), the window size is about 460 packets, which takes a little under 30 seconds to reach.

little bit about the path's bandwidth and could calibrate its behavior accordingly. Rather the problem is one of the length of the feedback loop over the network.

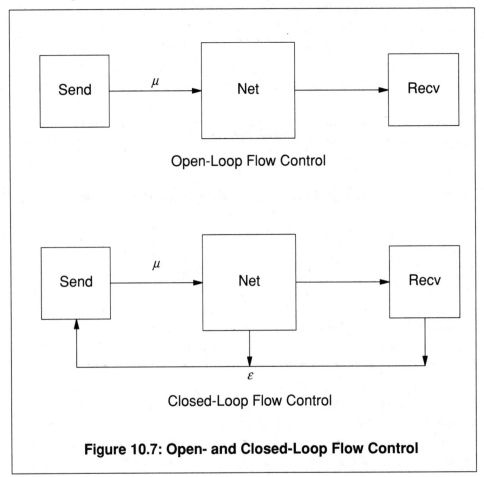

Figure 10.7: Open- and Closed-Loop Flow Control

Open vs. Closed Loop Flow Control

The terms *open-loop* and *closed-loop* come from control theory. The basic ideas are shown in Figure 10.7. The sender on the left sends data into the network according to some pattern, μ.

In closed-loop flow control, the receiver and the network can ask the sender to change μ by some amount, ε. Such a request may occur, for example, if the network is overloaded, or the receiver cannot keep up with the data rate, or the receiver is able to process data more quickly. Most of today's datagram networks use closed-loop flow control because it is very flexible — it can automatically respond to changes in the capabilities of the network or receiver. Slow-start is a closed-loop flow control scheme.

In open-loop flow control, the network, sender, and receiver negotiate μ at the start, and then there is no way for the network or the receiver to ask for changes. So the initial μ must be negotiated correctly at the start of the conversation. However, a potential advantage to open-loop flow control is that the sender does not need the capability to adapt to changes in the network. It can just send in pattern μ until it is finished. These are some of the reasons that telephone networks use open-loop flow control — it makes telephones simpler. The telephones do not need to adapt their transmission rates in response to changes in network performance.

The observation that telephones use open-loop flow control brings us to the crux of the problem with IP's (and thus TCP's) approach to flow and congestion control: it assumes that applications are willing to adapt almost arbitrarily to changes in the network. Many of the new applications discussed in Chapter 8 cannot easily adapt to changes in available bandwidth or network delay. Adaptive applications can adapt, but may be able to adapt only to limited range of behaviors. So although TCP/IP will work just fine at gigabit speeds for the kinds of networked applications we use today, it is imperfectly suited to supporting some of the new applications we can foresee using in the future. These applications will want a form of flow and congestion control that is closer to open-loop control, with fairly predictable bandwidths and delays.

Experiments with Multimedia and IP

Two incompletely answered questions are exactly how adaptable new applications will be to changes in bandwidths and delays and how much changes have to be constrained.

To try to learn answers to these questions, a number of experiments have been done sending real-time traffic like video and audio over IP. These experiments include use of the vat and nevot voice and video conferencing systems on the DARTNET testbed, the DECspin® conferencing system developed by Digital Equipment Corporation, and a conferencing system developed at INRIA in France [Schulzrinne 1993]. The experiments have ranged from small-scale conferences over half a dozen sites to successfully transmitting a lecture to a few hundred sites scattered all over the Internet. The goal of these experiments has been to see how much (if anything) needed to be added to the basic IP best-effort service to support real-time applications like voice and video.

All of the applications are adaptive applications as described in Chapter 8; they adapt to network delay by changing their playback point. What researchers found was that, using adaptive applications, they can do credible voice conferencing and useful (though less good) video conferencing over today's Internet. But there are frequent glitches. For example, the transmission of a lecture to hundreds of sites on the Internet completely overloaded some Internet paths. In a conference between two computers in the same city, researchers found that, to achieve good-quality voice, the playback point had to be set to over six seconds. Multimedia traffic does need some guarantee from the network about available bandwidths and delays to perform well. Similarly, to avoid overloaded links, the network needs some way to limit the number of multimedia sessions trying to use a link.

Multiple Receivers and Multicasting

Chapter 8 observed that a number of applications are one-to-many or few-to-many applications, where one or a few sources are sending to many receivers. A very efficient way to support this type of transmission is to use *multicasting*. Multicasting is an internetwork service that permits sources to send a single copy of a datagram (or cell) to an address that causes the datagram to be delivered to multiple recipients. Multicasting is far more efficient than requiring sources to send individual copies of a message to each recipient. If the sender transmits multiple copies, then some links in the network will have to carry the same message (to different receivers) multiple times. Under multicasting only one copy of a message will pass over any link in the network, and copies of the datagram will be made only where paths diverge. Furthermore, there is an obvious performance improvement for the sender if it need send only one copy of a message, even if the message is going to thousands of receivers.

Local area networks have supported multicasting for many years. For networks where machines share a common cable, multicasting is easy to support. A specially addressed packet can be read off the wire by multiple hosts. Similarly, wide area networks, like satellite networks in which all receivers can hear all transmissions, can easily support multicasting.

Extending multicasting capabilities to internetworks, however, has been achieved only in the past few years, primarily through the work of Deering [1991; 1988]. Essentially what Deering devised was a method for routers to figure out dynamically how to forward the datagram. The basic idea is that, when a router gets a multicast datagram, the router examines its routing table to figure out how it would transmit to the *source* of the datagram. If the datagram came in via the path the router would use to send to the datagram's source, then the router forwards the datagram out its other interfaces, otherwise the datagram is discarded.[10] This algorithm results in the routers dynamically generating a tree-shaped delivery graph from sender to all the recipients. Of course, some multicast datagrams need not go to all the networks in an internetwork. To allow individual networks to express interest in receiving multicast datagrams or a desire not to receive them, Deering has defined extensions to routing protocols to allow networks to advertise (through their routers) whether they wish to receive datagrams sent to particular multicast groups. Furthermore, to allow hosts on networks to indicate whether they wish to receive a particular multicast group, there is a protocol called the Internet Group Message Protocol (IGMP). Parts of Deering's work are now part of the TCP/IP protocol suite.

A nice feature of Deering's approach is that routing information for a particular multicast group is shared. There is no need to set up explicit delivery trees for each sender. The trees are implicitly computed when multicast datagrams arrive, and if trees from two different sources overlap, the same routing information can be used.

It is now possible to do multicasting on networks and internetworks, but there remains an unsolved problem: reliable multicasting. Although reliable multicasting can be done in a number of ways, all have very serious limitations that make them inappropriate for a general solution. The central problem is that reliable transmissions require that receivers acknowledge the sender's transmissions. This means that a sender must keep track of all recipients of its transmissions, even if there are several hundred recipients. The central goal of multicasting was to reduce the load on the sender by making it possible to send datagrams to one address and let the network distribute the datagram to all recipients. The requirement for acknowledgements upsets that goal. There are some smart schemes for reducing the number of acknowledgements (such as multicasting acks and having hosts that hear an acknowledgement suppress their own acknowledgements), but the need to track all the recipients remains.

Thankfully, to date, almost all applications that require multicasting are applications like voice and video, which can tolerate at least a little bit of loss.

---

[10] This algorithm is an extension of Dalal and Metcalfe's work on reverse path broadcasting.

So the current focus is on trying to minimize (but not eliminate) loss in multicast delivery.

Multiple Receivers and Heterogeneity

Providing internetwork support for multicasting is only the first step in the problem of delivering service to multiple receivers. The next, and equally difficult, step is dealing with the fact that receivers can be heterogeneous.

To take a simple example, consider a video transmission to multiple receivers. Some receivers may display the output in black and white whereas others will display the image in color. Less bandwidth is needed to deliver images to the receivers using black and white. Indeed, a receiver is probably displaying only black-and-white images to minimize the bandwidth required to receive the video (the receiver may be at the end of a low-bandwidth link).

This example suggests that a flow may behave differently for each receiver: providing high-bandwidth color video to some receivers and low-bandwidth black-and-white video to others. The implication is that any setup procedure must be able to accommodate receivers with differing needs.

10.6. Converging on the Shape of Gigabit Protocols

It is time to pull together the various threads in this chapter. It seems likely that gigabit networks will be internetworks like those of today: different gigabit networking technologies interconnected by some sort of router. Furthermore, based on recent work in protocol performance it is clear that today's protocols can transmit and receive data at gigabit rates.

However, today's datagram protocols do not completely address the needs of gigabit networks because they cannot provide performance guarantees. Applications like file transfers will be quite comfortable with algorithms like slow-start, which adapt to changes in available bandwidth, but a video application will not be happy if its bandwidth is suddenly chopped in half. At the same time, the ability of applications to adapt to more modest changes in bandwidth (and delay) suggests that modest extensions to the datagram networking paradigm might achieve the kinds of guarantees applications require. Keep in mind that one goal of gigabit networking has been to integrate new protocols with existing ones so extending a popular approach like datagram networking has the appeal of building on a known and working architecture.

Although there is still much work to be done, this line of thinking appears to be leading the data communications community to converge slowly on a general model of how flow and congestion control might be done in gigabit internetworks. Currently, this model appears in a number of different proposals using different terminologies. This book uses the terminology described in this section.

The flow and congestion control model works in terms of *flows*. A flow is a delivery graph from a sender to one or more receivers. Packets transmitted by the sender are carried down the graph, through various routers inside the internetwork to the receiver(s).

Traffic within a flow is divided into two types: guaranteed packets and best-effort packets. Guaranteed packets must be delivered according to some time constraint and with high reliability. Best-effort packets are delivered to the best of the internetwork's ability, after the needs of the guaranteed packets have been met. Furthermore, the model assumes that a single flow may mix guaranteed and best-effort packets. In other words, an application may transmit a mix of guaranteed and best-effort data to achieve the type of flow it requires.

It is usually assumed that to be able to send guaranteed packets over a flow, some sort of negotiation must occur between the sender, receiver(s), and the internetwork. During this negotiation, the sender tells the internetwork how it will *shape* the transmission of its guaranteed packets. In other words, the sender has some mechanism to ensure its traffic will look a certain way. Given information about how the sender's traffic will behave, the internetwork then arranges for individual networks (e.g., DQDB networks or HIPPI networks) and routers to schedule the flow's traffic such that the traffic has a guaranteed delay.

Most versions of the model assume that best-effort packets can be transmitted at any time, without advance reservation.

Few proposals say so explicitly, but the assumption is that the way to discourage applications from asking for guarantees they do not need is to charge the applications for guarantees.

Summarizing this model, one can see that it has three elements:

1. *Traffic shaping*. The sender has some way to describe the shape of transmission behavior of its guaranteed packets and to monitor its transmission behavior to ensure it keeps to that shape.

2. *Special queueing schemes*. Routers have a scheme for managing their queues so they can make performance guarantees. Similarly, local subnets have mechanisms to allow them to make guarantees.

3.   *A setup mechanism.* There is a mechanism to request guaranteed ser-
     vices from the internetwork, with the concomitant supporting features
     to allow the internetwork to decide whether to accept the flow.

The justification for this model comes from a variety of theoretical work
that has shown that certain combinations of particular traffic shaping schemes
and particular queueing schemes can guarantee performance. Perhaps the most
general result is that of Parekh [1992], which proved that, if a sender characterizes its traffic using one of the most flexible variants of the *leaky bucket* traffic
shaping algorithm and routers use a queueing scheme known as *fair queueing*, it
is possible to give firm guarantees on the delay that any packet will take through
the internetwork.

The next three chapters will examine pieces of this model in detail and consider some important variations and alternative schemes.

10.7. Summary

Today's protocols, with modest extensions to deal with sequence space
issues, will scale up to sending at gigabit rates. Techniques such as header prediction, caching, and combining checksum and copy loops have been shown to
achieve high performance.

But today's protocols cannot provide all the services required of the new
applications we expect to deploy on gigabit networks. New applications will
require tighter bounds on available bandwidth and delays through internetworks.
To provide these services, today's protocols will have to be enhanced.

Further Reading

A book on practical protocol performance remains to be written. Indeed,
most operating system texts, even the good ones, barely discuss the issues related
to implementing networking protocols. This chapter was really able only to
scratch the surface and much was left out. Probably the most notable work left
out is Peterson's [1990] work on the *x-kernel*, which is an attempt to build a protocol toolkit that makes it easy to write protocols with high performance.

The two most careful studies to date of TCP protocol performance and processing costs are Clark et al. [1989b] and Pasquale and Kay [1993].

Jain [1991] has written a good book on performance analysis which is
essential reading for anyone reading protocol performance results. Unfortunately, all too many protocol performance results are from poorly designed tests

and are at best useless and at worst misleading. (My favorite example is the scientist who measured throughputs of several different protocols over an FDDI ring and then, because they did not achieve 100 Mb/s throughput, claimed that none of the protocols was good enough. FDDI performance can be tuned for either high bandwidth or low delay around the ring. In other words, 100 Mb/s throughput may not possible if the FDDI is not configured for it. The scientist had no idea how his FDDI network had been configured and dismissed questions about configuration as "irrelevant.") Jain's book is a good guide to detecting such silliness.

Recently, another approach to multicasting called *core-based trees* has been proposed [Ballardie 1993]. Core-based trees have designated multicast servers, which serve as the core of a multicast distribution system. Data to be multicast is sent to the servers for multicast distribution. The developers of core-based trees have suggested this scheme may scale better to large internetworks than Deering's approach.

Chapter 11

Traffic Shaping

11.1. Introduction

The last chapter explained that congestion control in gigabit networks will probably be achieved with a mix of traffic shaping, queue management, and call admission (using setup protocols). This chapter studies the particular problem of traffic shaping.

The basic idea behind traffic shaping is that a source promises the network that the traffic a flow sends into the network will conform to a particular shape. The network uses this information to decide whether to accept the flow and, if it accepts the flow, how to manage the flow's traffic. A simple way to think of traffic shaping is as a set of rules that describe a flow's traffic.

11.2. Why Shape Traffic?

Traffic shaping has three major purposes. First, it is a way for a flow to describe its traffic so the network knows what kind of traffic to expect. Second, given a description of a flow's traffic, the network can determine if the flow should be allowed to send. Third, given a description of the flow's traffic, the network can periodically monitor the flow's traffic and confirm that the flow is behaving as it promised.

Regulating Traffic

Why does a flow need to regulate its traffic? Consider the following situation: a flow agrees with a gigabit network that the flow will transmit data no faster than 100 Mb in a second. Now contrast two transmission patterns: one in which the flow transmits a single 100 Mb packet every second, and another in which the flow transmits a 1 Kb packet, every 10 μs. Both transmission patterns are within the agreed 100 Mb per second, but their effects may be very different. In particular, the single large packet may cause problems. A 100 Mb packet may be too big for the buffer space in a switch. Unless the packet can be broken apart, it will take 100 ms to serialize onto a gigabit link and may interfere with the timing of other traffic. In short, one can see that how a flow injects its data into the network can be as important as the amount of data it sends.

Deciding Whether to Accept a Flow's Data

When a flow is being established, a switch or router in the network may be asked if it has the capacity to forward the flow's data. For example, in the last paragraph, it was observed that a switch may be unable to buffer a 100 Mb packet. By providing a description of its planned behavior, a flow makes it possible for a network to decide whether it has the facilities to support the flow.

Policing a Flow

Finally, it must be possible to see if a flow is indeed shaping its traffic in the way it promised when the flow was set up. A misbehaving flow can disrupt the traffic of other flows. Looking at the example one last time, if the flow promised to send 1 Kb packets and a node gets a 100 Mb packet, it knows the flow's traffic does not conform to the promised shape. A good traffic shaping scheme should make it easy for nodes inside the network to detect misbehaving flows. This activity is sometimes referred to as *policing* the flow's traffic.

Properties of a Good Traffic Shaping Scheme

To fullfill all these needs, a good traffic shaping scheme should have the following properties:

1. The shaping scheme should be able to describe a wide range of behaviors. Chapter 8 suggested that applications will vary widely in the way they send data, and a good shaping scheme needs to characterize this diversity.

2. The shaping rules should make it easy to describe traffic patterns to the network.

3. The shaping scheme should be easy to police.

Furthermore, it would be nice if shaping schemes for cell networks could be implemented in hardware. Processing small cells separately will likely continue to be difficult for most computers, so putting the shaping scheme in hardware would be useful. If the packet sizes are large, then the shaping scheme can be implemented in software.

The rest of this chapter will examine various shaping schemes that have been proposed, according to these criteria. The discussion will start with some simple schemes that are easy to describe, implement, and police but are rather limited in their abilities to describe traffic and work up to more sophisticated schemes. Most of these schemes work equally well for packets or cells, and unless the scheme is specific to cells, the term *packet* will be used to mean packet or cell throughout this chapter.

11.3. Isochronous Shaping

The simplest traffic shaping schemes simply try to shape all traffic into isochronous flows, with regular amounts of data being emitted at regular intervals. (Recall that Chapter 8 defined *isochronous media* as media with regular time intervals between samples at output. An *isochronous flow* has regular time intervals between samples as they are sent into the network.)

Simple Leaky Bucket

The original leaky bucket scheme was proposed by Turner [1986]. His goal was to find a way to shape bursty traffic into a regular stream of cells.

Conceptually, a simple leaky bucket shaping scheme works as shown in Figure 11.1. Each flow has its own leaky bucket. When data is to be sent over on the flow, the sending host places the flow's cells into bucket. Cells drain out the bottom of the bucket and are sent on the network at rate ρ. The rate is enforced by a regulator at the bottom of the bucket. The bucket size, β, limits how much data may build up waiting for the network. If the flow presents more data than the bucket can store, the excess data is discarded.

The primary effect of simple leaky bucket shaping is to coerce a bursty source of data into a flow of equally spaced cells, each cell being emitted $1/\rho$

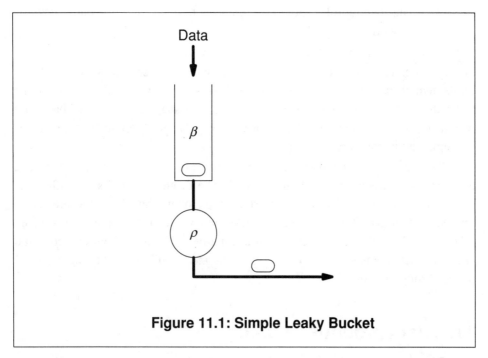

Figure 11.1: Simple Leaky Bucket

units of time after the last one (unless no data is in the bucket). Thus, the network knows that the flow will never inject traffic faster than rate ρ. The effect of the bucket size, β, is both to bound the amount of delay a cell can incur before getting into the network and to limit the maximum burst size the sender can try to send. (Bursts bigger than β will cause data to be discarded.)

Simple leaky bucket was designed for cell traffic, but it can also be used to regulate datagram traffic. The easiest way to think of leaky bucket used for datagrams is to assume that the bucket size β and rate ρ are measured in bytes. When a flow sends a datagram of size d, it tries to place the datagram into the bucket. If there are d bytes of space in the bucket, the datagram is placed in the bucket; otherwise it is discarded. When the datagram gets to the bottom of the bucket, the regulator holds the datagram for d/ρ time units before sending the datagram. As before, data is injected into the network at a rate of ρ.

The major appeal of simple leaky bucket is how easy it is to implement. In a cell network, each flow's traffic can be managed by a simple FIFO buffer with a timer set to go off every $1/\rho$ units of time. Whenever the timer goes off, if there is a cell at the start of the FIFO, the cell gets sent. A simple leaky bucket is equally easy to describe and police. A flow's pattern is described simply by ρ and if a flow ever sends two cells together in less time than $1/\rho$, the flow is violating its promised traffic pattern.

(r,T)-Smooth Traffic

The (r,T)-smooth algorithm was developed by Golestani [1990b] as part of his work on *stop-and-go* queueing algorithms (which will be considered in the next chapter).

In an (r,T)-smooth traffic system, a flow is permitted to inject no more than r bits of data into the network in any T bit times. T is a fixed constant throughout the internetwork. The ration, r, varies on a per-flow basis. If the next packet to be sent over the flow would cause the flow to use more than r bits in the current frame, the flow must hold the packet until the next frame starts. A flow that obeys this rule is said to have traffic that is (r,T)-smooth.

One can think of (r,T)-smooth traffic shaping as a slightly relaxed form of simple leaky bucket. Rather than sending one cell of size c every $1/\rho$ time units, the flow can send Tc/ρ bits of data every T bit times.

One major limitation of this scheme is that one can never send a packet larger than r bits long. (Technically one could send a packet $2r$ bits long, with r bits at the end of one cycle concatenated with r bits at the start of the next cycle, but philosophically, the algorithm is designed to treat each time cycle as independent, and so there is no guarantee that the bits would stay together through the network. Hence the limit is r bits.) Therefore, unless T is very long, the maximum packet size may be very small. Unfortunately, as we shall see in the next chapter, the *stop-and-go* queueing scheme prefers to keep the value of T rather small, to minimize delays. As a result, (r,T)-smoothing is a traffic shaping policy somewhat more suitable for cells than for datagrams.

Like the simple leaky bucket, the (r,T)-smooth scheme has the virtues that it is easy to describe a flow's behavior to the network and easy for the network to check. And a flow's traffic can be regulated by a simple bit counter that is refreshed every T bit times.

Limitation of Isochronous Shaping

Isochronous shaping schemes are easy to implement and lend themselves to easy descriptions and traffic policing, but they have a major limitation. The range of behavior that they can describe is limited to fixed-rate data flows. Variable-rate flows must request data rates equal to their peak data rates. Having the network allocate capacity for a flow's peak rate is wasteful, because a variable-rate flow only rarely sends at its peak rate.

11.4. Isochronous Shaping with Priority Schemes

To avoid giving up the simplicity of implementation of the isochronous shaping schemes, some researchers have proposed combining isochronous shaping schemes with *priority schemes*.[1]

The basic idea behind priority schemes is that every packet is tagged with a a bit pattern that tells the network how upset the flow's application would be if the packet was lost. If the network finds itself congested at any point, it just discards some or all of the traffic that is marked as less important.

Priorities are appealing because a number of applications that use high-speed networks can recover quite well from loss. For example, video is often sent in structured groups of packets. Recall the MPEG example in Chapter 8. Within a group, some packets are far more important than others. For example, losing **I** frames affects picture quality more than losing a **P** frame because the **I** frame can serve a reference point for creating several frames. However, if all **B** frames were lost, an observer would notice. A few packets can be lost, but not too many of them.

Another reason priority schemes are appealing is that some forward error correction schemes (such as the cell recovery schemes described in Chapter 3) make it possible to recover from the loss of a few cells. ATM supports a two-priority scheme using the CLP bit.

How Prioritizing Is Done

The essential idea is that when a flow exceeds its rate, the excess packets are given a lower priority. If the network is heavily loaded, these packets will be preferentially discarded. The decision about which priority to assign to a cell can be done in one of two places.

The sending application can mark its own packets or cells. Because the application presumably knows which data units are less important, it can mark

---

[1] Some literature uses the term *coloring* to convey the idea that the priority scheme is not a strict priority scheme (i.e., that packets colored red and green may have different priorities at different places in the network). However coloring has unfortunate overtones (the quality of service given to a packet is determined by its color), so the term *priority* will be used in this discussion.

the less important ones with a lower priority. For example, some bits in a voice sample can be dropped with little loss of voice quality. If the application separates those bits into separate cells, it can mark those cells with a lower priority.

The other option is to have the network mark the cells. The network watches the flow's packets or cells as they enter the network. If the flow is exceeding its promised rate, the network marks enough of the flow's cells so that the remaining high-priority cells are within the promised rate. This practice is probably useful only for policing, as the network typically does not know the relative importance of each cell or packet to the application. However, as a policing scheme it is very customer friendly. If the network is underloaded, the customer's excess cells will get through. The customer is penalized only in periods of high network load.

An Aside about Priority Schemes

For a variety of reasons, many users get very emotional about priority schemes, because they object to the network discarding their data. My favorite story on this subject is the video codec designer who reportedly said: "I write very good compression algorithms. If there were any bits you could throw away, my codec would not have sent them in the first place."

This fear is irrational. Certainly, if the network does packet recovery so a lost packet can be recovered, one should not care if the network occasionally loses a packet. Furthermore, today's data networks routinely throw away packets under overload and force hosts to recover from the loss. Priority schemes actually improve the situation by allowing the applications to manage their loss, so they can recover more easily from the losses.

Limitations of Priority Schemes

There are at least two more reasonable concerns about combining priority schemes with isochronous traffic shaping. One concern is that the amount of traffic that can be guaranteed is rather low: typically no more than 50% of the total bandwidth of a link. The reason for this restriction is that the likelihood that a low-priority packet will get through needs to be quite high, or no one will bother to mark any packet as low priority. To ensure that low-priority traffic is likely to get through, a large part of the bandwidth of each link needs to be kept free for low-priority traffic. Whether this limitation is important is unclear — it may be that the amount of traffic that needs to be guaranteed is small enough that 50% of the bandwidth is enough to satisfy all needs.

The second concern is how easy it is to selectively discard packets. Many communications devices use FIFOs to store queues of packets. FIFOs are memories that can be accessed only at front and back. So when a device determines that it is overloaded and needs to discard some low-priority packets, it will be unable to look inside its queues to locate and discard the low-priority packets. The implication is that such devices may have to anticipate increased load and discard the low-priority packets as they arrive (before they are queued). It is not clear how effective such anticipatory schemes can be. However, the scheme of isochronous shaping combined with priority schemes is sufficiently flexible that a number of vendors are using it in their first-generation cell switches.

11.5. Shaping Bursty Traffic Patterns

Although isochronous shaping with priorities appears to be a useful service, some traffic shaping schemes can support a far richer range of traffic patterns than isochronous shaping. Because they describe the traffic patterns more accurately, these schemes can make it possible for the network to allocate resources more efficiently.

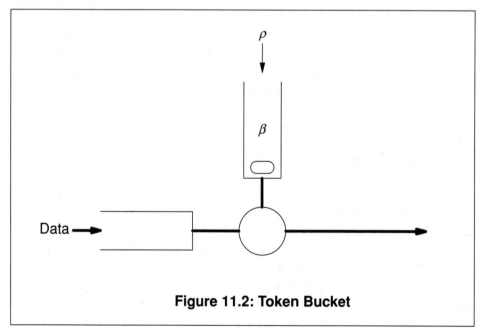

Figure 11.2: Token Bucket

Token Bucket

Token bucket is a variation on the simple leaky bucket. As shown in Figure 11.2, token bucket changes the simple leaky bucket scheme so that, instead of placing a flow's data into the bucket, the bucket is used to manage a device that regulates the flow's data.

In a token bucket system, the rate, ρ, is the rate at which tokens are placed in the bucket, which has capacity β. If the bucket fills, newly arriving tokens are discarded. When a packet is sent it is placed in the buffer on the left. To transmit the packet, the regulator must remove a number of tokens equal to the packet size from the bucket. (In cell networks, each token is equal to one cell.)

The effect of token bucket is a very different type of traffic shaping from simple leaky bucket. To see why this is so, consider trying to send a packet of size b tokens ($b < \beta$) under the following three scenarios:

1. *The token bucket is full.* The packet is sent, and b tokens are removed from the bucket.
2. *The token bucket is empty.* The datagram must wait for b tokens to drip into the bucket, at which time it is sent.
3. *The bucket is partially full.* There are B tokens in the bucket. If $b \leq B$, the datagram is sent immediately; otherwise it must wait for the remaining $b - B$ tokens before being sent.

The examples highlight the key difference between simple leaky bucket and token bucket. Whereas simple leaky bucket forces bursty traffic to become a steady stream, token bucket permits burstiness but bounds it. So where simple leaky bucket guarantees that the flow will never send faster than ρ worth of packets per second, token bucket merely guarantees that the burstiness is bounded so that the flow never sends more than $\beta + \tau/\rho$ tokens worth of data in an interval τ and that the long-term transmission rate will not exceed ρ.

Another difference is that token bucket has no discard or priority policy. Simple leaky bucket throws away data or marks with a lower priority any data that overfills the bucket. Token bucket discards tokens and leaves to the flow the problem of managing its transmission queue if the flow starts overdriving the regulator.

Like simple leaky bucket, token bucket is easy to implement. Each flow needs just a counter to count tokens and a timer to determine when to add new tokens to the counter.

Policing the flow, however, becomes a bit more difficult. The problem is that, in any period of time, the flow is allowed to exceed rate ρ by β tokens. So, if the network tries to police flows by simply measuring their traffic over intervals of length τ, a flow can cheat by sending $\beta + \tau/\rho$ tokens of data in every interval. (This is cheating because the flow would send data equal to $2\beta + 2\tau/\rho$ tokens in the interval 2τ, and it is supposed to send at most $\beta + 2\tau/\rho$ tokens worth of data.) So the network needs a more sophisticated policing scheme, one capable of examing a flow's behavior over longer periods.

Token Bucket with Leaky Bucket Rate Control

Token bucket is more flexible than simple leaky bucket but has one potential problem. If a flow has been idle for a while, its bucket will fill. When the flow begins sending again, it can conceivably send up to β tokens worth of data on the network without stopping. In other words, the flow can hog the network until the token bucket is emptied. As earlier chapters have already noted, allowing one flow to consume all the bandwidth is harmful. Cell switches do not respond well to steady streams of traffic heading for the same destination. Long bursts of high-priority traffic may interfere with other high-priority traffic. And long bursts can encourage super-token behavior in LANs. So we would like to limit how long a token bucket sender can monopolize the network.

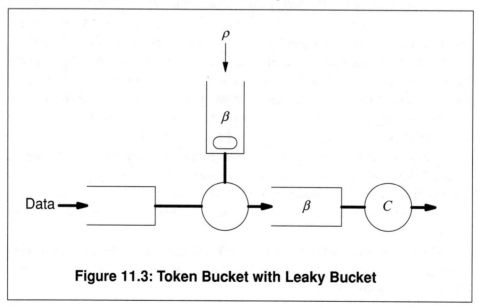

Figure 11.3: Token Bucket with Leaky Bucket

One option is simply to limit the size of β, but that is arguably too restrictive. The network may not mind getting a lot of data close together from a flow, provided there is some space for other traffic. Instead, researchers have developed a traffic shaping scheme that uses a token bucket combined with a simple leaky bucket. This scheme is shown in Figure 11.3.

The token bucket on the left side works as before with rate ρ and size β. But when the regulator lets data through, the data is then placed in a simple leaky bucket (also of size β), from which the data is drained at rate C. For this scheme to make sense, C should be substantially greater (faster) than ρ, because the goal is to make the scheme behave like a token bucket but with a little bit of interleaving. This scheme permits bursty traffic but regulates it so that the maximum transmission rate at any time is C while the long-term average has an upper bound of ρ.

In terms of implementation, this variation requires more work than token bucket. Each flow requires two counters and two timers (one timer and one counter for each bucket). Policing remains hard, although confirming that the flow's data rate does not exceed C is easy.

11.6. Summary

There is a diversity of traffic shaping schemes. This chapter has illustrated the range of shaping schemes with several examples. The assumption in this chapter has been that a more accurate description of a flow's traffic pattern helps the network more effectively manage its resources.

The simplest shaping schemes such as simple leaky bucket can describe only fixed data rates. Priority schemes can make the traffic descriptions more general, by combining high- and low-priority traffic within a flow.

Slightly more complex schemes, exemplified by token bucket and token bucket with a leaky bucket rate control, make it possible to describe more diverse traffic patterns.

Further Reading

Turner's [1986] paper was one of the first to discuss traffic shaping. Petr and Frost [1990] and Shacham and McKenney [1990] have considered interactions of priority schemes with cell recovery schemes.

Chapter 12

Performance Guarantees

12.1. Introduction

The last chapter sketched out a number of ways to describe how a flow's traffic behaves as it enters a network. The assumption motivating these schemes was that, by asking sources to provide information about a flow's behavior, it would be possible to construct networks that could guarantee performance for individual flows.

The purpose of this chapter is to verify that assumption, by presenting a number of ways that networks can manage their traffic. Each of these schemes is capable (at least under special conditions) of giving performance guarantees to flows.

Another way to think about the work presented in this chapter is to recall that Chapters 3 and 7 discussed the possible importance of serialization delay in achieving guaranteed services. One of the underlying assumptions in that discussion was that routers and switches would recognize time critical packets and treat them preferentially. This chapter explains how routers and switches manage their traffic so they can decide which packet or cell to send next over a link.

Essentially, every traffic management scheme involves *queue management* in the devices connecting networks, possibly combined with controls (e.g., MAC layer support) within each network. The network-specific support for guarantees that different technologies can offer was discussed earlier in the chapters on network technology, so this chapter will focus on queueing management in the devices.

In almost all cases, the proposed queueing schemes can be used for either cells or variable-sized packets. As a result, except where there exist important differences between the cell and packet versions of a scheme, this chapter will not distinguish between cells and packets and will use the term *packet* to generically refer to packets and cells. Also, to simplify terminology, devices that forward packets will be referred to as *routers*, unless the particular example only works for cell switches.

12.2. Terminology and Issues

Queues can be managed in a wide number of ways. Different methods for managing queues have different effects on the traffic that flows through the queues and place different requirements on the system implementing the queueing. To try to characterize these effects for guaranteed flows, a body of terminology has developed.

Statistical vs. Deterministic Guarantees

First, it is useful to consider the type of guarantee a queueing scheme can provide. Some schemes can provide *deterministic guarantees*; others offer only *statistical guarantees*. Deterministic guarantees take the form of a promise that all data will arrive within a delay, D, of being transmitted. One might also guarantee that a flow will have access to at least B bits per second of bandwidth at all times or that loss would not exceed some value. Statistical guarantees promise rather that some (typically very large) percentage of the data will arrive within the delay D or that the average bandwidth available to the flow will be ρ bits per second. Whether statistical or deterministic guarantees are to be preferred is a debated topic.

The general argument in favor of statistical guarantees is that permitting occasional (if rare) exceptions to the promised delay or loss rate or data rate provides useful flexibility. Also, statistical guarantees typically give far lower values for delay, because they need not worry the about rare worst case delay. Proponents of statistical guarantees point out that the experiments with adaptive applications show that applications are flexible enough to accept statistical guarantees.

In general, the argument for deterministic guarantees states that they allow for simpler attachment of hosts to the network. Instead of having to worry about statistical intervals, the receiving device knows exactly when to expect its data. A major limitation of deterministic guarantees is that they tend to require more complex (and expensive) queue management mechanisms to implement.

Conservation of Work

Another way to distinguish among queue management schemes is by whether or not they are *work conserving*.[1] Work conserving systems neither increase nor destroy work in a system (for example, a packet does not leave the server before it has completed service). Furthermore, the server may not be idle if there is work in a queue. Two good examples of work conserving schemes are FIFO and LIFO queues. An example of a non-work conserving scheme is one where a router waits a random amount of time before serving the next packet in a queue, even if packets are waiting in the queue.

From a theoretical perspective, the notion of work conserving systems is important because it has been proven that, given the same input traffic patterns and the same time to service (e.g., forward) each packet, all work conserving systems have identical average queue lengths and waiting times, regardless of the order in which the packets are served. Thus, a system designer who proves that a proposed queueing scheme is work conserving can draw on a whole body of existing work to determine buffering requirements and delay times for the device.

It is widely believed that work conserving schemes are better for serving bursty data traffic, though the justification for this view is unclear. (Most data communications experts would not recommend putting LIFO queueing in routers, but LIFO is work conserving.)

What Is Guaranteed

Applications typically want guarantees for three properties of a flow: the worst-case loss rate, the worst-case bandwidth, and the worst-case queueing delay. These three properties are closely related.

With the low loss rates of gigabit media, the effective loss rate for a flow is determined primarily by two factors. First, packets may effectively be lost by arriving too late to be useful. The degree to which packets arrive late is determined by queueing delay. Second, packets may be lost because routers get overloaded by too much traffic and their queues overflow. Queue overflow is a function of how well the bandwidth is allocated.

Allocating bandwidth is a matter of determining (by either estimating or counting) how many flows are going through a path and making sure that the

---

[1] Queueing theorists define work conserving systems different ways. The definition here is from Kleinrock [1976, p. 113]. For an alternative definition, see Wolff [1989, Chapter 10].

average sum of their data rates does not exceed the link bandwidth. If the flows' aggregate data rate is less than the link bandwidth then all their traffic can get through. One concern, however, is that a general result of queueing theory is that the closer the sum of the flows' data rates are to the link bandwidth, the longer the queues have to be in the routers attached to the link.

The size of a queue is important for two reasons. First, from a theoretical perspective, queue lengths and queueing delay are related. The maximum time a packet can wait in a queue is largely a function of the number of packets that can get ahead of it in the queue. Second, from a practical perspective, if a queue is too small for the traffic load, then loss will occur. There is a trade-off between queue length and loss rate that has to be balanced.

Because queueing sizes and queueing delays are related, if the queueing delay can be computed for a given traffic load, then the amount of memory required for queueing is also known. The effective loss rate is determined by delay and queue sizes, which suggests that delay is the key metric for performance. Once delay bounds are found, queueing capacity can be determined, as can the effective loss rate due to late packet arrivals. Computing delay bounds will be the focus of this chapter.

Integration With Switches and Routers

Most of the algorithms described in this chapter are queue-management schemes. They require switches and routers to regularly examine the queues on each outbound link and decide which cell or packet is to be sent next.

Some queueing schemes can be quite expensive; for example, requiring special table lookups and sorted queues. Typically, extra work makes devices more expensive to build or slower, so it would be nice to minimize the extra cost. Simpler schemes are preferred, where they give service comparable to more complex schemes.

Integration with Different Networks

Even if switches and routers manage their traffic perfectly, traffic still may not achieve performance guarantees, depending upon the performance of the network to which the switches or routers are attached. Recall from Chapters 6 and 7 that only some of the gigabit local area networks were able to provide explicit performance guarantees or bound the maximum time before a node would have access to the network. As a result, it is possible that a router might decide to send a packet, only to have the packet's transmission delayed by the local network's MAC layer access protocol.

One topic to keep in mind when considering the different approaches is how well they accommodate occasional variations in delay due to MAC layer transmission rules.

12.3. Statistical Multiplexing

Statistical multiplexing is a fancy term for taking traffic from a number of sources and forwarding it out the same output line. It is what routers already do. The idea behind statistical multiplexing ideas is to find some way to let routers continue to forward packets essentially the way they do today. The appeal of this approach to the problem is that it keeps routers simple.

All the proposed statistical multiplexing schemes rely, in some fashion, on the strong law of large numbers. The strong law of large numbers states that, given a large set of uncorrelated flows, the total amount of bandwidth required to satisfy all the flows stays nearly constant, even though the individual flows may substantially vary the amount of traffic they send. Intuitively one can see this might be so by noticing that if several hundred applications are sending data through the network, then, at any given moment, a few applications are probably increasing the amount of bandwidth they use, while a few other applications are probably reducing the amount of bandwidth they use. These changes will likely roughly balance each other out. The little bit that does not balance is probably so small compared to a gigabit per second that it does not matter. It is important to keep in mind that this balancing only works if the traffic is not correlated (i.e., each application's traffic is unrelated to traffic from any other application). If everyone on the network is watching the same video program, then no application will reduce its bandwidth when the video applications send more data.

The strong law of large numbers offers a potential way to support service guarantees. If the network knows the approximate statistics of the traffic it is currently handling (both guaranteed and nonguaranteed traffic because we are proposing to handle them together), it can determine if it can provide the requested guarantees for another flow. Obviously these guarantees can be only statistical, but if the behavior of traffic in the network is well understood, the guarantees can be quite good (e.g., 1 error in 10^8 packets).

Keep in mind that, although the strong law of large numbers says that the aggregate amount of bandwidth required is nearly constant, it does not state what the required aggregate bandwidth will be. In fact, for highly variable traffic, especially unguaranteed traffic, the required aggregate bandwidth may be quite large, far more than the sum of the average bandwidths of the flows. To truly understand how the mixing will work requires an understanding of the interaction between the guaranteed flows and the unguaranteed traffic.

Several proposals assume that unguaranteed traffic is purely random. Assuming that traffic is purely random is nice because then the combined traffic of even a modest number of flows will typically obey the strong law of large numbers, and the unguaranteed traffic can be considered as if it were a single well-behaved stream of traffic, unlikely to interfere with the guaranteed traffic. Unfortunately, although random arrivals are a fair model of traffic in telephone networks, it is generally accepted to be a rather poor model of traffic in data networks. Rather, data traffic is known to generally travel packet trains, or correlated clumps of packets [Jain 1986]. A variety of experiments have verified that packet trains, and more generally, correlated traffic, can be found in data networks even when highly loaded with traffic from a very large number of sources. (See, for example, Heimlich's [1989] study of NSFNET backbone traffic, and Feldmeier's [1988] study of route usage in routers.)

Many researchers had hoped and expected that data traffic from a large number of aggregated data flows would still obey the law of large numbers. Unfortunately, a recent study by a team of researchers from Bellcore and Boston University [Leland 1993] strongly suggests that data traffic, even from a large number of flows, does not obey the law of large numbers. Rather, they have showed that data traffic is self-similar, or fractal. Self-similar traffic has the property that aggregated traffic is just as bursty as the individual flows. (The term *self-similar* comes from the fact that if one examines the traffic patterns of the individual flows and the traffic pattern created by aggregating the flows, the patterns are statistically similar to each other.)

An important implication of this work is that proposals that employ statistical multiplexing must assume that data traffic is always bursty, even if the traffic is combined from a number of different sources.

Makrucki's Proposal

Makrucki has proposed a scheme for management of guaranteed flows in ATM networks.[2] Although the proposal is somewhat specific to ATM and will be

---

[2] Most of this work has been presented in the form of proposals to standards committees

described in terms of ATM, it could presumably be extended to cover packet networks as well.

Guaranteed sources are controlled by a leaky bucket with priority. If a source decides to exceed its leaky bucket rate, it must turn on the cell loss priority bit for cells in excess of its rate. If the source fails to turn on the bit, a traffic regulator in the network will detect the extra cells and turn on the CLP in enough of the flow's cells to bring it into conformance. Cells with the CLP bit off are guaranteed to get through. Cells with the CLP bit on may be dropped. Any unguaranteed traffic can be treated as a guaranteed flow with zero guaranteed bandwidth. Its cells are all unguaranteed and the CLP bit is always turned on.

A new guaranteed flow is permitted to start only if, for each link between switches, the sum of the new flow's leaky bucket rate, plus the leaky bucket rates of the existing flows on that link, is less than some (typically) large fraction of the hop's bandwidth between two switches. For example, one might allow new flows until the sum of all the leaky bucket rates equalled 50% of the link's bandwidth.

Queues in the switches have limits on the total number of cells from each particular VCI that can be in the queue at one time. The threshold is based on the number of cells that might appear in the queue if the cell were obeying its leaky bucket transmission rate. If a cell with the CLP bit on arrives when its VCI is over the threshold, the cell will be dropped. Cells with the CLP bit off are always queued if there is space in the queue.

Makrucki has simulated this scheme over a number of small network topologies using random Poisson sources mixed with a few bursty sources. The results suggest that the number of cells with the CLP bit set that are discarded can be kept low (0 to 4%) in most cases, though problem cases like heavily loaded networks (85%) with large bursts and low queue thresholds have very high loss rates (as high as 31%).

Makrucki's scheme is appealing because it is quite simple to implement (a counter per VCI and a FIFO queueing system). A concern is that it may make inefficient use of network bandwidth because of its somewhat conservative loading requirements.

---

and is not easily accessible, but some of the basic work behind these ideas can be found in Makrucki [1991].

Performance Bounds for Statistical Multiplexing

A major concern about Makrucki's simulation work is that it assumes that traffic is largely random (rather than in trains) and the simulations are all done on networks of only one to three switches. The problem with assuming traffic is random has already been discussed. But a growing body of evidence also suggests that, as an individual flow's traffic goes through several routers or ATM switches, it becomes less random. Packet train effects (burstiness) becomes stronger as a flow's path gets longer. Thus, simulations on small networks may be misleading.

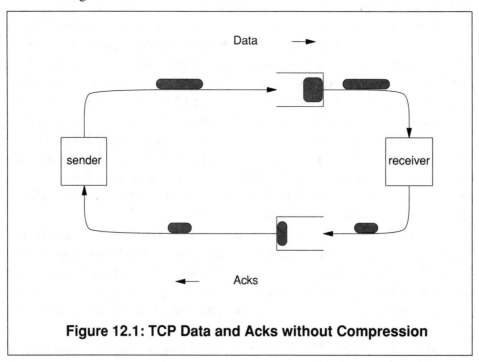

Figure 12.1: TCP Data and Acks without Compression

Simulations by Zhang, Shenker, and Clark [1991] later confirmed by observations by Mogul [1992], have shown that TCP acknowledgements can get compressed together by routers, with the result that when sources receive the compressed set of acknowledgements, they send out bursts of TCP data packets, which can overload router queues, causing the routers to discard packets. Acknowledgement compression is illustrated in Figures 12.1 and 12.2. In Figure 12.1, regularly spaced TCP data is being transmitted along the top path, and acknowledgements are being returned along the bottom path. The spacing of acknowledgements reflects the spacing of the data segments, and the sender

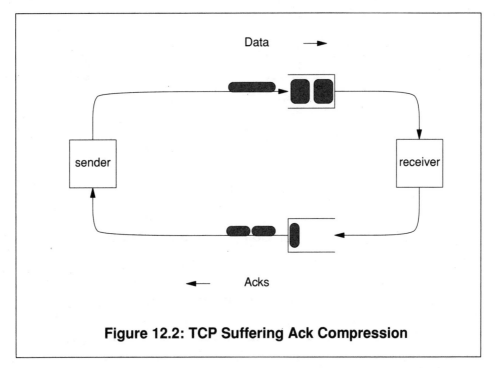

Data →

sender

receiver

← Acks

Figure 12.2: TCP Suffering Ack Compression

generates a new data packet every time an acknowledgement is received, so transmission proceeds smoothly. In Figure 12.2, however, the acknowledgements have been compressed, causing the sender to transmit data in bunches that threatens to overload the queue in the path on the top. The cause of acknowledgement compression is traffic from other connections that interferes with the spacing of the acks.

Less is known about the behavior of traffic in switches. It is clear, however, that traffic can become less random. Figure 12.3 illustrates an example, in which cells from connection 3 get moved closer together as they go through the switch, effectively increasing their burstiness to switches farther away. Kurose [1992] has developed rough approximations of per-flow performance bounds that suggest this kind of bunching occurs.

Work by Cruz [Cruz 1991a; Cruz 1991b] has shown that bunching is generally a function of the number of hops in a network and that, in the worst case, performance can be truly awful. Cruz studied the situation in which traffic sources were shaped by token buckets with leaky bucket filters (a general source model), and packets were served by FIFO queues. He then proved that, in the worst case, packet bunching occurs at each router, and furthermore, bunches of

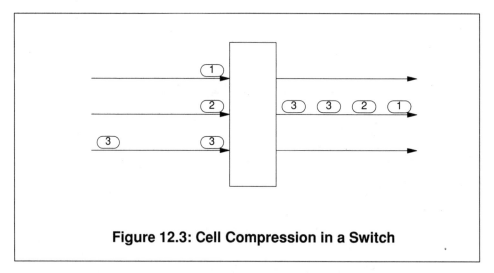

Figure 12.3: Cell Compression in a Switch

packets leaving one router can interfere with other bunches at the next router. The longer the path, the worse the interactions between compressed bunches and the worse the potential queueing delay becomes. Indeed, for a set of k identical sources with token bucket rate ρ and token bucket initially containing δ_0 credits, the maximum per-connection queueing delay is

$$\left[l_*(1 - k\rho) + \frac{\delta_0}{\rho} \right] \left[\frac{1}{(1 - k\rho)^h} - 1 \right]$$

where l_* is the maximum packet size and h is the number of hops in the path. The essential point of the equation is in the second bracketed term. Because ρ is the rate at which each flow sends and $k\rho$ must be less than 1 if the network is not to be overloaded, the right term becomes a very large number (the result of dividing 1 by the very small number $1 - k\rho$ raised to the exponent h). The left term is probably close to 1, so the resulting delay is large and grows exponentially with the number of hops in the path.

How to Deal with Worst Case Performance?

Given the existence of packet bunching, the self-similar nature of data traffic (which implies that packet bunching effects will not be smoothed out in aggregate traffic), and Cruz's disturbingly high bounds on worst-case delays, how can one make statistical multiplexing viable? One option is to more tightly constrain the sources, so that it is harder to form bunches. For example, Makrucki calls for simple leaky bucket shaping.

Another way to deal with bunching is to remix the traffic periodically using some sort of mixing device. Essentially, a mixing device tries to break up bunches by randomly mixing together traffic from several sources. (In cell networks, mixers must take care not to reorder cells within a VCI.) Informal reports of simulations done at Bellcore by Woloszynski suggest that mixers can make traffic substantially more random. Making traffic more random tends to make statistical multiplexing more viable, because the traffic becomes more predictable.

Mixers need not be separate devices. They can be incorporated into routers. For example, the input port controller of the MONET switch discussed in Chapter 5 is a mixer.

Interval Bounds

Another concern about statistical guarantees is that most of them are expressed in terms of connections with infinite lifetimes, whereas most flows exist for a finite time. For example, Nagarajan and Kurose [1992] describe a case where the statistical loss guarantee for infinitely lived flows is a loss of no more than 1 in 10^3, but for flows of just five minutes in duration, over 40% have loss rates that exceed this value. A voice application designed to handle a 10^3 loss rate would be nastily surprised by this "guarantee." More broadly, this example points out the need to clarify the interval over which a guarantee is good. Just as simply stating that a flow will generate data at 100 Mb/s is not enough to characterize a flow, providing a statistical loss guarantee is not enough. The guarantee needs to indicate the time interval over which the guarantee will hold (e.g., the loss rate over a two-minute period will never exceed 1 in 10^3). These guarantees are sometimes referred to as *interval-based guarantees*.

What Role for Statistical Multiplexing?

Recall that using statistical multiplexing to provide flow guarantees works only if the law of large numbers applies. In other words, a network using statistical guarantees can work only if a large number of uncorrelated flows exist in the network. However, it is easy to cite examples where the flows through a router will be correlated (e.g., if lots of the flows are related to a single multimedia conference), or where the number of flows will be small (e.g., a line used to carry a few flows, each consuming a few hundred megabits of bandwidth). Clearly, statistical multiplexing will not solve all the problems of providing performance guarantees. So why even consider it?

The major reason for considering statistical multiplexing is that, compared with the other solutions (discussed later), it is by far the simplest to implement. In particular, it does not require tracking information on a per-flow basis. Furthermore, there will be places in the network, particularly in high-speed backbones, where traffic will likely take the form of a large number of flows. In these high-speed backbones, there is an interest in keeping the designs of routers (or switches) simple, because simple designs (especially designs that do not require a lot of per-flow overhead) are usually faster. So an important part of gigabit internetworks, namely the backbones, could benefit substantially from using statistical multiplexing, if mechanisms can be found to manage the burstiness of data traffic.

12.4. Weighted Fair Queueing

Fair queueing is an idea originally developed by Nagle [1987] and then substantially revised and refined by Demers, Keshav, and Shenker [1990].

Nagle was interested in solving a particular problem in congestion control. Assume we have a router attached to a link whose bandwidth is oversubscribed by unguaranteed traffic such as TCP traffic. As discussed in Chapter 10, TCP implementations are expected to reduce the rate at which they send in the face of congestion. But suppose that one greedy rogue TCP connection does not reduce the rate at which it sends. What tends to happen is that the well-behaved TCP connections will reduce their sending rates to accommodate the unreasonable demands of the greedy TCP connection. Nagle wanted to find a way to manage the bandwidth of the oversubscribed link so that the greedy TCP connection would suffer and well-behaved TCP connections would get good service.

Nagle's solution was to require routers to maintain a queue for each source host and to forward the packets at the start of the queues in round-robin order. Empty queues are skipped, so given *n* active sources, the effect of the scheme is to allow each source to send one packet in every *n* packets sent over the oversubscribed link. A nice feature of the scheme is that, if a TCP connection does not scale back its sending rate to 1 in *n*, then its queue, and only its queue, in the router will overload. This phenomenon is sometimes called *isolation*, because the effects of being ill-behaved are isolated to the ill-behaved connection.

Nagle's initial proposal had a number of important limitations. First, it ignored packet lengths, so a TCP that sent big packets got far more bandwidth than a TCP that sends small packets. Second, it was quite sensitive to the patterns of packet arrivals. A packet that arrived into an empty queue just after the queue was examined in the round-robin cycle had to wait until n other queues had been examined before being sent.

To remedy these problems, Demers, Keshav, and Shenker developed a revised version of fair queueing. Central to the revised version is the notion of bit-by-bit round-robin service. As its name implies, bit-by-bit round-robin service can be thought of as serving n queues in round-robin order, sending one bit from each queue that has a packet in it. Clearly this scheme is more fair than doing round-robin by packet, because it takes into account packet length and requires a packet to wait, at worst, $n - 1$ bit times before it starts to be sent.

Given a particular bit rate and a count of the number of active connections, it is possible to compute when the last bit of the packet of length l would have been sent under bit-by-bit round robin. Demers, Keshav, and Shenker proposed ordering the transmission of packets according to the time by which their last bit should have been sent. One can show that this scheme is asymptotically the same as bit-by-bit round robin.

The scheme is not identical to bit-by-bit round robin because, in the worst case, a packet may leave somewhat later than it would under bit-by-bit round robin. To see why this might be so, consider a case where the router has to pick the next packet to send. It may be that the next packet that would have gone out via bit-by-bit round robin has not yet arrived at the router! The service rules state that the router should simply pick the packet from its queues that has the soonest delivery time. However, particularly if it is big, the transmission of this packet may delay the forwarding of a yet-to-be received (small) packet that would have gone out first under bit-by-bit round robin. One can prove, however, that no packet is delayed from when it should have been sent by more than the maximum packet size of the network.

One limitation of fair queueing is that it gives every host the same fraction ($1/n$) of the bandwidth. In many cases, this equal division may not be desirable. For example, forcing a supercomputer or file server to use no more bandwidth than an individual's workstation is usually not reasonable. A simple extension to fair queueing is to divide the bandwidth up into m-bit cycles, where m is more than the number of queues (n), and then allocate the extra bits to those hosts that deserve extra bandwidth. This extension is called *weighted fair queueing*.

The final extension to the scheme is to allocate bandwidth by flow rather than by host. This extension makes weighted fair queueing into a scheme for dividing up bandwidth among flows that pass through a router.

Parekh's Thesis

Because it isolates flows from each other's traffic, one might suspect that weighted fair queueing can give strong performance guarantees to flows. This is indeed the case, and was proved by Parekh [1992].

Parekh proved that, given a flow, i, whose traffic was shaped at the edge of the network by a token bucket with leaky bucket rate control and a network that did weighted fair queueing in all its nodes, the queueing delay (D_i) suffered by data sent in flow i has an upper bound of[3]

$$D_i = \frac{\beta_i}{g_i} + \frac{(h_i - 1)l_i}{g_i} + \sum_{m=1}^{h_i} \frac{l_*}{r_m} \tag{12.1}$$

where β_i is the flow's token bucket size, g_i is the weighted rate given to the flow (it must be greater than or equal to ρ_i, the rate at which the flow's token bucket fills), l_i is maximum packet length for the flow, l_* is the maximum packet length permitted in the network, h_i is the total number of hops taken by the session, and r_h is the outbound bandwidth at hop m. Furthermore, this delay bound is valid, even if none of the rest of the traffic through the networks is shaped at all. This result is important and worth taking some time to explain. We will consider each term separately.

First, consider a network in which the packet length is negligible. Assume that, at some time, all the flows are quiet and have full token buckets. Then all the flows empty their buckets onto the network and continue sending, as fast as they can (i.e., at rate ρ_i for flow i). One can prove that this scenario will maximize the queue lengths in the network. Now consider a situation in which for every flow the leaky bucket rate, C, is infinite and $g_i = \rho_i$. In other words, there is no limit on the leaky bucket rate into the network and the rate at which the network drains data from the session's queues is the same rate at which the session fills its bucket. Further assume that the values of the ρ_is add up to the total bandwidth of each hop in the network. It should be clear that the burst of data represented by the flow's bucket size (β_i) will never drain out of the network, because the network is running at capacity, and as fast as data is drained from the flow's queues, at rate ρ_i, new data is injected by the flow at rate ρ_i. As a result, the flow's delay through the network is the bucket size divided by the token bucket rate, or

---

[3] This equation is a variation on Eq. 4.36 of Parekh's dissertation. Parekh has confirmed that this version of the equation is also correct.

$$\frac{\beta_i}{\rho_i} \qquad (12.2)$$

The first term of Eq. 12.1 is this term generalized for a rate, g_i, which must be greater than or equal to ρ_i.

The next step is to treat the packet size as nonnegligible. Recall that under fair queueing a packet may be delayed from its appropriate transmission time by up to the maximum length of a packet (l_*). The time that this delay takes is the length of the packet divided by the bit rate (r_m) at the hop where the packet is being delayed, so the maximum possible delay through all the hops (h_i) taken by the flow is

$$\sum_{m=1}^{h_i} \frac{l_*}{r_m}$$

which is the third term of Eq. 12.1. Finally, there are some possible packetization effects within the flow, which are bounded by the second term of Eq. 12.1.

Equation 12.1 is important for a number of reasons. First, and most important, it says that using the most general shaping and admission scheme (token bucket with a leaky bucket regulator), strong guarantees on delay bounds can be given, even if the rest of the traffic on the network is not shaped. This result is somewhat surprising and therefore very interesting.

Second, the queueing required in the network is proportional to the worst-case delay. In particular, the queueing required in the network for flow i is approximately $g_i D_i$. (Parekh gives a more exact definition of the queue length but several pages of text are needed to explain it.)

Third, the result is easy to compute. One could very easily compute a delay bound while setting up the path for a flow.

Fourth, it highlights the issue of serialization effects and the relationships between the packet sizes on a network and delay suffered by a session. As bit rates get large (as $r_m \to \infty$), the last term drops away and the equation becomes

$$\frac{\beta_i}{g_i} + \frac{l_i}{g_i}$$

which says that a flow's delay is purely a function of its own bit rate and its own maximum packet size.

Fifth, because bit-by-bit round robin is about as general a scheme as one could hope for, it is suspected that this queueing delay bound plus the nonqueueing transmission delay may be very close to the minimum deterministic guarantee that a network can give. If Eq. 12.1 is the best one can hope for, that is something of a problem, because its delay bounds are rather long. (This topic is discussed in more detail later, under FIFO+.)

Performance Issues

Weighted fair queueing combined with Parekh's result offers the combination of a system that can guarantee each flow a given share of network bandwidth (namely, its weighted fair share) plus a firm delay bound (Eq. 12.1). These are all the properties we have identified as desirable for a system supporting guaranteed flows, so this scheme is very exciting. Unfortunately, it also has some limitations.

Although the delay bound is far better than Cruz's for token bucket through a FIFO queueing network, the delay bounds are still very long. Another limitation is that fair queueing is expensive to implement. It requires that a system be able to map each incoming packet to its particular flow (an $O(\log f)$ operation, where f is the number of flows) and also to maintain a queue ordered on the desired departure time of a packet (typically an $O(\log q)$ operation, where q is the size of the queue). Work has been done to explore which queue ordering algorithms have the best average performance [Keshav 1991] and methods for approximating fair queueing behavior using less expensive operations [McKenney 1991], but fair queueing is still viewed as an expensive algorithm to implement.

12.5. Jitter Control Schemes

Weighted fair queueing can guarantee that the delay a packet experiences will be less than a given value, but so long as the delay is within the bound, it does not guarantee exactly what the delay will be. For example, given a packet sent at time t_0, over a path whose minimum delay is d, weighted fair queueing will guarantee the packet will arrive no later than time $t_0 + D$. But individual packets may arrive any time between $t_0 + d$ and $t_0 + D$.

Some queueing schemes will guarantee a much tighter delivery time. So, for example, they may guarantee that a packet sent will arrive at time $t_0 + x$. In most cases, x is not an exact value, but rather a value plus or minus some small value. The amount by which x can vary is called *jitter*. This section looks at two schemes to control jitter.

Stop-and-Go Queueing

Stop-and-go queueing was designed by Golestani [1990a; 1990b; 1991] and is designed to be used with traffic that has been shaped to be (r,T)-smooth.

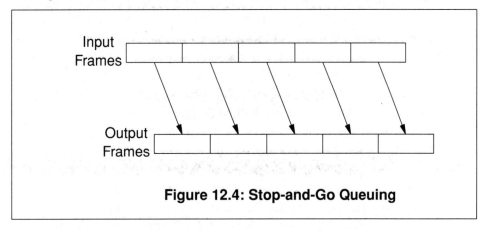

Figure 12.4: Stop-and-Go Queuing

The essential idea is to treat all traffic as frames of length T bits. A frame is considered to have arrived at a router only when the router has received the entire frame. A packet arriving in a frame cannot be forwarded until the entire frame is received. Stop-and-Go queueing then requires that any packet in the incoming frame be forwarded in the first outgoing frame that starts transmission after the packet's frame has arrived. This forwarding policy is illustrated in Figure 12.4.

Consider the delay, D, experienced by a packet. Define D to be a sum of three values: p, the propagation delay; Δ, a fixed delay; and δ, a small variance. Then observe that, under the queueing scheme described, if a flow is (r,T)-smooth in the arriving frame, the traffic will be (r,T)-smooth in the flow's departing frame. From this observation, two points quickly follow.

First, the fixed delay, Δ, for a flow with a path of length h is bounded by the range

$$hT \leq \Delta \leq 2hT$$

because at best the packet is delayed at each hop by the time it takes to receive its frame, and at worst the incoming frame arrives just after an outgoing frame has started. Because the interleaving of incoming and outgoing frames is fixed, Δ is constant. Note that the value of Δ is also the buffering required for the flow.

Second, the only source of variation in the packet's delay is the result of the packet being placed in a different place in an outbound frame than it occupied in an inbound frame. This means that δ must fall in the range $-T < \delta < T$. To see why this is so, consider the case where the packet enters the network as the first packet in the frame. The greatest time displacement is achieved if, by the time it reaches the destination, the packet is at the end of the frame, resulting in a displacement of $+T$. Similarly, a packet entering the network at the end of a frame can leave the network at the front of the frame, with a displacement of $-T$.

Because the propagation delay is fixed, these points show that a packet's delay in the network is strictly bounded by $p + \Delta \pm \delta$. If T is kept small, then the jitter is also kept small. However, the jitter bound does not come free. The jitter-bounded delay under Stop-and-Go is far higher than the average delay would be if Stop-and-Go were not used. To see why this is so, note that under Stop-and-Go's rules, packets arriving in the start of an incoming frame must be held by a full time T before being forwarded. So all the packets that would arrive quickly (and thus drive the average delay down) are instead being delayed. Furthermore, Parekh has proved that the delay for Stop-and-Go queueing must be longer than that of weighted fair queueing unless Stop-and-Go queueing substantially under-utilizes the network.

A quick outline of Parekh's proof is to view T as a time interval (rather than a set of bits) and note that the output from a token bucket shaped output is (r,T)-smooth if

$$rT \geq \beta + \rho T$$

Solving for T, one finds

$$T \geq \frac{\beta}{r - \rho}$$

So the minimum delay through a Stop-and-Go network is hT. If one assumes the packet effects are negligible, then the worst-case delay through a weighted fair queueing network is defined by Eq. 12.2. So if Stop-and-Go queuing is to have a better delay, then

$$hT \leq \frac{\beta}{\rho} \quad \text{or} \quad h\frac{\beta}{r - \rho} \leq \frac{\beta}{\rho}$$

Solving for r, one finds that r must be greater than $\rho(1 + h)$. Given that ρ is, at most, the average bandwidth of the flow, this implies that r is far in excess of the average bandwidth and therefore wasteful.

Stop-and-Go and weighted fair queueing both require buffer space proportional to the length of the path. One important difference is that Stop-and-Go queueing requires buffering proportional to T, whereas at high speeds, weighted fair queueing requires buffering proportional to l_*, so one would generally expect weighted fair queueing to require somewhat less buffering.

Jitter-EDD

Jitter-Earliest-Due-Date (jitter-EDD) is a scheme proposed by the Tenet group at U.C. Berkeley[4] to limit delay jitter [Verma 1991]. It is similar in spirit to Stop-and-Go queueing but differs in some useful ways in its mechanics.

When a flow is established, jitter-EDD gives each hop in the flow's path a queueing budget, b. Each hop also computes its jitter bound, j, which represents the maximum variation in the time a packet may take to get through the hop's service queues. At each hop, a packet is eligible to be transmitted $b - j$ time units after the packet arrives and must be transmitted by a deadline time of b. When the packet is transmitted, the hop records in the packet's header the difference τ between the actual time transmitted t and deadline b. At the next hop, this difference is added to the hop deadline, so that the packet only becomes eligible for transmission at time $\tau + b - j$, and its deadline is $\tau + b$. Thus the next hop compensates for the queueing jitter in the previous hop. The result is that the flow's jitter at the receiver is determined entirely by the variation in queueing delay at the last hop.

Flows are regulated by a leaky-bucket-like admission scheme, so that packets are generated at rate ρ_i and thus are separated at admission to the network by interval $1/\rho_i$. The forwarding scheme described earlier will preserve this spacing through all the hops, because any packet that gets ahead of the $1/\rho_i$ spacing at one hop, due to the queue jitter, will be delayed at the next hop. Note that if a flow exceeds its agreed-on rate, it may overfill the queue and cause packets to miss their deadlines. To guard against this behavior and penalize flows that send packets faster than their agreed rate, ρ_i, jitter-EDD computes a packet's deadline as the maximum of $\tau + b$, and the deadline time of the last packet in the flow, plus $1/\rho_i$.

Jitter-EDD is very similar to Stop-and-Go queueing. The major difference is that although Stop-and-Go queueing thinks in terms of frames and delays serving packets until their entire frame has arrived, jitter-EDD computes a per-packet delay budget and delays serving the packet until the delay has elapsed. The

---

[4] The Tenet group is part of the Blanca testbed. (See Chapter 16).

queueing and delay bounds are similar.

Do We Need to Control Jitter?

When they were first proposed, Stop-and-Go queueing and jitter-EDD were both very interesting because they presented ways to offer deterministic delay guarantees to flows shaped with simple input shaping schemes. However, now that a more flexible scheme with better delay and queueing bounds exists, namely, weighted fair queueing with token bucket shaping, these two schemes are of interest mostly for their ability to bound jitter. This raises the question of whether jitter control is a useful service.

The question of jitter control is still debated. Proponents of jitter control tend to argue that jitter control minimizes the buffering needed to smooth delay at hosts and generally makes host implementations simpler. Those who believe that jitter control in the network is unnecessary tend to argue that memory is sufficiently cheap that building a design around reducing memory costs is irrational. Furthermore, delivering data within strict jitter bounds does not significantly help host implementations, which must still worry about keeping data timing intact inside the host. (Expressing this point another way, the host already has to worry about internal jitter due to queueing in the local operating system, so stamping out jitter in the network does not eliminate the need for jitter management code in the hosts.)

The memory issue is the more important one. (The benefit of jitter management to host implementations does appear to be small.) Unfortunately it is a hard issue to resolve. Essentially it is an argument about two countervailing trends. The cost of additional memory, c, is dropping fast. The number of hosts attached to data networks, n, is growing quickly. So the issue boils down to determining the value of

$$n \times c \quad \text{as} \quad n \to \infty, \quad c \to 0$$

If this value is large, do jitter control in the network. If it is small, jitter control is not needed. Proponents of putting memory in the hosts will point out that the true test is a bit more subtle, because to reduce memory in hosts, one has to put somewhat more memory into routers, which are also being installed in ever-increasing quantities. Thus, if the number of routers is r, the equation should be restated as

$$(n - r) \times c \quad \text{as} \quad n \to \infty, \quad r \to \infty, \quad c \to 0$$

The equation goes to 0, which would seem to give a clear answer in favor of leaving out jitter control. But the equation is sufficiently abstracted from the original problem to call its relevance into question. So the jury on jitter control is still out.

12.6. Statistical Multiplexing Revisited

Weighted fair queueing, Stop-and-Go and jitter-EDD all suffer from one major problem: although they provide delay guarantees, the guarantees are often very long. For example, an experiment done by Kurose [1993] simulating a four hop path through a T1 network carrying 48 identical 32 Kb/s flows showed that although well over 99.9% of all traffic going through a simple FIFO queueing network arrived within 15 ms, weighted fair queueing would have given a delay guarantee of about 65 ms and Stop-and-Go's delay guarantee would have been in excess of 113 ms. Even though this traffic pattern (largely random traffic at high loads) is likely to make statistical multiplexing using FIFO look very good, it strongly suggests that firm delay bounds may often be far longer than applications wish to accept, particularly given that the three schemes require more overhead in routers than simple statistical multiplexing.

FIFO+

Clark, Shenker, and Zhang [Clark 1992] have developed a queueing scheme called FIFO+ that tries to incorporate the low delays of statistical multiplexing, with some of the delay guarantees of other schemes.

They observed that, because both are work conserving, FIFO queueing and weighted fair queueing have the same average delay times through a network. What distinguished the two schemes was that weighted fair queueing more tightly bounds the worst-case delay. As discussed earlier, the bad worst-case performance for FIFO comes from the chance that, at each hop, a packet may find itself caught behind a burst of traffic from other flows. Over several hops, it is possible to accumulate a large, worst-case delay.

The idea behind FIFO+ is to try to limit the accumulation of delay across hops, to bring down the worst-case delay. The approach is very similar to that of jitter-EDD. Each hop groups flows into *classes*. Each class tracks its average queueing delay for the hop. For each packet, the hop computes the difference between the queueing delay the packet experiences and the average queueing delay for the packet's class. It then adds (or subtracts) this difference from an offset field in the packet's header. Over the hops, this offset will record how far ahead or behind the packet is from its class's average. Each hop is required to schedule a packet in its queues as if it had arrived at the packet's real arrival time plus the packet's offset (which may be negative). The result is that packets that are ahead of average get pushed back in the queue and packets that are behind get pushed ahead.

Simulations by Zhang suggest that FIFO+ gives better worst-case delay bounds than FIFO over paths of more than one or two hops. Furthermore, those delay bounds are lower than those of weighted fair queueing. (Cruz [1992] has done an analytical study that tends to support this conclusion.)

It is important to keep in the mind that FIFO+, unlike weighted fair queueing, is a statistical multiplexing technique. Because it does not provide strict isolation, FIFO+ may occasionally violate its delay promises. Applications that require strict delay guarantees will have to be satisfied with the longer delay bounds of queueing schemes like weighted fair queueing.

12.7. Summary

This chapter has identified two general classes of queueing schemes that, when combined with the shaping schemes described in the last chapter, make it possible to give performance guarantees. Statistical schemes like Makrucki's scheme and FIFO+ give probabilistic guarantees. Deterministic schemes like weighted fair queueing, Stop-and-Go queueing, and jitter-EDD give firm performance bounds.

With the exception of FIFO+, statistical schemes based on FIFO are the easiest to implement but, again with the exception of FIFO+, require traffic to be essentially random and long lived for the guarantees to be valid. We observed some common cases where this assumption does not hold.

Deterministic schemes can give firm performance bounds. One exciting result was the work of Parekh, which combines the most flexible shaping algorithm (token bucket with a leaky bucket filter) with weighted fair queueing to give delay bounds, thus making it possible to offer delay bounds to highly variable traffic sources. Weighted fair queueing simply bounds the maximum delay, but does not tightly bound the interpacket delay jitter. If jitter bounds are desired, Stop-and-Go queueing and jitter-EDD both offer ways to bound jitter, albeit with longer delays than weighted fair queueing.

Because the deterministic schemes tend to give delay bounds that are quite long (far longer than the delay experienced by the vast majority of a flow's packets), the chapter considered FIFO+, a queueing scheme that tries to take advantage of statistical multiplexing, but incorporates an algorithm to compensate for the worst-case behavior of FIFO queues.

Overall, the message of this chapter is tremendously cheering. A variety of choices exist for combining queueing schemes and shaping algorithms into coherent schemes to provide performance guarantees to flows. The remaining problem is developing protocols to establish and route flows. This problem is taken up by the next chapter.

Further Reading

A short overview of some of the problems discussed in this chapter, from a slightly different point of view, is presented by Kurose [1993].

For those interested in a more theoretical treatment, a good understanding of queueing theory is useful. (Queueing theory is the mathematics of the study of queues.) The standard treatment of queueing theory as applied to data networking remains Kleinrock's two-volume work [1975; 1976] even though it is now nearly twenty years old. This longevity probably reflects both Kleinrock's talent for explaining material clearly and the fact that, because Kleinrock was a networking pioneer, the books have a stronger data communications orientation than more recent books. For those interested in a more up-to-date treatment of queueing theory in general, Wolff's [1989] book is good.

A number of approaches to the traffic guarantee problem have not been presented in this chapter due to lack of space. Some of the most interesting are the MARS protocol developed for TeraNet and by Guerin et al. at IBM [1991]. The MARS protocol, described by Hyman, Lazar, and Pacifici [1991] divides traffic into classes based on the statistical profiles of the traffic.

Chapter 13

Flow Setup and Routing

13.1. Remaining Problems

The last two chapters have described two important parts of any architecture to support performance guarantees: the queueing algorithms inside the (inter)network and the traffic rules (shaping) required to make those queueing algorithms work. But a number of loose ends remain.

The three most important loose ends are:

1. *How does an application, or a host acting on an application's behalf, request a flow?* Some mechanism, probably a protocol but at least a data structure, is required to allow an application or host to ask the network for a flow with particular performance guarantees. This mechanism also needs to include some way for the network to accept or refuse the request for the flow.

2. *How does the network figure out whether to say yes or no to a flow request?* The network needs some source of information about current usage to allow it to determine whether to accept or reject a requested flow. This problem is generally considered part of a larger routing problem, in which the network determines if it can accept the flow, and if so, via what path or paths the flow should send its data.

3. *How to support multicast flows?* Many applications require multicasting — the ability of one source to send to multiple receivers. Flows will not be just between two points (source and receiver) but rather from one source to an innumerable number of receivers, who may join or drop out of the flow at any time. So, flows will be tree-shaped distribution graphs rather than point-to-point connections, with guarantees required for each arc of the graph. Also, recall from Chapter 10

that the presence of multiple receivers raises heterogeneity issues. For example, two receivers of a video broadcast may want the video delivered at different data rates.

None of these problems is straightforward, and multicasting makes the first two problems harder to solve.

Currently, proposals exist for data structures and protocols to allow hosts to request both unicast and multicast flows. Only incomplete solutions exist for the problem of routing flows, however, and there is still debate about how to handle multicast delivery of data.

Several proposals are presented in this chapter.

13.2. The Host's Role in Flow Setup

A good place to start the study of flow set up is from the perspective of the host that requests a flow be established. The basic model is the following: an application on the host asks the host operating system (or some setup service on the host) to establish a flow and notifies the operating system of the application's requirements. The operating system translates the application's requirements into requirements for a flow (keep in mind that some of the application's requirements may be met by the sending or receiving operating systems) and sends a flow request into the internetwork. At some point, the internetwork either accepts or rejects the flow and returns some sort of identifier to label datagrams or cells affiliated with the flow. For datagrams, this identifier is typically called a *flow id*; for cells this identifier is the VPI/VCI.

What Does a Request Look Like?

The primary purpose of a request for a flow is to convey a description of the flow's requirements into the internetwork, so that the internetwork can determine if it can accept the flow. The description of a flow's requirements is sometimes called a flow specification or *flow spec*.

There is surprisingly wide (though by no means unanimous) agreement about what a flow specification looks like: it is either one or two values that identify a general class of behavior, or it is a multivalued explicit specification of the flow's requirements. Although these proposals may sound like they are at extremes, in fact they are quite close — the only difference is a question of how many different types of flows there will be.

Those who prefer very small flow specifications with one or two values generally believe that flows can be different in only a small number of ways. The idea is that there will be video flows, voice flows, big file transfer flows, and a few others and their burstiness, delay requirements, and sensitivity to loss will be well known. All switches and routers can be preconfigured with information about the different classes of behavior, and then the flow spec need simply identify which general class of traffic the flow falls into and perhaps indicate its average bandwidth so that, for instance, low bit rate video and high-definition video flows can be distinguished. One can see this approach, for example, in the work of the ACORN project [Hyman 1991].

Those who prefer more complete flow specs argue that the range of flow behavior is application specific (e.g., one type of video encoding may behave differently from another) and therefore the set of classes of behavior will be so big as to be unwieldy. The set of classes will also change constantly as new applications are developed. In this environment it makes sense for each application to describe its particular requirements. Examples of this approach can be found in the RCAP protocol [Banerjea 1991], and the research flow spec defined in RFC 1363.

The two approaches are just different sides of the same coin. Both approaches believe that basic information about the flow, such as its delay and bandwidth needs and sensitivity to loss, needs to be conveyed into the network. The disagreement is only over whether this information can be conveyed in the form of a macro (a class identifier) or must be stated explicitly.

An Example Flow Spec

To give a more concrete example of what a flow spec might look like, let us look briefly at the experimental flow spec defined in RFC 1363, which is shown in Figure 13.1. Ignoring the version number field, which is to allow for revisions, the flow spec serves four purposes.

First, the flow spec characterizes how the flow will shape its traffic. This flow spec uses a token bucket with simple leaky bucket rate constraint.

Second, the flow spec describes the flow's sensitivity to delay and delay variation. This flow spec does not permit applications to specify a maximum delay they will accept, only a minimum delay below which further improvement is not noticed. The logic for not including a maximum delay is that the maximum delay changes according to the context of the application and its user. For instance, consider a video "phone call." If a user in Tokyo is presented with a

bit 0	8	16	24	31
Version		Max. Transmission Unit		
Token Bucket Rate		Token Bucket Size		
Max. Transmission Rate		Min. Delay Noticed		
Max. Delay Variation		Loss Sensitivity		
Burst Loss Sensitivity		Loss Interval		
Quality of Guarantee				

Figure 13.1: RFC 1363 Flow Spec

choice between holding a one-hour meeting with someone in London over a link with a 750 ms delay and flying for most of a day to England to be able to participate in the meeting in person, the user will likely accept the 750 ms delay. But that same delay would probably not be acceptable for a conference with someone else in Tokyo. There's no easy way for an application to guess what the maximum acceptable delay is, so it should just establish the flow. The user can decide if the delay is acceptable. However, note that the application does know (based on human factors) below what point improving delay becomes silly and can provide that information to the internetwork to avoid having the internetwork search for overoptimized paths.

Third, the flow spec describes the flow's sensitivity to various types of loss. Sensitivity is characterized in terms of the maximum number of total losses and maximum number of successive losses (bursts) of packets of the maximum transmission unit size during a particular loss interval. The loss interval is used because long-term guarantees are often not valid during short intervals. (Recall the work of Nagarajan and Kurose mentioned in the previous chapter.)

Finally, the flow spec indicates whether the flow wants a statistical or deterministic guarantee. As Chapter 12 indicated, statistical queueing schemes are likely to be able to offer lower delays than deterministic queueing schemes. This flow spec was designed to permit experimentation with either type of queueing.

How the Network Answers a Request

There are three schools of thought about how a network should answer a request for a flow. The first school believes the answer should be a yes or no answer. The network either can agree to support the flow as requested, or reject it.

The second school believes the network should always establish a flow that represents the best service the network can currently offer. If this best case is not acceptable, the application can end the flow. An intermediate solution between this approach and the first one is to refuse flows that cannot be accepted without modification but indicate what level of service might be acceptable. A serious problem about this approach is that it may be possible to trade off the multiple requirements of the flow in different ways (e.g., more bandwidth for longer delay or higher loss for lower delay) and it is difficult for the internetwork to know which trade-offs the requesting host or application is likely to prefer.

The third school believes that negotiations should be interactive. If the network can accept the flow it does. If it cannot accept, it provides feedback about which parameters in the flow spec were problematic, and the requesting host modifies its request based on the network's feedback. The idea behind this approach is that the application knows which parameters are more important and can modify its flow spec accordingly. However, there is a potential for protracted negotiation in this scheme that some people find unattractive.

There would appear to be a benefit to keeping the flow request and response scheme as simple as possible and just allowing yes or no responses to flow requests (perhaps with hints about what requests might be more successful). However, there remain differences of opinion on this topic.

13.3. Protocols to Establish a Flow

A number of flow setup protocols have been proposed. Some are internetworking setup protocols, and some are proposals for specific technologies like ATM.

General Requirements

In addition to the preceding comments about how a network should respond to requests for flows, there are a few broader requirements on setup protocols.

A setup protocol should be able to easily accommodate multiple receivers for a single flow. It is highly desirable that the setup protocol make it possible to support multiple receivers efficiently with facilities like sharing reserved bandwidth among multiple senders. In a voice conference, few people are typically speaking at any time, even if many people are participating in the conference. Obviously, one would prefer a setup scheme that allows all the senders to share a set of reserved bandwidth equal, to say, capacity for three to five speakers.

The setup protocol should probably set up flows quickly, in tens or hundreds of milliseconds. Users expect delays to be brief when joining a conference or changing their display from one video conference to another.

The setup protocol should result in robust reservations. A setup protocol that results in reservations that are easily lost or ignored is not useful. Whatever reservation scheme is used should have some mechanism to cope with occasional glitches in the network.

It may be useful to be able to change the properties of a flow once a flow is established. A good example of this need is a video phone call in which a user decides she would like a better video quality and requests that the sending application send more bits of video. Suppose the old video rate was about b bits per second and the new video rate will be B bits per second. If the available network bandwidth between the sender and receiver is p bits per second, where p is greater than $B + b$, then the sender can establish a new flow to carry the higher quality video and use the old flow to receive images while the new flow is being set up. But if p is less than $B + b$, then the link can sustain a flow of B or b but not both. Rather than forcing the receiver to stop receiving while the old flow is destroyed and the new one established, it would be useful if the old flow could just have its bit rate increased. An important question is whether the situation of wanting to change the flow's bandwidth over a path with very limited bandwidth will occur frequently enough to warrant the headache of being able to change flow parameters while a flow is in progress.

It may also be useful to support advance reservations. Consider the case of a group of busy executives who schedule a multimedia conference with each other for a given day and time. They would likely be willing to pay extra for the network to ensure that resources are available for their meeting.

A Simple Idea

It is easier to see the relationships between the various protocols if there is a strawman proposal to compare them all against. The particular strawman proposal here is one that a number of different research teams have apparently discussed, though none has written it up as a proposal — probably because of concerns about its limitations. However, the strawman comes very close to being a good setup protocol and nicely illustrates some of the issues.

The strawman proposal is that one enhance an existing internet protocol like IP by adding a flow id field, and a flow spec option that can be sent as part of the IP header. Any sender that wants to establish a guaranteed flow chooses a unique flow id, and starts sending regular IP datagrams with the flow id field filled in. In the first IP datagram sent over the flow, the sender also includes a flow spec for the flow, in the flow spec option.

Routers forward IP datagrams as before unless the datagrams have the flow id field set. If the flow id field is set, then routers forward the datagram based on the information the router has about the flow's requirements. Routers get information about a flow's requirements by reading the flow spec option in the first datagram. If a router receives a datagram with an unknown flow id, the router forwards the datagram as if it were a regular IP datagram, but sends a message to the sender of the datagram asking for a copy of the flow's flow spec. The sender retransmits the flow spec by adding the flow spec option to another IP datagram in the flow. An alternative proposal is for the sender to periodically send a datagram with the flow spec option, say every nth packet. Either approach works, but because in most cases all the routers will know about the flow, having them explicitly request the flow spec if they do not have it seems more efficient.

This scheme has been proposed for datagram networks, but it can also be used for cell networks. Keep in mind that most cell networks require both the delivery of flow information to each switch and the allocation of a VPI/VCI for each hop. As revised for cell networks, the sender places the destination address and flow spec in the first cell and chooses a VPI/VCI that is unique for the first hop in the network. Because VPIs and VCIs are unique per hop, and the sender always knows which VPI and VCIs are in use, it can always choose a unique VPI/VCI.[1] Switches in the path read the first cell to find the destination address

---

[1] Well, almost always. Cell LANs, which may have multiple hosts attached, make allocating VPIs and VCIs a bit harder. But the VPI/VCI space is big enough that each host could have its own portion of the space.

and flow spec, determine the outbound port for the connection, allocate a unique VPI/VCI for that hop, and forward the cell on. Observe that, unlike routers in the datagram case, cell switches cannot recover from crashes because the VPI/VCI typically contains no information about a cell's source, and therefore the switch cannot request a new copy of the flow spec.

This approach has at least five major virtues. First, it is extremely easy to implement. Second, if done carefully, there is no setup delay. The sender can send the setup datagram or cell and then start sending data. Third, multicasting does not require much special handling. Datagrams or cells for setup are simply forwarded down all the paths in the multicast distribution tree. If a flow is rejected down a particular path, one can either notify the source or silently suppress the flow. Fourth, recovery from router failure (at least in the datagram case) is easy. When the router comes back up it will be able to forward the guaranteed traffic while waiting for a new copy of each flow's flow spec. The fifth and final advantage is that, if it wishes, the router or switch may be able to completely ignore the flow spec. For example, a backbone router doing statistical multiplexing could (in most situations) just ignore the flow id and route purely based on a datagram's destination IP address.

However, this strawman setup scheme has several minor but disturbing limitations. In some situations the recovery scheme of just forwarding datagrams to the flow's destination while waiting for a new copy of the flow spec does not work. What if a flow's datagrams would be routed differently if the router had the flow's flow spec? For example, suppose that a router can forward packets to destination X via one of two paths: the usual path is a 100 Mb/s link, the other path is a 2 gigabit satellite link with a long delay. Suppose a flow, f, requires 200 Mb/s of bandwidth and must go over the satellite link. If X crashes and comes back up, it may initially route traffic for f over the 100 Mb/s link, which is both insufficient for f's traffic and also raises the possibility that f's traffic will disrupt traffic of other flows over the 100 Mb/s link. One possible solution is to have special flow ids that forbid routers to forward a flow's traffic if the router has no flow spec for the flow. Note that the problem of routes that are based on the flow's flow spec can also cause trouble for backbones that wish to statistically multiplex.

If flows are allowed to send data immediately after the setup datagram (or cell), refusing a flow requires that the router refusing the flow also be prepared to discard the datagrams that follow the setup. This problem may not seem very important, because it is hoped that refusals will be very rare. But keep in mind that a flow is likely to be refused because the router is already heavily loaded and one probably does not want to add to the router's workload.

A more serious problem is that the scheme does not seem to reflect heterogeneous receivers. It is not clear how to reflect differing requirements of various receivers in this scheme. If one receiver wants just the black and white portion of a video stream and another receiver wants color, they have no way of conveying this information to the network. The scheme also fails to support advance reservations.

Attempts to solve these problems lead to substantially more complex setup protocols. We will look at two of the notable examples: ST-II and RSVP.

Version 2 of the Stream Protocol

Version 2 of the Stream Protocol (ST-II) is probably the most sophisticated internetwork flow setup protocol that has been implemented [Topolcic 1990]. (ST-II uses the term *streams* in place of flows.) As its name implies, it is a successor to an experimental protocol that was used for experimenting with multimedia conferencing in the early 1980s [Casner 1990]. ST-II is really two protocols: a datagram forwarding protocol, called *ST*, and a connection management protocol called the *ST Control Message Protocol* (SCMP). ST just forwards datagrams down routing trees created by SCMP. This section is concerned with how SCMP works.

There are seventeen different SCMP messages, corresponding to different flow management services that SCMP provides. These messages can be used to establish a flow to one or more recipients, remove one or more recipients from an existing flow, add one or more recipients to an existing flow, change an existing flow's flow spec, and manage a flow by doing error recovery and status checks. In ST-II, a flow's distribution graph is source specific — only an individual sender may use a particular distribution tree. If more than one sender is transmitting to a set of receivers, each sender must establish its own flow and distribution tree.

Flow setup is done on a hop-by-hop basis. Each router in the path must negotiate with the routers downstream from it in the flow distribution graph to establish the flow. Most flow setup operations work in two stages: a request from the sender works its way hop by hop down the distribution tree, and then responses from the receivers work their way back up the tree.

To get the flavor of how ST-II works, consider how ST-II sets up a flow. A sender starts the process by sending a CONNECT message, which contains a flow spec, a list of all of the flow's receivers, a flow name (a unique flow id), and a proposed hop id (a hop-specific shorthand identifier for the flow) to the router on the sender's network.[2] The router immediately acknowledges receipt of the CON-NECT message. The router also decides if the proposed hop id is acceptable and, if so, accepts the hop id. If the hop id is not acceptable, the router starts a negotiation with the sender to choose a better hop id.[3] Concurrent with negotiating the hop id, the router examines the list of destinations. If there is a destination the router cannot reach, it sends a REFUSE message for that destination. For those destinations it can reach, the router sorts the destination list by the next hop routers through which each destination is reached. For each next hop, the router determines if it can meet the requirements of the flow spec over that hop; if not, the router reduces the requirements of the flow spec to match the service it can actually achieve. The router then sends its own CONNECT message to each of the next hop routers. Each CONNECT message contains the revised flow spec for the particular hop and those destinations that are reachable through the next hop router. These routers in their turn examine the CONNECT message and decide whether to accept the proposed hop id, and what destinations they can reach.

Eventually, if all goes well, CONNECT messages reach the individual destinations. Each destination examines the version of the flow spec that it receives and either accepts or refuses the connection, using an ACCEPT or REFUSE message. As part of the acceptance process the destination can reduce the requirements flow spec it receives to match its particular requirements (e.g., just black-and-white video). The ACCEPT or REFUSE message works its way back hop by hop to the sender. At each hop, the router examines the message to see which destination has accepted or rejected the flow and if the flow requirements have been reduced. If the destination has accepted, then the flow has been established. If none of the destinations through a router accepts, then the partially established flow is torn down.

SCMP is hop-by-hop reliable. All messages are retransmitted if the next hop does not acknowledge them. Furthermore, once a flow is established, routers participating in the flow keep track of each other, and they can dynamically

---

[2] For simplicity, this example assumes that one router is used to get off the sender's network. If there are more routers, then the sender must generate different connection messages, one for each router, that list the flow destinations reached through that router.

[3] ST-II allows systems remarkable flexibility in how they manage their hop ids. The idea is that each system can allocate hop ids in whatever way makes lookups most efficient, and two adjacent systems have to negotiate a common hop id that is efficient for both.

reroute flows when routers fail and reload information about flows into routers that reboot.

Despite its complexity, ST-II has been implemented by several research projects. Their experiences suggest that although implementable, ST-II is sufficiently complex that it may not be the type of setup protocol one wants to deploy in an internetwork [Partridge 1992c]. One concern is that ST-II has an extremely complex state space, in which a flow could be simultaneously adding new receivers, removing some receivers, and updating the flow spec, which made coding very complex. Another problem is that ST-II does not scale well to large multicast groups, because every destination must be explicitly listed in the CON- NECT message and every destination must acknowledge the CONNECT message. As a result a connection to a few hundred hosts requires the sender to process hundreds of ACCEPT or REFUSE messages. Also, all messages to change streams must originate at the sender, which means the sender must periodically be interrupted from sending to process messages from receivers asking for changes to their branches of the flow.

ST-II was designed for datagram internetworks but fits reasonably well in the cell networking model. ST-II requires that a flow be established before one sends and that senders request flows to receivers. It is not farfetched to think of building an ST-II delivery tree using hop-by-hop cell connections between hops.

Overall, ST-II is probably best viewed as near the high end of setup protocol complexity. Save for advanced reservations, it offers most of the desired services. Receivers can modify flow specs, so diversity of receivers is supported. Multiple receivers are supported. Flows are quite robust. There is some question about how fast ST-II setup times are. Experimental implementations have been somewhat slow but this may simply reflect the maturity of the implementations. However, in supporting all these requirements, ST-II has become a complex and hard-to-implement protocol. Furthermore, its design places an extraordinary burden on the sender to maintain the flow and forces each sender to establish a different flow.

RSVP

The resource ReSerVation Protocol (RSVP) takes a different approach to the setup problem. Instead of having the sender manage the flow, RSVP has each receiver manage its piece of the flow's distribution graph. RSVP was developed by a team of researchers at XEROX and the University of Southern California [Zhang 1993].

In RSVP, senders simply multicast their data flow. It is the job of the internetwork's routing system to decide what, if any receivers should receive the data. Along with their flow traffic, senders periodically transmit *path* messages that include a flow spec describing their flows. RSVP assumes that the flow may be multilayer encoded (such as video) and that there may be multiple flow specs (one for each layer of encoding).

If interested in receiving one or more senders' flows, a receiver tunes to the appropriate multicast group and looks for path messages. Based on the path messages, the receiver decides what part of the senders' flows it would like to receive (e.g., just black-and-white bits or full color) and generates a *reservation* message, which contains a *filter* and a flow spec for each sender's flow. The filter indicates what parts of the individual senders' flows the receiver wishes to receive, and the flow spec describes the properties of the path that each filtered flow will require. The reservation message is propagated in the reverse direction along the route from the sender, through the tree established by the path messages.

There are three classes of filters. In *no-filter* mode, the sender's flow is not filtered at all — all datagrams from any sender are forwarded to the receiver. In *fixed-filter* mode, a sender's traffic is filtered according to a fixed filter for the duration of the receiver's reservation. Finally, in *dynamic-filter* mode, the receiver can change how a sender's traffic is filtered over time.

Filters have three important purposes. First, they provide support for heterogeneity. Receivers at the end of slow links can still participate in flows by using a filter to restrict what portion of a flow is passed to it. Second, dynamic filtering allows receivers to modify flow properties. An obvious case where this would be useful is if the receiver is alternately listening to multiple flows: it can change filters to "drop all packets from sender A" to "accept all packets from sender B" to change which flow it is listening on. Third, filters are used to try to reduce load and improve bandwidth management.

To see how filters are used, let us look at how reservation messages are handled. When a receiver generates a reservation message, the message is forwarded through the internetwork toward the senders. At each router, the reservation message is examined. If the reservation requests no filtering or fixed filtering, the router tries to aggregate the reservation with other reservations with the same filter (or lack of filter). If there already exists a reservation with the same filter for a given sender, then the new receiver can simply be added to the flow distribution tree at the current router. Otherwise, the reservation needs to be forwarded farther up the flow distribution tree.

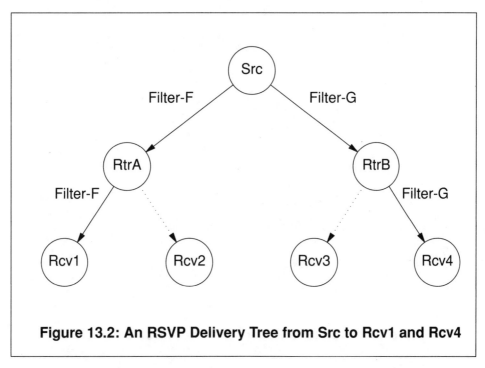

Figure 13.2: An RSVP Delivery Tree from Src to Rcv1 and Rcv4

Figures 13.2 and 13.3 illustrate how this aggregation of reservations is done. Figure 13.2 shows an existing routing tree through two routers (RtrA and RtrB) to two receivers (Rcv1 and Rcv4), who have reserved particular filters. In Figure 13.3, a new receiver, Rcv2, has been added. Note that because Rcv2 requested the same filter (Filter-F) as Rcv1, the reservation message from Rcv2 needed only to go to RtrA, not all the way up to the sender. Comparing RSVP with ST-II, one can see that a sender in RSVP is involved far less in managing the delivery tree.

RSVP uses *soft state* to maintain information about reservations. Soft state is information that is periodically refreshed by interested parties. In RSVP, senders and receivers refresh the state at routers. Senders are required to periodically retransmit path messages to allow new receivers to learn of the flow, to remind routers that the flow exists, and to adapt to routing changes. Receivers periodically retransmit their reservation messages to remind routers of their reservation. An advantage of soft state is that it makes error recovery easy. Receivers or senders that crash stop sending reservation and path messages. So if a reservation is not refreshed within a given period of time, the router discards it. Similarly, if a router crashes, its state will be refreshed by the periodic path and

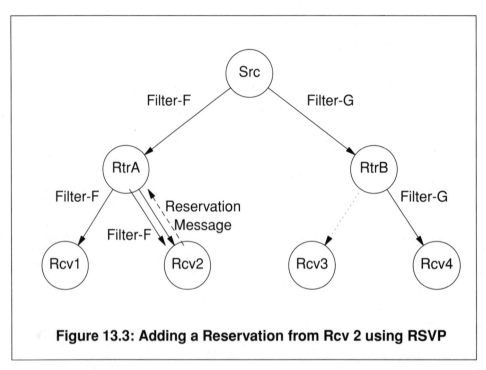

Figure 13.3: Adding a Reservation from Rcv 2 using RSVP

reservation messages when it reboots.

RSVP is less easily made to fit the cell networking model than ST-II. RSVP expects receivers to be able to listen to flows to decide if they want to reserve resources. Most cell network designs assume that senders will establish connections to receivers who want their data.

RSVP falls somewhere between ST-II and the strawman proposal in complexity. It offers the same services as ST-II and like ST-II lacks support for advance reservations. But RSVP allows multiple senders to share the same bandwidth and it places a much smaller burden on the senders.

ATM Connection Setup

Discussion of the ATM connection setup was deferred to this chapter from Chapter 4 so that it could be presented in relation to other work on setup and signalling.

Q.93B is a simplified version of the ISDN call setup protocol, Q.931. When this book went to press, ATM Forum and CCITT were still working on the Q.93B specification, and the specification may undergo substantial revision before it is released in 1994. The presentation here tries to focus on those elements of the protocol that seem least likely to change before the specification is released.[4]

Q.93B supports dynamic creation of ATM virtual channels. If a system needs a virtual circuit to be created to another system, it uses Q.93B to establish the virtual circuit. Once created, the virtual circuit stays open until either it is closed by its users or a network failure occurs. These dynamic virtual circuits (also called *demand virtual circuits*) can be contrasted with *permanent virtual circuits*, which are reestablished after network failures.

Q.93B supports the creation of three types of connections. A requester can establish a unidirection channel to a destination, a two-way channel to a destination (but only if the bandwidth in both directions is identical), or a unidirectional multicast delivery tree.

As currently defined, Q.93B is simply a set of rules for how the sending and receiving ends of a virtual circuit negotiate connectivity with the ATM network. How switches within the ATM network communicate with each other is not standardized. They can use Q.93B or their own protocol. However, whichever protocol is used, Q.93B defines the services the setup protocols must offer.

The exchange of Q.93B messages required to establish a simple one-way connection between a sender and receiver is shown in Figure 13.4. The sender begins by sending a SETUP message. The SETUP message contains information about the call, including a flow spec, which AAL is to be used (and AAL-specific parameters like the largest packet that can be sent if using AAL 5), and the address of the receiver. The network acknowledges the SETUP message with a CALL PROCEEDING message. The primary purpose of this message is to acknowledge the SETUP message but it also contains the network-assigned VCI/VPI for the connection.

Although the flow spec is capable of expressing traffic behavior in terms similar to that of token bucket shaping, the current standard requires that the cell transmission rate be expressed as a fixed rate (e.g., as a simple leaky bucket) and the other fields be ignored. The destination address can be expressed in a number of forms, including E.164 addresses (which one can think of as extended telephone numbers) and IEEE 802 addresses.

The network notifies the receiver that a call is being requested by sending a SETUP message to the receiver. The receiver acknowledges with a CALL PROCEEDING message and then decides, based on information in the SETUP

---

[4] The presentation here is based on the ATM Forum specification of April 1993.

message, whether to accept the call. If the receiver decides to accept the call, it sends a CONNECT message to the network. The network acknowledges the receiver's message with a CONNECT ACKNOWLEDGE and in turn sends a CON-NECT to the sender indicating the call is established. (The sender may optionally acknowledge the CONNECT message.)

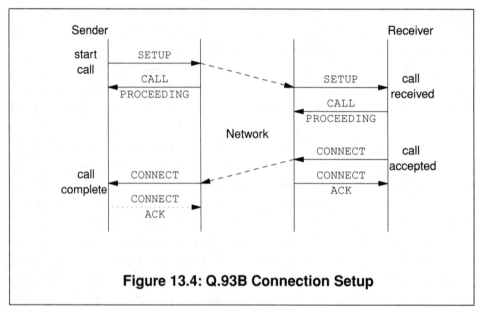

Figure 13.4: Q.93B Connection Setup

If there are errors in the negotiation, the typical response is for the party that detects the error to send a RELEASE COMPLETE message which indicates that the call has failed and all information on the call should be discarded.

To ensure reliable transmission of messages between the endpoints and the network, the SETUP and CONNECT messages are retransmitted if they are not acknowledged after a certain interval. It is not possible to send data until a CON-NECT message is received, so if the network detects the sender transmitting data on the new VCI, this information is taken to be an implicit acknowledgement that the CONNECT message has been received. Q.93B does not state how long it may take to set up a connection, but some experts estimate that over networks larger than a LAN, the setup time may be long (measured in seconds).

Multicast calls are achieved by establishing a one-way connection and then adding receivers using the ADD PARTY message. Multiple new receivers can be added in parallel. All receivers receive the same type of service requested in the original flow spec. Two-way connections are accomplished by including a flow spec for the reverse channel in the initial SETUP message.

As a setup protocol, Q.93B is somewhat minimalist. It supports the essential services. Flow requirements are specified and multicasting is supported. But it also cuts some corners. The setup times may be long, and the bandwidth allocation scheme (fixed bandwidth) is wasteful. In addition, it supports only homogeneous receivers (all receiving the same service). It is unclear whether these limitations will prove troublesome or can be worked around.

It is possible that the long setup times could be effectively reduced by caching connections (leaving idle connections open for some period of time in the expectation another application will start to use them). This technique has been used in the past to try to improve performance of IP over X.25. One problem with this approach is that leaving idle connections around can be expensive in terms of unused bandwidth and idle connection information in switches. A more serious concern about connection caching is that, even if two applications wish to communicate with the same remote system, there is no promise their performance requirements will be the same. A low-bandwidth connection left after a remote login application used it will be of little use to a high-bandwidth file transfer application — the file transfer application will have to request a new connection be established.

The wasteful fixed-rate allocation of bandwidth could be improved by using priorities. However, slow receivers in a multicast group may still be overwhelmed with unwanted bandwidth.

13.4. Routing

ST-II, RSVP, and Q.93B all assume the existence of a routing system that will help them find paths through a network. Unfortunately, building such routing systems is proving difficult.

Historically, routing has been the problem of determining if a path exists between two points in a network. Supporting flows changes routing into a far more difficult problem of determining if a path achieves a flow's requirements. Unfortunately, routing on multiple requirements can easily become an NP-complete problem in the number of links. Therefore the current challenge in routing is to find ways to route flows that are not hideously expensive.

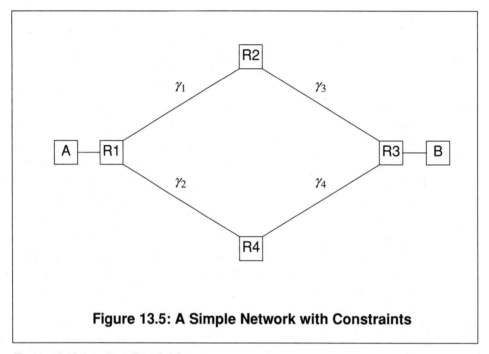

Figure 13.5: A Simple Network with Constraints

Examining the Problem

Considered abstractly, routing is the problem of finding a path through a graph, subject to one or more constraints. (The graph is an abstraction of the network's connectivity.)

Today's protocols, such as the Bellman-Ford algorithm (implemented in protocols like the Routing Information Protocol (RIP)) and Dijkstra's algorithm (implemented in protocols like the Open Shortest Path First (OSPF) and Intermediate-System to Intermediate-System (IS-IS) routing protocols), are capable of routing based on one constraint. In other words, given a connectivity graph and a single *metric* associated with each link in the graph, both Bellman-Ford and Dijkstra's algorithms can quickly find the path between two points that minimizes the sum of link metrics in the path. For example, given the simple network shown in Figure 13.5, both algorithms will discover that two paths exist from A to B and choose the path that minimizes the sum of the metrics. Thus if $\gamma_1 + \gamma_3 < \gamma_2 + \gamma_4$, the algorithms will pick the route (A,R1,R2,R3,B); otherwise they will pick the route (A,R1,R4,R3,B).

The major difference between two algorithms is that Dijkstra's algorithm distributes complete routing information to all routing agents, whereas the

Bellman-Ford algorithm tries to minimize routing information by requiring routers to pass along information only about the best routes they are aware of. Both approaches have strengths and weaknesses. Having full topology information, however, appears to be necessary to do routing for flows (see the following discussion) so it may be that approaches based on Dijkstra's algorithm will be preferred for routing flows.

It is important to note that in either algorithm, the metric can be anything. It can measure delay, bandwidth, cost of the link, or any other metric one desires, provided the metric can be expressed as a single (typically nonnegative) number.

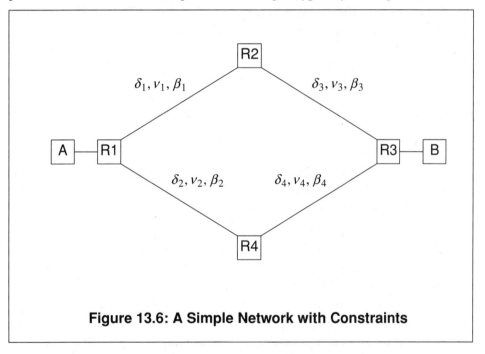

Figure 13.6: A Simple Network with Constraints

Routing for flows complicates the problem in two ways. First, each link has to be described in terms of multiple metrics. Second, whether a link can participate in a path depends on the requirements of the flow being routed.

To illustrate why these changes are a problem, consider the following scenario. Figure 13.6 illustrates the same simple network, but with each link having three metrics: a delay, δ; a delay variance, v; and an available bandwidth, β. Such a multimetric description of a link is sometimes called a *hop spec*. Now suppose that we are trying to find a path for a flow, f, from A to B, which has the requirements that delay be minimized, delay variance be less than v_f, and a minimum bandwidth of at least β_f. Because both Bellman-Ford and Dijkstra's algorithms can minimize only one metric, suppose that we try to find a path by minimizing the delay. It is entirely possible that we will find that the path with the minimum delay has unacceptably low bandwidth or high delay variance. Similarly, if we routed solely on bandwidth or delay variance, we might pick a path with an unacceptable delay.

What is really required is an algorithm that, given a flow spec and information about the links in the network, chooses a path that meets the flow spec's requirements. In this simple example, one such algorithm would be to just compute the combined metrics of all the paths and compare the combined metrics with the flow spec. This algorithm only works for very small networks, however. An algorithm that is efficient for large networks is needed.

Possible Solutions

How might one find an algorithm for routing flows in large networks? A few proposals have been made. All have problems.

One proposal is to find some way to reduce the multiple metrics into one metric. In other words given a flow spec and a complete map of the network (such as the one Dijkstra's algorithm provides), one could examine the capabilities of each hop and based on the flow's requirements generate a single metric for each of the hops. One could then run Dijkstra's algorithm over the network graph, using the flow-specific metric.

This approach is a version of a well-known problem called *policy routing*. Policy routing finds a path based on Boolean constraints that may differ on a per-flow basis. Because all the constraints are Boolean, one can examine each hop and generate a cost metric of 1 if the hop meets the constraints and infinity if the hop fails to meet the constraints. (Recall that the routing algorithms find the shortest path, so an invalid path should have an infinite length.) If a valid path exists, Dijkstra's algorithm will find it.

It does not appear that, in the general case, it is possible to completely express the flow's requirements as a single metric. However, some hops can certainly be eliminated from consideration in this fashion. For example, if a flow's required minimum bandwidth is β, one can certainly eliminate from consideration all hops with available bandwidth less than β. Also, it is possible to build networks where certain constraints can always be met. The world's telephone networks, for example, are carefully engineered so that the paths that a phone call may take will meet the delay requirements for voice. It might be possible to construct an internetwork in such a way that meeting a flow's requirements is a matter of solving for a path using just one metric.

If we cannot reduce the problem to one of solving for one metric, maybe we could get the problem down to solving for two metrics. Castiñeyra has developed an algorithm that can find the set of paths that minimize two metrics on moderately complex topologies in less than a second.[5] In this context, *minimizing* has a special meaning. A minimum point is a point a, b such that any point with a better value than a must have a worse value for b and vice versa. So Castiñeyra's algorithm generates a list of potential minimum-cost paths. How one chooses a particular path from this list has not yet been determined.

Multicasting and Multiobjective Routing

If finding a path for a flow between two points is hard, discovering a delivery tree from a source to multiple destinations which meets the divergent requirements of the different destinations is even harder.

Q.93B supports delivery to multiple destinations but completely ignores the problem of differing receiver requirements.

If one examines ST-II carefully, ST-II's approach is that each hop computes the point-to-point path and then combines all destinations that share the same next hop. Note, however, that ST-II does not know each receiver's requirements until the receiver gets the CONNECT message and can modify the flow spec, so the path ST-II chooses for establishing the path may not be optimal. Hence, ST-II supports differing receiver requirements, but may overallocate resources in the network.

Because it is receiver based, RSVP will typically find the best path between the existing delivery tree and the receiver. And because the receiver initiates the reservation, the path will reflect the receiver's particular requirements. Intuitively, one would expect this approach to better use the network than ST-II, but this problem has not yet been seriously studied.

13.5. Summary

For people interested in seeing multimedia networking made into a reality, this chapter is probably somewhat depressing. Even though Chapters 11 and 12 sketched out mechanisms to support real-time flows in a network, this chapter

---

[5] Personal communication from Castiñeyra.

says that we do not yet know how to access those mechanisms. The research community is only just getting its hands around the critical problem of handling multicast flows — and routing looks hard.

On the more optimistic side, protocols like RSVP do exist, and there has been considerable work developing flow specs and hop specs to support setup protocols and routing. There are also some promising approaches to routing based on multiple constraints.

Further Reading

Perlman [1992] has written a study on bridges and routers which includes a very easy to understand explanation of Bellman-Ford and Dijkstra's algorithms. The most complete study of multicasting is Deering's [1991] doctoral dissertation.

For two treatments of policy routing, see Estrin [1989] and Clark [1989a].

Chapter 14

Distributed Systems

14.1. Introduction

The preceding several chapters have sketched out most of a network layer cake. Working up from the bottom, various chapters have examined media capable of gigabit transmission rates, the protocols like HIPPI and ATM that encapsulate data sent over the media, the internetworking protocols that allow the interconnection of different networks, and how to connect hosts to such networks. Looking down from the top layer, Chapter 9 discussed how applications may wish to make use of the network. It is now time to look at the piece in the middle: distributed systems.

A distributed system is a programming infrastructure that makes it possible to use a collection of hosts and networks as a single integrated system. The goal of a distributed system is to hide from applications the fact that resources may be scattered across a number of hosts. Distributed systems vary widely in how successfully they achieve this hiding. Some systems are just a simple library of routines intended to make communication between hosts easier, while other systems link the various hosts so tightly together that the applications effectively see one system. These extremes are sometimes referred to as *loosely* and *tightly coupled* distributed systems.

Designing and building distributed systems remains tremendously difficult. Operating system design is influenced by the advent of new types of computer hardware. Networking is influenced by changes in communication technology. Because distributed systems are built on both operating systems and networking, work on distributed systems is buffeted by trends in both fields. (Arguably, distributed systems are also affected by a third field, programming languages, because one of the goals of distributed systems is to make it easier to write applications that use networks.) As Chapter 9 showed, operating systems are changing and this entire book is about how networks are changing. As a result, a lot of stress is being placed upon distributed systems.

This chapter examines the relationship between distributed systems and gigabit networks from three perspectives. First, it will look at the way distributed systems are built today and show how difficult it will be to scale those approaches to gigabit speeds. Second, it will look at alternative ways to build distributed systems that may scale better. Finally, it will look at how to extend distributed systems to support the new services that gigabit networks will make possible.

14.2. Distributed Systems Today

Currently, the field of distributed systems is somewhat chaotic. A number of loosely coupled distributed computing systems are available commercially, but there is still no general agreement about most of the key problems in distributed systems design.[1]

Nonetheless, there is a certain similarity among various distributed systems in that nearly all of them are implemented using one or the other of two communications paradigms: *remote procedure call* (RPC); or *distributed shared memory*. This section looks at both paradigms and considers how they might scale to gigabit speeds.

The Duality of Shared Memory and Message Passing?

RPC is a version of a communication technique known as *message passing*, in which communications between applications take the form of messages. Distributed shared memory is simply a networked form of shared memory. These classifications are notable because of an important, but oft-misunderstood, paper by Lauer and Needham [1978], which showed that shared memory and message passing are equivalent.

---

[1] For example, in April 1992, Andrew Tanenbaum circulated a list of what he believed were generally accepted truths about distributing computing to *comp.os.research*, a mailing list devoted to topics in operating systems research. The result was over 100 responses from leading researchers, violently disagreeing with both Tanenbaum and each other!

Lauer and Needham made two points. First, they proved that shared memory and message passing were *semantically* equivalent. Second, they showed that *on a single system*, shared memory and message passing could, in most cases, have equally good performance.

The importance of Lauer and Needham's result is that programmers can choose whichever paradigm they prefer, message passing or shared memory, confident that neither scheme allows them to solve a problem the other does not. However, Needham and Lauer's result is sometimes misunderstood to say that message passing and shared memory should have the same performance in a distributed system, which is emphatically not the case. Lauer and Needham showed equivalent performance only within a single host. Indeed, an important question in distributed systems design is whether message passing or shared memory will give better performance in gigabit networks.

The Challenge of Long Delays

Chapter 2 observed that gigabit networks get faster by packing bits closer together in the fiber (or wire), but that the time (the *delay* or *latency*) it takes for a single bit to traverse a wire stays about the same. This observation has an important impact for distributed systems, because it says that it will take about the same time to exchange small messages between applications on a gigabit network as it does over a 10 Mb/s Ethernet. Furthermore, because the network can send more bits per unit time and the hosts attached to the network can perform more instructions per unit time, the *relative* delay is increasing.

Table 14.1 Minimum Round-Trip Time in Nanoseconds		
Net Type	Distance (in km)	Time (in ns)
LANs	1.5	17,000
	10	110,000
WANs	5,000	55,600,000
	14,000	155,600,000
1 Satellite Hop	60,000	400,000,000

To see the severity of the delay problem, look at Table 14.1. The table measures the minimum time to send a single bit across a network and get a one-bit answer back.[2] In other words, the table represents the amount of time it would

---

[2] For the local and wide area network calculations, times were derived using the speed of light in fiber (approximately 180,000 km/s). For the satellite link, the speed of light in a

take for a one-bit message to travel from an application at one end of a network to an application at the other end of the network and back again (with zero processing done at the remote end), as seen by the computer waiting for a reply to a query.

One way to put the numbers in Table 14.1 into perspective is to measure the number of instruction cycles that the sending application must wait for an answer to its message. Recall that CPU cycle times are getting as small as a single nanosecond. So the application would wait for between 17,000 and 400 *million* instruction cycles. The last time a careful study was made of the execution times of applications, it showed that the average application performed less than 1 million instructions [Cabrera 1986]. Therefore, in the worst case, a system could probably run tens or possibly hundreds of applications from start to finish in the time it takes to exchange a single pair of messages across a wide area network.

An analysis by Gray [1988] a few years ago came to a similar conclusion. Examining the performance of distributed databases, Gray concluded that network delays were rapidly becoming the largest single cost in distributed systems.

Another aspect of distributed systems to consider is the people using the system. Chapter 8 talked a little bit about user sensitivity to delays. It is worth repeating that people's reaction times to events are measured in tens of milliseconds at the fastest, and that users are often tolerant of delays of hundreds of milliseconds or more.

In other words, human reaction times are close to the network delay times, which leads to odd sensitivities. A user will notice that a program that does 10 RPC calls across a wide area network to a file server is much slower than the same program doing 10 RPC calls across a LAN, because the WAN version will take at least a half-second longer to complete. But if the user used the WAN to log into the remote file server and ran a program on the server, the extra delays across the WAN would simply cause slightly longer keystroke delays. The increase in delay would be so small that the user probably would not notice it.

Human reaction times matter because, fundamentally, computer performance is measured in terms of how fast users perceive their systems to be. So when one worries about distributed system performance, in the end, one is worrying about how fast a system appears to its users. Performance is measured by people. Character echo times across the network will not look slow because a

---

vacuum (300,000 km/s) was used. The two wide area distances are approximately the distance across the North American continent and the distance between New York and Tokyo.

single round-trip delay is small relative to human response times. However, an application that does dozens or hundreds of RPCs will look very slow, because the sum of the RPC times is big enough that people will notice. A useful rule of thumb is that applications are usually more sensitive to delays than people are.

Having briefly tried to get a sense of the delay problem, it is now time to see how the various distributed system paradigms are affected by the delay problem.

Remote Procedure Call

RPC is by far the most popular programming interface for distributed systems. Developed in the 1970s and refined and popularized by Nelson and Birrell [1981; 1984], RPC makes all communication across a network look like simple procedure calls.

Nelson and Birrell's version of RPC posits the existence of *servers*, each of which supports some set of procedures that applications may call. Applications that call on remote procedures are called *clients*. each of which supports some set of procedures that applications may call. When a client needs access to a remote service, it determines (via some mechanism) which server or servers support the desired service and makes a remote procedure call to one or more of the servers.

The mechanics of a remote call are implemented through a combination of a message protocol and programming entry points called *stubs*. To make a remote call, a client application calls on a local stub procedure. To the client, calling the stub procedure looks just like calling a regular procedure, but when called, the local stub encapsulates (or *marshalls*) its arguments into a message and sends the message to a server. When a server receives a message, it unpacks the arguments from the message and calls the actual procedure with the arguments it received. When the procedure completes, the server packages the return value into a message and sends the message to the local stub. The local stub then returns to the application, using the remote return value as the local return value.

Almost all the difficult communication problems, such as making sure that messages get reliably transmitted between client and server, finding the right server to send the message to, and data type checking, are handled by a message protocol between the local stub and the server. As a result, in most RPC systems, a remote procedure call looks just like a regular procedure call.

The genius of RPC is that it hides networking behind a familiar programming interface: the procedure call. Programmers are already accustomed to procedure calls that cause actions outside their application (e.g., system calls) and to handling error values (such as a value indicating that the network has failed) returned by procedure calls. Little in an RPC system will surprise a programmer. Furthermore, RPC explicitly supports heterogeneous computing environments. A program written in one language on one host can easily call a procedure written in an entirely different language on another host, because the stubs will convert between argument formats. With such a familiar and general interface, it should come as no surprise that RPC is by far the most popular programming interface for distributed systems and is used by almost every distributed system.

However, classic RPC is also extremely poorly suited for gigabit networks. Because communication is achieved by sending a message then waiting for the reply, the time for each remote call incorporates at least one round-trip delay. As the relative delay increases, a remote call will look increasingly expensive.

In fact, RPC is already viewed as an expensive way to communicate, and a number of attempts have been made to improve its performance. Most of this work has taken the form of trying to make the RPC stubs faster,[3] which although important, has increasingly little effect as computers get faster. However, a few projects have tried to extend the RPC concept to improve performance over the network. Two are examined here: parallelism and caching. A third approach, called *remote evaluation*, is considered later in the chapter.

Extending RPC — Parallelism

One way to try to improve the performance of RPC is to support parallel remote calls. The idea is to convert sequential calls to remote procedures into parallel calls as shown in Figure 14.1. The figure shows the time taken by three sequential remote calls on the left compared with the time taken by the same three calls done in parallel on the right.

The most general and programmer-friendly version of parallel RPC, called *promises,* was developed by Liskov and Shrira [1988]. The essential idea is that, when a remote call is made, instead of waiting for the reply from the server, the remote stub returns a unique token, called a *promise*. The program then continues execution until the time it needs the data requested in the remote call, at which point it tries to "claim" the promise. If the server has replied before the promise is claimed, then the program immediately gets the result of the remote

---

[3] See for example, Schroeder and Burrow's work [1989] on Firefly RPC.

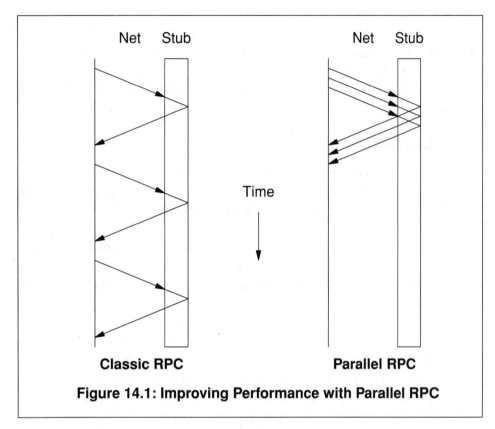

Figure 14.1: Improving Performance with Parallel RPC

call, otherwise the program is blocked until the remote call completes. (Note that promises are very similar to processor scoreboarding of registers, which tries to minimize the effects of delays between processors and their memory.)

A good example of a case where promises work well is searching through a file for a pattern. The program starts by issuing read requests for n blocks in the file and then waits for the first block to arrive. When the program receives the first file block, it requests the $n+1$ block and starts searching the first block. When the program finishes searching the first block, the second block is almost certainly ready to be claimed, and so the program can request the $n+2$ block and start searching the second block. Assuming n is chosen correctly (i.e., that it is approximately the right window size for the delay between the program and the file server it is reading from), the program will never have to wait for a file block after the first one is received.

Promises work well in situations where the program is conducive to parallel implementation. But there are situations where execution must be sequential;

situations in which the program cannot determine its next RPC until it has seen the results of its last RPC. For instance, consider the last example again, but assume that the searching program must first contact a resource server to learn what file server the to-be-searched file is located on. The call to the resource server must be completed before the program can start requesting file blocks from the server.

Extending RPC — Caching

Another way to improve RPC performance is to use caching. Consider the example of searching the file yet again. What if, when the program requested the first block of the file, the RPC stub in the server returned the first block plus n additional blocks? Assuming the local stub cached the extra blocks, the next several requests to read a block could be satisfied by the local stub, without using the network. A nice thing about this example is that the server can compute the optimal number of blocks to return. For instance,[4] if the request took 100 μs to reach the server and it takes about 8 μs to write a block onto the network, the time cost of sending (and having the remote stub receive) n extra blocks is $100 + 8(n + 1)$ μs. But the time cost to the program to request a block that was not sent is 100 μs. Assuming the server can estimate the likelihood that an extra block will be read, the server can compute the cost-benefit equation and solve for n.

In general, caching works well if most data is read-only. If the data changes (and assuming that applications typically want the most up-to-date information) then caching works less well, because servers and clients will have to spend considerable time ensuring that obsolete cached data is purged. Here lies a problem. As caches get larger, the chance that an application on another host will change data that has been cached becomes larger. To illustrate the magnitude of the problem, suppose that there is a 10% chance that if an application accesses one file on a file system, it will access another file in the file system. If the client and server are communicating via a 20 gigabit WAN link and the file system contains less than 40 megabytes of data, it is cost effective to return the entire file system in response to a single read request! If multiple applications are accessing the file system, then the likelihood is that a cached copy of the file system will rapidly become out of date, however, and hosts will have to frequently communicate with the server to check that their cached copies are up to date.

---

[4] This cost-benefit analysis closely follows a talk given by Jonathan Smith at the IRSG Gigabit Workshop in 1990 [Partridge 1990b].

Obviously this situation is hypothetical (20-gigabit WAN links are some years in the future), but it points out the key problem in caching in high-speed networks: to be effective, caches must get quite large, but large caches increase the chance that some data in the cache may be changed and thus can require so much maintenance that the costs of maintaining the cache negate much of the advantage of keeping a cache.

One interesting approach for reducing maintenance costs is called *leases* [Gray When a server sends a piece of data to a remote host to be cached, it also stamps an expiration time on the data. The server guarantees that the data will remain valid and unchanged until the expiration time. Programs that wish to change a piece of data must wait until all the expiration time stamps have expired (or request that the server explicitly ask that all copies be deleted). To check if a piece of cached data is still valid, a host need simply check its expiration time. Because process lifetimes tend to be short, the expiration times can also be short, not much longer than the network delay. The effect is to reduce cache maintenance while ensuring that applications doing writes need not wait terribly long.

Distributed Shared Memory

Distributed shared memory comes in two forms. One form, called *distributed memory*, supports a single memory space that is kept consistent among all hosts. In the other form, called *distributed virtual memory*, applications share selected chunks of a large virtual memory space maintained by the network.

Distributed memory was developed in an era when the time needed to send a message over a local area network was close to the memory access time in many computers. In other words, a message could be sent across a network in about the same time it took to read a word out of memory. This observation led researchers to develop schemes to share a single address space among multiple computers. Whenever a computer updated a word in the memory, all the other computers saw the change too. The act of sending data across a network was converted into the task of writing words into memory. Probably the best known of these systems is MEMNET [Delp 1988], in which a set of IBM PCs attached to a token ring shared a common memory space.

However, computer memory has gotten much faster, and memory access times are now orders of magnitude smaller than the time required to send a message over the network. The increasing relative delays mean that getting a piece of memory from a remote system is increasingly expensive, and keeping copies in sync with each other takes an increasingly long time.

One approach to cope with the delay problem is to use distributed virtual memory. The idea of distributed virtual memory is much the same as regular virtual memory. Data is broken up into discrete chunks that can be selectively retrieved, much as pages of virtual memory can be retrieved from a backup store. Applications can choose to share a chunk of memory, so that if one application changes the memory, the other applications see the change. The advantage of virtual memory is that rather than keeping all memory consistent, virtual memory makes it possible to worry about consistency on a per-chunk basis. This approach makes it easier to use techniques like caching and leases.

By weakening the consistency requirements, network delay problems can often be avoided. Hutto and Ahmad [1990] have developed a type of weakly consistent memory that they call *slow memory*, and have shown that, provided the programmer is aware that slow memory is being used, any algorithm that can be written using regular memory semantics can be implemented using slow memory.

The primary appeal of shared memory is that operating systems programmers have considerable experience with hierarchies of memory with varying access times and transfer speeds. As a result, although the access times over the network may be exceptional, the basic concept is familiar.

A limitation of shared memory is that it is essentially homogeneous — all hosts have to understand the same memory organization and format their data in memory in a common form. One frustration with much of the shared memory work is that it tends to focus on building the distributed memory infrastructure while ignoring the limitations of homogeneous systems. Some work is underway in the Aurora gigabit networking project to study heterogeneous shared memory but it is still in the early stages [Delp 1991].

14.3. Alternative Approaches to Distributed Systems

Neither of the current approaches to distributed systems looks like a perfect match for gigabit networks. RPC has delay problems that are only partially solved by caching and parallelism. Distributed memory does not deal well with heterogeneity. This section looks at some alternative approaches.

Putting the Delay Where Users Will Not Notice — Plan 9

Plan 9 is a research operating system developed and distributed by AT&T Bell Laboratories [Pike 1990; Presotto 1991; Pike 1991]. The name comes from an infamous movie, *Plan 9 from Outer Space*, considered in some circles to be the worst science fiction movie ever produced. (The first paper on Plan 9 was titled "Plan 9 from Bell Labs.")

In brief, Plan 9 posits a computing environment composed of *servers* and *terminals*. Servers come in two flavors: compute servers, which are multiprocessor computers without disk space, and file servers, which are computers whose sole purpose is to manage a large number of disks containing file systems. The terminals are bit-mapped graphics systems. Servers for an organization reside in a computer room, interconnected by a very high-speed LAN. The terminals are connected to a *distribution network*, which is envisioned as a somewhat lower speed network that connects terminals to the cluster of servers in the computer room.

All computation in Plan 9 is done on the compute servers. All files are stored on the file server. The purpose of the terminals is simply to provide a graphical user interface through which users access the computer servers.

The logic underlying Plan 9 is that it is far more efficient, in terms of both capital investment and personnel costs, to buy and maintain shared special purpose hardware to provide the functions of computing power, file storage, and user interface, than to buy and maintain general purpose workstations. There are arguments both for and against this point of view. For example, the difficulties of managing and backing up the disks on dozens (or hundreds) of different workstations have led many organizations to purchase specialized central file servers. However, the widespread use of workstations is, in part, a reaction against the costs and limitations of centralized computing centers, and it is not clear that Plan 9 addresses these problems.

Motivations for Plan 9 aside, from the perspective of gigabit networking, the interesting feature of Plan 9 is that, by concentrating the computing and file servers, it minimizes the delay between computing engines, while increasing the delay between the user's keyboard and the processor that does the computing. The beauty of this scheme is that users are far less sensitive to the network delay between their keyboards and processors than applications are to the delays between applications and file servers.

An important question about Plan 9 is whether it scales well to multiple organizations. The system is currently designed such that a set of servers would provide service to an organization of between a few dozen and a few hundred users. Clearly one cannot scale this design up to worldwide size (although it is fun to imagine building a single worldwide Plan 9 computing center, located, say, in the Arctic to minimize cooling costs). Rather one has to think about interconnecting different organizations' Plan 9 clusters and worry about whether intercluster communication will suffer from network delay problems.

There is no good answer to this question; one can argue either way. On one side, most traffic studies show that the vast majority (90% or more) of all data communication stays within an organization. If this trend continues, the fact that Plan 9 optimizes communication among an organization's servers may outweigh the cost of the occasional long-distance RPC. One can also observe that whatever schemes are found to minimize delay costs can be used between Plan 9 clusters. On the other side, one can point to perceived increasing trends toward an information culture in which a lot of information is stored in repositories outside the local organization. In this world, an increasing amount of communication is with resources outside the organization, which may make Plan 9's cluster approach less useful.

Object-Oriented Distributed Systems

Object-oriented distributed systems like *Clouds* [Wilkenloh 1989], *Emerald* [Jul 1988], and *Cronus* [Schantz 1986] have experimented with extending the idea of object-oriented programming to distributed systems.

In brief, object-oriented programming asks the programmer to program in terms of *objects* and *messages*. An object is a combination of data structures and a set of rules about how to behave in response to messages. To change an object or force it to do something, another object must send it a message. So for example, to increment an integer by 1, a process object sends an increment message to the object that maintains the integer. Examples of object-oriented programming languages include *SmallTalk* [Goldberg 1980], which forces everything into the object model, and *C++* [Stroustrup 1991], which provides object-oriented enhancements to the C programming language.

There is an obvious affinity between object-oriented programming and distributed systems. Both send messages: in distributed systems, applications send messages to each other; in object-oriented systems, objects send messages to each other. An object-oriented distributed system tries to take advantage of this affinity by making the applications and their data structures into objects and making all communication over the network take the form of messages between objects.

Some experimental object-oriented systems have tried to migrate objects within the system so that objects that communicate frequently are close together, thus minimizing delay costs. So far, these experiments have not gone well. Optimizing a dynamically changing communications graph has proven hard. But if someone finds a solution to this problem, object-oriented systems may become very interesting.

Moving Applications to Their Data

RPC, caching schemes, distributed memory, and to some extent, Plan 9 are all attempts to optimize the delivery of data from servers to the applications that use the data. An alternative approach is to try to move the applications closer to their data. Moving applications to the data they use is exciting because one can prove that, for some distributed applications, moving applications to their data will give optimal performance.

Consider an application that meets the following three conditions:

1. The application accesses data and does computation on several different hosts;

2. Only when it reaches a host does the application learn which host it will visit next;

3. The application cannot start its computation on a new host until it has completed at least some of its computation on the previous host.

Examples of such applications include database lookups (where the application must search an index before learning where the next level of the index lies) or looking up a file in a distributed file system (where each directory level may be stored on a different machine). What is the minimum number of trips across the network that the application needs to make?

Expressing this idea slightly more formally, consider an application, A, that visits a sequence of n hosts: $a_1, a_2, \ldots, a_n$, where n may be determined during the computation (i.e., n is not fixed when A starts), a_1 is the host on which A starts, host a_{i+1} is determined only after A reaches host a_i, and the correct evaluation of A on a_{i+1} depends on computation done on host a_i. For convenience (and without loss of generality) assume that each host is distinct and $a_i \neq a_{i+1}$. What is the minimum number of trips between hosts that A must make?

The answer is $n - 1$ trips. The simplest proof is by induction. To take the minimum number of trips to get to a_i, A should take the minimum number of trips to a_{i-1} and then go directly from a_{i-1} to a_i. This statement follows from the fact that A neither knows that it is visiting a_i nor can perform its computation on a_i until it has visited a_{i-1}. One then observes that the minimum number of trips required to get from a_1 to a_2 is one (the direct trip) and the proof is done.[5] If one assumes that A is visiting the various hosts to retrieve data, this proof suggests that migrating A from host to host will give optimal performance. Note, too, that classic RPC would take $2n$ trips, (one trip to a_i and one trip back with the result for every a_i) so the migration approach gives much better performance.

Clearly, not all distributed applications will meet the three conditions (though a fair number do), and it is interesting to observe that, if one removes one of the requirements, the problem of finding an optimal path becomes much harder. Consider removing the second condition and assuming that the application knows a priori at least some of the hosts it will visit. An example of such an application might be some of the modelling applications discussed in Chapter 8 — the programmer may know which supercomputers the application is going to visit, and in what order. The problem of finding optimal paths for this application is NP-complete [El-Dessouki 1978]. So although it may be possible to use the additional information to improve on delay costs, trying to find the best possible route becomes harder.[6] Similarly, if one removes the third condition and assumes that the computation on a_{i+1} is not dependent on the computation of a_i (but might, for example, be dependent on the computation of a_{i-1}), then parallelism could be used to do computations in parallel on a_i and a_{i+1}.

For a fairly wide class of applications, however, the three conditions hold. Accordingly, the next two sections look at ways to implement paradigms that support the migration of applications to their data.

---

[5] There is a subtle nit in this proof. What it really proves is how to minimize trips, not delay. Consider a situation in which the path the network uses from a_{i-1} to a_i is longer than the path that would be taken if the computation stopped at host b, even if no computation was done at b. Such situations exist in real life because networking routing algorithms are not always able to pick the shortest route between two points. But there is no reason to believe that the application is better suited than the network to find the optimal route, so it is probably reasonable to assume that trips can be equated with delay.

[6] But not impossible. Consider that if computers are very fast, it may be worth solving the NP-complete problem, for applications that visit a small number of hosts, because the cost of computing the solution once in advance is much less than the cost of choosing a nonoptimal route.

Process Migration

The most obvious way to move applications to their data is to use *process migration*. In brief, a process migration is a scheme where, when a process needs to access data on a remote host, the current system it is running on sends a copy of the process's running image to the remote host. The remote host then restarts the transferred image. The basic concept is simple, however, making process migration work has proven back-breakingly hard. To quote one team of researchers, "Successful migration facilities are not common in distributed operating systems, due largely to the inherent complexity of such facilities," [Artsy 1989].

There appear to be at least three difficult problems in implementing a process migration scheme:

1. *How to migrate control of a process?* Operating systems keep a lot of control information about processes, such as which files are open, the process's privileges, and information on its relationships to other processes. Migrating this information to other hosts has proven difficult.

2. *How to migrate the binary information, the instructions and data associated with the process*? The method used to transfer the (potentially) large quantity of instructions and data across the network has been shown to have a significant effect on performance.

3. *How to support heterogeneity?* Computer networks have an increasingly heterogeneous mix of hosts attached to them. But process migration exports binary images. How can we make heterogeneity and binary images compatible?

Many process migration schemes also worry about a fourth issue: when to migrate. In this case, however, the migration policy is well defined: migrate whenever the data being accessed is not local.

Migrating control of a process is a thorny problem. The information required to control a process includes data structures like file descriptor tables, page tables, and register variables. Much of this information is not embedded in the individual process but is kept in operating system tables such as page maps, parts of which must migrate with the process. Furthermore, not all information can migrate. For example, if a process is accessing a local frame buffer, one cannot casually move from one frame buffer to another. (We cannot assume the user is willing to run from one workstation to another, to keep observing the screen as the program migrates.)

The most productive approach so far to migration of control information has been a two-pronged approach: work hard to find ways to migrate control information the exported process is likely to access, and use *call-backs* to the original host to access control information that is rarely used. This approach was developed to support process migration in the Sprite operating system [Douglis 1989]. For example, file descriptors were designed so that they could migrate from host to host, but some system calls, notably calls to get the correct time (so that the age of files could be compared using a consistent clock), were sent back to the originating host. The Sprite designers report that call-backs proved infrequent enough that they did not seem to limit performance.

One particularly knotty problem in migration of control is relationships to other processes. If the migrated process is communicating with other processes (which may also migrate), keeping all related processes up to date on where a process is located can be difficult. The current approach is to keep a series of forward references, so that if a process migrates from host A to host B, messages for the process sent to host A are forwarded to host B. In some systems (notably DEMOS/MP [Powell 1983]), the source of the message is also notified that the process has moved and future messages should be sent to B. This scheme means that messages may incur expensive additional time in the network, as they are forwarded from host to host.

Finding effective ways to migrate the binary instructions and data of a process has historically been difficult. Migrating binaries is a two-part puzzle: how to get the process running on its new host as quickly as possible; and how to minimize the cost of migrating the process, for both sending and receiving hosts, while keeping the process running.

Currently, the most effective solution to the binary migration problem is a technique called *lazy evaluation,* developed by Zayas [1987]. When a process is migrated, lazy evaluation transfers the operating system control information and the process's current working set of pages and tells the new host to use the old host as the swap store for the process. This scheme gets the process running quickly, because some of the first information the new host gets is copies of the pages in which computation is currently underway, and tries to minimize migration costs by transferring subsequent pages only as the migrated process swaps them in. As part of his work, Zayas showed that most processes access only a small part of their total image space, so by transferring pages on demand, lazy evaluation minimized use of network bandwidth and the number of bytes that the old and new host had to transfer, and the savings from reducing the transfer size made up for the additional delay in retrieving pages from the old host.

If one tries to scale lazy evaluation to gigabit speeds, it becomes clear that using the old host as the swap space is no longer useful. Looking back at the marginal cost equations for caching earlier in this chapter, it is pretty obvious that sending all the pages of a process, even if most pages are never touched, is far more time efficient than selectively retrieving them. But it still appears wise to transmit the pages currently in use first, to allow the new host to start running the process as soon as possible.

Finally, process migration has to deal with heterogeneity, both in host architectures and operating systems. Heterogeneity is a hard problem and has only recently received attention. However, if one is interested in using process migration to migrate computation to data, then the heterogeneity problem must be addressed. There is no guarantee that the host having the data a process needs to access also supports the same binary instruction format and same operating system as the host from which the process originated.

Shub [1990] has developed a prototype system that supports process migration between heterogeneous host architectures, provided all the hosts support the same operating system. In his system, a program is simultaneously compiled in multiple instruction formats (one for each architecture to be supported). The compiler also includes information about how to map data structures from one architecture to another and how compiled code in one architecture maps to compiled code in another architecture. To migrate a process, the system determines where in its code the process has stopped on the old host and starts the process in the equivalent piece of code on the new host. Data formats are also converted from one host format to the next when the process migrates.

To date, little or no work has been done on migrating processes between heterogeneous operating systems. Because of incomplete support for heterogeneity, process migration cannot currently be used to implement the idea of moving code to the data it wishes to process. However, some ideas from the process migration work appear useful. First, one should make control information as portable as possible, and in those very rare cases where portability is not possible, one can use call-backs. Second, send the code that is currently running first, to minimize startup time on the remote host. Third, after reconsidering the lazy evaluation principle at gigabit speeds, send all the code at the start to avoid the large time costs of going back to pick up additional data.

Remote Evaluation and Late Binding

Arguably, part of the difficulty with implementing process migration is that process migration tries to do too much: pick up an entire running process and migrate it to another machine. What if one tried a narrower approach and migrated only pieces of the process? Perhaps by migrating only select pieces of a process, and leaving behind those parts of a process that are hard to move, migration could be made easier.

The basic work on migrating pieces of a process was done by Stamos [1986]. His idea was to revise the notion of remote procedure call, so that, instead of calling well-defined stub routines at a server, an application would send the server the procedure code to be run. Stamos called this scheme remote evaluation or REV (pronounced R, E, V).

Stamos's original reason for developing REV was a desire to make RPC more flexible. His concern was that programmers trying to design structured applications would find themselves unduly constrained by the limitations of the stub RPC interfaces. REV frees programmers of these constraints by allowing them to determine what pieces of their code run on a given host in a distributed system. Indeed, Stamos solved a number of problems to help give programmers extra flexibility, including not only making it possible to export procedures, but also making it possible to export arbitrary pieces of code.[7]

Beyond making RPC more flexible, REV also can help distributed applications make better use of the network. For instance, consider the example of having to ask a resource manager which file server to use (the example considered earlier when discussing parallel RPC). In an REV system, an RPC can be made to the resource manager to learn the file server, and then the resource manager can in turn directly make an RPC to the file server to retrieve the file. The extra trip back to the originating client can be skipped.

As defined by Stamos and implemented by him in CLU, and implemented by others in Avalon Lisp [Clamen 1989], REV has some limitations. It is programming language and machine specific. So it is even less easy to migrate than binary images, because it can migrate only between two hosts of the same type that support the same programming language environments. These limitations

---

[7] The insight for exporting arbitrary pieces of code is to analyze the piece of code as a block in which some variables are accessed and possibly changed. By analyzing what variables are used and treating them as call by reference parameters to a procedure, one can make the block of code into a pseudo-procedure and export it.

have been addressed in a set of proposed extensions to REV, called *late-binding RPC* [Partridge 1992a].

Late-binding RPC extends REV in two ways. First, it makes procedures machine and operating system independent by exporting an intermediate code representation and a standard interface. The idea of a machine-independent representation builds on prior work, most notably the printer-independent printing language, PostScript®, and an operating system independent management language called NICL [Falcone 1986]. (One important assumption in the late-binding design is that it is worth the cost of interpreting machine-independent code, if it saves just a few, or even one, trips across the network.) Second, late binding allows procedures to be reexported from one host to another, with a structure that allows routines to return execution to whatever host seems appropriate (not just to the host that was visited previously). Using these extensions, late binding shows that the REV approach can be used to migrate selected pieces of a program in whatever pattern seems most efficient.

Because REV is an extension to RPC, all the extensions developed for RPC work with REV. So mechanisms to support parallelism, such as promises, can be incorporated into REV. Also, because REV always causes computation to be done on the host on which the data resides, the concurrency problems that can hinder caching are no longer a concern. And REV could comfortably be used to communicate between servers in Plan 9. As a result, REV is in some ways more powerful than process migration — it can comfortably support both parallelism and migration in a familiar RPC package.

At the same time, REV does have limitations. The problem of how much of a process can be made migratable remains. REV solves the problem of hard-to-migrate operating system state information by offering the opportunity to leave it behind. It is not clear whether this solution is any better than call-backs. Also, like process migration, there remain the problems of communicating with other processes, which may also have migratory pieces. REV offers a partial solution in that the piece of the process that has stayed on the original host may be able to reply to messages from other processors. However, getting two migrating pieces of processes to communicate remains a hard problem. Also there are some pathological cases for which REV is not suited. Consider, for example, an application comparing two files on different file servers. A naive REV implementation would have procedures bouncing between file servers as each block is read, when a file caching approach would do much better.

Finally, there is a nagging problem of the impact on servers of sending applications to data. Do data servers get overloaded? The answer seems to be "it depends." It is more efficient for the server to receive one request for n writes to a file system, than to receive n requests, each of which does one write, because the cost of handling each request, especially the interrupt costs and context switches (recall the discussion in Chapter 9), is much larger than the cost of interpreting a little bit of code between each write. But a single REV request to do a write is generally larger and more expensive to process than an equivalent RPC request. Only experimentation with REV over a wide range of applications can definitively answer the question of impact on servers.

14.4. Enhancing Distributed Services

An earlier portion of this chapter examined how existing distributed systems paradigms might be extended to gigabit speeds. However, gigabit networks will also permit the use of new distributed applications, such as multimedia, and new types of computing that require more sophisticated handling of data or fast authentication and encryption.

Distributed Timekeeping

Early in this chapter it was noted that one of the call-backs used by the Sprite process migration scheme was to get the time, so that comparisons of time stamps were made using a consistent clock. That call-back would not be necessary if host clocks could be kept consistent across the network. This problem has been the subject of considerable research, most notably by Mills, over the past decade. For practical purposes, it is now possible to have a group of host clocks keep consistent and accurate time. (Consistent clocks agree with each other about what time it is. Accurate clocks keep the right time. There have been examples of algorithms that caused clocks to be consistent, but the clocks ran fast or slow, so that the times they displayed soon had nothing to do with real time of day).

Mills's protocol, the Network Time Protocol (NTP), has been in use on the Internet for several years [Mills 1992; Mills 1990]. In brief, the protocol creates a hierarchy of time servers. At the top of the hierarchy are a modest number of hosts with very accurate clocks (e.g., cesium oscillators or radio GPS clocks), known as stratum-1 time servers. Below these time servers in the hierarchy are hosts that synchronize their clocks with the stratum-1 time servers. These second level time servers are called stratum-2 time servers. To limit load on stratum-1 servers, most time servers synchronize to stratum-2 time servers (which are slightly less accurate than stratum-1 time servers).

To synchronize its clock using NTP, a host exchanges timing information with one or more time servers. (Typically the number is three, preferably three stratum-2 servers that get their clock information from different stratum-1 servers. Using multiple sources of time minimizes the chances that a bad host will corrupt the host's clock.) At periodic intervals, the host sends a small burst of NTP packets to each of its peer time servers. The time servers echo the NTP packets back.

Each NTP packet gets timestamped four times. The first time stamp, t_1, is put in by the sending host when the packet is sent. The second time stamp, t_2, is put in the packet by the receiving peer as soon as the packet is received. The third time stamp, t_3, is put into the packet when the packet is sent back. The fourth time stamp, t_4, is put into the packet as soon as the packet is received back at the sending host. From these four values it is possible to compute a packet delay, δ, and the apparent clock offset, o:

$$\delta = (t_4 - t_1) - (t_3 - t_2) \quad o = \frac{(t_2 - t_1) + (t_3 - t_4)}{2}$$

In general, lower values for δ give better values for o, so NTP has a filter that discards samples with exceptionally long delays.

After filtering, the values of δ and o from a burst of packets are combined to estimate the difference in clock times. Using the estimate of the clock difference, the frequency of the local clock can be adjusted to bring the clock slowly into sync with its time servers. Over several sampling periods, the clocks will be very nearly synchronized (to well under a second), and after a day or so clocks typically achieve synchronization to within a few milliseconds.

If all it did was eliminate call-backs, NTP would probably be just a novelty. However, it has proved to have a far wider range of uses. For example, network monitoring and management is much easier when time stamps in logs at different measuring stations are known to be in sync, and can be compared. A wide variety of uses for time stamps in distributed systems have been identified by Liskov [1991], including uses in improving the implementation of authentication, suppression of duplicate messages [Liskov 1990], cache leases, and distributed commit protocols. NTP has also made it simpler to suppress potentially harmful duplicate copies of messages in distributed systems. Finally, and perhaps most significant, clock synchronization has helped in the development of a protocol to synchronize multimedia flows.

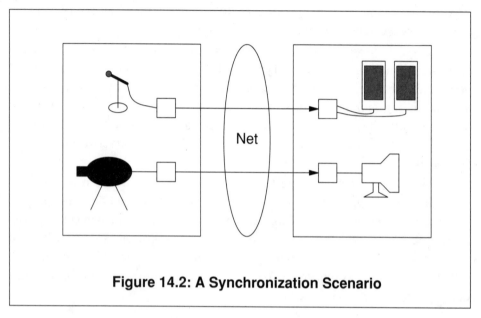

Figure 14.2: A Synchronization Scenario

Flow Synchronization

Consider the situation shown in Figure 14.2. Two computers in the area on the left are recording voice and video and transmitting that voice and video over a network to two computers in the area on the right, where the voice and video are played. The goal of *flow synchronization* is to make sure that the output is in sync (in particular, that lip-sync is achieved). To present the most general version of the synchronization problem, the example intentionally keeps the voice and video flows completely separate from source to destination. Possible advantages to combining the streams are discussed later in this section.

The problem of synchronizing the two flows can be solved using synchronized clocks, in a protocol developed by Escobar, Deutsch, and Partridge [1992]. Both source computers timestamp each piece of voice and video data with the time it was received at the microphone or camera and then send the data to their respective receiving computers. Assume that each receiving computer knows how long, in the worst case, it will take for a piece of data to get to the receiving computer from its source. (This information may be provided when the flow is set up.) The receiving computers can then exchange their delay information and determine the maximum time it will take before all of them have received samples that were recorded at the same time. (For the two-computer case, this value is simply the maximum of the respective delays.) The receivers agree to delay all samples for this amount of time and then play them out. The outputs will be in sync. This timestamping approach also implicitly accounts for variations in sample delays within a single flow.

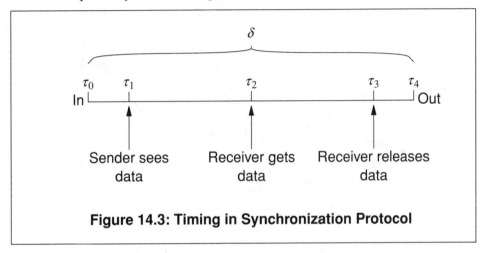

Figure 14.3: Timing in Synchronization Protocol

Although the basic protocol is pleasantly simple, a number of subtle features make implementation complex. For example, the timestamping and delay calculations must be done carefully. Figure 14.3 illustrates the problem. Data is received at the microphone at time τ_0, but there is some time before the digital samples get from the input device to the sending machine for timestamping at time τ_1. The sending host must take this time into account and timestamp the data with τ_0, the time the samples were taken. Similarly, on output, the receiver must account for the time it will take from when the receiver writes the data to the output device (at time τ_3) until the time the receiver plays the data (at τ_4).

Another problem is what to do if the network delay changes. If the application cannot adapt to changes and if the new delay is too long, the application must stop. If the application can adapt to changes, however, then the synchronization protocol permits the receivers to renegotiate their synchronization delay to accommodate the new network delay.

A third problem to consider is what to do if the voice and video are being multicast to a large number of sites. In many cases, it is not necessary to synchronize across all the sites; one simply needs to synchronize the voice and video at each site. The synchronization protocol permits receivers to be arbitrarily assigned to synchronization groups and maintains synchronization only within a group. So each site can be a separate group. (The alternative, synchronizing all the sites, requires considerable negotiation among sites and also has the unfortunate consequence of synchronizing all receivers to the longest network delay that any of the receivers sees.)

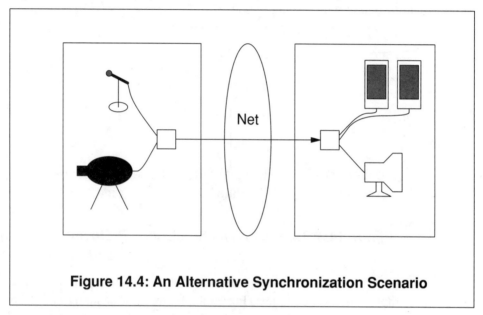

Figure 14.4: An Alternative Synchronization Scenario

So far, this section has viewed the flows to be synchronized as being completely independent. What if all samples originate on one computer and are transmitted as a single flow to the receiving computer to be played, as shown in Figure 14.4? From a theoretical perspective, this scenario is the same as the first one: some mechanism like a time stamp must be used to link samples (e.g., voice and video samples) created at the same time, and the receiving system must use that information to make sure the samples are played in sync. However, from a practical perspective, combining the samples at the sender and receiver has some advantages (and disadvantages) that make the approach interesting [Nahrstedt 1992].

First, the mechanisms for showing the timing between samples can be made much simpler. For example, related voice and video samples could be put in the same packet for transmission. Keeping the data synchronized on output is also easier. If related data is in the same packet it is implicitly synchronized. Accounting for variations in sample delays within a flow is somewhat harder but techniques exist for restoring intersample delays without using time stamps if all the data is going to one receiver [Alvarez-Cuevas 1993]. Finally, it is may be true (for the same reasons that justify the strong law of large numbers) that a flow combining the data from several bursty sources of data will be less bursty than each of the individual sources, because some of the burstiness will balance out. If so, it may be of benefit to the network to try to manage the single, less bursty stream. (See, for example, Vakil [1993].)

A limitation of combining the samples into one flow is that the one flow model is less general. Sources have to be attached to the same sender and output devices have to be attached to the same receiver. Another concern is that combining samples to ease synchronization may make it more difficult to selectively discard samples. Recall that RSVP proposed to filter samples to reduce a flow's transmission rate to one that the receiver could support.

Better External Data Formats

Chapters 9 and 10 discussed the data copying problem and how it can affect protocol throughput. Distributed systems have their own version of the data copying problem: processing external data formats.

Different types of hosts may have different internal representations of data. An obvious example is that some hosts use ASCII to represent characters while others use EBCDIC. Differences also commonly exist in floating point number representations and the order of bytes within integers. External data formats like ASN.1 and XDR solve this problem by defining standard representations for all the data types and requiring hosts to convert their data into this format before sending it across the network. When hosts receive external data, they must convert the data into their internal formats.

External data formats are intended to avoid the *m×n problem*. In brief, the *m×n* problem points out that if *m* types of hosts are sending data to *n* types of hosts, all using their own data formats, then each of the *n* hosts has to support *m* conversion routines, one for each of the *m* sending host types. Worse still, adding a new type of host to the network requires all *n* hosts to add another set of conversion routines. External data formats solve this problem by defining one standard representation, so each machine need only implement one set of conversion routines (to and from the standard representation).

The problem is that converting to and from external formats is typically very time consuming. Data conversion is a byte-by-byte, or bit-by-bit, process. As a result, in a number of cases, two high-speed hosts have been connected with 800 Mb/s HIPPI links but, due to the costs of data conversion, have only achieved 10 Mb/s effective throughput between applications.

Results like this have focussed attention on finding ways to reduce external data format conversion costs. One obvious approach is to try to improve the performance of the conversion routines. There has been considerable improvement here. For example, a team at the Pittsburgh Supercomputer Center reported improving throughput between a Cray and Connection Machine from 20 Mb/s to 180 Mb/s by recoding the data conversion routines in the Connection Machine [Mahdavi]. A study by Sample and Neufeld [1993] showed that conversion code for the ASN.1 encoding rules could be made substantially faster by employing better buffering and memory management. Results like these suggest that better coding may reduce the costs of external data format conversion, but 180 Mb/s is still well short of the 800 Mb/s HIPPI bit rates. Accordingly, many researchers believe better ways to handle external data formats are needed.

One popular approach is to try to find ways to avoid using external data formats at all. For example, if two hosts with the same type of hardware are communicating, no external data format is needed. This approach has the obvious commercial advantage that computers from the same manufacturer communicate more quickly, but it is not a general solution to the externalization problem.

A more complex solution is offered by the Network Data Representation (NDR) [Zahn 1990]. The NDR designers observed that the majority of computers used data formats that were permutations of a few basic representations. In other words, it was fairly likely that a host used either ASCII or EBCDIC for its characters, used one of a few floating type representations, and used one of the two possible byte orders within integers. So NDR defines a data representation that allows data to be sent using any one of these permutations and requires all receivers to be capable of converting from any of the permutations into the local format. The NDR approach offers better performance in two ways. First, in almost all cases, the sender's internal data representation matches one of the permutations, so the sender can transmit data without any conversion. Second, in some cases, the receiver's data formats will be at least partly compatible with the sender's data formats, so the receiver will not have to do a conversion either.

A more radical approach, which has been suggested informally by several researchers[8] but for which performance results are ambiguous, is to expand on the idea of combining the checksum and copy loop discussed in Chapter 10 and roll the external data format code into the loop as well. Clark and Tennenhouse have suggested that, to make it easier to combine the operations, applications

---

[8] Most notably Eric Cooper, Dave Clark, Per Gunningberg, and Dave Tennenhouse.

should be able to determine how data is encapsulated, so that the data is sent in the best possible chunk sizes to facilitate combining of operations. They call this idea *application level framing,* or ALF [Clark 1990]. One problem that ALF has yet to resolve is how to handle multicast applications, where different receivers may prefer different chunk sizes.

14.5. Authentication

A critical problem in distributed systems is confirming that a message, an RPC, or a distributed memory access is authentic. If a message says it is from Alice, the receiving system should be able to confirm the message is really from Alice and not from Bob. (Alice and Bob are the canonical examples in many security papers.)

The problem of authentication is essentially one of confirming that the message or packet a host or application has received is indeed from whom it says it is from and its contents are indeed what the sender originally transmitted.

A good way to do authentication is through the use of *public key encryption,* or PKE [Diffie 1988], combined with a hash function. The basic idea behind PKE is that a person (or host or program) has two keys: a public key and a private key. Data encrypted with the public key can be decrypted only with the private key; similarly, data encrypted with the private key can only be decrypted with the public key. Although several schemes for supporting PKE have been proposed, the most widely accepted algorithm is the Rivest-Shamir-Adelman (RSA) algorithm [Rivest 1978], which uses large prime numbers for both keys.

To "sign" a message, the sender computes a hash function on the data and then appends the hash value, encrypted with the sender's private key, to the message. When the message is received, the receiver computes the same hash function on the data and then uses the sender's public key to decrypt the transmitted hash value. If the two hash values match, the message is authenticated. The authentication relies on two assumptions: first, that the likelihood that two different messages will give the same hash is extremely small (therefore a different hash value means the message was corrupted in transit or the decryption failed), and, second, that the receiver has the right public key for the sender. Obviously, to make this system go fast, having a fast hash algorithm is essential, and efforts have been made to devise fast hashing algorithms, such as MD5 [Rivest 1992].

Making sure the receiver has the right public key is very important. Suppose Bob wants to get authenticated messages from Alice and asks his friend

Charles for Alice's key. Rather than giving Alice's key to Bob, Charles makes up a new set of keys and gives Bob one of the new keys. Charles can now send messages to Bob, signed as Alice, and Bob will believe they are really from Alice. What is worse, Bob will believe that real messages from Alice are not authentic, because Bob has the wrong key.

If Bob and Alice are real people and know each other, there is an obvious solution to this problem: Bob should get Alice's key directly from Alice. But what if one or both of Bob and Alice are applications or hosts? Some mechanism is required for applications and hosts to be able to validate each other and users.

One way to allow applications to validate each other is using a *certificate hierarchy*. A certificate hierarchy is a tree of entities with a trusted root; an entity that everyone believes is trustworthy. The public key of the trusted root is made known to everyone. Parties can then come to the trusted root, which will issue them a key pair[9] and a certificate. The certificate states that a party has a given public key and is validated by a hash encrypted with the root's private key. When a program receives a message signed with a public key, it contacts a certificate server to get the certificate of the message's sender and then uses the public key in the certificate to decrypt and check the message's hash code. In more sophisticated schemes, a chain of certificates is built. For example, Alice might get a certificate from the trusted root and then in turn give certificates to Bob and Charles. Thus to verify Charles's signature, a program would have to get Charles's certificate (to confirm Charles's key as signed by Alice), and then get Alice's certificate (to confirm Alice's key as signed for by the trusted root).

It may appear that confirming the validity of a certificate will require several network messages to certificate servers (with the concomitant delay), but one of the nice features of certificate chains is that they are self-authenticating. For example, along with a message he has written, Charles could send his certificate *and* Alice's certificate. If the recipient of the message has the trusted root's public key (and it seems likely that the root's public key could be widely distributed), it can verify Alice's certificate and then use Alice's certificate to verify Charles's certificate and message. This is a very useful result. It says applications and hosts can freely send around authenticated public keys and thus authenticate messages (or even packets) without incurring additional network delays.

---

[9] There are ways to allow this to occur such that the root never sees the private key in the key pair. See Kent and Linn [1989] for details.

14.6. Summary

This chapter has examined the issues of making distributed systems ready for gigabit networks.

The fundamental performance problem appears to be delay, and a number of ways to address the delay problem have been presented, including complete schemes like REV, Plan 9, and caching, but also additional services like NTP and certificate based authentication, which make it possible to avoid incurring latencies to do simple functions like compare time stamps or authenticate packets.

Another performance problem is data conversion and it was repeatedly observed that many systems ignore this problem. However, the benchmarks for data conversion suggest that ignoring data conversion problems is probably a mistake, as it can have a tremendous impact on performance. Unfortunately, there currently is no magic bullet for the data conversion problem.

Finally, we examined the problem of flow synchronization and showed how, by building on sychronized clocks, the flow synchronization problem can be solved.

Further Reading

Mullender's [1989] book is a fine introduction to distributed systems. It is a compilation of chapters by outstanding researchers, on their respective fields of expertise, and is based on a conference course they taught together. It does not, however, cover external data formats or process migration in any detail. The short tutorial on data formats by Partridge and Rose [1989] may be useful. The $m \times n$ problem was first described by Padlipsky [1983].

For a near-complete listing of all the major distributed systems activities in the world, see Borghoff and Nast-Kolb [1989].

Birrell and Nelson's [1984] paper remains the standard reference on RPC. Readers looking for a more complete perspective should read Nelson's [1981] doctoral dissertation which continues to be the most detailed study of basic issues in RPC.

There is a wide range of literature on process migration. Beyond the works already mentioned in this chapter, Smith's [1988] survey of process migration is outstanding, and Theimer's [1986] Ph.D. thesis is valuable reading.

For a thought-provoking approach to distributed shared memory, readers may wish to look at ParaDiGM [Cheriton 1991] which proposes a scheme in which networks and distributed memory are combined into a unified architecture.

Chapter 15

The State of Gigabit Networking

15.1. Introduction

The past fourteen chapters have covered a wide range of topics in gigabit networking. However, gigabit networking is still a dynamic field, with several unsolved problems. The focus of this chapter is to pull together the material of the preceding chapters, plus bits and pieces of other work, and highlight what problems lie ahead.

15.2. Putting the Pieces Together

It is easier to start with what one knows, so we will start by building a networking infrastructure with the material from the previous chapters.

An essential first step toward gigabit networking is to develop methods for transmitting data over various media at gigabit rates. That problem is fairly well understood. There is a wide range of gigabit technologies to choose from, including WDM networks, ATM/SONET, and HIPPI. If any problem has received insufficient attention in this area, it is the relative shortage of packet network solutions. However, this concern is a modest complaint in an environment of plenty — there is clearly a wide range of gigabit architectures to choose from.

Given this profusion of networking technologies, what internetworking protocols should be run over them? One suggestion is ATM, but fitting ATM over packet networks is a rather clumsy solution. A better solution would appear to be some form of internetworking protocol. Chapter 10 showed that today's internetworking protocols like IP and CLNP are generally capable of achieving gigabit data rates, as are the transport protocols like UDP, TCP, and TP4 that run over them. Furthermore, Chapter 9 showed that developments in operating systems and network interfaces seem likely to keep up with gigabit speeds.

For many applications, such as bulk transfers of data, existing protocols will be sufficient. These protocols, however, do not have quite all the features needed to support new real-time applications like conferencing. However, Chapters 11, 12, and 13 showed how today's protocols could be extended to support real-time flows, using a number of approaches that combine traffic shaping (using leaky bucket or another shaping scheme) and queueing paradigms like Stop-and-Go Queueing or Weighted Fair Queueing with setup protocols like RSVP. The queueing and shaping work, although much of it is still very new, has already made important progress. It is no longer a question of whether real-time applications can be supported, but rather which of the several workable shaping and queuing schemes should be used.

Moving up to look at the distributed systems infrastructure that is built over internetworking protocols, the picture becomes somewhat fragmented. Pieces of the distributed system infrastructure exist. Distributed timekeeping, which makes many other tasks easier, is widely available. Protocols for synchronizing multiple flows have been developed and successfully tested. However, there is still a rather large muddle about how to avoid the latency problem when communicating between systems. A number of proposals exist, but there seems to be no consensus about which one to choose.

Finally, looking at applications that use a gigabit network, we can see a large number of interesting applications ranging from multimedia conferencing, to visualization applications, to medical applications.

15.3. Lingering Problems

A lot of the work discussed in the preceding chapters is not yet mature and needs to be completed if gigabit networks are to achieve their promise.

Flow Setup and Routing Are Not Yet Mature

First, none of the proposed flow setup protocols is mature. What may be the best candidate, namely, RSVP, is still in the early stages of development. It will probably be some time before there will be enough experience with flow setup protocols to make it possible to choose one and deploy it widely. This problem is particularly troubling because ATM, as a connection-oriented protocol, requires some sort of flow setup protocol just to be usable, and it appears likely that to achieve quick deployment ATM will be forced to select a protocol that will rapidly become obsolete.

Second, the problems of finding routes for flows that desire performance guarantees have received little attention and appear to be quite hard. It will probably be several years before these routing problems are well understood.

Finding the Right Paradigm for Distributed Systems

Distributed systems are also struggling to deal with the relatively long latencies of gigabit networks. Despite a number of thought provoking ideas like Plan 9 and remote evaluation, there is no consensus about what solutions are workable. Furthermore, given the rather muddled state of distributed systems research, it is unclear how long it will be before widely accepted solutions are developed.

Another distributed system problem is how to handle external data formats efficiently. The recent work of Sample and Neufeld suggests this problem may not be quite as severe as once thought, but the problem of efficient format conversions is far from solved.

Changing Operating Systems

Operating systems also have their challenges. Although the essential problems of allowing operating systems to handle large volumes of data appear to be well understood, the mechanisms needed to support real-time requirements are still being investigated. Real-time support appears to be much easier than first thought. Thanks largely to the high speeds of new processors, relaxed scheduling schemes like workahead scheduling may suffice to support most real-time applications. However, there is little experience with these systems to date and certainly nothing approaching a commercial product.

Fast Encryption

Another concern is encryption. Authentication (discussed in Chapter 14) protects against impersonation, but it does not protect data from being read by others as it crosses a network. Some work on pipelined Digital Encryption Standard (DES) systems has been done [Broscius 1991], but little else has been published.

15.4. Unaddressed Problems

There are also some minor issues for which so little work has been done that they were not discussed in earlier chapters. However, gigabit networks would benefit from more attention being given to these problems.

Protocol Verification

Verification of protocols is one such issue. A major task in developing data networking protocols is proving that they work. Unfortunately, verifying a protocol typically requires exhaustive evaluation of all the protocol's states, where the set of states is defined as the set of possible messages multiplied by the number of possible receiving states. For a protocol like TCP, which has a 20-byte message header (where each different field value represents a different message) and 11 states, the total number of states is over 1.6×10^{48} states. Current verification languages and tools are only just beginning to be able to verify protocols of this complexity, with the result that most of the major protocols in use today have not been verified to work. Gigabit protocols, with their timing constraints and other requirements, seem likely to make the state space even larger, further challenging our ability to verify them.

Better Traffic Models

The dynamics of traffic inside networks is still very poorly understood. Cruz, Parekh, and others have had considerable success finding worst case bounds on the delay of data sent through networks, but solutions for common problems like determining the maximum buffer sizes required to achieved a certain loss rate in a cell switch are still poorly understood. There are two parts to this problem. First, we lack a generally accepted probabilistic model of data traffic. The popular exponential distributions (of M/M/1 and M/D/1 fame), although wonderful for modelling telephone traffic, are known to be inadequate to model data traffic. Indeed, the recent work showing data traffic is fractal suggests a far more sophisticated traffic model is needed. Second, even if a new model were developed, there is a shortage of well-developed queueing theory tools for solving queueing theory problems that do not have exponential arrival or service times.

These theoretical limitations are not just interesting problems for theorists. The inability to accurately predict traffic and buffer requirements has forced switch designers to rely on extensive simulations or to try to find ways to mix data traffic so that it approximates the well-understood exponential distribution.

Gigabit Network Management

Another understudied topic is gigabit network management. (Recall from Chapter 2 that even the link-level management protocols for SONET have yet to be defined.) Two interesting questions are, What effect will bigger bandwidths have on management and Will providing service guarantees make management more complex?

Those who believe that larger bandwidths will have an effect on management tend to argue that, with bigger amounts of bandwidth, more can go wrong (e.g., more data misdirected) in a unit of time. The inference is that management systems might have to put more intelligence closer to the devices being managed. One can contrast this approach, for example, with that of the Simple Network Management Protocol (SNMP), which tries to limit the management information kept in devices.

Service guarantees might also require that devices become more intelligent, because the devices will need to recover in ways consistent with trying to preserve previously guaranteed flows.

Note that, with the exception of network management, these problems do not have to be solved to deploy gigabit networks. For instance, we have muddled along with unverified protocols for 20 years. However, in the long term, these problems need to be addressed.

15.5. After Gigabits, Terabits?

Chapter 2 noted that the theoretical capacity of a single fiber was measured in terabits per second. The obvious, and unanswered, question is whether it is possible to build true terabit networks, in which individual hosts can transmit data at rates in excess of a terabit per second.

The hardest problem in building a terabit link appears to be converting between the optical and electrical signals at high speeds. Signals from the fiber will be arriving at the rate of one every picosecond. This requires sub-picosecond logic inside the receiver, which is currently beyond our ability to construct.

One intriguing area of research is trying to avoid this optical-electrical conversion entirely by developing all-optical computers, computers that use photons instead of electrons to effect their computations.

Finally, one must ask if a terabit network is useful. The answer is unclear. It is possible to imagine systems that could use a terabit link. Several processor designers predict that, in about ten years, processors will have instruction cycle times measured in hundreds of picoseconds (tens of BIPS). If a hundred of those processors were assembled into a parallel system, the system might well be able to generate or receive at a terabit per second. However, one might ask whether forcing the parallel processors to use a single serial fiber is the right design. It may make more sense to have multiple parallel network connections into the system, where each connection runs at a few tens of gigabits.

15.6. Final Thoughts

The past five years have seen an explosion in research and development of high-speed networks, with the result that the field is mature enough for this book to be written. Solutions to many of the hard problems have been developed. In cases where the solutions do not exist, the problems at least appear to be well defined. The outlines and many of the details of how to deploy gigabit networks appear fairly firm.

At the same time, the field remains dynamic. There are a number of loose ends to tidy up and ideas to refine. Furthermore, experience with real gigabit networks is rather limited. As this book goes to press, several of the major wide area testbeds have been operational only for about half a year and if past history is any guide, operational experience with these testbeds will turn up a number of vexing problems that will need to be solved.

Further Reading

Most of the topics mentioned in this chapter were discussed in prior chapters, and readers are referred to the references in those chapters and at the end of the book.

For readers interested in protocol verification, Holzmann [1991] has written a highly readable book on the field.

A popular introduction to network management is Marshall Rose's [1991] book.

Chapter 16

Where to Learn More

16.1. Introduction

In a field that is still evolving, it seemed appropriate to provide more than the usual few paragraphs of general advice about where to look for additional publications. Currently, a large number of major research programs are underway, each generating results and publications. There has also been a proliferation of networking journals and conferences in recent years. This chapter is an overview of these activities, designed to guide readers interested in tracking the field over the next few years. An annotated bibliography follows this chapter.

16.2. Testbeds and Research Programs

Contrary to the popular image of the average researcher as a single professor with a small group of graduate students, most research in gigabit networking is being done by large teams of senior researchers. Some of these teams are made up of people from a single organization, such as AT&T's LuckyNet project, while others, such as Aurora, combine researchers from several organizations. Many of these teams have built experimental gigabit networks, which are called *testbeds*.

Probably the best known testbeds are the five U.S. testbeds funded, in part, by the National Science Foundation (NSF) and the Advanced Research Projects Agency (ARPA). The testbeds combine government research funding with substantial funding from industry and, in conjunction with some smaller testbed activities, form the core of gigabit research activities in the United States. The work of the testbeds, which were created in 1989, is being coordinated primarily by Bob Kahn and Dick Binder at the Corporation for National Research Initiatives (CNRI).

Because some (though by no means all) of the best research is coming from the organized research teams, knowing something about the projects can be useful. This section looks briefly at most of the major gigabit programs around the world. For each project, it describes each program's goals and the organizations involved. It also lists some of the more prolific authors involved in the project (knowing individuals' names is useful when scanning the literature, because project names often do not appear in the titles of papers) and some of the important results of the project to date. The programs are discussed in roughly the order of when they started.

BERKOM, Germany

BERKOM was the first gigabit program, started in 1986 by the German telephone company and the Berlin Senate to do research into gigabit speed networks and high-speed computers. Funded for five years, BERKOM has recently ended, but a successor program, BERKOM II, is expected to begin shortly.

BERKOM	
Participants	GMD-FOKUS, German PTT, the Berlin Senate
Authors	B. Butscher, R. Popescu-Zeletin, M. Walch

The project was centered in Berlin, which has a large installed base of optical fiber, and examined protocols and workstation architectures for high-speed networks. In its later stages, the project primarily worked with ATM.

Most of the BERKOM work has been published in IFIP conference proceedings in Europe. Because the circulation of IFIP conference proceedings is rather small (and it often takes up to twelve months after the conference for the proceedings to be published), the BERKOM work has not received as much attention as perhaps it should.

University of Cambridge, United Kingdom

Although Cambridge does not have a formal gigabit program, it has been the source of much innovative work on very high-speed networking, particularly in the area of cell networks and multimedia. Current research has centered around building multimedia distributed systems using special multimedia workstations attached to the Cambridge Backbone Ring as the experimental platform.

Some of the work has been done in conjunction with the Olivetti Research Laboratory in Cambridge.

University of Cambridge	
Participants	University of Cambridge, Olivetti Research Lab, University of Twente
Authors	A. Hopper, I. Leslie, D. McAuley, R. Needham, D. Greaves

Beyond the development of the Cambridge Backbone Ring [Greaves 1990], the project has published interesting papers on the role of ATM [Leslie 1993b] and has recently started a joint distributed systems project with the University of Twente called *Pegasus* [Leslie

Blanca Testbed, United States

In 1986, AT&T started a program called the Experimental University Network (XUNET) in conjunction with the University of California at Berkeley, the University of Illinois and the University of Wisconsin to study wide area networking using a cell networking technology developed at AT&T. In 1990, the XUNET program was expanded to include a gigabit testbed called *Blanca*, which is one of the five ARPA/NSF testbeds.

The Blanca Testbed	
Participants	Lawrence Berkeley Laboratory, National Center for Supercomputing Applications (NCSA), University of California at Berkeley, University of Illinois at Urbana-Champaign, University of Wisconsin at Madison, Ameritech, Astronautics, Bell Atlantic, Pacific Bell and AT&T
Authors	C. Catlett, R. Campbell, D. Ferrari, A. G. Fraser, B. Johnston, C. Kalmanek, L. Landweber, R. Palmer, P. Rupert

The Blanca testbed's research program is quite broad, covering work in network protocols (especially work in call setup, multiplexing and congestion control in cell networks), the interface between computers and networks (both integration of supercomputers and the development of network virtual memory schemes), and gigabit applications (particularly applications involving supercomputing applications at NCSA). Work is centered around a cross-country testbed called XUNET-II.

The project has produced a number of interesting results including work on support for multimedia protocols [Verma 1991] and congestion avoidance and control [Faber 1992]. Catlett of NCSA is widely viewed as an expert on high-speed applications [Catlett 1992], and Fraser of AT&T was one of the pioneers of cell networking [Fraser 1993].

The XUNET project also includes some participants who are not part of the Blanca testbed: Columbia University, University of Pennsylvania, and CAIP Rutgers.

Aurora, United States

Aurora is another of the ARPA/NSF testbeds. (Some of the participants were members of an earlier project called DAWN.)

The Aurora Testbed	
Participants	Bellcore, IBM, MIT, University of Pennsylvania, Bell Atlantic, MCI and NYNET
Authors	B. Davie, D.D. Clark, D.J. Farber, I. Gopal, R. Guerin, A. McAuley, J.M. Smith, D. Sincoskie, D. Tennenhouse

Sometimes referred to as "the project with too many Daves,"[1] the research activities in Aurora cover a wide range of problems. Central to Aurora is an OC-12 testbed on the East Coast of the United States, incorporating both the Bellcore Sunshine ATM switch and the IBM plaNET switch. The project is connecting workstations to the testbed and doing experiments in internetworking protocols, applications, distributed system paradigms, workstation operating systems, and performance guarantees.

The project has produced a large body of notable work. Beyond the work on the Sunshine and plaNET switches [Giacopelli 1991; Cidon 1988], the team members have published outstanding papers on ATM error correction [McAuley 1990], flow and congestion control [Clark 1992; Guerin 1991], protocol architecture [Clark 1990; Tennenhouse 1990], and ATM protocol interfaces [Davie

---

[1] Dave Clark, Dave Farber, Dave Sincoskie, and Dave Tennenhouse. DAWN was widely rumored to be an acronym for Dave's Awesome and Wonderful Network.

1993a; Traw 1993]. A survey of the project can be found in [Clark 1993].

Nectar, United States

Confusingly, there have been two Nectar projects in which Carnegie-Mellon University has participated. The first was an experiment in nongigabit data communications. The second is an ARPA/NSF testbed. The Nectar testbed's purpose is to experiment with local area applications of gigabit networks, by connecting participants within greater Pittsburgh.

The Nectar Testbed	
Participants	Carnegie-Mellon University (CMU), Pittsburgh Supercomputer Center, Bellcore and Bell Atlantic/Bell of Pennsylvania
Authors	H. T. Kung,[2] P. Steenkiste

The project has used a combination of local HIPPI switches and ATM/SONET links connecting the switches to interconnect the Pittsburgh Supercomputing Center with various computer systems at CMU. The project is now investigating questions of protocol and operating system design to improve distributed computing performance between the various machines.

Project Zeus, United States

A multiphase project at Washington University at St. Louis, Project Zeus is probably best known as the project on which Jon Turner is working.

Project Zeus	
Participants	Washington University at St. Louis, Southwestern Bell, SynOptics, Ascom Timeplex, and Bellcore
Authors	M. Gaddis, G. Parulkar, J. S. Turner

The project's goal is to build, from scratch, an ATM network connecting several departments within Washington University. The network will combine video over ATM services with support for more standard packet protocols such as IP. The basic technology for the testbed, such as the switches, has been built and

---

[2] Kung recently moved to Harvard University.

the construction of the campus network is currently underway.

The project team has produced a number of important papers, most recently an interesting paper on congestion control by Turner [1992]. A survey of the project appears in *IEEE Network Magazine* [Cox 1993].

ACORN, United States

In 1989, the Columbia University Center for Telecommunications Research and its industrial partners started a research program in high-speed optical networks. This project was dubbed the Advanced Communications Organization for Research Networks (ACORN).

ACORN	
Participants	Columbia University, AT&T Bell Labs, Bellcore, GTE, Merrill-Lynch Teleport, NEC, Northern Telecom, Phillips, Southwestern Bell
Authors	A. Acampora, R. Gidron, A. Lazar, M. Schwartz, Y.Y. Yemini

The project has built the TeraNet gigabit network [Gidron 1992] and is now using it as a research testbed at Columbia. Related to TeraNet, the project has reported some interesting work on admission control in support of multimedia [Hyman 1991].

BBN, United States

The gigabit research project at Bolt Beranek and Newman (BBN) started work in 1988 with funding from ARPA. The project has focussed on protocols and technologies important to the development and experimentation with gigabit internetworks.

BBN Gigabits Project	
Participants	BBN
Authors	D. Deutsch, J. Escobar, C. Partridge

To date, the project has made useful contributions in the areas of ATM segmentation and reassembly protocols [Escobar 1991], multiflow synchronization [Escobar 1992], and flow setup [Partridge 1992b]. In addition, in conjunction with Motorola, BBN is building the ground stations for the ACTS gigabit satellite network.

CASA, United States

The CASA testbed is another of the ARPA/NSF testbeds established in 1990. The focus of the project is to experiment with applications of distributed supercomputing, by connecting major supercomputing centers at labs in the southwestern United States. The applications being studied generally involve multiple supercomputers communicating over the network and include chemical reaction computations, interactive geological applications using rich data sources such as Landsat images, and climate modelling.

The CASA Testbed	
Participants	Los Alamos National Laboratory (LANL), California Institute of Technology (CalTech), Jet Propulsion Laboratory (JPL), San Diego Supercomputer Center (SDSC), UCLA, MCI, Pacific Bell, ParaSoft, and US West
Authors	L. Bergman, H.-W. Braun, R. Mechoso, P. Messina, J. Morrison

The project is using HIPPI, adapted to work over eight SONET OC-3 long-distance lines, to connect up LANL, JPL, CalTech and SDSC. CASA's technical reports are available via e-mail. Send requests to *techpubs@ccsf.caltech.edu*.

VISTAnet, United States

VISTAnet is a small B-ISDN testbed built in the Research Triangle Park area in North Carolina. It is dedicated to studying high-bandwidth medical and visualization applications and their protocols using B-ISDN and HIPPI gigabit networks.

The VISTAnet Testbed	
Participants	BellSouth, GTE, University of North Carolina at Chapel Hill, MCNC, North Carolina State University
Authors	V. Chi, H. Fuchs, A. Nilsson, H. Perros, N. Ransom, J. Rosenman, D. Stevenson

The major application of the testbed is experiments with collaborative medical systems involving doctors planning oncology radiation treatments using three-dimensional images of cancerous tumors. To do these experiments, CAT scanners are integrated with high-performance supercomputers and 3D graphics workstations. The computers are attached to the network via HIPPI to B-ISDN adapters.

A more detailed survey of the testbed's activities can be found in the *Journal of High Speed Networks* [Ransom 1992].

MultiG, Sweden

MultiG is the Swedish national gigabit research program and started in 1990. It is a cooperative program made up of interrelated projects at several major research and industrial labs in the Stockholm area.

MultiG	
Participants	Ellemtel, Ericsson Telecom, Swedish Institute of Computer Science, Swedish Board for Technical and Industrial Development, Televerket, Swedish Telecommunications Area Stockholm, Royal Institute of Technology
Authors	P. Gunningberg, G. Q. MaGuire, B. Pehrson, S. Pink

The program is working in two broad areas: computer supported cooperative work (CSWC) and networking protocols. The CSCW activities are building and using applications, such as multimedia conferencing systems, video servers, and virtual reality, to learn about the requirements of new gigabit applications. The networking activities are trying to develop protocols and network hardware to support the needs of the CSCW applications.

The project holds a workshop every six months, which contains copies of recently completed papers. Notable papers published in other journals include a discussion of an access protocol for a proposed MultiG cell network [Gauffin 1992], and a study of an implementation of a flow setup protocol [Partridge 1992c]. A survey of the MultiG project was published in *IEEE Network Magazine* [Pehrson 1992].

LuckyNet, United States

While participating in the Blanca testbed, AT&T felt it needed to do additional research into how it should best support B-ISDN. So it established the LuckyNet testbed, named for Bell Lab's then Executive Director, Robert Lucky, in 1991. The project's dual research focus is on various aspects of networking with B-ISDN, including ATM switching, transport protocols, network reliability and restoration, and signalling protocols, and application that use B-ISDN, including multimedia conferencing and document retrieval.

LuckyNet	
Participants	AT&T Bell Labs
Authors	K. Y. Eng, R. Gitlin, Z. Haas, M. Karol, T. London, L. Greenstein

A survey of the project has been published in the *Journal of High Speed Networks* [Gitlin 1992].

MAGIC, United States

MAGIC is one of the newest gigabit testbeds, funded by ARPA in early 1992. It is a SONET/ATM network built in the midwestern United States.

The MAGIC Testbed	
Participants	Sprint, Minnesota Supercomputer Center, US Army Battle Lab, USGS Earth Resources Observation Systems Data Center, University of Kansas, SRI International, Lawrence Berkeley Laboratories, US Army Command Battle Laboratory, Digital Equipment Corporation
Authors	V. Frost, T. Salo, M. Sobek, C. Thacker

The purpose of MAGIC is to study two general topics: gigabit visualization applications over high-speed networks, especially military problems involving terrain visualization and simulation, and integration of protocols such as TCP/IP into high-speed SONET/ATM environments.

SuperJANET, United Kingdom

SuperJANET is a national OC-24 (622 Mb/s) gigabit testbed for the United Kingdom. Deployment of the network started in late 1992, with six pilot members: Cambridge, Edinburgh, and Manchester Universities, Imperial College of Science, Technology and Medicine, University College London, and Rutherford Appleton Laboratory. (This pilot group is quite strong. In addition to the team at Cambridge, University College London has long had a world-wide reputation for outstanding networking research and Rutherford has participated in several major network testbeds).

The testbed is to expand to include over fifty participants by late 1994. The name was chosen to indicate the network's role as a complementary network to the existing Joint Academic Network, JANET, which has served the UK research community for many years.

SuperJANET	
Participants	Most networking research centers in the United Kingdom

The scope of the testbed is so broad that it seems likely that most networking research centers in the UK will be part of SuperJANET and be able to participate in experiments on the network. Some information on the plans for Super-JANET can be found in the December 1992 issue of *Network News*, a publication of the organization that runs JANET. (Contact JANET-LIAISON-DESK@jnt.ac.uk for more information.)

Smaller Programs

In addition to these rather large and established gigabit projects, a number of smaller or emerging gigabit projects are worthy of mention.

Greg Finn and Bob Felderman at USC Information Sciences Institute have established an active and growing gigabit project centered around the ATOMIC network. Also at USC and ISI, Deborah Estrin is working on reservation protocols for gigabit networks. Finally, ISI is managing the DARTNET, a low-speed ARPA testbed where a number of ideas about multimedia flow control for gigabit networks are actually being tested.

Similarly, Hewlett-Packard's Bristol Laboratories has an active program based around the HANGMAN network. Greg Watson, Dave Banks, and John Limb (now at Hewlett-Packard, Palo Alto) have written a number of interesting papers based on this work.

Eight organizations (Bellcore, Columbia University, Hewlett-Packard, Hughes Aircraft Company, Lawrence Livermore National Labs, Northern Telecom, Rockwell International, and United Technologies Research Center) with additional funding from ARPA established an optical networking project called the *Optical Networks Technology Consortium* in 1993. The purpose of the consortium is to conduct research in all-optical networking, in particular, to build an experimental all optical data networking.

The XEROX Palo Alto Research Center (PARC) has been actively involved in work on ATM (Bryan Lyles), congestion control and flow setup (Lixia Zhang), and multicasting (Steve Deering).

At MIT, Bob Kennedy and Pierre Humblet have an active fiber optics laboratory. Members of their lab have worked with IBM in the development of Rainbow.

The University of Massachusetts has a number of active gigabit researchers. Jim Kurose has done interesting work on traffic behavior. (A good source of pointers to a lot of his work is Kurose [1993].) Aura Ganz and Imrich Chlamtac have been working on fiber optic networks.

ESPRIT, a European Community funding agency, has begun to actively fund gigabit research projects such as OSI '95, a collaboration project including the University of Liege (e.g., André Danthine) and the University of Lancaster, studying how to enhance OSI for gigabit speeds and multimedia protocols [Danthine 1992].

Singapore has announced plans for a national gigabit testbed. See [Catlett 1993] for more information.

Despite active gigabit research activities at a number of Silicon Valley firms, Silicon Valley does not have a gigabit testbed to call its own. Over the past few years, there has been an effort to correct that problem and create a gigabit network known as the *Bay Area Gigabit Network* (BAGNET). Potential participants include XEROX, Hewlett-Packard, Digital Equipment Corporation, NASA, and Pacific Bell.

16.3. Conferences and Journals

Figuring out which conferences and journals to read for information on gigabit networking is rather hard. The difficulty comes from a number of causes. First, the field is becoming interdisciplinary, with important work in fiber optics, data networking, telephony, and distributed systems. Second, the communications field as a whole has grown enormously over the past few years and has spawned a ridiculous number of new conferences and (to a lesser extent) new journals. The result is that readers (and authors) must selectively choose which journals, magazines and conferences to read. What follows is a personal guide to the journals, magazines, and conferences I have found most useful to read while writing this book.[3]

---

[3] This list probably reflects, in part, my own professional activities. As an active member of IEEE and ACM and a past and current editor of ACM SIGCOMM and IEEE Communica-

Major Journals and Conferences

Three major professional groups sponsor journals and conferences in high-speed networking: the Association for Computing Machinery's Special Interest Group on Data Communication (SIGCOMM), the Institute of Electrical and Electronics Engineers (IEEE), and the International Federation for Information Processing (IFIP).

ACM SIGCOMM sponsors an annual SIGCOMM conference, which is probably the hardest data communications conference in which to get a paper accepted. The rejection rate is typically over 75%, but the results are wonderful — SIGCOMM usually publishes about half of the most important data communications conference papers presented in any given year. SIGCOMM also publishes an entry-level research journal called *ACM Computer Communication Review* (CCR). CCR emphasizes timely publication of interesting work. The SIGCOMM proceedings are published each year as a special issue of CCR.

IEEE hosts a profusion of data communications conferences, many of which are a waste of time and paper. However, two of the conferences regularly present outstanding papers on high-speed networking. IEEE INFOCOM is widely considered the major IEEE conference on data communications and typically includes a large number of notable papers. And some notable papers are presented at *IEEE GLOBECOM*.

IEEE publishes two magazines on communications: *IEEE Communications Magazine* and *IEEE Network Magazine*. Both magazines publish refereed articles intended for the average technical reader (as contrasted with journal papers, which are typically written by researchers for researchers). *Communications Magazine* covers the entire communications field, whereas *Network Magazine* covers only data communications. Both magazines have published a number of important articles (in particular, surveys) on high-speed networking and expect to continue to do so.

IEEE also publishes *IEEE Journal on Selected Areas of Communications,* generally known as JSAC. JSAC exclusively publishes special issues on key topics in the field of communications. Many of the issues represent the best work in the field at the time they are published. So although JSAC may publish only one or two issues each year related to high-speed networks, they typically contain some of the best papers of the year.

ACM and IEEE started joint publication of a new journal, *IEEE/ACM Transactions on Networking,* in 1993. It is too early to tell how important this journal will be for high-speed networking. But the senior editors, Jim Kurose

(Editor-in-Chief) and Gary Delp (Publications Editor), are both widely respected in the high-speed networking community, so it seems likely the journal will become an important publication.

IFIP hosts two major conferences devoted exclusively to high-speed networks: the IFIP 6.1 Conference on Protocols for High-Speed Networks (PfHSN), and the IFIP 6.1/6.4 Conference on High Performance Networking (HPN), formerly, the Conference on High Speed LANs (HSLAN). Generally, HPN has been focussed slightly more on work within Europe, while PfHSN has been slightly more successful at drawing papers and attendees from around the world. Both conferences have their proceedings published by North-Holland/Elsevier. Unfortunately, the conference proceedings are typically available about a year after the conference is held, which has limited the impact of the conferences somewhat.

Other Journals and Related Conferences

John Wiley and Sons publishes a journal called *Internetworking: Research and Experience,* whose editor-in-chief is Doug Comer. Although relatively new (it started publication in 1989), the journal has published some valuable papers, particularly in the area of flow and congestion control.

In 1992, IOS Press started publishing the *Journal of High Speed Networks,* edited by Deepinder Sidhu. It is too early to tell what role this journal will play, but the early issues have been very good. Sidhu also hosts a popular annual workshop on high-speed networks at the University of Maryland each spring.

For readers interested in distributed systems and operating systems issues, there are three notable conferences. The first is the Symposium on Operating System Principles (SOSP), sponsored by the ACM's Special Interest Group on Operating Systems (SIGOPS). Held every two years, SOSP is extremely competitive (the 1991 SOSP accepted 18% of the papers submitted) and typically publishes a large fraction of the important operating systems papers for the years it is held.

ACM sponsors a conference called ASPLOS (Architectural Support for Programming Languages and Operating Systems) about every eighteen months, which sometimes publishes distributed systems papers.

The USENIX association holds a Symposium on Experience with Distributed and Multiprocessor Systems (SEDMS), which is highly regarded.

16.4. Getting Items in the Bibliography

Most of the items in the bibliography are books or articles in widely available journals and should be available from any major technical library.

Doctoral dissertations from most major universities (with the annoying exception of MIT) can be purchased from University Microfilms Incorporated in Ann Arbor, Michigan.

Technical reports from universities are typically available for a copying fee. In many cases these reports are now available on-line on the Internet, so it is worth checking with the department that issued the report before buying a copy.

I have tried to refrain from citing standards and technical contributions to standards committees, because locating copies can be extremely difficult. Internet standards (RFCs) are all freely available on-line. Drafts of some other standards documents have been put on-line, so ask around. And, if all else fails, contact the appropriate standards body to try to get a copy.

Bibliography

"Gigabit Network Testbeds." [1990]. *IEEE Computer*, Vol. 23, No. 9, IEEE, September 1990.

> Lists the NRI testbeds and who to contact at each for more information.

AKHTAR, S. [1987]. *Congestion Control in a Fast Packet Switching Network,* Washington University, St. Louis, Miss., December 1987

> First major study of leaky bucket.

ALVAREZ-CUEVAS, F., M. BERTRAN, F. OLLER, and J.M. SELGA [1993]. "A Novel Algorithm for Voice Synchronisation in Packet Switching Networks," *IEEE Network*, Vol. 7, No. 5, September 1993.

> Intersample variation management for single flows.

AMDAHL, G.M. [1967]. "Validity of the Single Processor Approach to Achieving Large Scale Computing Capabilities," *Proc. AFIPS 1967 Spring Joint Computer Conf.,* Vol. 30, Atlantic City, N.J., April 1967, pp. 483-485.

> An insightful and widely cited discussion of trade-offs in computer performance.

ANDERSON, D.P. [1993]. "Meta-Scheduling for Distributed Continuous Media," *ACM Trans. on Computer Systems*, Vol. 11, No. 3, August 1993.

> Scheduling techniques for operating systems supporting multimedia applications.

ANDERSON, T.E., H.M. LEVY, B.N. BERSHAD, and E.D. LAZOWSKA [1991]. "The Interaction of Architectures and Operating System Design," *Proc. 4th Intl. Conf. Architectural Support for Programming Languages and Operating Systems*, ACM, Santa Clara, Calif., 8-11 April 1991.

> Suggestions on how operating systems may need to adapt to changes in processor architectures.

ARNOULD, E.A., F.J. BITZ, E.C. COOPER, R.D. SANSOM, and P.A. STEENKISTE [1989]. "The Design of Nectar: A Network Backplane for Heterogeneous Multicomputers," *Proc. 3rd Intl. Conf. Architectural Support for Programming Languages and Operating Systems (ASPLOS)*, April 1989, pp. 205-216.

> Describes the CAB network interface.

ARTHURS, E., J.M. COOPER, M.S. GOODMAN, H. KOBRINSKI, M. TUR, and M.P. VECCHI
[1986]. "Multiwavelength Optical Crossconnect for Parallel-Processing Computers," *Electronic Letters*, Vol. 24, pp. 119-120.
The FOX network.

ARTSY, Y., and R. FINKEL [1989]. "Designing a Process Migration Facility: The Char-
lotte Experience," *Computer*, Vol. 22, No. 9, September 1989, pp. 47-58.
A good paper on process migration.

ASTHANA, A., C. DELPH, H.V. JAGADISH, and P. KRZYZANOWSKI [1992]. "Towards a
Gigabit IP Router," *Jour. of High Speed Networks*, Vol. 1, No. 4, pp. 281-288.
Describes an experimental router built at AT&T.

BALLARDIE, T., P. FRANCIS, and J. CROWCROFT [1993]. "Core Based Trees," *Proc. ACM
SIGCOMM '93*, San Francisco, September 1993, pp. 1-11.
Describes an alternative to Deering multicasting.

BALOMBIN, J. [1992]. "TDMA System and Gigabit Earth Station," *Proc. DARPA Principle Investigators Meeting*, New Orleans, 1-2 September 1992.
Slides describing the ACTS system in general.

BANERJEA, A., and B.A. MAH [1991]. "The Real-Time Channel Administration Protocol," *Proc. 2nd Intl. Workshop on Network and Operating System Support for Digital Audio and Video*, Heidelberg, November 1991.
Describes RCAP.

BANKS, D., and M. PRUDENCE [1993]. "A High Performance Network Architecture for a
PA-RISC Workstation," *IEEE Jour. Selected Areas in Communications*, Vol. 10,
No. 1, February 1993, pp. 191-202.
Describes the Medusa Interface.

BARAN, P. [1964]. "On Distributed Communications," RM-3420-PR, Rand Corp.,
August 1964.
Arguably the first research work to discuss the idea of packet switching.

BATCHER, K.E. [1968]. "Sorting networks and their applications," *Proc. AFIPS Spring
Joint Conf.*, Vol. 32, pp. 307-314.
How to build Batcher sorting networks.

BERGAMO, M. [1992]. "TDMA System and Gigabit Earth Station," *Proc. DARPA Principle Investigators Meeting*, New Orleans, 1-2 September 1992.
A talk on the ACTS system as used for data networking.

BIERSACK, E.W., C.J. COTTON, D.C. FELDMEIER, A.J. MCAULEY, and W.D. SINCOSKIE
[1992]. "Gigabit Networking Research at Bellcore," *IEEE Network Magazine*,
Vol. 6, No. 2, March 1992, pp. 42-48.
Survey of Aurora project from Bellcore's perspective.

BIRRELL, A., and B. NELSON [1984]. "Implementing Remote Procedure Calls," *ACM Trans. Computer Systems*, Vol. 2, No. 1, February 1984, pp. 39-59.

A very influential paper on RPC.

BJORKMAN, M., and P. GUNNINGBERG [1993]. "Locking Effects in Multiprocessor Implementation of Protocols," *Proc. ACM SIGCOMM '93*, San Francisco, September 1993.

A parallel TCP/IP implementation based on the X-kernel.

BLAHUT, R.E. [1983]. *Theory and Practice of Error Control Codes,* Addison-Wesley, Reading, Mass.

A good textbook for theory of CRCs.

BOGGS, D.R., J.C. MOGUL, and C.A. KENT [1988]. "Measured Capacity of an Ethernet: Myths and Reality," *Proc. ACM SIGCOMM '88*, Stanford, Calif., August 1988, pp. 222-234.

Boggs and colleagues point out the deficiencies of most theoretical studies of Ethernet performance and show actual measured throughput of about 9 Mbit/s.

BORGHOFF, U.M., and K. NAST-KOLB [1989]. "Distributed Systems: A Comprehensive Survey," TUM-I8909, Technical Univ. Munich, Munich, Germany.

The most comprehensive listing available of distributed systems research world-wide.

BORMAN, D.A. [1989]. "Implementing TCP/IP on a Cray Computer," *ACM Computer Communication Review*, Vol. 19, No. 2, April 1989, pp. 11-15.

A real example of a fast TCP/IP.

BRACKETT, C.A. [1990]. "Dense Wavelength Division Multiplexing Networks: Principles and Applications," *IEEE Jour. Selected Areas in Communications*, Vol. 8, No. 6, August 1990, pp. 948-964.

A good survey of the problems in dense WDM, as of 1990.

BRADEN, B., D. BORMAN, and C. PARTRIDGE [1988]. "Computing the Internet Checksum; RFC 1071," *Internet Request for Comments*, No. 1071, Network Information Center, September 1988.

Summarizes techniques for making implementations of the Internet checksum run fast.

BRADEN, R. [1989]. "Requirements for Internet Hosts — Communication Layers; RFC-1122," *Internet Requests for Comments*, No. 1122, DDN Network Information Center, October 1989.

Establishes what protocols must be supported by an IP host and fixes errors in the specifications.

BRADY, P.T. [1971]. "Effects of Transmission Delay on Conversational Behavior on Echo-Free Telephone Circuits," *Bell System Technical Jour.*, Vol. 50, No. 1, January 1971, pp. 115-134.

A careful study of delay issues in voice speech. One of the best at isolating equipment issues from human factors.

BROSCIUS, A.G., and J.M. SMITH [1991]. "Exploiting Parallelism in Hardware Implementation of the DES," *Proc. CRYPTO 1991 Conf.*, Santa Barbara, Calif., August 1991, pp. 367-376.

> Describes a high-speed DES system.

CABRERA, L-F. [1986]. "The Influence of Workload on Load Balancing Strategies," *Proc. 1986 Summer USENIX Conf.*, Atlanta, Georgia, 11-13 June 1986, pp. 446-458.

> Studies the behavior of processes, with a view toward deciding which processes to migrate. Arguably most interesting for its results, which show the average process (in UNIX at least) is very short lived.

CACERES, R. [1991a]. *Efficiency of Asynchronous Transfer Mode Networks in Tranporting Wide-Area Data Traffic,* International Computer Science Institute, University of California Berkeley, July 1991

> Takes traces of packet sizes from IP traffic and computes cost of encapsulation in ATM.

CACERES, R., P.B. DANZIG, S. JAMIN, and D.J. MITZEL [1991b]. "Characteristics of Wide-Area TCP Conversations," *Proc. ACM SIGCOMM '91*, Zurich, September 1991, pp. 101-112.

> Discusses the statistical behavior of TCP connections made by various applications.

CASNER, S., K. SEO, W. EDMOND, and C. TOPOLCIC [1990]. "N-Way Conferencing with Packet Video," *Proc. 3rd Intl. Workshop on Packet Video*, Morristown, N.J., March 1990.

> Reports on experience with ST.

CATLETT, C.E. [1992]. "In Search of Gigabit Applications," *IEEE Communications Magazine*, Vol. 30, No. 4, April 1992, pp. 42-51.

> Discusses some of the applications being used in the gigabit testbeds.

CATLETT, C., and S.M. TAN [1993]. "Singapore Gigabit Networks," *Internet Society News*, Vol. 1, No. 4, Winter 1993, pp. 12-13.

> Describes planned Singapore gigabit testbed.

CHEN, W.-T., H.-J. LIU, and Y.-T. TSAY [1991]. "High-Throughput Cell Scheduling for Broadband Switching Systems," *IEEE Jour. Selected Areas in Communications*, Vol. 9, No. 9, December 1991, pp. 1150-1523.

CHERITON, D.R., H. GOOSEN, and P. BOYLE [1991]. "ParaDiGM: A Highly Scalable Shared-Memory, Multi-Computer Architecture," *IEEE Computer*, Vol. 24, No. 2, February 1991.

> Describes an innovative idea for distributed shared memory.

CHESSON, G. [1987]. "Protocol Engine Design," *Proc. 1987 Summer USENIX Conf.*, Phoenix, Az., 8-12 June 1987, pp. 209-216.

Generally considered the paper that launched the idea of lightweight protocols.

CHEUNG, N.K., K. NOSU, and G. WINZER [1990]. "Dense Wavelength Division Multiplexing Techniques for High Capacity and Multiple Access Communication Systems (Special Issue)," *IEEE Jour. Selected Areas in Communications*, Vol. 8, No. 6, August 1990.

An entire special issue on dense WDM, including a fine survey paper by C.A. Brackett.

CIDON, I., J. DERBY, I. GOPAL, and B. KADABA [1992a]. "A Critique of ATM from a Data Communications Perspective," *Jour. of High Speed Networks*, Vol. 1, No. 4, pp. 315-336.

Discusses various shortcomings of ATM.

CIDON, I., and I. GOPAL [1988]. "Paris: An Approach to Integrated High-Speed Private Networks," *Intl. Jour. Digital and Analog Cabled Systems*, Vol. 1, pp. 77-85.

The Paris (now plaNET) switching system.

CIDON, I., I. GOPAL, J. JANNIELLO, and M. KAPLAN [1992b]. "The plaNET/ORBIT High Speed Network," RC-18270, IBM.

The most recent overview of the plaNET and ORBIT architectures.

CISNEROS, A., and C.A. BRACKETT [1991]. "A Large ATM Switch Based on Memory Switches and Optical Star Couplers," *IEEE Jour. Selected Areas in Communications*, Vol. 9, No. 8, October 1991, pp. 1348-1360.

An intriguing design for a cell switch with optical switching fabric.

CLAMEN, S.M., L.D. LEIBENGOOD, S.M. NETTLES, and J.M. WING [1989]. *An Overview of Avalon/Common Lisp,* Carnegie-Mellon University, Department of Computer Science, 22 September 1989

An environment that uses REV. See Stamos.

CLARK, D. [1989a]. "Policy Routing in Internet Protocols; RFC-1102," *Internet Request for Comments*, No. 1102, Network Information Center, May 1989.

A discussion of policy routing. See Estrin.

CLARK, D.D. [1982]. "Modularity and Efficiency in Protocol Implementation; RFC-817," *Internet Request for Comments*, No. 817, Network Information Center, July 1982.

Still one of the best papers on how to do a protocol implementation.

CLARK, D.D., B.S. DAVIE, D.J. FARBER, I.S. GOPAL, B.K. KADABA, W.D. SINCOSKIE, J.M. SMITH, and D.L. TENNENHOUSE [1993]. "The AURORA Gigabit Testbed," *Computer Networks and ISDN Systems*, Vol. 25, No. 6, January 1993.

A joint survey of the Aurora testbed.

CLARK, D.D., V. JACOBSON, J. ROMKEY, and H. SALWEN [1989b]. "An Analysis of TCP Processing Overhead," *IEEE Communications*, Vol. 27, No. 6, June 1989, pp. 23-29.

Valuable reference on protocol processing overhead.

CLARK, D.D., S. SHENKER, and L. ZHANG [1992]. "Supporting Real-Time Applications in an Integrated Services Packet Network: Architecture and Mechanism," *Proc. ACM SIGCOMM '92*, Baltimore, August 1992, pp. 14-26.

Describes FIFO+.

CLARK, D.D., and D.L. TENNENHOUSE [1990]. "Architectural Considerations for a New Generation of Protocols," *Proc. ACM SIGCOMM '90*, Vol. 20, No. 4, Philadelphia, September 1990, pp. 200-208.

Suggestions for how to structure gigabit protocols. Presents ALF.

COHEN, D., G. FINN, R. FELDERMAN, and A. DESCHON [1992]. *ATOMIC: A Local Communication Network Created Through Repeated Application of Multicomputing Components*, USC-Information Sciences Institute

COMER, D.E. [1991]. *Internetworking with TCP/IP, (*Vol I*): Principles, Protocols and Architecture*, 2nd edition, Prentice Hall, Englewood Cliffs, N.J.

A widely used textbook on TCP/IP.

COX, J.R., M.E. GADDIS, and J.S. TURNER [1993]. "Project Zeus," *IEEE Network Magazine*, Vol. 7, No. 2, March 1993.

A survey of Project Zeus.

CROWCROFT, J., I. WAKEMAN, Z. WANG, and D. SIROVICA [1992]. "Is Layering Harmful?," *IEEE Network Magazine*, Vol. 6, No. 1, January 1992, pp. 20-25.

Discusses how layered implementations can lead to surprising bugs.

CRUZ, R.L. [1991a]. "A Calculus for Network Delay, Part I: Network Elements in Isolation," *IEEE Trans. on Information Theory*, Vol. 37, No. 1, January 1991, pp. 114-131.

First piece of two-part work on queueing bounds.

CRUZ, R.L. [1991b]. "A Calculus for Network Delay, Part II: Network Analysis," *IEEE Trans. on Information Theory*, Vol. 37, No. 1, January 1991, pp. 132-141.

Second piece of two-part work on queueing bounds. Contains most of the interesting delay results.

CRUZ, R.L. [1992]. "Service Burstiness and Dynamic Burstiness Measures: A Framework," *Jour. of High Speed Networks*, Vol. 1, No. 2, pp. 105-128.

Extends his work and that of Parekh to cover queueing algorithms similar to FIFO+.

DALLY, W.J., and C.L. SEITZ [1987]. "Deadlock-Free Message Routing in Multiprocessor Interconnection Networks," *IEEE Trans. on Computers*, Vol. 36, No. 5, May 1987.

Describes routing approach taken in Mosaic chip.

DANTHINE, A. [1992]. "Esprit Project OSI'95: New Transport Services for High-Speed Networking," *Computer Networks and ISDN Systems*, Vol. 25, pp. 384-399.

Presents the goals of OSI'95.

DAVIDSON, J., W. HATHAWAY, J. POSTEL, N. MIMNO, R. THOMAS, and D. WALDEN [1977]. "The ARPAnet Telnet Protocol: Its Purpose, Principles of Implementation and Impact on Host Operating System Design," *Proc. Fifth Data Communications Symp.*, Snowbird, Utah, September 1977.

Includes an early discussion of layering.

DAVIE, B.S. [1991]. "Host Interface Design for Experimental Very High-Speed Networks," *Proc. ACM SIGCOMM '91*, Zurich, September 1991, pp. 307-315.

Describes an ATM interface for the DEC 5000 workstation.

DAVIE, B.S. [1993a]. "The Architecture and Implementation of a High-Speed Host Interface," *IEEE Jour. Selected Areas in Communications*, Vol. 11, No. 2, February 1993, pp. 173-180.

More on the OSIRIS interface.

DAVIE, B.S., J.M. SMITH, and C.B.S. TRAW [1993b]. "Host Interfaces for ATM Networks," *High Performance Communications*, Kluwer Academic Publishers.

DEERING, S.E. [1988]. "Multicast Routing in Internetworks and Extended LANs," *Proc. SIGCOMM '88*, Stanford, Ca., August 1988.

The short paper on multicasting.

DEERING, S.E. [1991]. *Multicast Routing in a Datagram Internetwork,* Stanford University, December 1991, pp. 55-64

The big work on multicasting (his doctoral thesis). Also available as Stanford Computer Science Department technical report no. STAN-CS-92-1415.

DELP, G. [1988]. "The Architecture and Implementation of Memnet: A High-Speed Shared-Memory Computer Communication Network," Udel-EE 88-05-1, University of Delaware, May 1988.

An implementation of shared memory, considered in detail.

DELP, G., D. FARBER, R. MINNICH, J.M. SMITH, and M.-C. TAM [1991]. "Memory as a Network Abstraction," *IEEE Network*, Vol. 5, No. 4, July 1991, pp. 34-41.

Modelling high speed networks as distributed memory.

DEMERS, A., S. KESHAV, and S. SHENKER [1990]. "Analysis and Simulation of a Fair Queueing Algorithm," *Internetwork: Research and Experience*, Vol. 1, No. 1, John Wiley & Sons, September 1990, pp. 3-26.

> Presents an enhanced version of fair queueing and weighted fair queueing. An earlier version of the paper appeared in *Proc. ACM SIGCOMM '89.*

DEPRYCKER, M. [1993]. *Asynchronous Transfer Mode: Solution for Broadband ISDN* (2nd edition), Ellis Horwood, Chichester, England

> Most up-to-date survey of ATM.

DE VRIES, R.J.F. [1990]. "Gauss: a simple high performance switch architecture for ATM," *Proc. ACM SIGCOMM '90; (Special Issue Computer Communication Review)*, Vol. 20, No. 4, September 1990, pp. 126-134.

> One of the nicer crossbar variants. Published after Jacob's [1990] survey.

DHAS, C., V.K. KONANGI, and M. SREETHARAN [1991]. *Broadband Switching: Architectures, Protocols, Design, and Analysis*, IEEE Computer Society, New York

> A good collection of papers on cell switching, though biased toward papers published in IEEE journals.

DIFFIE, W. [1988]. "The First Ten Years of Public Key Cryptography," *Proc. IEEE*, Vol. 76, No. 5, May 1988, pp. 560-577.

> A good survey of public key algorithms by one of the inventors of public key.

DOERINGER, W., D. DYKEMAN, M. KAISERSWERTH, B.W. MEISTER, H. RUDIN, and R. WILLIAMSON [1990]. "A Survey of Light-Weight Transport Protocols for High-Speed Networks," *IEEE Trans. on Communications*, Vol. 38, No. 11, November 1990, pp. 2025-2039.

> The broadest survey of lightweight protocols.

DOUGLIS, F., and J. OUSTERHOUT [1989]. "Transparent Process Migration for Personal Workstations," UCB/CSD 89/540, Computer Science Division, Univ. California, Berkeley, Calif., November 1989.

> Process migration in Sprite.

EL-DESSOUKI, O.I. [1978]. *Program Partitioning and Load Balancing in Network Computers*, Illinois Institute of Technology

> A doctoral dissertation. Theoretical study of problems of partitioning computation across multiple machines.

ESCOBAR, J., D. DEUTSCH, and C. PARTRIDGE [1992]. "Flow Synchronization Protocol," *IEEE GLOBECOM '92*, Orlando, Fl., December 1992, pp. 1381-1387.

> Describes a general solution to multiprotocol synchronization.

ESCOBAR, J., and C. PARTRIDGE [1991]. "A Proposed Segmentation and Re-assembly (SAR) Protocol for Use with Asynchronous Transfer Mode (ATM)," *Protocols for High-Speed Networks, II (Proc. IFIP 6.1/6.4 Workshop)*, Elsevier, San Jose, Calif., pp. 353-368.

> A general SAR and thoughts about SAR design are presented.

ESTRIN, D. [1989]. "Policy requirements for inter Administrative Domain routin; RFC-1125," *Internet Request for Comments*, No. 1125, Network Information Center, November 1989.

> A discussion of policy routing. See Clark [1989].

FABER, T., L. LANDWEBER, and A. MUKHERJEE [1992]. "Dynamic Time Windows: Packet Admission Control with Feedback," *Proc. ACM SIGCOMM '92*, Baltimore, August 1992, pp. 124-135.

> An interesting scheme for congestion avoidance and control at high speeds.

FALCONE, J.R., and J.S. EMER [1986]. "A Programmable Interface Language for Heterogeneous Distributed Systems," DEC-TR-371, Digital Equiment Corporation, August 1986.

> Migrating code to manage distributed systems. See Stamos [1986].

FELDMEIER, D.C. [1988]. "Improving Gateway Performance with a Routing-Table Cache," *Proc. IEEE INFOCOM '88*, New Orleans, March 1988, pp. 298-307.

> Measurements of cache sizes and their hit rates.

FELDMEIER, D.C. [1990]. "Multiplexing Issues in Communications System Design," *Proc. ACM SIGCOMM '90*, Philadelphia, September 1990, pp. 209-219.

> Discussion of the role of (and problems with) multiplexing in network protocols.

FERRARI, D. [1992]. "Real-Time Communication in an Internetwork," *Jour. of High Speed Networks*, Vol. 1, No. 1, pp. 78-103.

> An architecture paper that describes the larger approach that the Jitter-EDD and other mechanisms are designed to achieve.

FERRARI, D., and D. VERMA [1990]. "A Scheme for Real-Time Channel Establishment in Wide-Area Networks," *IEEE Jour. Selected Areas in Communications*, Vol. 8, No. 3, April 1990, pp. 368-379.

> A design of setup rules.

FLETCHER, J. [1982]. "An Arithmetic Checksum for Serial Transmissions," *IEEE Trans. on Communication*, Vol. 30, No. 1, January 1982, pp. 247-252.

> Explains the OSI checksum algorithm.

FOUDRIAT, E.C., K. MALY, C.M. OVERSTREET, S. KHANNA, and F. PATERRA [1991]. "A Carrier Sensed Multiple Access Protocol for High Data Rate Ring Networks," *ACM Computer Communication Review*, Vol. 21, No. 2, April 1991, pp. 59-70.

> An interesting design for a CSMA high-speed ring.

FRASER, A.G. [1993]. "Early Experiments with Asynchronous Time Division Networks," *IEEE Network Magazine*, Vol. 7, No. 1, January 1993, pp. 12-27.
> Fraser's retrospective, complete with copies of early drawings, on early work on cell networks.

GANS, M.J., T.S. CHU, P.W. WOLNIANSKY, and M. CARLONI [1991]. "A 2.5 Gigabit 23-Mile Radio Link for LuckyNet," *Proc. IEEE GLOBECOM '91*, Phoenix, Az., 2-5 December 1991, pp. 1065-1068.
> Describes the design of a fast radio link.

GARRETT, M.W., and M. VETTERLI [1993]. "Joint Source/Channel Coding of Statistically Multiplexed Real-Time Services on Packet Networks," *IEEE/ACM Trans. on Networking*, Vol. 1, No. 1, February 1993, pp. 71-80.
> Priority schemes for real-time traffic.

GAUFFIN, L., L. HAKANSSON, and B. PEHSON [1992]. "Multi-Gigabit Networking Based on DTM: A TDM Medium Access Technique with Dynamical Bandwidth-Allocation," *Computer Networks and ISDN Systems*, Vol. 24, pp. 119-130.
> Describes the access protocol for an experimental network being built for MultiG.

GIACOPELLI, J.N., J.J. HICKEY, W.S. MARCUS, W.D. SINCOSKIE, and M. LITTLEWOOD, [1991]. "Sunshine: A High-Performance Self-Routing Broadband Packet Switch Architecture," *IEEE Jour. Selected Areas in Communications*, Vol. 9, No. 8, October 1991, pp. 1289-1298.
> One of the latest Batcher-Banyan switch.

GIDRON, R. [1992]. "TeraNet: A Multi-Gigabits Per Second ATM Network," *Network Architecture*.
> The best description of TeraNet.

GITLIN, R., and T.B. LONDON [1992]. "Broadband Network Research and the LuckyNet Testbed," *Jour. of High Speed Networks*, Vol. 1, No. 1, pp. 1-48.
> An overview of LuckyNet.

GOLDBERG, A., and D. ROBSON [1980]. *SMALLTALK-80 - The Language and Its Implementation*, Addison-Wesley, Reading, Mass.
> SMALLTALK described by some of its designers.

GOLESTANI, S.J. [1990a]. "Congestion-Free Transmission of Real-Time Traffic in Packet Networks," *Proc. IEEE INFOCOM '90*, San Francisco, June 1990, pp. 527-536.
> Expansions on (r,T)-smoothing.

GOLESTANI, S.J. [1990b]. "A Stop-and-Go Queueing Framework for Congestion Management," *Proc. ACM SIGCOMM '90*, Vol. 20, No. 4, September 1990, pp. 8-18.
> (r,T)-smoothing.

GOLESTANI, S.J. [1991]. "Duration-Limited Statistical Multiplexing of Delay-Sensitive Traffic in Packet Networks," *Proc. IEEE INFOCOM '91*, Bal Harbor, Fl., April 1991, pp. 323-332.

GOODMAN, M.S., H. KOBRINSKI, M.P. VECCHI, R.M. BULLEY, and J.L. GIMLETT [1990]. "The LAMBDANET Multiwavelength Network: Architecture, Applications, and Demonstrations," *IEEE Jour. Selected Areas in Communications*, Vol. 8, No. 6, August 1990, pp. 995-1004.

    One of the best known single-hop WDM network experiments.

GRAY, C.G., and D.R. CHERITON [1989]. "Leases: An Efficient Fault-Tolerant Mechanism for Distributed File Cache Consistency," *Proc. 12th ACM Symp. on Operating Systems Principles*, Litchfield Park, Arizona, December 3-6, 1989.

    A method for reducing the costs of maintaining a cache.

GRAY, J. [1988]. "The Cost of Messages," *Proc. 7th Annual ACM Symp. on Principles of Distributed Computing*, Toronto, Canada, 15-17 August 1988, pp. 1-7.

    Analyzes the cost of sending a message over a network, c. 1988.

GREAVES, D.J., D. LIOUPIS, and A. HOPPER [1990]. "The Cambridge Backbone Ring," *IEEE INFOCOM '90*, San Francisco, June 1990, pp. 8-14.

    One of the best papers on high-speed cell LANs.

GREEN, P.E. [1993]. *Fiber Optic Networks,* Prentice Hall, Englewood Cliffs, N.J.

    A rigorous treatment of fiber optics intended as a graduate textbook.

GREENE, D., and B. LYLES [1992]. "Reliability of Adaptation Layers," *Protocols for High-Speed Networks, III (Proc. IFIP 6.1/6.4 Workshop)*, Elsevier, Stockholm.

    Shows that the far simpler AAL 5 has superior error handling properties to AAL 3/4.

GUERIN, R., H. AHMADI, and M. NAGHSHINEH [1991]. "Equivalent Capacity and its Application to Bandwidth Allocation in High-Speed Networks," *IEEE Jour. Selected Areas in Communications*, Vol. 9, No. 7, September 1991, pp. 968-981.

    Thought provoking work on bandwidth management and congestion avoidance.

GUERIN, R., and L. GUN [1992]. "A Unified Approach to Bandwidth Allocation in Fast Packet-Switched Networks," *Proc. IEEE INFOCOM '92*, May 1992, pp. 1-12.

    Interesting thinking on congestion and flow control.

HAHNE, E.L., A.K. CHOUDHURY, and N.F. MAXEMCHUK [1990]. "Improving the Fairness of Distributed-Queue-Dual-Bus Networks," *Proc. IEEE INFOCOM '90*, San Francisco, June 1990, pp. 175-184.

    How to fix fairness problems in dual-bus networks.

HANDEL, R., and M.N. HUBER [1990]. *Integrated Broadband Networks; An Introduction to ATM-based Networks,* Addison-Wesley, Reading, Mass.

    Good basic introduction to B-ISDN.

HAYTER, M., and D. MCAULEY [1991]. "The Desk-Area Network," *ACM Operating Systems Review*, Vol. 25, October 1991, pp. 14-21.

> Describes using ATM as a computer bus.

HEIMLICH, S.A. [1989]. "Traffic Characterization of the NSFNET National Backbone," *Proc. 1989 Winter USENIX Conf.*

> A study of traffic patterns on the NSFNET backbone.

HEINANEN, J. [1993]. "Multiprotocol Encapsulation over ATM Adaptation Layer 5; RFC 1483," *Internet Requests for Comments*, No. 1483, July 1993.

> While issued by an Internet standards body, this proposed standard is expected to be adopted as the way to encapsulate all datagram protocols over AAL 5.

HENNESSY, J.L., and D.A. PATTERSON [1990]. *Computer Architecture: A Quantitative Approach,* Morgan Kaufmann, San Mateo, Calif.

> Probably the best computer architecture textbook available.

HOLZMANN, G. [1991]. *Design and Validation of Computer Protocols,* Prentice Hall, Englewood Cliffs, N.J.

> Fast becoming the standard reference on protocol validation.

HOPPER, A. [1977]. "Data Ring at Computer Laboratory, University of Cambridge," *Computer Science and Technology; NBS Special-Pub 500-31*, US National Bureau of Standards, Washington, D.C., 23-23 August 1977.

> Possibly the earliest cell network.

HOPPER, A. [1990]. "Pandora — An Experimental System for Multimedia Applications," *ACM Operating Systems Review*, Vol. 24, No. 2, April 1990.

> Multimedia experiments at University of Cambridge.

HUANG, A., and S. KNAUER [1984]. "STARLITE: A Wideband Digital Switch," *Proc. GLOBECOM '84*, Atlanta, Georgia, 26-29 November 1984, pp. 121-125.

> The first widely known Batcher-Banyan switch.

HUITEMA, C., and A. DOGHRI [1990]. "A High Speed Approach for the OSI Presentation Protocol," *Protocols for High-Speed Networks, I (Proc. IFIP 6.1/6.4 Workshop)*, Elsevier, Zurich, pp. 277-288.

> Illustrates the costs of supporting the ASN.1 external data representation and suggests an alternative representation which is faster.

HUTTO, P.W., and M. AHAMAD [1990]. *Slow Memory: Weakening Consistency to Enhance Concurrency in Distributed Shared Memories,* Georgia Institute of Technology, Atlanta

> Interesting ideas about memory consistency rules.

HYMAN, J., A.A. LAZAR, and G. PACIFICI [1991]. "MARS: The MAGNET II Real-Time Scheduling Algorithm," *Proc. ACM SIGCOMM '91*, Zurich, September 1991, pp. 285-294.

> Scheduling algorithms for TeraNet.

IEEE [1991]. *Distributed Queue Dual Bus (DQDB) Subnetwork of a Metropolitan Area Network (MAN)*, Institute for Electrical and Electronics Engineers, Piscataway, N.J., 3 July 1991

> The DQDB Standard.

IRVIN, D.R. [1993]. "Making Broadband-ISDN Successful," *IEEE Network Magazine*, Vol. 7, No. 1, January 1993, pp. 40-45.

> A useful discussion of how trends in data communications and telephony are likely to impact telephone companies.

JACOB, A.R. [1990]. "A Survey of Fast Packet Switches," *ACM Computer Communication Review*, Vol. 20, No. 1, January 1990, pp. 54-64.

> A good place to start reading about switches. Has references to most of the key papers.

JACOBSON, V. [1988]. "Congestion Avoidance and Control," *Proc. ACM SIGCOMM '88*, Stanford, Calif., August 1988, pp. 314-329.

> A classic paper on TCP congestion and flow control.

JACOBSON, V. [1990b]. "4BSD Header Prediction," *ACM Computer Communication Review*, Vol. 20, No. 1, April 1990, pp. 13-15.

> Slides illustrating the basic header prediction algorithms.

JACOBSON, V. [1990a]. "Compression TCP/IP Headers for Low-Speed Serial Links; RFC-1144," *Internet Request for Comments*, No. 1144, Network Information Center, February 1990.

> Describes how to compress TCP/IP headers based on observations about how the fields are used.

JACOBSON, V. [1990c]. *Tutorial Notes from SIGCOMM '90,* , Philadelphia, September 1990.

> Now available only from people who were at the tutorial, these notes provide code for and insightful comments about developing very high-speed TCP/IP implementations.

JACOBSON, V., R. BRADEN, and D. BORMAN [1992]. "TCP Extensions for High Performance; RFC-1323," *Internet Request for Comments*, No. 1323, Network Information Center, May 1992.

> Defines extensions to TCP for high delay×bandwidth paths.

JAIN, R. [1990a]. "Myths About Congestion Management in High-Speed Network," DEC-TR-724, Digital Equipment Corporation.

> A good discussion of some of the ways one can get confused about congestion management.

JAIN, R. [1990b]. "Performance Analysis of FDDI Token Ring Networks: Effect of Parameters and Guidelines for Setting TTRT," *Proc. ACM SIGCOMM '90*, Philadelphia, September 1990, pp. 264-275.

    A careful study of the relationship between token rotation times and network efficiency.

JAIN, R. [1991]. *The Art of Computer Systems Performance Analysis: Techniques for Experimental Design, Measurement, Simulation and Modelling,* Wiley, New York.

    An award-winning book on performance analysis.

JAIN, R. [1992]. "A Comparison of Hashing Schemes for Address Lookup in Computer Networks," *IEEE Trans. on Communications*, Vol. 40, No. 10, October 1992, pp. 1570-1573.

    Hashing schemes for routers.

JAIN, R., and K.K. RAMAKRISHNAN [1988]. "A Binary Feedback Scheme for Congestion Avoidance in Computer Networks with a Connectionless Network Layer," *Proc. ACM SIGCOMM '88*, Stanford, Calif., 16-19 August 1988, pp. 303-313.

    The DEC-bit congestion control scheme.

JAIN, R., and S. ROUTHIER [1986]. "Packet Trains: Measurements and a New Model for Computer Network Traffic," *IEEE Jour. Selected Areas in Communications*, Vol. 4, No. 6, May 1986, pp. 1162-1167.

    A good model of how data traffic tends to behave.

JANNIELLO, F.J., R. RAMASWAMI, and D.G. STEINBERG [1992]. "A Prototype Circuit-Switched Multi-Wavelength Optical Metropolitan-Area Network," *Proc. IEEE Intl. Communications Conf.*, Geneva.

    Describes RAINBOW WDM network as demonstrated in late 1991.

JOHNSON, M.J. [1991]. *Protocols for High-Speed Networks, II (Proc. IFIP 6.1/6.4 Workshop),* Elsevier, San Jose, Calif.

    Proc. 2nd IFIP 6.1/6.4 workshop. A number of notable papers on issues such as SAR protocols, congestion control, and gigabit protocol and interface design.

JUL, E., H. LEVY, N. HUTCHINSON, and A. BLACK [1988]. "Fine-Grained Mobility in the Emerald System," *ACM Trans. Computer Systems*, Vol. 6, No. 1, February 1988, pp. 109-133.

    An interesting object-oriented distributed system.

KANAKIA, H., and D. CHERITON [1988]. "The VMP Network Adapter Board (NAB): High-Performance Network Communication for Multiprocessors," *Proc. ACM SIGCOMM '88*, Stanford, Calif., August 1988, pp. 175-187.

    Describes the NAB network interface.

KARN, P., and C. PARTRIDGE [1991]. "Improving Round-Trip Time Estimates in Reliable Transport Protocols," *ACM Trans. on Computer Systems*, Vol. 9, No. 4, November 1991, pp. 364-373.

> Defines Karn's algorithm for filtering out potentially misleading round-trip time samples.

KAROL, M.J., M.G. HLUCHYJ, and S.P. MORGAN [1987]. "Input Versus Output Queueing on a Space-Division Packet Switch," *IEEE Trans. Communications*, Vol. 35, No. 12, December 1987, pp. 1347-1356.

> Classic study on cell switch design.

KAY, J., and J. PASQUALE [1993]. "The Importance of Non-Data Touching Processing Overheads in TCP/IP," *Proc. ACM SIGCOMM '93*, San Francisco, September 1993.

> A detailed study of the various overheads in a TCP/IP implementation. Most interesting for its careful measurements of where the costs lie in a particular implementation.

KENT, C.A., and J.C. MOGUL [1987]. "Fragmentation Considered Harmful," *Proc. of ACM SIGCOMM '87*, Stowe, Vt., 11-13 August 1987, pp. 390-401.

> Classic study of fragmentation and reassembly issues.

KENT, S., and J. LINN [1989]. "Privacy Enhancement for Internet Electronic Mail: Part II - Certificate-Based Key Management; RFC-1114," *Internet Requests for Comments*, No. 1114, DDN Network Information Center, August 1989.

> How certificate trees work.

KESHAV, S. [1991]. "On Efficient Implementation of Fair Queuing," *Internetworking: Research and Experience*, Vol. 2, No. 2, September 1991, pp. 157-174.

> Fast queueing ordering schemes in support of fair queueing. See Demers [1990] and McKenney [1991].

KLEINROCK, L. [1975]. *Queueing Systems; Vol. 1: Theory,* John Wiley, New York

> The first volume of the classic work on queueing theory.

KLEINROCK, L. [1976]. *Queueing Systems; Vol. 2: Computer Applications,* John Wiley, New York

> The second volume of the classic work on queueing theory.

KLEMMER, E.T. [1967]. "Subjective Evaluation of Transmission Delay in Telephone Conversations," *The Bell System Technical Jour.*, Vol. 46, July-August 1967, pp. 1141-1147.

> Study of user sensitivity to delays in the network. A successor to Riesz and Klemmer [1963].

KUROSE, J.F. [1992]. "On Computing Per-Session Performance Bounds in High-Speed Multi-Hop Computer Networks," *Proc. ACM SIGMETRICS '92/IFIP Performance '92 Conf.*, Newport, R.I., June 1992, pp. 128-139.
> A study of the probability distributions of delays for traffic routed through multiple switches.

KUROSE, J.F. [1993]. "Open Issues and Challenges in Proving Quality of Service Guarantees in High-Speed Networks," *ACM Computer Communication Review*, Vol. 23, No. 1, January 1993, pp. 6-15.
> A nice overview of the problems of providing service guarantees.

LAUER, H.C., and R.M. NEEDHAM [1978]. "On the Duality of Operating System Structures," *Proc. Second Intl. Symp. on Operating Systems*, IRIA, October 1978.
> Shows that shared memory and message passing are semantically equivalent.

LEE, T.T. [1988]. "Nonblocking Copy Networks for Multicast Packet Switching," *IEEE Jour. Selected Areas in Communications*, Vol. 9, No. 9, December 1988, pp. 1455-1467.
> The standard reference for building multicast copy networks for cell switches. Also contains a nice proof showing how to build nonblocking banyans in the appendix.

LEINER, B. [1988]. "Critical Issues in High Bandwidth Networking; RFC-1077," *Internet Requests for Comments*, No. 1077, DDN Network Information Center, 5 August 1988.
> A study requested by ARPA (then DARPA). Out of date, but sometimes thought provoking.

LELAND, W.E., M.S. TAQQU, W. WILLINGER, and D.V. WILSON [1993]. "On the Self-Similar Nature of Ethernet Traffic," *Proc. ACM SIGCOMM '93*, San Francisco, September 1993.
> Shows that data traffic, as measured on several different networks, is fractal.

LESLIE, I. [1991]. "Fairisle: An ATM Network for the Local Area," *Proc. ACM SIGCOMM '91*, Zurich, September 3-6, 1991, pp. 327-336.
> The Fairisle ATM Switch.

LESLIE, I.M., D.R. MCAULEY, and D.L. TENNENHOUSE [1993b]. "ATM Everywhere?," *IEEE Network Magazine*, Vol. 7, No. 2, March 1993.
> A discussion of the challenges of making ATM ubiquitous.

LESLIE, I.M., D. MCAULEY, and S.J. MULLENDER [1993a]. "Pegasus — Operating System Support for Distributed Multimedia Systems," *Operating Systems Review*, Vol. 27, No. 1, January 1993, pp. 69-78.
> A joint research project between University of Cambridge and University of Twente.

LEWIS, H.R., and L. DENENBERG [1991]. *Data Structures and Their Algorithms,* Harper Collins, New York

> A useful algorithms text. Has a good discussion of perfect hashing.

LIMB, J. [1990]. "A Simple Multiple Access Protocol for Metropolitan Area Networks," *Proc. ACM SIGCOMM '90*, Philadelphia, September 24-27, 1990, pp. 69-78.

> A simple access protocol used in HANGMAN.

LISKOV, B. [1991]. "Practical Uses of Synchronized Clocks in Distributed Systems," *Proc. 10th ACM Symp. Principles of Distributed Computing*, August 1991.

> Describes a number of ways that synchronized clocks can be used to improve or simplify distributed algorithms and systems.

LISKOV, B., and L. SHRIRA [1988]. "Promises: Linguistic Support for Efficient Asynchronous Procedure Calls in Distributed Systems," *Proc. ACM SIGPLAN '88*, Atlanta, Georgia, June 22-24, 1988, pp. 260-267.

> Describes a method for supporting parallel RPC.

LISKOV, B., L. SHRIRA, and J. WROCLAWSKI [1990]. "Efficient At-Most-Once Messages Based on Synchronized Clocks," *Proc. ACM SIGCOMM '90*, Philadelphia, September, 1990.

> A method for supressing possibly harmful duplicate messages using clocks synchronized with NTP.

MAHDAVI, J., G.L. HUNTOON, and M. MATHIS "DHSC Performance Bottleneck: Current Progress," *Proc. Third Gigabit Testbed Workshop*, Corp. National Research Initiatives, pp. 377-380.

> Slides from a talk about the data conversion costs between a Cray Y-MP and a Connection Machine.

MAKRUCKI, B.A. [1991]. "A Study of Source Traffic Management and Buffer Allocation in ATM Networks," *Proc. 7th ITC Specialist Seminar; Broadband Technologies: Applications, Control and Performance.*

> Ideas about how to use statistical multiplexing in ATM networks.

MAXEMCHUK, N. [1985]. "Regular Mesh Topologies in Local and Metropolitan Area Networks," *AT&T Technical Jour.*, Vol. 64, No. 7, September 1985, pp. 1659-1685.

> Early description of the Manhattan Street Network.

MAXEMCHUK, N. [1987]. "Routing in the Manhattan Street Network," *IEEE Trans. on Communications*, Vol. 35, No. 5, May 1987, pp. 503-512.

> Routing techniques for the MSN.

MCAULEY, A.J. [1990]. "Reliable Broadband Communication Using a Burst Erasure Correcting Code," *Proc. ACM SIGCOMM '90*, Philadelphia, 24-27 September 1990, pp. 297-306.

> Develops a variant of Reed-Solomon codes for correcting burst erasures in ATM networks.

MCKENNEY, P. [1991]. "Stochastic Fair Queueing," *Internetworking: Research and Experience*, Vol. 2, No. 2, June 1991, pp. 113-131.

> An approximation to fair queueing that may have a less expensive implementation. See Demers [1990] and Keshav [1991].

MCKENNEY, P., and K. DOVE [1992]. "Efficient Demultiplexing of Incoming TCP Packets," *Proc. ACM SIGCOMM '93*, Baltimore, 17-20 August 1992, pp. 269-279.

> A careful study of various techniques for looking up protocol control blocks.

METCALFE, R.M. [1993]. "Computer/Network Interface Design: Lessons from Arpanet and Ethernet," *IEEE Jour. Selected Areas in Communications*, Vol. 11, No. 2, February 1993, pp. 173-180.

> A wonderful perspective on the challenges of building network interfaces.

METCALFE, R.M., and D.R. BOGGS [1976]. "Ethernet: Distributed Packet Switching for Local Computer Networks," *Communications of the ACM*, Vol. 19, No. 7, July 1976, pp. 395-404.

> Classic Ethernet paper by its designers.

MILLS, D.L. [1990]. "On the Accuracy and Stability of Clocks Synchronized by the Network Time Protocol in the Internet System," *ACM Computer Communication Review*, Vol. 20, No. 1, January 1990, pp. 65-75.

> Experience with NTP.

MILLS, D.L. [1992]. "Network Time Protocol (Version 3): Specification, implementation, and analysis; RFC-1305," *Internet Requests for Comments*, No. 1305, DDN Network Information Center, March 1992.

> Specification of NTP.

MOGUL, J.C. [1991b]. "Network Locality at the Scale of Processes," *Proc. ACM SIGCOMM '91*, Zurich, September 1991, pp. 273-284.

> Describes locality of packet traffic at hosts.

MOGUL, J.C. [1992]. "Observing TCP Dynamics in Real Networks," *Proc. ACM SIGCOMM '92*, Baltimore, August 1992, pp. 305-317.

> Shows that acknowledgement compression exists in real networks. See Zhang, Shenker and Clark [1991].

MOGUL, J.C., and A. BORG [1991a]. "The Effects of Context Switches on Cache Performance," *Proc. 4th Intl. Conf. Architectural Support for Programming Languages and Operating Systems (ASPLOS)*, ACM, Santa Clara, Calif., 8-11 April 1991.

> How cache misses hurt and will continue to hurt on RISC systems.

MUKHERJEE, B. [1992b]. "WDM-Based Local Lightwave Networks; Part 2: Multihop Systems," *IEEE Network Magazine*, Vol. 6, No. 4, July 1992, pp. 20-33.

> Second part of the survey.

MUKHERJEE, B. [1992a]. "WDM-Based Local Lightwave Networks; Part 1: Single-Hop Systems," *IEEE Network Magazine*, Vol. 6, No. 3, May 1992, pp. 12-27.

Excellent survey of techniques for WDM networks.

MULLENDER, S. [1989]. *Distributed Systems,* ACM Press/Addison-Wesley, Reading, Mass.

A good survey, made up of chapters on various topics by the experts on those topics.

NAGARAJAN, R., and J. KUROSE [1992]. "On Defining, Computing, and Guaranteeing Quality-of-Service in High-Speed Networks," *Proc. INFOCOM '92*, May 1992, pp. 2015-2026.

Has examples of how poorly statistical multiplexing can perform.

NAGLE, J. [1984]. "Congestion Control in IP/TCP Internetworks; RFC-896," *Internet Requests for Comments*, No. 896, DDN Network Information Center, January 1984.

One of the earliest works on congestion control. Defines Nagle's algorithm.

NAGLE, J. [1987]. "On Packet Switches with Infinite Storage," *IEEE Trans. on Communications*, Vol. 35, No. 4, April 1987, pp. 435-438.

Presents initial version of fair queueing. Also available as RFC 970.

NAHRSTEDT, K., and J.M. SMITH [1992]. "An Integrated Multimedia Architecture for High-Speed Networks," *Proc. Multimedia '92 Conference*, Monterey, CA, April 1992.

Describes a method for combining multimedia samples into a single flow.

NAKASSIS, A. [1988]. "Fletcher's Error Detection Algorithm: How to Implement It Efficiently and How to Avoid the Most Common Pitfalls," *ACM Computer Communication Review*, Vol. 18, No. 5, October 1988, pp. 63-88.

How to improve implementations of the OSI checksum. See also Sklower [1989].

NELSON, B.J. [1981]. *Remote Procedure Call,* Carnegie-Mellon University

His doctoral dissertation. Probably still the best basic study of RPC.

OUSTERHOUT, J.K. [1990]. "Why Aren't Operating Systems Getting Faster as Fast as Hardware?," *Proc. 1990 Summer USENIX Conf.*, Anaheim, Calif., June 11-15, 1990.

Nice thinking about the future of operating systems.

OUSTERHOUT, J., H. DA COSTA, D. HARRISON, J.A. KUNZE, M. KUPFER, and J.G. THOMPSON [1985]. "A Trace-Driven Analysis of the UNIX 4.2 BSD File System," *Proc. Tenth Symp. Operating System Principles*, ACM, Orcas Island, Wa., 1-4 December 1985, pp. 15-24.

A careful study of file system behavior with lots of implications for caching strategies.

OUSTERHOUT, J., and F. DOUGLIS [1988]. "Beating the I/O Bottleneck: A Case for Log-Structured File Systems," UCB/CSD 88/467, Computer Science Division, Univ. California, Berkeley, Calif., October 1988.

> Some researchers feel this is the most innovative idea for file system design in some time.

PADLIPSKY, M.A. [1983]. "A Perspective on the ARPANET Reference Model," *Proc. INFOCOM '83*, San Diego, Calif..

> Describes the m×n problem in Padlipsky's unique prose style.

PALMER, R. [1992]. "DECspin," *Report on the Workshop on Quality of Service Issues in High Speed Networks*, AT&T Bell Labs, 23-24 April 1992.

> Describes a video conferencing system.

PANCHA, P., and M. EL ZARKI [1992]. "Prioritized Transmission of Variable Bit Rate MPEG Video.," *Proc. IEEE GLOBECOM '92*.

> Describes a scheme for layered MPEG encoding.

PAREKH, A.K.J. [1992]. "A Generalized Processor Sharing Approach to Flow Control in Integrated Services Networks," LIDS-TH-2089, MIT Laboratory for Information and Decision Systems, Cambridge, Mass., February 1992.

> A doctoral dissertation. Gives delay bounds for traffic through a network controlled by fair queueing.

PARTRIDGE, C. [1990b]. *Internet Research Steering Group Workshop on Architectures for Very-High-Speed Networks; RFC-1152*, Cambridge, Mass., 24-26 January 1990.

> Proceedings of a by-application-only workshop on gigabit networking. Beginning to be dated.

PARTRIDGE, C. [1990a]. "How Slow Is One Gigabit Per Second?," *ACM Computer Communication Review*, Vol. 20, No. 1, January 1990, pp. 44-53.

> Argues, based in part on Clark et al. [1989] that TCP/IP could be used over gigabit networks.

PARTRIDGE, C. [1992a]. *Late-Binding RPC: A Paradigm for Distributed Computation in a Gigabit Environment,* Harvard University

> A doctoral dissertation. Describes how to do late-binding RPC.

PARTRIDGE, C. [1992b]. "A Proposed Flow Specification; RFC-1363," *Internet Request for Comments*, No. 1363, Network Information Center, September 1992.

> Defines a flow spec to use for experimentation.

PARTRIDGE, C., and S. PINK [1992c]. "An Implementation of the Revised Internet Stream Protocol (ST-2)," *Internetworking: Research and Experience*, Vol. 3, No. 1, pp. 27-54.

> Describes experience with an implementation of a multimedia protocol.

PARTRIDGE, C., and S. PINK [1993]. "A Faster UDP," *IEEE/ACM Trans. on Networking*, Vol. 1, No. 4, August 1993.

Describes optimizations to reduce UDP processing costs by over 30%.

PARTRIDGE, C., and M.T. ROSE. [1989]. "A Comparison of External Data Formats," *Message Handling Systems and Distributed Applications*, Elsevier/North-Holland.

Compares the major external data formats.

PARTRIDGE, C., and G. TREWITT. [1988]. "The High-Level Entity Management System (HEMS)," *IEEE Network*, March 1988.

A network management protocol that achieves management in large part by sending mini-programs to managed devices to be executed.

PATTERSON, D.A. [1985]. "Reduced Instruction Set Computers," *Communications of the ACM*, Vol. 28, No. 1, January 1985, pp. 8-21.

A short description of RISC processors. For a more detailed explanation, see Hennessy [1990].

PATTERSON, D.A., G. GIBSON, and R.H. KATZ [1988]. "A Case for Redundant Arrays of Inexpensive Disks (RAID)," *Proc. ACM SIGMOD Conf.*, pp. 109-116.

What the disk system of the future might look like.

PEHRSON, B., P. GUNNINGBERG, and S. PINK [1992]. "Distributed Multimedia Applications on Gigabit Networks," *IEEE Network Magazine*, Vol. 6, No. 1, January 1992, pp. 26-35.

Survey of the MultiG project.

PERLMAN, R. [1992]. *Interconnections: Bridges and Routers,* Addison-Wesley, Reading, Mass.

A good textbook on bridging and routing.

PERSONICK, S.D. [1985]. *Fiber Optics: Technology and Applications,* Plenum Publishers

A detailed overview of fiber optics for the nonengineer.

PETERSON, L., N. HUTCHINSON, S. O'MALLEY, and H. RAO [1990]. "The x-kernel: A Platform for Accessing Internet Resources," *Computer*, Vol. 23, No. 5, IEEE, May 1990, pp. 23-34.

A protocol programming package designed to make efficient protocol implementation easier.

PETR, D.W., and V.S. FROST [1990]. "Optimal Packet Discarding: An ATM-Oriented Analysis Model and Initial Results," *Proc. IEEE INFOCOM '91*, June 1990, pp. 537-542.

Discusses discarding of cells based on priority.

PIKE, R. [1991]. "8½, the Plan 9 Window System," *Proc. Summer 1991 USENIX Conf.*, Nashville, June 1991, pp. 257-265.

>   Describes the Plan 9 user interface. Available on-line on research.att.com.

PIKE, R., D. PRESOTTO, K. THOMPSON, and H. TRICKEY [1990]. "Plan 9 from Bell Labs," *Proc. Summer 1990 UKUUG Conf.*, London, July 1990, pp. 1-9.

>   The Plan 9 overview. Also available on-line on research.att.com.

POSTEL, J. [1980]. "User Datagram Protocol; RFC-768," *Internet Request for Comments*, No. 768, Network Information Center, August 1980.

>   The UDP specification.

POSTEL, J. [1981]. "Transmission Control Protocol; RFC-793," *Internet Request for Comments*, No. 793, Network Information Center, September 1981.

>   The TCP specification.

POWELL, M.L., and B.P. MILLER [1983]. "Process Migration in DEMOS/MP," *9th ACM Symp. Operating System Principles*, October 1983.

>   A notable process migration scheme.

PRESOTTO, D., R. PIKE, K. THOMPSON, and H. TRICKEY [1991]. "Plan 9, a Distributed System," *Proc. Spring 1991 EurOpen Conf.*, May 1991, pp. 43-50.

>   Fleshes out some of the distributed systems ideas of Plan 9 a bit more than the 1990 paper (Pike et al.). Available on-line on research.att.com.

RANSOM, M.N. [1992]. "The VISTAnet Gigabit Network Testbed," *Jour. of High Speed Networks*, Vol. 1, No. 1, pp. 49-60.

>   Overview of VISTAnet.

RIESZ, R.R., and E.T. KLEMMER [1963]. "Subject Evaluation of Delay and Echo Suppressors in Telephone Communications," *The Bell System Technical Jour.*, Vol. 42, November 1963, pp. 2919-2941.

>   Studies of user sensitivity to delays in the network. See also, Klemmer's [1967] paper that revises some of the results.

RIVEST, R. [1992]. "The MD5 Message-Digest Algorithm; RFC-1321," *Internet Requests for Comments*, No. 1321, DDN Network Information Center, April 1992.

>   A fast hashing scheme for use in authentication.

RIVEST, R.L., A. SHAMIR, and L. ADLEMAN [1978]. "A method for obtaining digital signatures and public key cryptosystems," *Communications of the ACM*, Vol. 21, No. 2, February 1978, pp. 120-126.

>   Describes RSA and digital authentication.

ROBINSON, J. [1990]. "The Monet Switch," *Internet Research Steering Group Workshop on Architectures for Very-High-Speed Networks; RFC-1152*, DDN Network Information Center, Cambridge, Mass., 24-26 January 1990.

>   A blocking Banyan switch.

ROSE, M. [1991]. *The Simple Book: An Introduction to Management of TCP/IP-based Internets,* Prentice Hall, Englewood Cliffs, N.J.

A good reference for the Simple Network Management Protocol (SNMP).

RUDIN, H.R., and R. WILLIAMSON [1990]. *Protocols for High-Speed Networks, I (Proc. IFIP 6.1/6.4 Workshop),* Elsevier, Zurich

Proceedings of the first IFIP 6.1/6.4 workshop. Papers on the Universal Receiver Protocol and the effects of multiplexing.

SALTZER, J.H., D.P. REED, and D.D. CLARK [1984]. "End-to-End Arguments in System Design," *ACM Trans. on Computer Systems*, Vol. 2, No. 4, November 1984.

The end-to-end argument is one of the few general principles of networking.

SAMPLE, M., and G. NEUFELD [1993]. "Implementing Efficient Encoders and Decoders for Network Data Representations," *Proc. IEEE INFOCOM '93*, San Francisco, 30 March - 1 April 1993, pp. 169-172.

Shows how to improve encoding and decoding performance for ASN.1.

SCHANTZ, R., R. THOMAS, and G. BONO [1986]. "The Architecture of the Cronus Distributed Operating Systems," *Sixth Intl. Conf. on Distributed Computing Systems,* May 1986.

Cronus was a notable object-oriented distributed system.

SCHROEDER, M.D., A.D. BIRRELL, M. BURROWS, H. MUARRY, R.M. NEEDHAM, T.L. RODEHEFFER, E.H. SATTERTHWAITE, and C.P. THACKER [1991]. "Autonet: A High-Speed, Self-Configuring Local Area Network Using Point-to-Point Links," *IEEE Jour. Selected Areas in Communications*, Vol. 9, No. 8, October 1991, pp. 1318-1335.

Describes a self-configuring local area network. The AN2 switch design was heavily influenced by ideas developed in this network.

SCHROEDER, M.D., and M. BURROWS [1989]. "Performance of Firefly RPC," *12th ACM Symp. Operating System Principles*, ACM SIGOPS, December 1989.

Arguably the best study of RPC performance.

SCHULZRINNE, H.G. [1993]. *Reducing and characterizing packet loss for high-speed computer networks with real-time services,* University of Massachusetts, May 1993

A doctoral dissertation. Nevot is described in Chapter 4.

SEXTON, M., and A. REID [1992]. *Transmission Networking: SONET and the Synchronous Digital Hierarchy,* Artech House, Norwood, Mass.

A good survey of SONET though skimpy in its coverage of how ATM might be used over SONET.

SHACHAM, N., and P. MCKENNEY [1990]. "Packet Recovery in High-Speed Networks Using Coding and Buffer Management," *Proc. INFOCOM '90*, June 1990, pp. 124-130.

> A scheme for recovering cells that have been discarded, with suggestions for how to discard cells so that they are likely to be recoverable by the receiver.

SHARON, O., and A. SEGALL [1992]. "A Simple Scheme for Slot Reuse Without Latency in Dual Bus," *Protocols for High-Speed Networks, III (Proc. IFIP 6.1/6.4 Workshop)*, Elsevier, Stockholm, May 13-15, 1992.

> A scheme for slot reuse in dual-bus networks.

SHNEIDERMAN, B. [1992]. *Designing the User Interface: Strategies for Effective Human-Computer Interaction* (2nd edition), Addison-Wesley, Reading, Mass.

> A thought provoking look at human factors issues in user interfaces.

SHUB, C.M. [1990]. "Native Code Process-Originated Migration in a Heterogeneous Environment," *ACM Conf. on Computer Science*, Washington DC, February 1990, pp. 266-270.

> Migrating processes between heterogeneous host architectures.

SILBERSCHATZ, A., and P. GALVIN [1994]. *Operating System Concepts* (4th edition), Addison-Wesley, Reading, Mass., November 1994

> Latest edition of a good operating systems book.

SITES, R.L. [1992]. *Alpha Architecture Reference Manual,* Digital Press, Bedford, Mass.

> Describes the architecture of the Alpha processor family.

SKLOWER, K. [1989]. "Improving the Efficiency of the OSI Checksum Calculation," *ACM Computer Communication Review*, Vol. 19, No. 5, October 1989, pp. 32-43.

> How to improve implementations of the OSI checksum. See also Nakassis [1988].

SMITH, J.M. [1988]. "A Survey of Process Migration Mechanisms," *ACM SIGOPS Operating Systems Review*, July 1988, pp. 28-40.

> A good survey of process migration.

SMITH, J.M., and G.Q. MAGUIRE, JR. [1989]. "Measured Response Times for Page-Sized Fetches on a Network," *ACM SIGARCH Computer Architecture News*, Vol. 17, No. 5, September 1989, pp. 71-77.

SMITH, J.M., and C.B.S. TRAW [1993]. "Giving Applications Access to Gb/s Networking," *IEEE Network Magazine*, Vol. 7, No. 4, July 1993, pp. 44-52.

> Issues in integrating operating systems and network interfaces so that applications actually see gigabit throughput.

SMITH, J.M., C.B.S. TRAW, and D.J. FARBER [1992]. "Cryptographic Support for a Gigabit Network," *Proc. INET '92*, Kobe, JAPAN, June 15-18, 1992, pp. 229-237.

SPEER, S., R. KUMAR, and C. PARTRIDGE [1993]. *Improving UNIX Kernel and Networking Performance using Profile Based Optimization,* Hewlett-Packard, July 1993

A technical report on using PBO to improve networking performance.

SPRAGINS, J.D., J.L. HAMMOND, and K. PAWLIKOWSKI [1991]. *Telecommunications: Protocols and Design,* Addison-Wesley, Reading, Mass.

A useful textbook on data communications from the telecommunications perspective.

STALLINGS, W. [1992]. *ISDN and Broadband ISDN* (2nd edition), MacMillan, New York

An overview of ISDN and Broadband ISDN, focussed mostly on ISDN.

STAMOS, J.W. [1986]. "Remote Evaluation," MIT/LCS/TR-354, MIT Lab for Computer Science, Cambridge, Mass., January 1986.

A doctoral dissertation. An approach to improving RPC performance by migrating code.

STRAYER, W.T., B.J. DEMPSEY, and A.C. WEAVER [1992]. *XTP: The Xpress Transfer Protocol (XTP),* Addison-Wesley, Reading, Mass.

The most complete discussion of XTP.

STROM, R.E., D.F. BACON, A.P. GOLDBERT, A. LOWRY, D.M. YELLIN, and S.A. YEMINI [1991]. *HERMES: A Language for Distributed Computing,* Prentice Hall, Englewood Cliffs, N.J.

An approach to distributed computing that tries to thoroughly hide underlying properties of the network.

STROUSTRUP, B. [1991]. *The C++ Programming Language* (2nd edition), Addison-Wesley, Reading, Mass.

C++ described by its designer.

TAM, M.-C., J.M. SMITH, and D.J. FARBER [1990]. "A Taxonomy-Based Comparison of Several Distributed Shared Memory Systems," *ACM Operating Systems Review,* Vol. 24, No. 3, July 1990, pp. 40-67.

Useful survey of distributed shared memory.

TANENBAUM, A.S. [1988]. *Computer Networks* (2nd edition), Prentice Hall, Englewood Cliffs, N.J.

A widely used data communications text.

TANTAWY, A., and M. ZITTERBART [1992]. "Multiprocessing in High-Performance IP Routers," *Protocols for High-Speed Networks, III (Proc. IFIP 6.1/6.4 Workshop),* Elsevier, Stockholm, May 13-15, 1992.

Thoughts on multiprocessor IP routers.

TENNENHOUSE, D.L. [1990]. "Layered Multiplexing Considered Harmful," *Protocols for High-Speed Networks, I (Proc. IFIP 6.1/6.4 Workshop)*, Elsevier, Zurich.
> Argues that multiple levels of multiplexing should be avoided in high speed protocol implementations.

THEIMER, M.M. [1986]. *Preemptable Remote Execution Facilities for Loosely-Coupled Distributed Systems*, Stanford University
> A doctoral dissertation on process migration.

TOBAGI, F.A., T. KWOK, and F.M. CHIUSSI [1991]. "Architecture, Performance, and Implementation of the Tandem Banyan Fast Packet Switch," *IEEE Jour. Selected Areas in Communications*, Vol. 9, No. 8, October 1991, pp. 1173-1193.
> Describes a parallel Batcher-Banyan switch.

TOKUDA, H., T. NAKAJIMA, and P. RAO [1990]. "Real-Time Mach: Towards a Predictable Real-time System," *Proc. USENIX Mach Workshop*, October 1990.
> Describes real-time extensions to Mach.

TOLMIE, D., and J. RENWICK [1993]. "HIPPI: Simplicity Yields Success," *IEEE Network Magazine*, Vol. 7, No. 1, January 1993, pp. 28-33.
> HIPPI described by its designers.

TOPOLCIC, C. [1990]. "Experimental Internet Stream Protocol, Version 2 (ST-II); RFC-1190," *Internet Request for Comments*, No. 1190, Network Information Center, October 1990.
> The ST-II specification.

TRAW, C.B.S., and J.M. SMITH [1991]. "A High-Performance Host Interface for ATM Networks," *Proc. ACM SIGCOMM '91*, Zurich, September 1991, pp. 317-325.
> Describes an ATM interface for the IBM RS/6000.

TRAW, C.B.S., and J.M. SMITH [1993]. "Hardware/Software Organization of a High-Performance ATM Host Interface," *IEEE Jour. Selected Areas in Communications (Special Issue on High Speed Computer/Network Interfaces)*, Vol. 11, No. 2, February 1993.
> More detailed presentation of the ATM interface originally described in Traw [1991].

TURNER, J.S. [1986]. "New Directions in Communications (or Which Way to the Information Age)," *IEEE Communications*, Vol. 24, No. 10, October 1986, pp. 8-15.
> For many people, the paper that opened their eyes to what cell switching could do.

TURNER, J.S. [1992]. "Managing Bandwidth in ATM Networks with Bursty Traffic," *IEEE Network Magazine*, Vol. 6, No. 5, September 1992, pp. 50-59.
> A perspective on congestion control.

VAKIL, F. [1993]. "A Mathematical Theory of ATM Communications," TM-ARH-022985, Bell Communications Research, May 1993.

> Intriguing thoughts on traffic combination rules for flows.

VERMA, D., H. ZHANG, and D. FERRARI [1991]. "Guaranteeing Delay Jitter Bounds in Packet Switching Networks," *Proc. TriComm '91*, IEEE, Chapel Hill, N.C., April 1991.

> One of the better schemes for jitter control.

WANG, Z., and J. CROWCROFT [1992]. "SEAL Detects Cell Misordering," *IEEE Network Magazine*, Vol. 6, No. 4, July 1992, pp. 8-9.

> Shows that CRC-32 is robust in detecting cell misordering.

WATSON, G., D. BANKS, C. CALAMVOKIS, C. DALTON, A. EDWARDS, and J. LUMLEY [1993]. "Afterburner," *IEEE Network Magazine*, Vol. 7, No. 4, July 1993, pp. 36-43.

> A successor interface to the Medusa.

WATSON, G., S. OOI, D. SKELLERN, and D. CUNNINGHAM [1992a]. "HANGMAN Gb/s Network," *IEEE Network Magazine*, Vol. 6, No. 4, July 1992, pp. 10-18.

> A gigabit LAN technology.

WATSON, G., and S. THOME [1992b]. "A Performance Analysis of S++: A MAC Protocol for High Speed Networks," *Protocols for High-Speed Networks, III (Proc. 3rd IFIP WG6.1/6.4 Workshop)*, North Holland, Stockholm.

> The successor to *S*.

WILKENLOH, C.J., U. RAMACHANDRAN, S. MENON, R. J. LEBLANC, M.Y.A. KHALDI, P.W. HUTTO, P. DASGUPTA, R.C. CHEN, J.M. BERNABEU, W.F. APPELBE, and M. AHAMAD [1989]. "The Clouds Experience: Building an Object-Based Distributed Operating System," *Workshop on Experiences with Distributed and Multiprocessor Systems*, Fort Lauderdale, Fl., October 5-6, 1989, pp. 333-348.

> A notable object-oriented distributed system.

WOLFF, R.W. [1989]. *Stochastic Modeling and the Theory of Queues,* Prentice Hall, Englewood Cliffs, N.J.

> One of the best queueing theory books since Kleinrock [1975; 1976].

YEH, Y-S., M.G. HLUCHYJ, and A.S. ACAMPORA [1987]. "The Knockout Switch: A Simple, Modular Architecture for High-Performance Packet Switching," *IEEE Jour. Selected Areas in Communications*, Vol. 5, No. 8, October 1987, pp. 1274-1283.

> A good prototype crossbar switch design. Its performance is often used as a baseline for comparison.

ZAHN, L., T.H. DINEEN, P.J. LEACH, E.A. MARTIN, N.W. MISHKIN, J.N. PATO, and G.L. WYANT [1990]. *Network Computing Architecture,* Prentice Hall, Englewood Cliffs, N.J.

> Describes the components of the NCA, most notably NDR.

ZAYAS, E. [1987]. "Attacking the Process Migration Bottleneck," *11th ACM Symp. Operating Systems Principles,* ACM SIGOPS, Austin, Tx., 8-11 November 1987, pp. 13-24.

> Thought provoking work on improving the performance of process migration.

ZEGURA, E.W. [1993]. "Architectures for ATM Switching Systems," *IEEE Communications Magazine,* Vol. 31, No. 2, February 1993, pp. 28-37.

> An overview of several novel switching architectures including Benes switches.

ZHANG, L., S.E. DEERING, D. ESTRIN, S. SHENKER, and D. ZAPPALA [1993]. "RSVP: A New Resource ReSerVation Protocol," *IEEE Network Magazine,* Vol. 9, No. 5, September 1993.

> A thoughtful design for a setup protocol.

ZHANG, L., S. SHENKER, and D.D. CLARK [1991]. "Observations on the Dynamics of a Congestion Control Algorithm: The Effects of Two-Way Traffic," *Proc. ACM SIGCOMM '91,* Zurich, September 1991, pp. 133-148.

> Notes the potential for acknowledgement compression, based on simulation work. See Mogul [1992].

ZIELINSKI, K., M. CHOPPING, D. MILWAY, A. HOPPER, and B. ROBERTSON [1991]. "The Metrobridge: A Backbone Network Distributed System," *ACM Computer Communication Review,* Vol. 21, No. 3, January 1991, pp. 45-60.

> Experiments connecting PCs via ATM.

ZIMMERMAN, H., [1980]. "OSI Reference Model — The ISO Model of Architecture for Open Systems Interconnection," *IEEE Trans. on Communications,* Vol. 28, No. 4, April 1980, pp. 425-432.

> Describes the outline and motivation for the seven-layer model.

Index

，電腦圖書的園地

電腦部

371-7725